The Reflexive Imperative in Late Modernity

WITHDRAWN

This book completes Margaret Archer's trilogy investigating the role of reflexivity in mediating between structure and agency. What do young people want from life? Using analysis of family experiences and life histories, her argument respects the properties and powers of both structure and agency and presents the 'internal conversation' as the site of their interplay. In unpacking what 'social conditioning' means, Archer demonstrates the usefulness of 'relational realism'. She advances a new theory of relational socialization, appropriate to the 'mixed messages' conveyed in families that are rarely normatively consensual and thus cannot provide clear guidelines for action. Life-histories are analysed to explain the making and breaking of various modes of reflexivity. Different modalities have been dominant from early societies to the present and the author argues that modernity is slowly ceding place to a 'morphogenetic society' as meta-reflexivity now begins to predominate, at least amongst educated young people.

MARGARET S. ARCHER is Professor of Social Theory at Ecole Polytechnique Fédérale de Lausanne and Directrice of its Centre d'Ontologie Sociale. She was Professor of Sociology at the University of Warwick from 1979 until 2010. She has written over twenty books including *Making our Way through the World: Human Reflexivity and Social Mobility* (2007), *Structure, Agency and the Internal Conversation* (2003) and *Being Human: The Problem of Agency* (2000).

The Reflexive Imperative in Late Modernity

Margaret S. Archer

Ecole Polytechnique Fédérale de Lausanne

CAMBRIDGE
UNIVERSITY PRESS

CAMBRIDGE UNIVERSITY PRESS
Cambridge, New York, Melbourne, Madrid, Cape Town,
Singapore, São Paulo, Delhi, Mexico City

Cambridge University Press
The Edinburgh Building, Cambridge CB2 8RU, UK

Published in the United States of America by Cambridge University Press,
New York

www.cambridge.org
Information on this title: www.cambridge.org/9781107605275

First published 2012

Printed in the United Kingdom at the University Press, Cambridge

A catalogue record for this publication is available from the British Library

Library of Congress Cataloguing in Publication data
Archer, Margaret Scotford.
The reflexive imperative in late modernity / Margaret S. Archer.
    p.   cm.
ISBN 978-1-107-02095-5 (hardback)
1. Socialization.   2. Families.   3. Reflection (Philosophy)   I. Title.
HM686.A73   2012
303.3′2 – dc23   2011053163

ISBN 978-1-107-02095-5 Hardback
ISBN 978-1-107-60527-5 Paperback

With gratitude to all my students at the University of Warwick from 1973 to 2010, good years for me and I hope for them

Contents

Figures

Acknowledgements

This book starts its life deeply in debt. Without my respondents' generous gift of their time over the last three years there would have been no book. I had never done longitudinal research before and it is amazing how the textbooks dehumanize it. Of course, we all know abstractly about interpretation and its pitfalls. But, what is hardly mentioned is the huge hermeneutic responsibility I came to feel towards my 'subjects' – to hear more than their words, to listen to what was not said and to grasp what they were articulating as much to themselves as to me. There were quite a few sleepless nights spent pondering over the real meanings behind the transcripts. I can only hope that no one feels they have been misconstrued but my sincere apologies go to any who may do. Equally, I had no idea how concerned I would become that each interviewee's life project worked out well and came to care very much that this was the case.

Quite a lot is said in the text about friendship and its importance, but there is a very special bond between a writer and those few to whom fledgling ideas are exposed trustingly. My deepest thanks go to three special ones, who have done this before and I hope will do it again. Firstly, to my indispensible friend Pierpaolo Donati who has read every chapter, was always urging me on to the next and, in the meantime, was developing my ideas well beyond what they had in them. Next, to Doug Porpora, especially for a week at the Alpbach Forum also spent talking and walking – thank you for patiently waiting for me to catch up with both. Finally, a big thank you to my goddaughter Nicoleta Cinpoeş, friend, supporter and grammarian extraordinaire, for correcting the errors I could no longer see.

There are many others that I can only acknowledge collectively, but particularly my realist friends in Britain and Italy for giving me opportunities to try out some of these ideas in public and for their detailed e-mails full of comments and encouragement.

Lastly, a big thank you to the Independent Social Research Foundation (ISRF) for enabling these themes to be developed further, to the Ecole

Polytechnique Fédérale de Lausanne for appointing me to do so and to my lakeside commune in France, which gives the most beautiful view possible from any study window and whose mayor cheerfully stops to get my car going.

Margaret Archer
Maxilly-sur-Léman

Introduction

In this book I attempt to sustain a single proposition, namely that for the first time in human history the imperative to be reflexive is becoming categorical for all, although manifesting itself in only the most developed parts of the world. This thesis does not rest upon any form of sociological Kantianism. There is no 'ought' attaching to intensified reflexivity and no stern voice of duty urging increased reflexive deliberation.

Instead, the thesis is that the emergence of a new conjuncture between the cultural order (ideationally based) and the structural order (materially based) is shaping new situational contexts in which more and more social subjects find themselves and whose variety they have to confront – in a novel manner. This is the practical consequence and manifestation of nascent morphogenesis. What each and every person has to determine is what they are going to do in these situations. Increasingly all have to draw upon their socially dependent but nonetheless personal powers of reflexivity in order to define their course(s) of action in relation to the novelty of their circumstances. Habits and *habitus* are no longer reliable guides. The positive face of the reflexive imperative is the opportunity for subjects to pursue what they care about most in the social order. In fact their personal concerns become their compasses. Its negative face is that subjects can design and follow courses of action that are inappropriate to realising their prime social concerns and whose negative outcomes rebound upon them.

As in the first two books of this trilogy,[1] reflexivity is defined as 'the regular exercise of the mental ability, shared by all normal people, to consider themselves in relation to their (social) contexts and vice versa'.[2] The imperative to engage in reflexive deliberations (which may also involve interpersonal as well as intra-subjective exchanges) derives, quite simply,

---

[1] Margaret S. Archer, *Structure, Agency and the Internal Conversation*, Cambridge University Press, 2003, and *Making our Way through the World: Human Reflexivity and Social Mobility*, Cambridge University Press, 2007.

[2] For a fuller discussion see Archer, *Making our Way through the World*, 'Introduction', above definition p. 4.

from the absence of social guidelines indicating what to do in novel situations. It is tempting to write 'in new games', but for the fact that not even the constitutive rules let alone the regulative ones are fully formed. Indeed, it will be agential reflexive deliberations and the actions stemming from them that are ultimately responsible for formulating such rules – for as long as they last. This will also be of shorter duration as morphogenesis engages increasingly.

Already it is necessary to enter a caveat. In *Making our Way through the World*, I defended the proposition 'No reflexivity; no society'.[3] That statement must be clearly distinguished from the present thesis about the reflexive imperative. The argument that any social order depends upon the exercise of human reflexivity rests on three counts. Firstly, that reflexive first-person awareness is indispensable in even the simplest society because without it, no rule, expectation, obligation and so forth could be incumbent upon anyone in particular without the 'sense of self' that is needed to bend such injunctions back upon oneself and know if the cap fits or not. Secondly, traditional practices require reflexive monitoring for competent performance, for coping when things go wrong and for meeting unexpected contingencies. Since all social life is lived in an open system, the very workability of tradition depends upon resort to reflexive ingenuity in order to cover unscripted eventualities, which often entail the elaboration of tradition itself.[4] Thirdly, traditional guidelines may be in conflict with one another because there is no guarantee that all norms are complementary at any given time. When they are not, as was the case for Antigone (torn between conflicting obligations to her king and her brother), only she could decide reflexively in which cause to act. All three points are under-girded by Garfinkel's demonstration that even the smooth accomplishment of everyday routine interactions involves a 'reflexive accounting', which makes this a constitutive feature of social life itself.[5] Nevertheless, this is universal reflexivity, which is part and parcel of being a member of society, and not the extended reflexivity that is the subject of this book.

'No reflexivity; no society' is also premised upon no culture ever being so comprehensive and coherent in its composition and no structure ever being so commanding or consistent in its organization as to maintain an enduring form of social life without making constant resort to the reflexively derived actions of its members. This is one major difference between

---

[3] Archer, *Making our Way*, pp. 25–29.

[4] For example, the traditional Massai initiation rite into male adulthood entailed killing a lion. When the Kenyan government banned lion killing, the 'continuation' of this tradition required elaborative ingenuity.

[5] Harold Garfinkel, *Studies in Ethnomethodology*, Oxford, Polity Press, 1984.

my own position and that of the proponents of 'reflexive modernization' for whom the intensive and extensive practice of reflexivity is a newcomer, only arriving on the scene during late modernity. Despite that, it is important to ask what else distinguishes the present argument about the reflexive imperative from what has come to be called 'the extended reflexivity thesis',[6] given that each is held to apply to the current period. The 'extended reflexivity thesis' is associated with Ulrich Beck and his collaborators, and maintains that 'in reflexive modernity, individuals have become ever more free of structure; in fact they have to redefine structure (or as Giddens puts it, tradition)', meaning that much greater demands are placed upon personal reflexivity to make a 'life of one's own'.[7] The answer to what differentiates the two positions is 'just about everything', beginning, as is already implicit, with Beck, Giddens, Lash and Bauman portraying the relationship between traditionalism and reflexivity as effectively a zero-sum one.[8] However, it is the following two differences that are crucial.

Firstly, in *Reflexive Modernization*, 'extended reflexivity' is presented as the direct counterpart of 'the demise of structure'. It is social destructuration that enables reflexive, narrative, serial and kaleidoscopic self-reconstructions by newly 'individualized' people. This is part and parcel of these authors conceptualizing late modernity as a period in which structures 'dissolve' into 'flows', structured groupings fade into 'zombie' status, differences in life chances yo-yo with increasing speed and what had once been structurally enduring now melts into 'liquidity'. Most 'liquid' of all is the free flow and endless recombination of ideas. Not only is culture itself viewed as (now) being unstructured, but the ideational domain comes to override any other in shaping social life. Hence, the assertion that, '[with] the emergence of a self-culture, it is rather a *lack* of social structures which establishes itself as the basic feature of the social structure'.[9]

On the contrary, I maintain that the general intensification of reflexivity (and the different modes of internal conversation through which it is practised) is directly related to mutually reinforcing changes in cultural

---

[6] See, for example, Matthew Adams, 'Hybridizing Habitus and Reflexivity', *Sociology*, 40:3, 2006, 511–528, where the phrase is used repeatedly.

[7] Ulrick Beck, 'Preface', in Ulrich Beck, Anthony Giddens and Scott Lash, *Reflexive Modernization: Politics, Tradition and Aesthetics in the Modern Social Order*, Cambridge, Polity Press, 1994, p. 177.

[8] My critique, of the 'central conflationary' theoriszation of *reflexive modernization*, will not be repeated here. See Archer, *Making our Way*, pp. 29–37.

[9] Ulrich Beck and Elizabeth Beck-Gernsheim, *Individualization*, London, Sage, 2002, p. 51.

and social structures. Specifically, it results from an unprecedented acceleration of morphogenesis in these two spheres simultaneously, rather than from the diminished importance of structure, that is, the diminution of its properties and powers to the advantage of an increasingly influential but formless culture. The effects of the 2007 banking crisis on other social institutions has rendered the structures involved, their interdependencies and causal powers sufficiently transparent to undermine any conviction that 'destructuration' has occurred. Rather than disappearing, the workings of finance capital had been partially and deliberately occluded.

Secondly, and more starkly, the reflexive imperative is *not a thesis that is tied to* modernity refusing to look beyond its 'project' – not to late modernity, not to high modernity and not to Second Wave modernity. The times (and places) examined are much the same in the two theses, that is, from the late eighties when the launch of the World Wide Web coincided with the expansion of multi-national corporations and the deregulation of finance markets. However, the onset of nascent morphogenesis, generated by human agency and working through nothing but human agents – singular and collective – points beyond modernity to the potential for its transcendence. What seems unique about this latest historical cycle of modernity is that it appears to be giving way to a morphogenesis that is increasingly unbound from its morphostatic fetters. My ultimate aim – one that will not be completed in this volume – is to ascertain whether or not the concurrence of morphogenesis in the realms of structure, culture and agency announces the advent of a thoroughly morphogenetic society.[10]

This book begins the upward journey from the micro to the macro level by considering this reconfiguring of the social order in relation to society's members.[11] However, the effects examined are limited to their impacts upon collectives of people and, in turn, to aggregate outcomes for social institutions in the new millennium. Although such effects point to a transformation of civil society *inter alia*, this investigation can do no more than gesture towards new possibilities for the taming of modernity's two Leviathans – the State and the Market. Nevertheless, even to look towards a horizon where modernity may be transcended as the distant result of today's nascent morphogenesis, is to be carried light years away from resignation to the future of the social order as nothing more than 'institutionalized individualism'.[12]

---

[10] This is the research project just launched by the *Centre d'Ontologie Sociale* at the Ecole Polytechnique Fédérale de Lausanne.

[11] For the stages in the development of my 'morphogenetic approach' in social theory, see Margaret S. Archer, 'The Trajectory of the Morphogenetic Approach: An Account in the First-Person', *Sociologia: Problemas e Práticas*, 54, 2007, 35–47.

[12] Beck and Beck-Gernsheim, *Individualization*, p. 2.

In short, the two theses about 'reflexive modernization' and the 'reflexive imperative' have entirely different theoretical starting points, they meet briefly and in superficial accord about the recently enhanced importance of reflexivity, but their destinations and modes of analysis are poles apart.

The acceleration of morphogenesis and the extension of reflexivity

This book is closely related to its predecessors, *Structure, Agency and the Internal Conversation* and *Making our Way through the World: Human Reflexivity and Social Mobility*, but it also links upwards to the institutional and cultural structures that were coming into being at the start of the new millennium. It looks forward to the elaboration of these structures at the hands of the young subjects (aged roughly 18–22) upon whom the empirical part of this study is based. The trilogy shares the same historical backcloth against which it is maintained that agential reflexivity increases in scope and range over time. It does so because, at the most macro level, the structural and cultural orders shift over recorded history from (i) an era of lasting social stability, generated by structure and culture mutually reinforcing morphostasis in one another, to (ii) the long period, coterminous with modernity, during which morphogenesis in one order gradually induced it in the other, with increasingly disruptive consequences for the population in general, to (iii) the current period of rapid social transformation deriving from the positive reinforcement of cultural morphogenesis by structural morphogenesis and vice versa. In other words, structure, culture and agency, each of which is relatively autonomous and possesses its own distinctive emergent properties and causal powers, are necessary to the existence of one another in a given form but simultaneously account for their combined elaboration. Together they 'make history'.

In sociological terms, the 'making of history' means that periods of stability – as opposed to mere quietude – are analysed as morphostatic, that is, with reference to relations that tend to preserve or maintain a system's given form of organization or state. Conversely, morphogenesis derives from those processes that tend to elaborate or change a system's given form, structure or state.[13] Both generative mechanisms are entirely

---

[13] These concepts were first introduced into social theory by Walter Buckley, *Sociology and Modern Systems Theory*, Englewood Cliffs, N.J., Prentice Hall, 1967, pp. 58–59. Buckley focuses upon 'system-environment exchanges'. Instead, my own use of these concepts places the emphasis upon internal relations. See also Magoroh Maruyama, 'The Second Cybernetics: Deviation–Amplifying Mutual Causal Processes', *American Scientist*, 5:2, 164–179.

and continuously activity-dependent. It is agency that generates both morphostasis and morphogenesis and, in turn, these very different relationships between components of the social system exert causal powers only by working through social agents. Where reflexivity is concerned, the key process through which societal morphostasis or morphogenesis influence the subjectivity of the populations in question is identical to the way in which any structural or culture property exerts an influence on human subjects, even if it is not perceived to do so. That is, by shaping the situations in which they find themselves, ones that are neither of their making nor choosing because they pre-date the agents in question.[14] Reflexivity has been advanced as the process mediating the effects of our circumstances upon our actions.[15] Our internal conversations define what courses of action we take in given situations and subjects who are similarly placed do not respond uniformly.

Morphostatic configurations, those whose effects are structurally and culturally restorative of the *status quo*, exert this causal power through shaping everyday situations into ones that represent 'contextual continuity' for subjects. The recurrence of these situations means that members know what to do because their repetition over time also means that appropriate courses of action have been defined intergenerationally – perhaps to the point of becoming tacit knowledge – and are readily transmitted through informal socialization. Conversely, thoroughly morphogenetic figurations would shape nearly all everyday situations as ones of 'contextual incongruity', where past guidelines become more and more incongruous with the novel situational variety encountered. Increasingly, each subject has to make his or her own way through the world without established guidelines – a process which cannot be conducted in terms of tacit knowledge or as 'second nature', but necessarily by virtue of internal deliberations. Between these extremes lies the vast majority of recorded history – that is modernity. Its hallmark was the simultaneous circulation of negative, structure-restoring feedback and positive, structure-elaborating feedback for structural, cultural and agential properties and powers. The precise forms taken describe the contours of the multiple modernities that have been historically distinguished.[16] As modernity

---

[14] See Margaret S. Archer, *Culture and Agency: The Place of Culture in Social Theory*, Cambridge University Press, 1988, chapter 6, and *Realist Social Theory: The Morphogenetic Approach*, Cambridge University Press, 1995, pp. 195–229.

[15] See Archer, *Structure, Agency and the Internal Conversation*, pp. 130–152.

[16] For example, see Eliezer Ben-Rafael and Yitzak Sternberg (eds.), *Comparing Modernities: Pluralism versus Homogeneity. Essays in Homage to Shmuel N. Eisenstadt*, Leiden and Boston, Mass., Brill, 2005.

advanced, these disjunctions constituted 'contextual discontinuity' for wider and wider sections of the population in any country.

The main proposition about the 'reflexive imperative' can be formulated with greater precision and placed within this broader historical panorama as follows: *the extensiveness with which reflexivity is practised by social subjects increases proportionate to the degree to which both structural and cultural morphogenesis (as opposed to morphostasis) impinge upon them.*[17] This is not the statement of a Humean constant conjunction (or correlation coefficient) because the main concern is to explain *how* the (objective) macroscopic features of social configurations have an effect upon the (subjective) mental activities of their members, at the micro level. Neither is this a statement about social hydraulics, that is, one conceptualizing social forces as pushes and pulls, which affect subjects willy-nilly, thus reducing them to 'passive agents'. Nor is it the final statement of the main proposition because it says nothing about *the modes of reflexivity* that predominate under given circumstances. It is these *changing modalities of reflexivity* that constitute the main concern of the present book. This begins to be unpacked in the first chapter, and it is the recent change in the dominant mode of reflexivity coming to be practised, along with the decline of those associated with earlier social configurations, that signals the restructuring of late modernity and the potential for its transcendence.

The study focuses exclusively upon the period from the late 1980s onwards, examining how the increasingly morphogenetic changes underway reshaped the situational contexts in which the new generation of 'active agents' grew up and with what effects for the making (and breaking) of the modes of reflexivity they developed and practised. The development of any reflexive modality is explained as a product of the formula 'social context + personal concerns'. In shorthand, its first term can be condensed into the differences between 'contextual continuity, 'contextual discontinuity' and 'contextual incongruity', which characterized the experience of growing up for different cohorts and sections of the population during the broad periods distinguished above and discussed in the following chapter. This means that a closer examination of young people, of their natal contexts and of their constellation of concerns (which give them their personal identities), will tell a great deal about their judgements upon the current institutional array because these always underlie the attempts of subjects to identify and attain social positions through

---

[17] For those who defend the durable influence of habit or habitus, counter-arguments are provided in Margaret S. Archer, 'Routine, Reflexivity and Realism', *Sociological Theory*, 28:3, 2010, 272–303.

which they can realize their ultimate concerns (which give them their social identities).[18]

It will, however, tell only part of the story about their subsequent impact upon it, through their *aggregate tendency* to seek and to shun particular positions within the array of roles currently available to them and their reasons for this. The full story also needs to include collective action through which groups expressly organize and articulate aims for the transformation or defence of the social order or particular parts of it. Nevertheless, the present study has something to contribute here, too, by documenting the connections between the modes of reflexivity practised and the proclivity or reluctance of their practitioners to engage in political involvement, participate in social movements and to associate themselves with new organizational initiatives – albeit at the individual level.

The present study

The crucial question in terms of its implications for a possible morpho-genetic society is 'does the nature of reflexivity remain unchanged' amidst these social transformations and opportunities for social subjects to be transformatory? The previous two studies have necessarily been mute on this topic because all data was collected at one point in time. For example, it was impossible to answer two of the most frequently asked questions: 'Do or can people change their dominant mode of reflexivity over their life courses?' and 'Can 'fractured reflexives' recover and regain some governance over their lives?' The current data should be able to supply some answers because it is longitudinal. The subjects are all the undergraduate students who took the foundation course in sociology at the University of Warwick during the Autumn of 2003, with thirty-six volunteers from among them being interviewed in depth once a year during their bachelor's degree.[19] This means that for the first time it is possible to say something about the making and breaking of human reflexivity over time.

However, there is something of more pressing interest about these students who entered university in 2003. Of course they are not representative of their age cohort. As students in Britain they have been selected for entry, they are much better educated than average, and they chose Warwick as much as it chose them, picking it, they tended to say, because of its image as a university for the future. They are, for the most part,

---

[18] See Margaret S. Archer, *Being Human: The Problem of Agency*, Cambridge University Press, 2000, pp. 283–305.

[19] Please consult the Methodological appendix for further details about the population.

extremely articulate and this is exactly what was required – young people who could be informative about what otherwise must remain entirely speculative.

What makes them of absorbing interest are their dates of birth. These are young adults who were born and grew up in the last two decades of the twentieth century. Their births were coterminous with structural and cultural morphogenesis entering into synergy with one another, their natal environments were shaped and shaken by its initial impacts and their schooling was the earliest that could have registered the spawning new opportunities open to them. They are the first generation to grow up with the computer as a standard feature in the home and the first for whom going online was the readiest source of information. Now, in their early twenties, they confront the transforming social landscape that I will be trying to describe with their help. They are seeking reflexively to make their way through the world but also, as will be seen, some of their internal conversations are agential deliberations about remaking the social order. Sadly, too many of them also become casualties of the process. In consequence, this is not a utopian book and neither does it hold out prospects of that indeterminate state called 'adaptation' for our one complex, global, social system that may currently herald morphogenetic society.

1   A brief history of how reflexivity becomes imperative

Does reflexivity have a history? It seems that, like language, upon which reflexivity depends – without being entirely linguistic – it must have a pre-history. That is, there must have been a time before which *homo erectus* or his kinfolk had learned to speak and to be capable of mentally reflecting about their intentionality. In other words, there was a before and an after. What is not obvious is whether or not 'afterwards' was a long, continuous and unfinished process of constant elaboration, or if reflexivity's biography consisted of distinct and discontinuous periods. Another way of putting the same question is: does human reflexivity show distinct variations in the modes through which it is practised and, if so, were such modalities subject to change over time in response to changing historical circumstances?

A difficulty arises in posing the question in this way, namely, that it would be acknowledged in some disciplines but not in others. On the one hand, in psycholinguistics and as early as 1934, Vygotsky was calling for a 'history of reflexivity'.[1] Certainly, his appeal resulted in very little take-up but not, it seems, because his request was unintelligible or unacceptable. It appears more likely that what accounted for the lack of response was the need for considerable historical probing and bold conjecturing at precisely the time when it was safer for his Russian collaborators to confine themselves to laboratory work and to seek political cover behind 'scientism'. On the other hand, Western social theorists have shared the same reluctance to respond to Vygotsky's call. Instead, their common denominator has been to regard *reflexivity as a homogeneous phenomenon*. Either people exercised it or they didn't but, when they did they were engaging in much the same kind of practice and for much the same kind of reasons. At most, they could do so more or less, as in what has recently become known as 'the extended reflexivity thesis'.[2]

---

[1] Lev S. Vygotsky, *Thought and Language*, Cambridge, Mass., MIT Press, 1964 (1934). His call was for a 'historical theory of inner speech', p. 153.

[2] For example, the phrase is used repeatedly in Matthew Adams, 'Hybridizing Habitus and Reflexivity', *Sociology*, 40:3, 2006.

Thus, with some oversimplification, the great American pragmatists – who alone took reflexivity seriously at the end of the nineteenth century and at the beginning of the twentieth – generically endorsed the formula that action would follow routine guidelines and resort would be made to reflexive deliberations only when subjects were confronted with unforeseen and problematic situations. Despite the enormous contribution of James, Dewey, Mead and in particular Pierce in conceptualizing reflexivity as operating through the 'internal conversation' (rather than as a process of introspection), there is nothing in their works that introduces a historical panorama of changes in relation to the type of reflexivity practised.[3] This was the case despite their willingness to engage boldly with the past and especially the future in other respects. In short, it seems that to them 'problematic situations' would be encountered at all times and the ahistorical response would be a resort to the mental activities and inner dialogue that constituted reflexivity *tout court*.[4]

Conversely, there is the current account proffered by Beck and Giddens which, again with oversimplifications, maintains that for a very long time traditionalism could operate as the guide to action and that only with the arrival of the 'juggernaut' or the 'risk' society did traditional action give way to reflexive action. This makes reflexivity itself a 'newcomer', largely confined by Beck to the onset of what he calls Second Wave modernity. Again, there is no suggestion that reflexivity – when it arrives – is other than a homogeneous mental practice. However, it does arrive on the recent historical scene and with the implication that its advent is for all. This is in contradistinction to Bourdieu's tenacious retention of the *socialized habitus* as the guide to action and his confinement of reflexivity to a practice that could be *collectively developed* only by members of the academic community. The same tenacity is shown by those of his successors who engage in concept-stretching and advance a *flexible habitus* to secure enduring conceptual relevance in the new millennium.[5] Whatever else may be said about this manoeuvre, it contains no suggestion that, if this notion truly seeks to incorporate reflexivity, it will be practised in different ways by different people and differently in different social settings.

---

[3] See William Lyons, *The Disappearance of Introspection*, Cambridge, Mass., MIT Press, 1986.

[4] For a more detailed examination of the contributions of James, Peirce and Mead to the theme of reflexivity-as-internal-conversation see Margaret S. Archer, *Structure, Agency and the Internal Conversation*, Cambridge University Press, 2003, chapter 2: 'From introspection to internal conversation', pp. 53–92.

[5] Both of these themes and associated thinkers are treated in greater detail in Margaret S. Archer, *Making our Way through the World: Human Reflexivity and Social Mobility*, Cambridge University Press, 2007, chapter 1: 'Reflexivity's Biographies', pp. 25–61.

These debates will not be re-entered now (their salient elements will be picked up in the next chapter). Instead, two propositions will be advanced here. Firstly, that *reflexivity is not a homogeneous phenomenon but is exercised through distinctive modes*, and that one such modality is dominant for almost every person at any given time. This is an empirical proposition about the present. Secondly, it will be suggested that there *is a historical succession in the dominance of such reflexive modes*. In other words, reflexivity does have a history. Although this is advanced largely in theoretical terms, nothing defies its empirical investigation in principle.

Different ways of being reflexive

The two earlier works in this trilogy outlined four modes of reflexivity *practised by all of us some of the time* through the internal conversations we hold with ourselves: communicative, autonomous, meta- and fractured reflexivity.[6] These are summarized in Figure 1.1.

They can be illustrated by the following everyday example, where someone is pictured using all four modes in relation to a single event. A man with little experience of dentistry begins to suspect that his persistent toothache might require an extraction. He shares these forebodings with friends, thus seeking their confirmation or otherwise by employing the communicative pattern of 'thought and talk'. The same man, now convinced of his need for dental attention, sets out alone, checks the traffic and safely crosses the road to a dentist, practising the self-contained autonomous mode. However, on closer inspection, this dental practice strikes him as appearing expensive and exclusive. He has second thoughts and decides to find a more modest one, thus meta-reflexively revising his first inclination and moving on. Finally, an unsympathetic receptionist at his revised choice of dental practice may leave him vacillating between his present pain and his enhanced fear of the extraction procedure she has just described to him; in the fractured mode, unable to decide, he mutters unhappily that he needs to think about it and may come back later.

Although we all do resort to each of the four modes of internal conversation on different occasions and in different situations, the vast majority of the Coventry sample (over 93 per cent) were shown to have a *dominant mode*, with the four being rather evenly distributed across the small, stratified sample.[7] Their dominant modalities were found to be very general

---

[6] For discussion in detail see Margaret S. Archer, *Structure, Agency and the Internal Conversation*, chapters 6–9 and *Making our Way through the World*, chapters 4–6.

[7] In Archer, *Making our Way*, the following dominant modes of reflexivity were estimated, using ICONI (the Internal Conversation Indicator), for the stratified sample of Coventry inhabitants: communicative reflexives = 21 per cent, autonomous

Communicative Reflexivity

Internal Conversations need to be confirmed and completed by others

before they lead to action

Autonomous Reflexivity

Internal Conversations are self-contained, leading directly to action

Meta-Reflexivity

Internal Conversations critically evaluate previous inner dialogues and are

critical about effective action in society

Fractured Reflexivity

Internal Conversations cannot lead to purposeful courses of action,

but intensify personal distress and disorientation resulting in expressive action

Figure 1.1 Modes of reflexivity

in their deployment by subjects, remaining consistent over the following range of mental activities, as interpreted by interviewees: 'mulling-over' (a problem, situation or relationship), 'planning' (the day, the week or further ahead), 'imagining' (as in 'what would happen if . . . ?'), 'deciding' (debating what to do or what is for the best), 'rehearsing' (practising what to say or do), 'reliving' (some event, episode or relationship), 'prioritising' (working out what matters to you most), 'imaginary conversations' (with people you know, have known or know about), 'budgeting' (working out if you can afford to do something, in terms of money, time or effort)

reflexives = 27 per cent, meta-reflexives = 23 per cent and fractured reflexives = 22 per cent (figures rounded up), p. 335. This compares with the following for students at point of entry in the present study: communicative reflexives = 13.5 per cent, autonomous reflexives = 19 per cent, meta-reflexives = 38.6 per cent and fractured reflexives = 17.4 per cent. For further details, especially concerning the development of ICONI, please consult the 'Methodological appendix' of this book.

and 'clarifying' (sorting out what you think about some issue, person or problem).

In other words, reflexivity is not conceptualized here in 'decisionist' or 'rationalist' terms. As can be seen from the above list, a given subject might (and approximately half agreed that they did) engage in self-talk in relation to most, though not all, of the above activities. That is quite compatible with various stock characters: the instrumental rationalist (who would spend most time on 'planning', 'deciding' and 'budgeting'); the archetypal academic (pre-occupied with 'mulling-over' and 'clarifying'); any kind of day-dreamer (lost in 'imagination', 'reliving' and 'imaginary conversations'); or a scrupulous moralist (preoccupied with 'debating' what is for the best, 'prioritising' and 'clarifying'). These are only lay stereotypes. In their private mental lives, real subjects will focus their intra-personal dialogues on any combination or permutation of the above activities because no rules govern what we choose to dwell upon in the privacy of our own heads. Doubtless, at times we have all been enjoined by others to 'wake up', to 'get real' or to 'switch on', but we also know how transitory were our propitiatory responses. Hence, we know too that our internal conversations defy external regulation. As Norbert Wiley puts it, 'we are little gods in the world of inner speech'.[8]

Because we are, it follows that nothing can ultimately prevent us from devoting the vast majority of our internal conversation to anything from contemplation, through trivial diversion to vituperation. Equally, nothing stops us from blocking out this self-talk with earphones and a music player. Wiley is also correct when he continues: 'This is our own private little world. It is nobody's business but our own, and it does tasks for us that could not be accomplished in any other way.'[9] Some of these tasks are my concern here, although there are no grounds for asserting that they dominate our inner dialogue to the exclusion of quotidian questions, trivial pursuits or abstract ruminations. Nor do they exclude the days and times when, though we wish to concentrate upon some particular issue or activity, our inner conversations are distracted and flit about like midges or are leadenly unproductive through fatigue.

Nevertheless, internal conversation 'does tasks for us that could not be accomplished in any other way'. Specifically, to have a personal identity is defined by our constellation of concerns and to have a concern is necessarily to be concerned about it.[10] If something matters to us it is

---

[8] Norbert Wiley, 'The Sociology of Inner Speech: Saussure Meets the Dialogical Self', paper presented at the meeting of the American Sociological Association, August 2004.

[9] *Ibid.*, p. 9.

[10] For a full discussion of this conclusion see Margaret S. Archer, *Being Human: The Problem of Agency*, Cambridge University Press, 2000, chapter 7: 'Personal identity: the inner conversation and emotional elaboration', pp. 222–252.

nonsense to say that we pay it no attention. The life of our minds is always, to some extent, taken up with the life we want to live. Because it is human life, it will mainly be lived socially and many (though not all) of our concerns will be explicitly social in kind.[11] Thus, the prime social task of our reflexivity is to outline, in broad brush strokes, the kind of *modus vivendi* we would find satisfying and sustainable within society – as we know it and know ourselves under our own fallible descriptions. What we are attempting to accomplish is to marry our concerns to a way of life that allows their realization, a way of life about which we can be wholehearted, investing ourselves in it with each personifying its requirements in our own and unique manner.[12] Hence we gain and maintain some governance over our own lives. This is a supremely reflexive task, entailing 'strong evaluation' of our social context in the light of our concerns and adjusting these concerns in the light of our circumstances.[13]

Whilst everybody has to do this for themselves reflexively through their internal conversations, that does not imply that subjects have to do it alone. To engage in inner dialogue is to activate our personal powers, but that does not make any of us individualistic monads.[14] We all receive and use external information, we all engage in external as well as internal conversation and, above all, being human refers to a quintessentially relational being.[15] Our human relations and the relationality between them form part of both our internal and our external conversations. Finally, it cannot be over-emphasized, that this reflexive task does not turn subjects into the humanoids of Rational Choice Theory. To seek 'a life worth living' – which is quite different from Beck's notion of 'a life of one's own' – is in no sense seeking to become 'better off' (unless this is a tautology) or to 'maximize one's preference schedule', precisely because *concerns are not preferences*. Rather, they are commitments that are ends in themselves and constitutive of who we are, for whose sake we will be

---

[11] I do not consider it helpful to make all possible concerns 'implicitly social' by definition. Analytically, people can have primary concerns in the natural, practical or transcendental orders, where social aspects are probably unavoidable but nevertheless remain ancillary.

[12] Harry Frankfurt, 'Identification and wholeheartedness', in Frankfurt, *The Importance of What We Care About*, Cambridge University Press, 1988 and see Martin Hollis' consistent defence of our active *personification* of roles, from *Models of Man*, Cambridge University Press, 1977, through *The Cunning of Reason*, Cambridge University Press, 1987 to 'Honour among Thieves', *Proceedings of the British Academy*, LXXV, 1989.

[13] Charles Taylor, *Human Agency and Language*, Cambridge University Press, 1985, chapter 1: 'What Is Human Agency?'.

[14] Granting such emergent personal powers and attaching causal efficacy to their use is wrongly held by some to lead directly to 'monadism'. See Anthony King, 'Against Structure: a Critique of Morphogenetic Social Theory', *Sociological Review*, 47, 1999, 199–227 and *The Structure of Social Theory*, London, Routledge, 2004.

[15] Pierpaolo Donati, *Teoria Relazionale della Società*, Milan, Franco Angeli, 1992, chapter 1: 'La relazione sociale come «presupposizione prima» della sociologia'.

altruistic, self-sacrificing and sometimes ready to die and always, at least, be trying to live. They are also definitive of our varying forms of social engagement.

Modes of reflexivity and situational logics of action

Drawing upon the findings of my previous two studies, the dominant mode of reflexivity practised by singular subjects did not appear to be psychologically determined because structural and cultural characteristics of subjects' social backgrounds were found to be closely associated with the predominance of different modes of reflexivity.[16] Specifically, those who grew up in a close, harmonious and geo-locally stable family – thus experiencing 'contextual continuity' – showed a strong tendency to be practitioners of communicative reflexivity; those experiencing exactly the opposite, that is, 'contextual discontinuity', displayed an equally marked proclivity for the practice of autonomous reflexivity. Subjects who had come to endorse concerns at some variance with those contested in their natal backgrounds – thus confronting 'contextual incongruity' – were the adults who tended to practice meta-reflexivity as their dominant mode. Fractured reflexivity was related to the experience of various severely disruptive occurrences, such as acute illness, involuntary redundancy, unexpected marital breakdown, none of which appears amenable to psychological reduction. However, neither is it ruled out that individual psychology may have a part to play here, nor that some subjects might be more psychologically susceptible to 'fractured reflexivity' under these kinds of circumstances, which are not universally associated with this effect. Individual psychology may indeed have an important contribution to make about the sources of these propensities towards a particular dominant mode.[17]

Nevertheless, the importance of contextual factors does raise historical questions about the distribution of the different dominant modes of reflexivity over time because contextual 'continuity', 'discontinuity' and 'incongruity' were respectively the lot of the majority of people during successive historical epochs. The answers must remain speculative, although they can be rendered rather more robust if taken in conjunction with a second question. It has been maintained that the new millennium is already a period of unprecedented morphogenesis and the aim of this

---

[16] This does not mean that individual and social psychology make no contribution. It is only to maintain that modes of reflexivity are not psychologically reducible.

[17] For a promising collaborative approach, see Edward. L. Deci and Richard M. Ryan, *Intrinsic Motivation and Self-Determination in Human Behavior*, New York, Plenum Press, 1985.

book is to ascertain what effects this has had upon young people coming to maturity during it. If such effects are indeed detected in the dominant modes of reflexivity they are now practising or beginning to practise seriously, then it is expected that these would be mediated through prior transformations in their respective contextual backgrounds – which is what will be explored in subsequent chapters. Were this to be so, the case would be strengthened for plotting the historical trajectory of reflexivity retrodictively and coming a step closer to answering Vygotsky's call for a 'history of reflexivity'. At the end of the day, it will not be incontrovertible, but must remain what Weber called a 'peculiarly plausible hypothesis'.[18] Like his own, it would be open to further substantiation, to some extent historical, through use of diaries, 'confessions' and novels, and today through investigation of those vast tracts of the Southern world where morphogenesis has not yet engaged.

In various sections of society, i.e. for those associated with particular institutional spheres, organizational activities and role occupancy, the conditions constituting 'contextual continuity', 'contextual discontinuity' and 'contextual incongruity' have doubtless been present to some degree throughout history. However, this is not the case if we consider the lineaments of societies at the most macro level, including the single global society now coming into being. Macroscopically, the structural relationships between parts of the social system and the ideational relationships between components of the cultural system together constitute a generative mechanism productive of one of the three types of context mentioned above, namely contextual 'continuity', 'discontinuity' or 'incongruity'.

However, just as all normal, adult human beings practise elements of all four reflexive modes today, yet nearly all have developed a dominant modality, so all social configurations too, will have shaped contextual pockets where the development of each mode of reflexivity was fostered among some portion of every given population. Nevertheless, specific macro-level configurations of the social system will have been especially favourable to the emergence of a particular mode as the dominant one in the reflexivity of the general population.

Morphostasis, 'contextual continuity' and communicative reflexivity

Although very little time will be devoted here to the morphostatic social formations pre-dating modernity, they will be briefly revisited for three

---

[18] Max Weber, *The Theory of Social and Economic Organization*, New York, Free Press, 1964, pp. 96–97.

reasons.[19] Firstly, they furnish an important contrast because *early societies, in which structure and culture supplied negative feedback to each other and thus contributed to the restoration and perpetuation of the status quo, were also the ones likely to have fostered communicative reflexivity amongst the large majority of the population.* Secondly, if this was the case, the processes responsible for it should also be (formally) similar to those continuing to have the same effects *sectionally* (in particular institutions, organizations and roles) across the centuries and up to the present day. Thirdly, they will reveal what generic types of contexts were shaped either for the majority of society's members or for those associated with (enduring sectors) of a similar kind. In turn, this will enable the next stage of the argument to be introduced, namely, how these different types of contexts also give rise to distinctive situational logics of action for the realization of subjects' personal concerns. These three points will be examined in turn.

Firstly and structurally, early societies were characterized by a low level of social differentiation and correspondingly small distinctions in material interests between people. In parallel, there were few available sources of alternative ideas and correspondingly small distinctions in ideational interests within the population. In these circumstances, where the structural and cultural elites were mutual beneficiaries of each other's activities, they often tended to coalesce into a single hegemonic group (Brahmin, Literati, the Privileged Estates) hence consolidating their control and exercising it to prevent challenge from the less advantaged and to preclude their access to countervailing ideas. Uses of power to contain the differentiation, organization and mobilization of new interest groups were paralleled by ideational containment strategies aimed at cultural unification of the population and the reproduction of a single conspectus of ideas. In short, what was sought by these elite groups served to promote 'contextual continuity' across society and onwards over future generations. This did not last forever, and there are internal reasons why it could not.[20] Nevertheless, 'contextual continuity' could endure and be made to endure for centuries.

Secondly, the maintenance of 'contextual continuity' was obviously not how elites defined their objectives under their own descriptions: chiefs, emperors and kings sought to render their leadership unassailable; witch doctors, high priests and literati sought to make their ideas inviolable.

---

[19] For a more detailed discussion, see Margaret S. Archer, *Realist Social Theory: the Morphogenetic Approach*, Cambridge University Press, 1995, pp. 213–245.

[20] For the socio-cultural dynamics of cultural change see Margaret S. Archer, *Culture and Agency: The Place of Culture in Social Theory*, Cambridge University Press, 1988, chapter 7: 'Socio-cultural Interaction'.

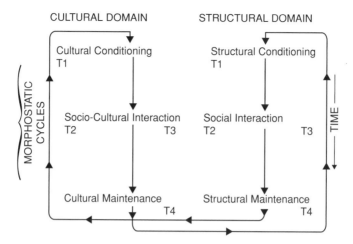

Figure 1.2 Structural and cultural configurations reproducing morphostasis in society and agency

'Contextual continuity' was, thus, the generative mechanism resulting from their successful and often conjoint implementation of a variety of power strategies. In so far as and for as long as their strategic containment of structural differentiation and ideational diversification proved effective, it worked *because the absence of variety* continued to shape situations for successive cohorts of the population in which neither new interests nor alternative ideas could be consolidated. This is what 'contextual continuity' means, although in 'old and cold' societies it is commonly known as 'traditionalism'.[21]

We can now identify the generic process by which morphostatic scenarios, both societally and sectionally, shape situations for their respective populations that predispose them to develop communicative reflexivity. The necessary condition is that structure and culture are mutually reinforcing through negative feedback, serving to maintain the *status quo* in both over time, as illustrated in Figure 1.2.

---

[21] Considered as a generative mechanism and one at work throughout modernity, 'contextual continuity', which is often empirically associated with routine action, is more general than traditionalism. This is of importance for instances where it continues to have the same generic consequences *sectorially*, in certain parts of the social order that no one would think of as being traditional and where what is required of those involved are not actions that could properly be called traditionalistic. For example, Kuhn's sociology of science maintains that in normal times only one paradigm enjoys monopoly, leading to the consolidation of new habits in research whose effect 'suppresses fundamental novelties because they are necessarily subversive of its basic commitments.' Thomas Kuhn, *The Structure of Scientific Revolutions*, Chicago University Press, 1962, p. 5.

The effect of such scenarios is to shape the situations that subjects confront as ones of 'contextual continuity': those encountered by one generation or cohort are much the same as they were for their predecessors. It is through such situational shaping that structural and cultural emergent properties are – as always – transmitted to the agents in question.[22] However, it could very properly be objected that for subjects to find themselves in much the same situation as one another, in no way elicits the same response from them. Indeed, that must be correct and it is impossible for any theorist consistently to maintain otherwise *if* subjects are held to possess their own irreducible, emergent properties and powers, both individually and collectively. Therefore, more is required to establish a linkage between morphostasis in the social order and the dominant practice of a particular mode of personal reflexivity. In other words, the generative mechanism is still incomplete. Two further points are needed to forge the linkage.

On the one hand, we have to note what the maintenance of morphostasis does to the subjects involved as well as to the situations in which they find themselves. Its effect – an intentional one where strategic uses of power are involved – is ultimately to distribute *similarities* throughout the population concerned. This is simply the reverse face of actively sustaining low levels of social differentiation and of ideational diversification; subjects develop few different interests or ideas from one another. Clearly, it approximates to Durkheim's characterization of the 'segmented society', whose members are very like one another, to the point of constituting 'a jumble of juxtaposed atoms'.[23] As is well known, this led Durkheim to query what, in that case, held them together and to answer this by reference to the 'collective effervescence' generated in religious rituals – a source of solidarity and of normativity. Without denying that shared religious practices can supply both, they seem to be a supplementary rather than a necessary condition of solidarity and of normativity. Instead, similarity and familiarity appear to contain within themselves all that is needed for their development from social interaction.

---

[22] 'Given their pre-existence, structural and cultural emergents shape the social environment to be inhabited. These results of past actions are deposited in the form of current situations. They account for what is there . . . to be distributed and also for the shape of such distributions; for the nature of the extant role array, the proportion of positions available at any time and the advantages/disadvantages associated with them; for the institutional configuration present and for those second order emergent properties of compatibility and incompatibility, that is, whether the respective operations of institutions are matters of obstruction or assistance to one another.' Archer, *Realist Social Theory*, p. 201.

[23] Emile Durkheim, *Division of Labour*, New York, Free Press, 1965, p. 130.

Given members' common experiential frame of reference (because of 'contextual continuity') and their shared topography and commonwealth of ideas, any issues to be resolved (where to hunt next, which nomadic halt to make and so forth) will find the majority vetoing innovative proposals in favour of established practices. Members increase in solidarity through defending established custom and practice and by repelling idiosyncratic suggestions, which is roughly what Durkheim also says about restitutive law and public punishment producing a return to the *status quo ante*. The interaction between 'similars and familiars' is its own source of normativity, one that endorses conventionalism and whose limited knowledge of alternatives effectively turns 'that's how things are done around here' from being a description of habit into something normatively binding.[24] It is when individuals share their hopes, dreams and aspirations with 'similars and familiars' that these are cut down to size, i.e. to the norms of established custom and practice, because when they seek confirmation and completion of their initial thoughts and inclinations, convention is re-endorsed through external conversations.[25] Since 'thought and talk' with 'similars and familiars' is the relational process making for communicative reflexivity – which, in turn, reinforces social solidarity – this is the first part of its linkage with morphostasis via 'contextual continuity'.

At this point, it might be queried why people engage in such 'thought and talk' at all. Whence the need to be reflexive rather than to respond in terms of tacit knowledge and simply 'knowing how to go on'? Precisely the same answer is given both by realists and by pragmatists. Problematic situations can always arise in any open system and appropriate responses to every eventuality cannot be part of traditionalism's coda because unprecedented circumstances cannot be covered by it. Reflexivity is necessary and predisposes towards 'thought and talk' because some have to come up with ideas but also must convince and carry the rest with them in what are collectively binding decisions. In other words, *some reflexivity is indeed universal but in morphostatic social configurations there is no general impetus whatsoever towards the reflexive imperative becoming incumbent on all.*

However, there is the final link to forge and this relates to the guidance supplied by situational logics for action embedded in contexts of different kinds, in this case ones of 'continuity'. At all times and in all places

---

[24] This is where historically the *proximal* norm circles, the *imagined* and the *actual* circles, distinguished by Dave Elder-Vass, tend to be superimposed. *The Causal Power of Social Structures*, Cambridge University Press, 2010, pp. 122–133.

[25] Archer, *Making our Way through the World*, pp. 270–284.

subjects acquire their personal identities through the constellation of concerns that they endorse. This is part of the exercise of their personal powers, the one that makes them unique persons. Those who vest their ultimate concerns within their natal context also seek to project this context forward in time – literally reconstituting it – in order that their concerns may continue to be realized. However, they do more *because*, by virtue of their concerns, they have acquired a vested interest in 'contextual continuity' itself. Undoubtedly, that gives them a generic interest in social reproduction, which is not an unintended consequence of their actions, much less a matter of tacit habituation or of an inarticulate knowing 'how to go on'.

If 'contextual continuity' is threatened, either internally by some accentuating their (minor) differences or selectively stressing some potentially incongruent element in the ideational conspectus, or externally through the importing of attractive differences from elsewhere, the result is the same. Those whose interests are vested in 'contextual continuity' must pursue *a situational logic of 'correction' or 'protection'* in order to defend (the conditions of) what they care about most. Correction and protection are vocal and active exercises against perceived threat. So-called 'mindless' traditionalism is a misnomer; some must be mindful about how generous syncretism needs to be in order to correct and contain 'wrong thinking', and be judicious about boundary maintenance in order to regulate intrusive elements and thus protect a stable environment against 'wrong doing'. In so far as they are successful they perpetuate 'contextual continuity' because it is part and parcel of actualizing their concerns, and thus they preserve the generative mechanism of communicative reflexivity.

Finally, it is important to avoid a possible source of misunderstanding. Namely, what is the exact force of saying that subjects '*must* pursue' a particular situational logic, given that agency is not seen as being socially determined? Any situational logic is of the 'if /then' variety and it is, therefore, the incidence of the 'if' that is primitive to the rest of the logic. In other words, it is our human concerns – especially our ultimate concerns – that are pivotal, not only because they make us what we are as persons but also because they serve to direct what we do with our agency.[26]

Our ultimate concerns are sounding-boards, affecting our (internal) responses to anything we encounter, according to it resonating harmoniously or discordantly with what we care about most. It is these reactions

[26] Mustafa Emirbayer and Ann Mische, 'What Is Agency?', *American Journal of Sociology*, 103:4, 1998, 962–1023.

that affect what we do, *not* because we have complete or accurate discursive penetration of the situation. Instead, discordant elements have the capacity to move ordinary people because they are emotionally registered as *offensive*.[27] They are shunned, repudiated or negatively sanctioned since they are antipathetic. This is the spur to action which invokes the 'then' of the 'if/then' logic. Conversely, elements harmonious with the ultimate concern are felt as *congenial*. They are welcomed, encouraged or positively sanctioned because that is what subjects' emotions, as transvalued by their commitments, motivate people to do.[28]

These internal prompts and restraints represent the exercise of personal powers and are what bind agents to following the situational logic of correction and protection. Its manifestations will be quotidian: how children and the young are disciplined or rewarded; what behaviours are positively or negatively sanctioned in a community; which practices are fostered or repressed in a religious group. In this way, the situational logic of correction and protection effectively, though non-teleologically, works to maintain and protract 'contextual continuity' – and with it the conditions propitious to the development and dominance of communicative reflexivity.

Morphostasis/morphogenesis, 'contextual discontinuity' and autonomous reflexivity

The central characteristic of modernity was not simply that differentiation and diversification had engaged in the structural and cultural domains respectively, but that these two domains no longer co-existed in synchrony with one another. Elsewhere, I have argued that it was of no moment whether the structural differentiation of oppositional groups pre-dated the cultural differentiation of ideational adversaries or vice versa.[29] In either case, the emergence of a morphogenetic scenario in the one later induced the same in the other. This is because a new promotive interest group, seeking to challenge the existing hegemonic elite, needed novel ideas to undermine existing legitimacy and to justify its own claims. Alternatively, it is because advocates of novel ideas required sponsorship

---

[27] Archer, *Being Human*, chapter 6 and summarized as 'Emotions as Commentaries on Human Concerns', in Jonathan H. Turner (ed.), *Theory and Research on Human Emotions*, Amsterdam, Elsevier, 2004, pp. 327–356.

[28] That there is some such second-ordering process involved for the emotions commands broad agreement. Jon Elster refers to it as 'transmutation' (*Alchemies of the Mind*, Cambridge University Press, 1999, p. 56), John D. Greenwood as 'transformation' (*Realism, Identity and the Emotions*, London, Sage, 1994, p. 156) and Charles Taylor as 'transvaluation' (*Human Agency and Language*, pp. 65–68).

[29] Archer, *Realist Social Theory*, pp. 308–324.

from amongst the powerful in order to promote their cultural agenda in the face of the dominant ideational conspectus.

However, the lack of synchrony between morphostasis in one domain and morphogenesis in the other meant that both negative feedback (restoring the *status quo*), and positive feedback (amplifying deviations from it), were circulating simultaneously. The effect was twofold. Firstly, a major consequence was to slow down the whole process of transformation. Secondly, the process was disjunctive, affecting some institutions faster than others, transforming certain bodies of ideas overnight and leaving others virtually unaffected, and reshaping the lives of part of the population whilst those of the remainder continued untouched.

Structurally, the key point about the transition to modernity was its unintended consequence of dichotomizing the peoples of Europe, who became the subjects of European nations, into those experiencing 'contextual discontinuity' and, indeed, seeking to extend it through political and, later, industrial unrest. On the other hand, the combined impacts of urbanization, politicization and industrialization appear to have left the rural populations in relatively undisturbed 'contextual continuity', whilst the slowness of change allowed the newly urbanized groups to reconstitute community on the basis of class in the towns. After several generations of urban living, everyday life could again take its guidelines from this newly established form of 'contextual continuity'.

The concurrent effects of cultural morphogenesis reinforced those of collective mobilization and vice versa. On the one hand, the organized contenders for power and position necessarily adopted novel ideas to legitimate their aims. On the other hand, those defending their positions elaborated upon their sources of justification in order to buttress their ideological defence and extend its appeal, thus attempting to (re-)establish ideational unification. During the great age of ideological debate, the populace did not remain immune in a cocoon of cultural traditionalism because, sooner or later, they became the targets of efforts to mobilize and manipulate them in order to determine the outcomes of issues that were not of their making. As they were dragged into the ideological fray, popular awareness of alternative ideas grew – and to be aware of an alternative to tradition spells the end of traditionalism.

In short, the spread of 'contextual discontinuity' was a sectional phenomenon, growing patchily throughout the course of modernity, even as it gathered momentum. However, only by unpacking the dynamics generating 'contextual discontinuity' it is possible to explain why the latter fostered autonomous reflexivity amongst larger and larger tracts of the population over time, although its practitioners seem likely to have remained in the minority throughout the nineteenth century. This is not simply an instance of 'elective affinity', which is a concept that fails to give an account of the causal powers that link 'interests' to 'ideas'. The concept of 'elective affinity' merely demonstrates their compatibility in principle and leaves the actual forging of the linkage to some kind of magnetic mutual attraction.[30]

Consequently, what is required is a closer specification of the new situations carved out for more primary agents as modernity developed, ones that impacted upon not only their 'contexts' but also their 'concerns', cumulatively resulting in the emergence of newly differentiated forms of collective agency, organized for the promotion of new sectional interests and articulating novel ideas for their advancement or vice versa.[31] Equally, the situational positioning of other groups (who probably constituted the majority of the population) was such that their 'contexts and concerns' induced and enabled newly routinized but non-traditional norms, values and practices to be elaborated and to take root. Without this being taken into account it will not be possible to explain the differential effects of unsynchronized morphogenesis and morphostasis throughout a given population. Without this, it will also remain a puzzle why a seemingly uniform change, which is what the singular term 'modernity' is often used to convey, simultaneously had differential consequences for the emergent social classes. It is this simultaneity that leads me to view the periodization of modernity – into early, high, late, second wave and so forth – as unhelpful because all of these sub-divisions imply homogenous effects within them and consequently downplay or ignore the differential effects, which are quintessential to modernity *because it is based upon a fundamental lack of synchrony between structural and cultural changes.*

In other words, at no stage and during no phase did the complex of institutional and ideational transformations, constitutive of the short-hand term modernity, ever work to foster a universally dominant mode of reflexivity. During the eighteenth, especially the nineteenth, and most of the twentieth centuries in Europe, collective agents were both the

---

[30] Indeed, Weber himself, when exploring the specific 'economic ethos' of different world religions, had to abandon his methodological individualism and introduce the interplay between structural and cultural factors to explain the variable nature of rationality in different historical social configurations. In other words, he too became a serious advocate of the notion that the impact of the macro-figurational upon micro-level mental processes was mediated through the combined structural and cultural shaping of the situational contexts of action. This seems to be the central point of his contrast between ancient India and China, on the one hand, and ancient Judaism, on the other.

[31] Primary agents are defined as those similarly positioned but deprived of having any say, in contrast with collective or corporate agents who have articulate aims and are organized for their strategic pursuit. See Archer, *Realist Social Theory*, pp. 257–265.

recipients of situations, pre-shaped as ones of 'contextual discontinuity', and also the protagonists of change whose exertions created further 'contextual discontinuities' for others. Simultaneously, primary agents were constrained to relocate geographically, to change their work place and nature of employment, and to lose a host of services associated with family life in rural communities. In turn, their urban–industrial life chances represented positive inducements towards redeveloping 'contextual continuity' in towns. Both of these effects, as experienced by different sections of the population, are needed to understand why 'modernity' simultaneously fostered both autonomous reflexivity and the continuation of communicative reflexivity, although not in any stable ratio.

The key distinction between these two influences, is that those finding themselves in situations of 'contextual discontinuity' – and through their own exertions often extending such discontinuity to others – also experienced and contributed to the creation and diffusion of new forms of difference throughout society. Thereafter, it was the collective agential interactions between promotive interest groups, both material and ideal, that unleashed the dynamics *leading autonomous reflexivity to become the distinctive mode associated with modernity*, if not the one practised by the majority of people. Conversely, those disrupted and dis-embedded, but remaining primary agents, were responsible for recreating a new and relatively durable form of 'contextual continuity' that accentuated the *novel similarities* of their lived reality out of need, giving rise to the urban community, to intergenerational solidarity and to working-class conviviality which were propitious to communicative reflexivity.

Whether structurally or culturally, *competitive contradictions* played a central role, without reference to which the eventual hegemony of Autonomous Reflexivity is condemned to remain an 'elective affinity'. Such contradictions are distinctive in that they were completely dependent upon modernist assailants – both materially and ideationally based – asserting themselves against traditional elites and ideas. There was no interdependence between the two that gave these contradictions any salience in society beyond that attained for them by the adversarial parties. The Reformation, the Enlightenment, the French Revolution and the Industrial Revolution were dependent upon their thinkers and leaders continuing their thinking and doing. Only because they did so were traditionalists compelled to reorganize into defensive formations and to overhaul their ideas defensively. Had the challengers somehow faded away, there would have been no impetus for existing dominant groups to persist with such manoeuvres. However, since they continued to lock horns, ideational and institutional elaboration continued to result on both sides. From compromise and concession between them emerged those hard-won agencies for participation and governance – representative democracy, unionism and scholarization. In turn, they themselves extended new forms of 'contextual discontinuity' to portions of the population previously untouched by it.

However, the increasing salience of conflict stemming from *competitive contradictions* is quintessentially fissiparous. It promotes competition *beyond* the tendency that Marx rightly identified for capitalism not only to generate conflicts with the working-class movement (which itself displayed the same fissiparousness in ideas and organization), but also the inherent process by which capitalist was set in competition with capitalist, and worker with worker. Equally, competitiveness attached to ideational conflicts, ones that cannot readily be assimilated to class conflict and its super-structural manifestations. Take for example, the unbridled competition between the established Church of England and the various kinds of dissenting denominations over church- and school-building, as the long-term effect of the Reformation having introduced 'private judgement' into religious matters, or the nineteenth-century battle between the Catholic Church and the State over the right to educate the French youth.[32]

This is not the place to enter into the details of any of the above save to note three general consequences. Firstly, that these initial manifestations of *competitive contradictions* spread to affect all social institutions – in state and civil society alike – where the actions of collective agents were a spur to acquire organization and to articulate goals on the part of disgruntled primary agents, as I have analysed at length for education.[33] Secondly, that this spelt increasing mobilization of greater and greater sections of the population, though far from the majority (see Figure 1.3). Nevertheless, not all of the latter could resist the pressures, coming from their own ranks, to mobilize them for enfranchisement, for educational provision and for unionization. Finally, the overall result for (European) society was *pluralism* in the realm of ideas and social *cleavage followed by sectionalism* amongst collective agents and their burgeoning and still fissiparous organizations and ideologies. This part of the dynamics of competition is summarized below.

In other words, the mobilization of significant numbers into promotive interest groups effectively divided national populations into those

---

[32] The Reformation not only stimulated the Counter-Reformation, but immediately unleashed competition within Protestantism: not only the variants contemporaneous with Lutheranism (Pietism, Anabaptism, Zwinglianism), but onwards to Presbyterianism, Methodism, Baptism and so forth, each with its own later clutch of schisms.

[33] Margaret S. Archer, *Social Origins of Educational Systems*, London and Berverly Hills, Sage, 1979.

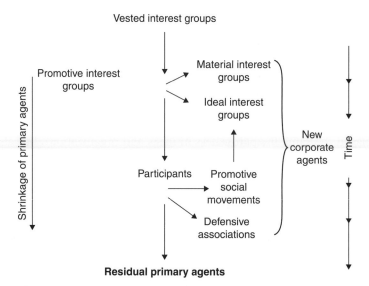

Figure 1.3 From primary to collective agency

promoting further 'contextual discontinuity' – even if for defensive purposes[34] – and a large residuum of others, more preoccupied with everyday concerns, whose practical actions fostered new geo-local forms of 'contextual continuity'. Only the former became subject to the *situational logic of competition* that accompanies the spread of ideational pluralism and sectional cleavages. That logic strongly induces instrumental rationality, which is the penultimate link to autonomous reflexivity.

Firstly, whatever reasons and values had led particular agents to become involved in sectional struggles also embroiled them in the dynamics of conflicts that were unrestrained by mutual interdependence. That is, competitive conflict involved the attempt to inflict injurious acts, with the ideal aim being the *elimination* of the oppositional party. However, since both sides of each confrontation had the same goal, it was rarely achievable. Instead, more and more strategic thinking had to be devoted to the question of how best to make headway. Thus, for example, the incursion of instrumental rationality into working-class radicalism can be traced throughout nineteenth-century Britain: from the eliminative violence of Luddism, through the strategic debates within and between

---

[34] For example, in the attempt to defend its educational hegemony, the established Church of England had to accept and actively contribute to a large extension of educational provisions – itself contributing to extensions in 'contextual discontinuity' for the newly scholarized – as part and parcel of the competition to retain control over education.

'moral force' Chartists and 'physical force' Chartism, and on through the subsequent disputes about the most effective form in which to develop Unionism – 'grand, national and consolidated' or trades-based. Equally, entrepreneurial interests had to weigh the concessions mooted for industrial quietude – restrictions on child labour, on working hours, on time for elementary education – against their competitive position in the increasingly European market.

Matters were no different for ideal interest groups. If the Church of England sought to defend its hegemony in education, strategically it had to extend instruction beyond its own needs and desires and to teach new material irrelevant to its concerns. On the other hand, some recipients of these strategic ploys were new collective agents who were driven to instrumentally rational considerations about, for instance, their ability to support independent mechanics institutes from their subsistence level wages in order to inculcate oppositional values and alternative skills.

Such examples are commonplace oversimplifications about the effects of competitive conflict upon the collective agents involved. However, the consequences of the situational logic of competition need to be taken down a level, from the promotive interest groups to their members, in order to secure the final linkage with autonomous reflexivity. The very concept of 'mobilization' can too often sound like a hydraulic process in which people are propelled to promote a cause because it is in their objective interests. What this neglects is the ideational and organizational bombardment that 'quasi-group' members are simultaneously receiving from both sides, in addition to the tension experienced between their own 'micro' life world concerns and the demands of larger scale interests.

In real life, each potential member for 'mobilization' is thrown back upon his or her own resources because they are increasingly badgered to make one of several choices. In Charles Taylor's terms, they are hassled into becoming even 'stronger evaluators'.[35] Each must (fallibly) think through their own concerns in their own currencies: deliberating between jam and justice for tomorrow compared with feeding their families today; determining if violence is being done to the church of their fathers by endorsing innovative practices today in order to defend it; deciding if the Primitive Methodists or Ebenezer Methodists had put matters right where the Methodists had gone wrong; debating if a particular factory should make a local concession to its disgruntled workforce at the risk of reducing its competitive position with rival manufacturers. The key point is that all these examples are of instrumentally rational deliberations.

[35] Charles Taylor, 'Self-Interpreting Animals', in his *Human Agency and Language*, pp. 65–68.

Autonomous reflexivity also expands because *pluralism, sectionalism and competitive conflict have increasingly deprived many people of disinterested 'similars and familiars'*, who could act as interlocutors, since most are in the same boat – and are mostly at sea.

This is because competitive situations are 'game-like' with their outcomes approximating to the zero-sum formula. Indeed, it is precisely their zero-sum character that helps to account for why more and more are drawn into competition through 'mobilization'. To be mobilized is not simply a socio-cultural matter of acceding to the persuasive pressure of class, status or party activists. It is also *motivated* by the nature of such games themselves. Either you compete, in the hope of winning (something), or you certainly lose through non-participation, because this allows others to win more easily. In effect, all subjects become part of these institutional 'games', whether or not they chose to play the hands that they had been dealt without choice on their part.

Formally, modernity's 'games' are very similar for all social institutions. Generically, they are about 'having, gaining or retaining a say' in order to obtain or secure benefits for the contending groups. Hence the sameness of competitive conflicts over representative politics, capitalist production and profits, and control of education or religion. For all social groups the zero-sum outcomes serve to place a premium upon strategic thinking of the means–ends variety. Even if, for argument's sake, we credited all members of the embattled churches and warring denominations (in Britain) with the highest other-worldly motives, they were still condemned to work in terms of instrumental rationality and to ask themselves if they would become *competitively* 'better off' by building a new school, orphanage, hospital or, for that matter, a church.[36] Of course, it is important to recall that these institutional dynamics are not necessarily mirrored at the individual level: there are statutory non-players (such as women and Catholics, until the Relief Act of 1829 in Britain), there are half-hearted players (some of those with nothing to sell but their labour power), non-conscripted players (as yet undisturbed in their rural redoubts) and conscientious objectors (various kinds of radicals), which is why autonomous reflexivity remained far from universal.

There were, of course, various agential options: to walk away, to vacillate at length, to give covert support without overt involvement, or to come down decisively on one side or the other. Yet, in any of these cases, this will be a novel – because autonomous – decision for agents

[36] The same was the case for continental struggles between the Church and the State. For example, see Antoine Prost, *L'Enseignement en France 1800–1967*, Paris, Armand Colin, 1968.

who have become caught up in the situational logic of competition. For those who actively assent to mobilization, the initial impetus to develop autonomous reflexivity is then sustained by the constant need to initiate, evaluate and arbitrate between alternative forms of strategic action. Those who decline such personal involvement could remain temporarily untouched by these struggles and their associated situational logic of competition, maintaining their 'contextual continuity' and sustaining their practice of communicative reflexivity – for the time being. Again, *this is why the reflexive imperative does not even begin to become universal during modernity.*

Morphogenesis, 'contextual incongruity' and meta-reflexivity

What is now coming into being is an entirely new phase in the relationship between structure, culture and agency. This is because structure and culture have each become morphogenetic and are coming to stand in a relationship of positive reinforcement towards one another. The new generative mechanism entailed by this is for variety to produce still more variety because, in pure form, nothing restrains it (such as defensive attachment to previous quasi-traditional interests and ideas or adherence to prior forms of routine action). Even more importantly, in pure form, it can develop because the very novelty of new variety means that no group has 'commandeered' it and acquired vested interests in it. These had played a significant part in the synchronic account of the maintenance of emergent structures in the morphogenetic approach when applied within modernity (as opposed to the diachronic account of their social origins). Effectively, they divided a population (non-exhaustively) into those with vested interests in prolonging the *status quo* versus those whose interests lay in transformation, and they structured conflict by influencing motivation accordingly, though not deterministically. Indeed, the rapidity of change means that the very notion of vested interests will become outdated if and when morphogenesis becomes truly unbound. Conversely, the objective benefits of opportunity could then represent an open promise to all, but these should not be construed in exclusively material terms.

References to 'pure form' do not signify an ideal type, which may never be actualized or encountered in reality, but simply refer to a process that is currently far from being complete. Indeed, the morphogenetic scenario has yet to come of age and its development is marked and blurred by its co-existence with many structural, cultural and agential properties robustly enduring from late modernity. Nevertheless, the advent of *faster morphogenesis introduces a completely unprecedented influence of structure and culture upon personal reflexivity, which promotes a distinctive mode of reflexive deliberation – meta-reflexivity.* This, of course, is not a completely new modality and evidence from classical writings and especially from the extensive Christian confessional literature bear ample witness to practices of self-examination, self-monitoring, self-critique and resolutions to self-amendment being conducted through the internal conversation.[37] What is new is that meta-reflexivity ceases to be a minority practice (a matter of small pockets of practitioners in all epochs) and, instead, becomes the mode associated with a historical period, in the same way that autonomous reflexivity was related (rather than merely correlated) to developed modernity through the situational logic of competition.

In other words, changes in social and cultural structure are held to be powerful influences (though neither necessary nor sufficient ones for particular subjects) accounting for the growth and dominance of particular modes of reflexivity amongst given populations. Where the developed world is concerned, the recent engagement of the morphogenetic scenario shapes situations for its constitutive members that predispose more of them towards meta-reflexivity. The initial necessary condition for this is that structure and culture are mutually reinforcing through positive feedback, thus serving to *augment deviations from the status quo*, as illustrated in the Figure 1.4.

In other words, contrary to the *reflexive modernization* thesis, changed structural and cultural conditions are held here to lie behind today's trend in reflexivity, rather than 'extended' individual reflexivity being the reverse face of structures 'shrunken' to the dimensions of Beck's 'institutionalized individualism'.[38] It is now necessary to show how these rapid changes generated by the morphogenetic scenario affect many subjects by shaping the situations they ineluctably confront as ones of 'contextual incongruity', and then to specify how this predisposes them towards the

---

[37] Religious practices may indeed represent a particular social sector that, of its own kind, tends to foster critical inner dialogue amongst those who are seriously committed. This is a proposition that I endorse but will not explore here. Perhaps it is worth noting, however, that in the morphostatic early medieval period, the routinized employment of confessional manuals seems likely to have somewhat depressed meta-reflexivity. Nevertheless, Thomas à Kempis' *Imitation of Christ* (1418) and, the anonymous *Cloud of Unknowing* (fourteenth century) cannot, in sociological terms, be seen as anything other than serious exhortations to deeper meta-reflexivity. See Pierpaolo Donati, *La Matrice Teologica della Società*, Soveria Mannelli, Rubbettino, 2010. Much the same point is made by Nicos Mouzelis about the anaphatic mysticism of the Orthodox Churches in 'Self And Self-Other Reflexivity: The Apophatic Dimension', *European Journal of Social Theory*, vol. 13:2, 2010, 271–284.

[38] Ulrich Beck and Elizabeth Beck-Gernsheim, *Individualization*, London, Sage, 2002, 'Preface', p. xxi.

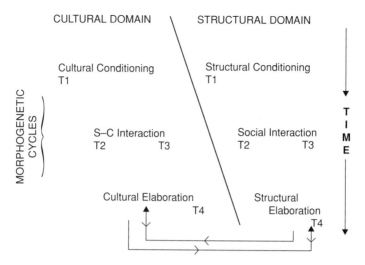

Figure 1.4 Structural and cultural configurations generating morpho-genesis in society and agency

practice of meta-reflexivity. Let us proceed by the *via negative* and ask why neither the communicative nor autonomous modes would be appropriate under these changed and quintessentially changing circumstances.

As has been seen, the practice of communicative reflexivity, exercised through 'thought and talk' with interlocutors who are also 'similars and familiars', strongly tends to reinforce normative conventionalism. In other words it enmeshes the subject in local custom and practice, it drags flights of fancy down to earth, it valorizes the familiar over the novel, it privileges the public over the private, today over tomorrow and certainty over uncertainty.[39] In sum, it encourages conventional, local-ized responses, even though these would be wrongly construed as routine actions in the contemporary social order. What end or personal concern does communicative reflexivity ultimately serve? It works according to the situational logic of protection and that is exactly its effect. It protects and protracts the micro-life world of, at most, a small community and, increasingly today, a handful of significant others. Such protectiveness towards (usually) the subject's family has been shown to involve objec-tive self-sacrifice, a refusal by subjects to avail themselves of accessible forms of advancement and a willingness to settle for 'living within their means'.[40] This is still possible under the morphogenetic scenario, if some version of 'the family' remains a subject's ultimate concern. However,

[39] Archer, *Making our Way*, 270–279.   [40] *Ibid.*, chapter 4.

there are three, big snags that make the maintenance of communicative reflexivity increasingly arduous.

Firstly, the price becomes steeper as increasing opportunities are turned down whilst many others 'get ahead' by taking advantage of them. Secondly, 'staying as we are' is diminishingly possible: new skills must be acquired if jobs are to be kept, new technology mastered if everyday life is to go on and new experiences weathered because they cannot be avoided. Thirdly, and most importantly, there will be a shrinking pool of 'similars and familiars' available as potential and durable interlocutors because many classmates, workmates, children and neighbours will embrace some element of their new opportunities or have novelty thrust upon them (through job retraining, relocation of employment, the difficulty of buying a 'simple' television, the irresistibility of cheap foreign holidays or the son/daughter-in-law from Asia). Communicative reflexivity remains possible, but it has become considerably more costly (in various currencies) and involves a great deal more effort to sustain. Above all, it has become a matter of active choice and bares no resemblance to a default setting. In other words, communicative reflexivity flourishes most easily and appropriately when similarities are continuously distributed throughout the population and similar situations are consistently encountered. This 'likeness' – integral to 'contextual continuity' – also reconfirms the appositeness of conventional responses and, in turn, fosters social reproduction. In return, as it were, communicative reflexivity made a quiet but major contribution to the continuous regeneration of social solidarity throughout modernity. This is now lost in direct proportion to the pronounced shrinkage of this category, augmenting both anomie and isolation during the transitional period.

Conversely, autonomous reflexivity is promoted by situations in which instrumental rationality advances subjects' concerns. These situations are distinctive because they confront subjects with 'contextual discontinuity', which means that conventional responses deriving from their natal repertoire are no longer appropriate guides to action. Because of the intrinsically competitive nature of these situations, subjects must determine where their own best interests lie and deliberate about the best means to achieve these ends – doing both fallibly and under their own descriptions. In other words, extreme practitioners of autonomous reflexivity come closest of all to acting like the 'rational man' of Rational Choice Theory.

Although instrumental rationality cannot flourish in highly stable environments, where traditionalism and conventionalism are the dominant guides to action and promote communicative reflexivity, nevertheless it requires relative predictability from its settings. This is simply an extension of the logical point that means–ends reasoning depends upon a calculability of pay-offs and sufficient knowledge about likely outcomes such that taking risks is a matter of calculated risk-taking. Otherwise it is impossible to act in a goal-seeking, risk-discounting manner with the aim of becoming better off. In other words, Durkheim appears to have been substantially correct that *anomie* – as a serious disjunction between means and ends – will increase the pathologies amongst those most severely affected by profound economic disruption.[41] Thus, instrumental rationality cannot operate in an unpredictable environment where calculability goes out of the window. Yet, quite fundamentally, this is what the beginnings of morphogenesis now represent.

However, this is not the so-called 'risk society', if that really means more than our very real human ability to wipe out our planet. The *situational logic of opportunity is something quite different because it is non-competitive and non-zero sum* in its outcomes. In principle, there is nothing that precludes it from generating 'win–win' outcomes for all. But what the exponential increase in variety rules out are both strategic 'maximizing' or 'satisficing' as well as the more elaborate 'mini-max' or 'maxi-min' strategies of rational choice. What the rapid release of novelty, innovation and synergy are doing is putting paid to calculability, including calculated risks. 'Venture capital' is becoming market betting. Yet, the last thing upon which capitalist competition was ever modelled was roulette. Moreover, morphogenesis cannot be approached in the spirit of the entrepreneurial adventurer or that of the Las Vegas punter because it is hostile to instrumental rationality just as it is inimical to irrational gambling.

If the intensification of morphogenesis spells a precipitous reduction in calculability, and if that, in turn, is inimical to instrumental rationality, should not a sharp and equivalent reduction in the practice of autonomous reflexivity also follow? This would seem to be the logical implication, but in practice the conditions that lead to this conclusion were, until the 2007 financial crisis, fairly effectively contained by the powerful interests involved. Specifically, the multinational corporations and finance capitalists tackled the root cause threatening their activities, namely incalculability. The former moved to an 'assurance game' in order to stabilize key aspects of the environment in which they operate. What this basically entailed was a series of mutual agreements that enabled those whose operations gained them a market advantage to continue to benefit from it for a certain number of years. This is why legal patents

---

[41] Emile Durkheim, *Suicide*, London, Routledge and Kegan Paul, 1968 (1897), chapter 5.

became crucially important. They served to 'freeze' uncertainty and, in guaranteeing profitability *ceteris paribus*, thus freed up internal resources to make the next innovative development which, if successful, would then be protected in the same manner. Calculability had been restored, the old game could continue with no more than the old absence of guarantees that new lines of research and development might turn out to be dead ends.[42]

However, the assurance game was not applicable to key areas, the most crucial being the finance market, but the latter had effectively tackled the incalculability of risk, from its own point of view, until the house of cards collapsed in 2007. Up to that date, the insurance game complemented the assurance game. Thus, the complex development of financial 'derivatives' and hedge funds represented forms of insurance by spreading risk over a variety of investments. If the development of 'derivatives' rendered risks calculable for the biggest players, investment supermarkets performed something of the same function for those with surplus capital. Assurance and insurance provided insulation against the quintessential unpredictability of morphogenesis and enabled the old game to continue – *pro tem*.

They were complemented by other devices that manipulate consumption to ensure rising 'demand' and to underwrite increased commodification. The proliferation of the credit card market, with a massive intensification of offers to transfer one's balance (read: 'debts') to a new interest free card for a limited period, was a direct inducement to increased indebtedness, at an exorbitant interest rate, for those who frequently could not pay. An identical role was performed by sub-prime mortgages and unsecured loans. This complete reversal of cautious issuing and lending in the past, on the basis of established 'credit-worthiness' and earnings, artificially stimulated demand over an increasing range of products, from housing to holidays to cosmetic surgery, thus introducing greater stability in market demand and extending this to the tertiary sector.

Market and state collaborated in buttressing finance capitalism, as pictured in Figure 1.5, as the expansion of public services in terms of benefits and employment kept 'demand' buoyant in European countries, which increasingly produced nothing but consumed more and more. Whilst ever the game went on and the devices for concealing the manipulative aspects of marketization became more sophisticated, so too could many continue to work on the basis of instrumental rationality in

---

[42] For example, Boots the chemists, not noted for their research leadership in pharmaceuticals, were buoyed-up by the patented protection of their big winner 'ibuprofen'.

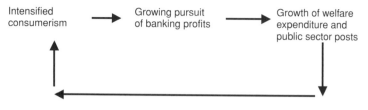

Figure 1.5 How market financialization and state redistribution work together. Adapted from Pierpaolo Donati, 'The Crisis of the World System and the Need for Civil Society', in José T. Raga and Mary A. Glendon (eds.), *Crisis in the Global Economy – Re-planning the Journey*, Vatican City Press, p. 144, 2011

planning their courses of action in the hope of becoming better off. With its collapse and a few of the most audacious financial players going under, European states were more concerned to re-establish 'business as usual' than to introduce stringent regulation of the finance services, which had replaced the production of goods as the source of national wealth. In other words, there are few grounds for supposing that the associated mode of reflexivity – autonomous reflexivity – would undergo a sudden and sharp decline.

Nevertheless, more and more people and especially the young who, on the whole, have fewer interests in artificially stabilizing the environment for finance capital, also have very good reasons to respond positively to *the situational logic of opportunity*. Why should they register the incalculability of rapidly intensifying variety as a threat to be tamed, particularly since they are badly placed to do the taming? Moreover, the positive feedback that spawns unlimited innovations also throws up novelties that appeal to the young and which they are remarkably adept at mastering: electronic games, mobile phones, iPods and the endlessly proliferating uses to be made of the Internet. New technology is 'cool'. The vista of opportunities presented by the Internet should not be underestimated: the chance to extend virtual experience far beyond the confines of the practical ones on offer at home and school, to encounter news and opinions wildly at variance with those of TV and family members, to explore the forbidden and even to extend it and to assume one or many cyber personas, these surely beat the children's encyclopaedias that had been the baby boomers' resort for flat information.

More importantly, an increasing proportion of those growing up after the1980s found themselves in a situation of 'contextual incongruity', particularly when they came to seeking their first jobs. For growing numbers and for the first time in history their natal social context fitted them for nothing, in total contrast to the simple societies of morphostatic times when the combination of imitation, induction and initiation supplied everything needed for entry to adult life. Because the context was substantially unchanging in the latter, the same skills and the same know-how could be slowly and informally acquired and smoothly applied to unchanged positions by successive generations as they reached adulthood. The name of the game was contextual replication and it depended on the mutual structural and cultural reinforcement of morphostasis continuing to generate 'contextual continuity'.

With the slowness of change characteristic of modernity, it was well known what additional skills or accomplishments were required for offspring to keep their social place or make slight improvements on it. By and large the returns upon these investments were predictable and the only calculation to be made concerned their affordability. Increasingly, as morphogenesis engaged either structurally or culturally, families had to cope with 'contextual discontinuity' by ingenuity or self-sacrifice: new industrialists seeking a practical education for their sons and successors sent them to the (independent) Scottish universities or to study engineering in Germany, whilst radicalized members of the working class scraped pennies together to send them to mechanics institutes – self-run and free from indoctrination by entrepreneurs or the clergy.

Significantly, 'contextual incongruity' was virtually unknown and confined to isolated pockets of society. The clearest historical examples are cultural instances of religious groups whose faiths were incongruous with the established Church, the longest and perhaps hardest case being the small percentage of recusant Catholics, practising illegally and sending their sons to Belgium or France for education and potential ordination, often not to see them again. Similarly, Jews and a century of nonconformists were denied a university degree in the UK until the abolition of the Test Acts in 1870. However, such instances implied an intergenerational solidarity of values within the family, which sets them apart from 'contextual incongruity' today.

Equally, three categories of women also experienced 'contextual incongruity': the 'fallen', placed beyond the pale, whatever the respectability of their backgrounds; the necessarily self-subsistent, whom Malthus sought to export abroad as governesses; and the intelligent home educated who, when novelists, often resorted to male pseudonyms or, as reformers, either married or else found themselves beyond the pale of any reputable context. Yet, at least in the latter cases, the consequences of 'wilful' persistence remained a matter of hard choice and predictable consequences, but it was a choice nonetheless – again setting such cases apart from today.

Predictability, calculability and thus instrumental rationality continued for most of the twentieth century. The increasing reach of 'contextual discontinuity' certainly acted as a spur to upward social mobility and the fear of its opposite to strenuous exertions on the part of parents to salvage the status of their offspring.[43] Nevertheless, it remained largely a question of what could be afforded, it became a very predictable matter in terms of the growing calibration of qualifications to posts throughout Europe, and its cadence represented slow, calculable and incremental intergenerational moves. The nineteenth-century French saying that it took three generations from the grandfather being an *instituteur* to the grandson becoming a *professeur* had not dramatically shortened.

With the onset of morphogenesis all of that began to change as the situational logic of opportunity engaged because of the proliferation of increasing variety. As far as the young were concerned, especially those transitional cohorts entering the job market in the late eighties and nineties, this confronted them with an array of new outlets, of short-term posts – rather than a job for life – whose names and contents were ephemeral, with expectations of postings abroad, with flexi-time, virtual offices and with the first broad hints that if they did not like what was (temporarily) on offer, then why not design what suited them. Why, though, did this represent 'contextual incongruity' for these young people?

It was because this major and unprecedented transformation meant that the parental background no longer possessed any corpus of *cultural capital* whose durable occupational value could be transmitted to their children, as opposed to cultural transmission *tout simple*.[44] Parental culture is rapidly ceasing to be a capital good, negotiable on the job market and counting as a significant element in the patrimony of offspring. *Les Héritiers* are being impoverished by more than death duties. Culture is still their inheritance but is swiftly becoming an internal good – valued at the estimate of its recipients, like the family silver – rather than an external good with a high value on the open market.[45] Consequently, strategies for ensuring the intergenerational transmission of cultural capital started to peter out, partly because it had been devalued almost overnight and partly because rapidly diminishing calculability made old

---

[43] These were well documented by Bourdieu and Passeron, which poses the question how such strategic actions could have evaded reflexive deliberation. Pierre Bourdieu and Jean-Claude Passeron, *La Reproduction*, Paris, Ed de Minuit, 1970, chapter 2.

[44] One indicator of which (in Britain) was the consistently better performance of Asian girls in state schools, compared with all other categories of pupil, over more than a decade.

[45] Alasdair MacIntyre, *After Virtue*, London, Duckworth, 1981, p. 187ff. See also Andrew Sayer, *The Moral Significance of Class*, Cambridge University Press, 2005, pp. 111–126.

forms of strategic action increasingly inapplicable. Many middle-class and upper-class parents who stuck to past routines, which had served their own parents well, of 'buying advantage' through private schooling began to face offspring who felt they had had an albatross tied round their necks. Confronting the incongruity between their background and their foreground, an increasing number of public school leavers began to blur their accents, abuse their past participles, make out they had never met Latin, refer to their school by its geographical location – all tokens of embarrassment reflecting their subjective recognition of the 'contextual incongruity' in which they were now placed.

Of course it will be objected that such an education still gained a disproportionate number of entrants to the oldest universities, but some of the sharpest public school leavers had no desire to go there and, in any case, such establishments were besieged by egalitarian-cum-meritocratic pressures which somewhat undercut their social point. Certain unlikely institutions themselves caught on and the Girls' Public Day School Trust quietly shed 'Public' from the name of its network at this time. Equally, it will be objected that their graduates still have preferential access to careers in the Civil Service, in diplomacy, in the traditional professions. But that is quite compatible with the fact that by the end of the twentieth century some of those from privileged backgrounds began to discount these openings. The fast learners had got the message: the Stock Exchange wanted the 'barrow-boy' mentality on the floor. Effectively, their possession of old-style cultural 'capital' was a disadvantage vis-à-vis new openings and opportunities, although it retains lingering value for the more traditional occupational outlets.

In a very different way, working-class parents found themselves in much the same position of literally having nothing of market value to reproduce among their children. With the rapid decline of manufacturing and frequent joblessness, their previous ability to recommend high wages and to 'speak for' their sons also disappeared. With the computerization of secretarial, reception and much work in retail, mothers found their daughters already more proficient than they were themselves. With involuntary redundancies, make-shift jobs and frequent visits to the job centre, there are less and less remnants of working-class culture to be reproduced – especially the old attractions of a lasting group of convivial workmates – and decreasing incentives to reproductory practices in employment among both parents and offspring. The latter, in any case, are now mostly 'at college', for varying amounts of time, but long enough for many to come to think that courses such as IT and Design represent a blue yonder of opportunity. Meanwhile, many of their parents retreat into a non-directive goodwill towards their children's futures, usually expressed as: 'We'll support them whatever they want to do.' This passes the burden of decision-making to the next generation and constitutes another dimension of 'contextual incongruity'. The parental generation has thrown up its hands in effective admission that their ways are not congruent with the new ways, which their offspring must navigate for themselves, albeit with diffuse family support.

Whereas the 'past', in the form of one's background, used to be a help in the present towards the future, it increasingly has nothing to give and, at worst, represents a hindrance to be overcome by the young. The old homology between socialized dispositions to accept positions, which the young were then dispositionally suited to occupy and pre-disposed to reproduce positionally, is coming to an end. As the very notion of *transferable* cultural capital becomes more and more tenuous, simultaneously all those intricate manoeuvres of substituting between different kinds of capital become outdated. Economic capital is always useful, but what can it purchase for the next generation that can be cashed out in terms of cultural advantage? A laptop, a gap year, a well-used passport, graduating debt free; these are certainly financially advantageous but they remain economic because what the offspring derive from them or do with them are at their discretion. Certainly, *social capital* does remain more enduring, but increasingly this is by transmitting a confidence and a lack of trepidation in pursuing the situational logic of opportunity. Nevertheless, *how* and *where* it is pursued is a task to be designed and followed up and often revised or corrected by the young themselves.

Reflexivity and nascent morphogenesis

How do the young launch themselves into the world and what pilots them in one direction rather than another? If past pathways are no guide and if the future speed of change is hostile to the very notion of defined paths to determinate ends, on what basis can they decide how to begin making their way through the world? Certainly, not in terms of instrumental rationality, because this requires strategic thinking about means and ends, which the unpredictability of novelty precludes more and more. Whilst the situational logic of competition was a logic that induced people to make choices, these were between well-defined alternatives. That logic operated through accentuating differences of class, status and power, by insisting upon their salience and pointing to objective gains and losses to make its point, thus undermining both openness and indifference, and making the question of alignment inescapable.

By contrast, the situational logic of opportunity is much looser and wider open. It constitutes an invitation to make what anyone will of complementary items in the cultural and social systems, to marry their existing knowledge and skills to some novel development without any certainty about the outcome of this combination, to experiment, to migrate, to innovate and to elaborate. If none of this synergy, syncretism or synthesis works, the reflexive imperative enjoins a return to the drawing board and trying again. In all of this, the burden is placed squarely upon the tyro entrants to chart their own courses of action. There are no fixed alternatives – as there were under the logic of competition. Certainly, in these transitional times, the option remains of joining the re-styled multi-national corporations, the banking sector, or public services, which is why autonomous reflexives are not short of congenial outlets.

Thus, it becomes imperative to deliberate about themselves in relation to the open opportunities they now confront. But in what terms can their deliberations be sensibly conducted? The response is 'in relation to their concerns'. This preserves the active agent without him or her degenerating into the wanton gambler. In the two preceding works, the general formula 'contexts + concerns' was presented as the key to what guided the reflexive process, accounted for its outcomes and, indeed, shaped the mode of reflexivity employed. Exactly the same recurs here; the 'context' is changing beyond recognition, 'contextual incongruity' is a newcomer in the sense that it now characterizes a growing tract of the population in the developed world as opposed to the previous small pockets of rather distinctive people. But, given its hallmark features of unpredictability, incalculability and the valorization of novelty, this means that personal 'concerns' play an increasing role in guiding deliberations and the conclusions arrived at. In sum, 'the importance of what we care about' has never been more important.

If subjects' constellations of concerns define their personal identities, then their ultimate concern and its realization will preponderate in their internal conversations.[46] In turn, this means that those (young people) who have committed themselves to a concern or 'cause' have a serious point of orientation from which to approach the situational logic of opportunity. Of course, endorsing such aims and values may well have the effect of intensifying their 'contextual incongruity' with their natal background, because nothing ensures that their values were derived from (consensual) parental socialization or are compatible with family normativity – where that remains. Given the changeable composition and definitions of 'the family', the values endorsed by offspring may represent a selection from what they encountered at home, an accentuation of

---

[46] Archer, *Being Human*, chapter 7.

one strand, or a rejection of all that was on offer in favour of something encountered elsewhere. In all such cases, the young subjects encounter a cultural element of 'contextual incongruity' in addition to those already discussed in structural terms.[47]

Not all have arrived at this point or will necessarily do so, but the fact that most can specify their concerns – as will be seen – gives them a grappling hook on the situational logic of opportunity. It enables them to engage in productive and purposeful internal conversation. This inner dialogue allows them to complete the following sequence: (a) defining and dovetailing their CONCERNS, (b) developing concrete courses of action as their PROJECTS and (c) establishing satisfying and sustainable PRACTICES. If conducted successfully, this enables subjects to realize their concerns and results in each person constituting his or her *modus vivendi*. What is novel is that its completion is becoming more and more reliant on *the practice of meta-reflexivity*. The defining features of this mode, namely for subjects to be critically reflexive about their own internal conversations and to be critical about effective action in society, are strongly fostered by nascent morphogenesis and the opportunities it presents. This is the case for three reasons.

To begin with, young subjects are necessarily at an epistemological disadvantage when they first confront the task of making their own match between their concerns and their first form of employment because they know too little about themselves and about swiftly changing opportunities. They have to crystallize both their concerns and to concretize them into a projected course of action in the world of work, yet know they are fallible in these two respects. *Self-critique thus becomes intrinsic to the very formulation and endorsement of a project*, which distinguishes it from the self-monitoring that was always required for the performance of skilled tasks. There are no formal apprenticeships in the morphogenetic society, only a plethora of courses extending dubious promises and always in need of being supplemented by shifting informal networks of proficients working at the cutting edge. During interview, this can appear as indecisiveness or vacillation as students (readily) proffer their lists of future jobs under consideration – lists which often contain seemingly very contrasting contenders, for example, training as a social worker or becoming an antiques dealer. Significantly, they themselves recognize this and, equally significant is the fact that they volunteer that they are sensibly 'keeping their options open' for the time being.

Some can readily define their three main concerns in life, but are incapable of prioritizing them; others do so but have revised their

---

[47] Socialization – in theory and practice – is discussed in Chapter 3.

priorities a year later; only a few, at the age of eighteen or nineteen, have disengaged an ultimate concern which proves lasting over their undergraduate years.[48] In other words, they are properly tentative or positively distrustful about their first inclinations and the first occupational matches that they suggest to themselves. This means that they rightfully linger long over the first stage of what I have termed the DDD scheme, made up of Discernment, Deliberation and Dedication.[49] That spells prolonged internal conversations, in which subjects critically explore and test their self-knowledge, and equally critically scrutinize the first 'matches' they have internally suggested to themselves. They do not know enough and are aware of it, but they appear fully cognisant of the fact that only through their own reflexive deliberations can they come to endorse a project, however much information they absorb from careers services and recruitment fairs. In other words, internal self-critique is accepted to be a predicate of safe landings and that is a hallmark of meta-reflexivity.

Secondly, when they feel reasonably – but of course fallibly – satisfied with the concerns they seek to realize, they still have to designate or design a project for future employment that is expressive of their concerns, thus making them prepared to invest themselves in it.[50] Additionally, but crucially, subjects have to deem their projects to be feasible in the outer world. In this they are hampered by their inadequate knowledge: some will temporize by awarding themselves an additional gap year; others will test the waters by taking an internship or placement; and still others will take a job for self-maintenance whilst their project takes shape. In this process, *all are driven to engage to some degree with the second aspect of meta-reflexivity, namely social critique*, even if this constitutes a relatively pain-free assent to the employment route taken – something which tends to be the preserve of autonomous reflexives. For others, the reflexive imperative drives them to further 'deliberation', in which feasible-sounding opportunities are discarded on closer inspection or from experience, and new opportunities are discovered and scrutinized. For still others, their internal critique of the outstanding array of institutionalized outlets is so profound that they recognize the situational logic of opportunity invites 'dedication' to a novel project of their own making, wherever they choose to make it.

Lastly, the growth and diversification of the third, voluntary or social–private sector has increasing attractions because it provides roles that can

---

[48] That is during their first of the three-year undergraduate degree, for the majority.
[49] For a more detailed discussion, see Archer, *Being Human*, pp. 230–241.
[50] A 'project' is used as a generic term for any intentional course of action pursued.

be personified in terms of the value commitments endorsed by many young subjects. Here, social critique represents profound disenchantment with both market and state and an attempt to locate an institutional base in which they are willing to invest themselves. In this context, Habermas has accentuated the 'colonization' of such new outlets and organizations by the old Leviathans.[51] Yet, as meta-reflexivity increases, it is equally important to emphasize the counter-flow of critique. Some of these young subjects are prepared to enter school teaching, for example, with the aim of encouraging their pupils to thrive in a manner that will clash with governmentally imposed 'performance indicators' and with the professional associations that have currently endorsed them.

As my elder son and his wife happily launched into their tenth season of running mountaineering courses abroad, having skilled and re-skilled themselves en route and at their own expense, the comment passed by their nonagenarian grandmother encapsulated what has been argued in this chapter about the newness of the reflexive imperative. 'What a pity', she remarked, 'that they're not using their degrees'. This is an understandable reaction from what had been a bright young girl, born into a numerous family, who was subject to the full brunt of the situational logic of competition in its war-time austerity. Degrees were then a means to an end and her enduring instrumental rationality resulted in ever overvaluing the university place that she was offered only for it to be turned down by her family. That missed degree would have been 'used' to open professional doors; when half of the (British) age cohort was destined to acquire one under New Labour and nearly 40% did so, the only door they were certain to go through was that which opens onto the reflexive imperative.[52]

Conclusion

This chapter has been futuristic in presenting the reflexive imperative as the necessary accompaniment of 'morphogenesis unbound'. Nevertheless, we remain in a transitional period and modernity has not yet breathed its last gasp. Above all, the global world remains a capitalist domain and capitalism has proved remarkably ingenious about

---

[51] Jürgen Habermas, *The Theory of Communicative Action*, Polity Press, Cambridge, 1989 (1981).

[52] When 'educational inflation' began to develop in the US, Green *et al.* advanced their thesis that as the educational level of the population approached x, the only advantage of attaining x was to avoid penalization because the prizes now went to those with x+1. Thomas F. Green, David P. Ericson and Robert M. Seidman, *Predicting the Behaviour of the Educational System*, Syracuse, N.Y.: Syracuse University Press, 1980.

developing a civilized ideational face and has adapted successfully towards critique from the better organized social movements (with green, organic and ecological marketing becoming big business, for example). Hints have been given about how it has sustained its hegemony and hence continued to provide the competitive conditions that foster autonomous reflexivity. Placing the emphasis upon autonomous versus meta-reflexivity, as constituting the major divide between educated young people today, assumes that the conditions propitious to developing and sustaining communicative reflexivity are becoming consistently harder to maintain (as will be illustrated in Chapter 4). In short, the diminution of communicatives appears to augment the ranks of both autonomous and meta-reflexives.

However, it also increases the proportion of fractured reflexives. This chapter should not be read as a peon of praise to the situational logic of opportunity. Welcome as it may be in terms of enhancing self-determination and of according increased governance over their own life courses for many, it has a negative face that has not yet been examined. The necessity of reflexively defining one's concerns, of deliberatively designating one's own projects and of determining one's own *modus vivendi* also means that responding to the reflexive imperative exposes subjects to the consequences of their own fallibility. It makes them vulnerable to the contingencies of life in an open system – one largely without a safety net, given the loss of community and overall reduction in social integration. The reflexive imperative produces casualties – the fractured reflexives – those who get it wrong and, in their fracturedness, simply cannot work out how to put it right.

2   The reflexive imperative versus habits and *habitus*

Introduction

The role of habit – habitual, routinized or customary action – has had an extremely long run in social theory. We are indebted to Charles Camic for demonstrating that 'habits' played a bigger part in classical theorizing than is usually acknowledged.[1] His definition is also nicely straightforward and Catholic: 'the term "habit" generally denominates a more or less self-actuating disposition or tendency to engage in a previously adopted or acquired form of action'.[2] However, it is hard to agree with his bold claims that 'contemporary sociology has virtually dispensed with the concept'; that 'there is no need to carry this investigation forwards in time' – meaning beyond the first decades of the twentieth century – or to accept that 'the end of habit' in social theory resulted from a successful take over by behavioural psychology abetted by Talcott Parsons' substitution of normative regulation for habituation.[3] Even harder to endorse is his judgement on reflexivity, the usurper of habitual action: 'So obviously appropriate has the reflective model come to appear that those who employ it seldom concern themselves with providing a reasoned defence, or even an explicit justification, for their practice of uniformly casting human conduct into this one mold'.[4] In what follows I want to question firstly, the death of habit; secondly, to query the absence of good reason for attending to reflexivity today; and thirdly, to doubt whether 'habit' and 'reflexivity' have stood in a zero-sum relationship over the last hundred years of theorizing.

Writing in 1986 and from translation, it was understandable that Camic did not detect the nascent revitalization of pragmatism but less so that he had no intimation that Bourdieu's reformulation of *habitus*

This chapter is a modified version of 'Routine, Reflexivity and Realism', 2010, *Sociological Theory*, 28:3, 272–303.

[1] Charles Camic, 'The Matter of Habit', *American Journal of Sociology*, 91:5, 1986, 1039–1087.
[2] *Ibid.*, p. 1044.   [3] *Ibid.*, pp. 1040 and 1076.   [4] *Ibid.*, p. 1041.

was already becoming what Scott Lash dubbed the only cultural game in town (there is a single reference to *reproduction*).[5] There were very good reasons indeed, which strengthened over the last two decades of the twentieth century, for paying more attention to reflexive action, although those I will advance are not identical to Alexander's prescience.[6] Finally, what has predominated amongst social theorists is far from an endorsement of 'one mold' of (reflexive) action, but rather diverse efforts to hybridize habit and reflexivity.

However, there is a puzzle about certain theoretical convergences that paved the way towards the hegemony of hybridization today. On the one hand, modern pragmatists have become much more concerned, not with the exorbitation of routine but, in their most emblematic book, with the *Creativity of Action*.[7] Conversely, a number of modern realists, brought up on Bhaskar's 'transformatory model of social action' and some on my 'morphogenetic approach', today rank among the strong defenders of routine action, habits and *habitus*.[8] In other words, pragmatists and realists appear on the 'wrong sides' in the discussion of reflexivity – with pragmatists ever more disposed to stress the contribution of innovative action whilst certain realists are strong supporters of habitual dispositions.

This crossover begs for explanation. It seems as if both parties are seeking to strengthen their weaker flanks in faster changing times. The great American pragmatists had always maintained that reflexivity (exercised through 'internal conversation') came into its own when habitual action was blocked by problematic circumstances. It might be argued in short hand that 'globalization' creates vastly more problems which are not amenable to traditional routine responses and hence augments reflexive deliberations. Yet, this is too pat, because Joas stresses the 'situated creativity' of *all* action (as against purposeful, normative or rational instrumental action orientations) without increasing the role of reflexivity, since 'creativity' – tantalizingly undefined – is not held to involve premeditation. Conversely, critical realism came on

[5] Pierre Bourdieu, *La Reproduction*, Paris, Ed. De Minuit, 1970.
[6] Jeffrey Alexander, *Theoretical Logic in Sociology*, vol. 1, *Positivism, Presuppositions, and Current Controversies*, Berkeley and Los Angeles, University of California Press, 1982, p. 67f.
[7] Hans Joas, *The Creativity of Action*, University Of Chicago Press, 1996 (1992).
[8] Roy Bhaskar, *The Possibility of Naturalism*, Hemel Hempstead, Harvester Press, 1989 (1979) and Margaret S. Archer, *Social Origins of Educational Systems*, London and Beverly Hills, Sage, 1979, *Culture and Agency: The Place of Culture in Social Theory*, Cambridge University Press, 1988 and *Realist Social Theory: the Morphogenetic Approach*, Cambridge University Press, 1995.

the scene with a depth ontology, but has encountered two recurring critiques.[9] On the one hand, the charge of reification has constantly been levelled, prompting some to emphasize synchronic analysis alone. This is clearest in Manicas who, despite including 'realism' in his latest title, concentrates exclusively upon the synchronic, treating the diachronic structuring of roles, rules, resources and interests as 'matters to hand'.[10] Thus, questions about how these had come to be 'so' rather than 'otherwise' remained unanswered, as with Searle's bundling them into the 'background'.[11] On the other hand, despite their insistence upon 'activity dependence' and 'relationality', realists largely view social relations as founded upon shared objective interests and their associated effects in motivating action. In brief, realism's weaker flank is that it does not have a robust and relational theory of social integration.[12] It seems to me that the otherwise puzzling invocation of 'habit' by so many realists is an attempt to plug this gap.

What these developments seek to satisfy are the basically reasonable – though often one-sidedly exaggerated – objections that the influences of the social order upon agency should not be located *fully within agents* or *entirely outside them*.

The former has been something of a problem for pragmatism and the latter for realism. Despite the high ratio of internalized sociality, especially in Meadian pragmatism, the very fact that agents encounter external obstacles defeating their habitual routines and exceeding their habitual repertoires does mean that all social influences cannot be subcutaneous – which would leave the 'spontaneous "I"' permanently unemployed. The constant interplay between 'situated problems' and 'situated creativity' in contemporary pragmatism does even out the workload between the 'I' (always more of a task-performer rather than a seething Freudian *id*) and the generalized other, thus balancing the-social-within and the-social-without.

For its part, realism has never placed sociality entirely outside agency; had it done so its frequent references to ideological mystification and, indeed, the living out of epistemic fallacies would have become incomprehensible. Those who have perversely tried to level a charge that realism subscribes to monadic individualism in a wholly exterior social

---

[9] Roy Bhaskar, *A Realist Theory of Science*, Hassocks, Harvester Press, 1978 (1975).

[10] Peter T. Manicas, *A Realist Philosophy of Social Science: Explanation and Understanding*, Cambridge University Press, 2006, p. 75f.

[11] John R. Searle, *The Construction of Social Reality*, London, Penguin, 1995, pp. 129–142.

[12] Margaret S. Archer, 'Critical Realism and Relational Sociology: Complementarity and Synergy', *Journal of Critical Realism*, 9:2, 2010, 199–207.

world[13] are hard pressed to account for the importance realism has always attached to explanatory and ideological critique.[14] Nevertheless, the recent annexation of habit and *habitus* presumably recommends itself to the above type of critic by letting more of the social get under the agential skin.

My own version of realist social theory – the morphogenetic approach – is not very hospitable to this current enthusiasm for habitual action among realists for three reasons. These relate to what the morphogenetic approach is and does: (i) it is an explanatory framework for examining the interplay between structure and agency and their outcomes, and (ii) it is a toolkit for developing the analytical histories of the emergence of particular social formations, institutional structures and organizational forms. In other words, the morphogenetic approach is both an explanatory programme (the methodological complement of critical realist meta-theory), but also a means of accounting for the trajectories, dynamics and contours of social formations, and (iii) it refers to 'morphogenetic society' as a new formation *in statu nascendi*.

Morphogenesis refers to 'those processes which tend to elaborate or change a system's given form, structure or state', and morphostasis to those processes in a complex system that tend to preserve the above unchanged.[15] As an explanatory framework, my morphogenetic approach endorses a stratified ontology for structures (1995), cultures (1988) and agents (2000), because each has its emergent and irreducible properties and powers – and it explains every social outcomes as the product of their interplay. Outcomes, which can be broadly reproductory or largely transformatory, depend upon the intertwining of structure, culture and agency, but not by rendering them 'inseparable', as in the 'central conflation' of Giddens, Bourdieu and Beck, which makes for an amalgam precluding the examination of their interplay.[16] Nor is this 'co-determinism', implying a dualistic – literally a dual factor approach – to Dépelteau; it is never anything but *analytical* dualism.[17] Crucially,

---

[13] Anthony King, 'Against Structure: A Critique of Morphogenetic Social Theory', *Sociological Review*, 47:2, 1999, 199–227 and 'Why I Am Not an Individualist', *Journal for the Theory of Social Behaviour*, 37:2, 2007, 211–219. But with greater perversity see François Dépelteau, 'Relational Thinking: A Critique of Co-Deterministic Theories of Structure and Agency', *Sociological Theory*, 26:1, 2008, 51–69.

[14] Andrew Collier, *Critical Realism*, London, Verso, 1994, pp. 101–104 and 170–190.

[15] Walter Buckley, *Sociology and Modern Systems Theory*, Englewood Cliffs, N. J., Prentice Hall, 1967, p. 58.

[16] Archer, *Realist Social Theory*, pp. 93–134.

[17] Dépelteau, 'Relational Thinking'. Leaving aside the *méchanceté* of this paper, whose author tortuously misrepresents my arguments, Dépelteau is insufficiently versed in either the realism he attacks or the relational sociology he defends. It is not

what is missed *inter alia* by such a co-determinist interpretation is the *double morphogenesis* in which actors themselves change relationally in the very process of actively pursuing changes in the social order. This should be viewed as one of the principal 'non-Meadian' ways by which the social gets inside us.

My generic aim is to account for what forms of interplay generate 'morphogenesis' at one extreme and 'morphostasis' at the other, be it at the micro-, meso- or macro-level. In order to discuss the bearing of this realist approach on the relationship between habit and reflexivity, it will be necessary to draw upon it as both an 'explanatory framework' and an 'analytical history' of emergence. Discussion of both requires a brief inspection of the *basic* morphogenetic cycle. From that, firstly, I will situate the differential importance of habit on the morphostatic–morphogenetic continuum, which is also the historical trajectory of the developed world. Secondly, far-reaching criticisms will be derived about the *ahistorical* nature of the debate surrounding habit/habitual action, which will also allow me to situate the importance of reflexivity in the historical panorama of *structural and agential* transformation (i.e. the double morphogenesis and its epochal consequences).

The relevance of the morphostatic–morphogenetic continuum

All structural properties found in any society are continuously activity-dependent. Nevertheless, it is possible to separate 'structure' and 'agency' through analytical dualism, and to examine their interplay in order to account for the structuring and restructuring of the social order. Fundamentally, this is possible for two reasons. Firstly, 'structure' and 'agency' are *different kinds of emergent properties*, although space precludes entering the debate about emergence here. This is shown by the differences in their properties and powers, *despite* the fact that they are crucial for one another's formation, continuation and development. As Bhaksar put

appreciated that in social realism, all emergent properties *are relational in kind*, that they may exist unexercised and be exercised unrealized, in what is an ontological and not, as is asserted, an epistemological position. Relational sociology fares worse, being attributed to Mustafa Emirbayer ('Manifesto for a Relational Sociology', *American Journal of Sociology*, vol. 103, n. 2, September 1997, 281–317), oblivious of the flourishing Italian school (*locus classicus* Pierpaolo Donati's *Introduzione alla sociologia relazionale* (Milan, Franco Angeli, 1983) and his many subsequent elaborations, the latest in his *Relational Sociology: A New Paradigm for the Social Sciences*, London, Routledge, 2010). This latter work overtly endorses critical realism. Instead, what Donati calls *relationalist* sociology, in order to distinguish his approach from it, is reduced to the repetition of the term 'transactions', as if no other concept were needed – with the exception of 'habits'.

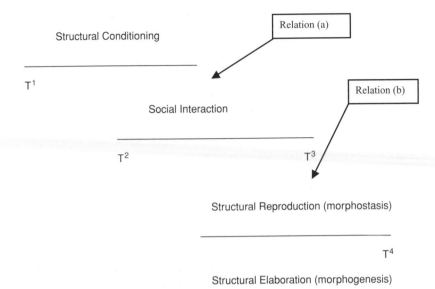

Figure 2.1 The basic morphogenetic sequence

it succinctly, 'people and society. . . do not constitute two moments of the same process. Rather they refer to radically different things'.[18] Thus, an educational system can be 'centralized', whilst a person cannot, and humans are 'emotional', which cannot be the case for structures. Secondly, and fundamental to the workability of this explanatory methodology, 'structure' and 'agency' operate diachronically over different tracts of time because: (i) structure necessarily pre-dates the action(s) that transform it and (ii) structural elaboration necessarily post-dates those actions, as represented in Figure 2.1. The possibility of employing analytical dualism rests upon nothing but this.

Full significance is accorded to the timescale through which structure and agency themselves *emerge, intertwine and redefine* one another, since this is the bedrock of the explanatory format employed in accounting for any substantive social change. Since all the lines in the Figure 2.1 are in fact continuous, delineating any cycle depends upon the problem in hand. The projection of all lines forwards and backwards connects up with anterior and posterior cycles of the historical structuring and restructuring process, enabling us to unravel and explain the processes involved in the *structuring* and specific forms of *restructuring* that take

[18] Bhaskar, *The Possibility*, p. 76.

place *over time*. Equally, it is what allows us to grasp agential change, occurring through the double morphogenesis and the crucial changes in relations and relationality that ensue.[19]

Finally, contra certain forms of friendly fire, this is both a diachronic *and* a synchronic account.[20] Nothing social is self-sustaining; a myriad of agential 'doings' (including reflecting, believing and imagining) and social relations alone (the cohesive and conflicting relations of groups) keep any higher level social entity in being and may render it relatively enduring. In other words, whilst ever something like the centralized French educational system lasts, then move a marker, second-by-second, from the system's inception until today and each and every moment of its 'centralization' depends upon agential doings and intentions (individual and collective). However, this is not equivalent to some Giddensian notion that *every* doing on the part of *everyone* somehow contributes to maintaining the whole.[21] On the contrary, some actors and actions are irrelevant to sustaining centralization, some are more important than others, and further 'doings' counteract one another so that the *status quo* continues *pro tem*. The point of the morphogenetic approach is precisely to specify the 'who's who' and 'who does what' in social transformation.

When a morphogenetic cycle is completed, by issuing in structural elaboration, not only is structure transformed but so is agency, as part and parcel of the same process – the double morphogenesis.[22] As it reshapes structural relations at any given T^4, agency is ineluctably reshaping itself in relational terms: of domination and subordination, of integration, organization, combination and articulation; in terms of the vested interests of some but not of other agents; in terms of what has become normalized and taken for granted; in terms of the new roles and positions that some occupy and others do not; and in terms of the novel situations in which all agents now find themselves, which are constraining to the projects of some and enabling to the projects of others, yet of significance for the motivation of all.

To appreciate fully the part played by either habit or reflexivity, it is necessary to look more closely at the interconnections between the relationships summarized in the basic diagram (Figure 2.1). Within any cycle

---

[19] Pierpaolo Donati, 'La teoria del realismo critico è una ragione sociologic anche fa esperienza della realità', in Andrea M. Maccarini, Emmanuele Morandi and Riccardo Prandini (eds.), *Realismo Sociologico*, Genoa-Milan, Marietti, 2008, pp. 163–181. Pierpaolo Donati, *Teoria Relazionale della Società*, Milan, Franco Angeli, 2009.

[20] Dave Elder-Vass, 'Reconciling Archer and Bourdieu', *Sociological Theory*, 25:4, 2007, 325–346.

[21] Anthony Giddens, *Central Problems in Social Theory*, London, Macmillan, 1979, pp. 77–78.

[22] Archer, *Realist Social Theory*, pp. 247–293.

this is to clarify {relation a}, that is, *how* structural/cultural conditioning effectively influences socio-cultural interaction. Without such clarification, the term 'conditioning' merely rules out any form of determinism, but does not arbitrate between two possible answers: conditional influences are exerted largely through 'traditional' socialization (of habit and associated repertoires of routine action) or through the exercise of reflexivity, entailing deliberation about the appropriate course of action in a given social context.

When first applying critical realism to the social order, Bhaskar was clear that in {relation a} 'the causal power of social forms is mediated through social agency'.[23] Whilst this (laudably) wards off charges about the reification of structural and cultural emergent properties or their hydraulic influences upon members of society by properly insisting upon their 'activity-dependence', it actually tells us nothing about the *process of mediation itself.* Hence, it does not arbitrate upon the two possible answers above: non-reflexive socialization versus reflexive deliberation. This may account for why realist social theorists freely opt for either 'habit' or 'reflexivity' being the key mediatory mechanism.

To provide guidelines for arbitration, rather than leaving the issue of what constitutes conditioning undefined, it is necessary to clarify {relation b}, namely, what kinds of social interaction issue in structural/cultural morphostasis versus morphogenesis. This is crucial because T^4 is the new T^1 of the next cycle of <conditioning → interaction → elaboration>, the end of one cycle being the beginning of the next. In other words, it is decisive for whether or not the conditional influence exerted further down the timeline on the next 'generation' of agents (who may or may not be the same people) is much the same as at the initial T^1, as would be the case where morphostasis was the outcome, or is distinctively different, where the sequence ends in morphogenesis.

A timeless, placeless, and societally unspecific debate on mediatory processes is futile, that is, one seeking a show of hands on the universal motion that 'habit is more important than reflexivity' or vice versa. Of course, most would rightly respond 'sometimes one and sometimes the other'. Quite properly, they are hedging their bets until the 'when', 'where' and 'under what conditions' have been specified. Attempts to short circuit this specification by performing a shotgun wedding between habit and reflexivity and calling its offspring 'hybridization' achieves nothing of theoretical utility. Obviously, the sponsors of this hybrid are usually more sophisticated than that. Conversely, strong defenders of habitual action almost uniformly assign a high and universal importance

---

[23] Bhaskar, *The Possibility*, p. 26.

to the pre-reflexive (years, practices, experiences, sociality, and socialization) upon habit formation. Alternatively, strong advocates of reflexivity attribute the same high and universal importance to people's ability to scrutinize, monitor and modify acquired habits through the internal conversation. These, too, are generalizations and call for the same specification as the blunt 'sometimes one and sometimes the other'.

What I will seek to argue in this first section is that if we put {relation a}, meaning how people are socially conditioned, together with {relation b}, standing for whether they reproduce or change their initial circumstances, it becomes possible to advance some specific propositions about the relative importance of habit and reflexivity in relation to time, place and conditions. Part of the usefulness of the three propositions advanced is that it enables us to identify from *which particular type of social configuration those defending the universality of habitual action are over-generalizing its importance*; the same goes for universal protagonists of reflexivity. A more useful theoretical contribution than either would be to offer a specific diagnosis of the place of habit and reflexivity in the past, present and future, as ventured in Chapter 1.

Generically, the conditioning influence of the structural/cultural context in {relation a} works through shaping the situations – from the accessibility of resources to the prevalence of beliefs – in which agents find themselves, such that some courses of action would be impeded and discouraged, whilst others would be facilitated and encouraged.[24] The use of these terms denotes objective effects upon subjectivity as Porpora makes crystal clear: 'among the causal powers that are deposited in social positions are interests . . . actors are motivated to act in their interests'.[25] However, if constraints and enablements are taken as illustrative of contextual conditioning, then it has to be acknowledged that this is only the first instalment of the story, the part accounting for how structural and cultural properties objectively impinge upon agents. This is because there are no constraints and enablements per se, that is, as entities. These are

---

[24] I formulated the transmission to social properties to agents as follows in Archer, *Realist Social Theory*, and quote it to re-endorse it: 'Given their pre-existence, structural and cultural emergents shape the social environment to be inhabited. These results of past actions are deposited in the form of current situations. They account for what there is (structurally and culturally) to be distributed and also for the shape of such distributions; for the nature of the extant role array; the proportion of positions available at any time and the advantages/disadvantages associated with them; for the institutional configuration present and for those second order emergent properties of complementarity and compatibility, that is whether the respective operations of institutions are matters of obstruction or assistance to one another. In these ways, situations are objectively defined for their subsequent occupants or incumbents.' P. 201.

[25] Douglas V. Porpora, 'Four Concepts of Social Structure', *Journal for the Theory of Social Behaviour*, 19, 1989, 195–211, p. 208.

the potential *causal powers* of emergent social properties, yet a constraint needs something to constrain and an enablement something to enable. In other words, for anything to exert the contingent power of a constraint or an enablement, it has to stand in a *relationship* such that it obstructs or aids the achievement of some specific agential enterprise as subjectively defined. The generic name for such enterprises is 'projects' – i.e. any end, however inchoate, that can be intentionally entertained by human beings. In short, the *activation* of objective constraints and enablements depends upon their subjective reception by individuals or groups. The reception phase $(T^1 - T^2)$, entailing social interaction is, by definition, profoundly relational in kind.

In short, three conditions are required for the conditional influence of structural and cultural properties to *exercise their powers* as constraints or enablements. Firstly, such powers are dependent upon the existence of human 'projects'; if *per impossible* there were no such projects, this would mean that there were no constraints or enablements. Secondly, to operate as either an enabling or a constraining influence, there has to be a relationship of congruence or incongruence respectively with particular agential projects. Thirdly, agents have to respond to these influences which, being conditional rather than deterministic, are subject to reflexive deliberation over the nature of the response, and their personal powers include the abilities to withstand them or to circumvent them.

However, this brief discussion of {relation a} remains indeterminate about *what* members of society (in what proportions) *will actually do*. In the first two books in this trilogy I have argued that this depends upon the mode of reflexivity employed by different agents, but have simultaneously maintained that the dominant mode practised is contextually dependent.[26] The general formula [social contexts + personal concerns] attaches equal importance to both elements in accounting for the extensiveness of reflexivity and its dominant modality. Thus, to advance the present discussion about when habit prevails over reflexivity or vice versa, it is necessary to link up {relation a} to {relation b} in order to introduce the overall historical sequence of morphostatic and morphogenetic cycle(s).

In the broadest terms there is a historical trajectory from morphostatic social formations (governed fundamentally by negative feedback) to morphogenetic ones (where positive feedback begins to predominate) – as discussed in the previous chapter – which accounts for the *variable* importance that habitual action has played societally. In other words,

---

[26] Margaret S. Archer, *Structure, Agency and the Internal Conversation*, Cambridge University Press, 2003 and *Making our Way through the World: Human Reflexivity and Social Mobility*, Cambridge University Press, 2003, pp. 317–325.

habit does, indeed, have a particular place in history – it belongs with morphostasis. Undoubtedly, habitual action can be prolonged (amongst large tracts of the population) whilst ever morphostatic and morpho-genetic feedback loops circulate simultaneously, which is the *durée* of modernity itself. But its days are numbered when morphogenesis begins to engage fully because this is also when the 'reflexive imperative' becomes ineluctable, even for the realization of 'traditional' concerns. To invoke 'hybridization' is to put a label on this complexity rather than to understand and explain what is going on, or so it will be argued.

In other words, I want us to heed Vygotsky's neglected call, made in 1934, for a history of reflexivity, rather than treating it as a human potential but one whose practice is historically indeterminate.[27] This aim broadly coincides with Emirbayer and Mische's injunction to 'look at agentic orientations supported by periods of stability and change', when seeking to understand the kinds of projects they entertain.[28] How-ever, although their injunction shows that the present argument appeals to a broader church than realism, nevertheless, realism can improve upon their empiricist appeal (above) to Swidler's distinction between 'settled' and 'unsettled' times.[29] This can be achieved by distinguishing between the contexts shaped for any given group of agents, {relation a}, being ones of 'contextual continuity', 'contextual discontinuity' or 'contextual incongruity'. It entails situating these three kinds of inher-ited contexts (not of contemporary agents' making or choosing) on the morphostatic–morphogenetic continuum and showing that they occupy distinctive tracts of the historical panorama stretching from the earliest societies to the present day {relation b}, as was sketched in Chapter 1. Variations of the contextual kind may also be differentiated for differ-ent sections of the population and distinct sectors of a relevant society, neither of which are necessarily in synch with one another or with the macro-trajectory of society.

Morphostasis–morphogenesis and contextual continuity, discontinuity and incongruity

From the summary discussion just presented, three propositions are advanced and will be examined in turn.

---

[27] Lev S. Vygotsky, *Thought and Language*, Cambridge, Mass., MIT Press, 1964 (1934), p. 153.

[28] Mustafa Emirbayer and Ann Mische, 'What is Agency', *American Journal of Sociology*, 103:4, 1998, 962–1023, 1006–1007.

[29] Ann Swidler, 'Culture in Action: Symbols and Strategies', *American Sociological Review*, 51, 1986, 273–286.

The hegemony of habit depends upon societal morphostasis

Here, 'habit' is used to embrace cognate terms (*habitus*, customary behaviour, habitual and routinized action). Habit denotes what William James termed 'sequences of behaviour that have become virtually automatic' or what Giddens designated as actions that are 'relatively unmotivated'.[30] Charles Camic has done sterling service by combing through the works of Durkheim and Weber to provide an overview of the respective parts they assigned to habit and habitual action. However, he is so concerned to demonstrate that habit remained a preoccupation for both theorists that he misses the connection each forged between early societies (or ancient civilizations) and their 'contextual continuity', which promoted the hegemony of traditional action – in short, Durkheim and Weber's characterizations of morphostasis and its consequences. Yet, we all know that the 'worried man of the Third Republic', like the delegate to the Conference of Versailles, were equally riveted by the transition to modernity and the discontinuities, differentiation and diversification of mental orientations and institutional operations that it represented – all of which are manifestations that morphogenesis had seriously begun to engage.

In other words and under their own descriptions, both founding figures seemed acutely aware of the pivotal role played by 'contextual continuity', which is shorthand for how action contexts are shaped for the members of structurally and culturally morphostatic configurations of the social order. Thus, Camic underlines that to Durkheim: 'Primitive peoples . . . live to a large extent under the "force of habit" and under the "yoke of habit" . . . for "when things go on happening in the same way, habit . . . suffice(s) for conduct" and moral behaviour itself is easily transformed "into habit mechanically carried out"' – which remained the case into the Middle Ages.[31] Durkheim's own summary statement is classically pragmatist, namely, whilst ever 'there is an equilibrium between our dispositions and surrounding environment', action bypasses reflexive deliberation, with 'consciousness and reflection' awakening only 'when habit is disrupted, when a process of non-adaptation occurs'.[32]

From this Camic concludes that for Durkheim 'human action, whether individual or collective, oscillates between two poles, that of consciousness or reflection on the one side, and that of habit on the other side, with

---

[30] William James, *The Principles of Psychology*, vol. 1, New York, Dover, 1950 (1890), p. 10 and Giddens, *Central Problems*, p. 218.

[31] Camic, 'The Matter of Habit', p. 1051.

[32] Emile Durkheim, *Pragmatism and Society*, Cambridge University Press, 1983 (1913–1914), pp. 79–80.

the latter pole being the stronger'.[33] However, the references substantiating this judgement were largely drawn from his works on moral education, civic ethics and future pedagogy.[34] We should not forget that the purpose of these writings was part of Durkheim's reformist and remedial recipe for modernity, in order to restore social integration to its level in the *status quo ante*. It is not part of his *description* of modernity but of his *prescription* for the *status quo post*. Moreover, Camic does acknowledge Durkheim's belief that 'under the dynamic conditions of the modern age, any viable morality entails as well continual reflection at the upper reaches of the social order'.[35]

Lacking Comtean dreams of sociologists becoming society's guides, Weber simply describes the ligatures binding early societies and ancient civilizations to traditionalism and habit: 'the further we go back in history [...] social action is determined in an ever more comprehensive sphere exclusively by the disposition (*Eingestellheit*) toward the purely traditional'.[36] 'Contextual continuity' is presented as the necessary condition for this 'sea of traditionalism', with peasant life revolving around the seasons. Camic's failure to highlight the significance of morphostasis (and its transformation) is because he leapfrogs over Weber's world religion studies as a whole, since the emergence of Western rationalism and capitalism is 'sufficiently familiar that it can largely be passed over'.[37] In so doing, the significance that Weber attributed to 'contextual continuity', stemming from the mutual reinforcement of structural and cultural morphostasis, is lost. So, too, is the point of the comparative studies of world religions, where the absence of these conditions was precisely what he held to account for the origins of rationality in ancient Judaism (whose prototype in theodicies of misfortune was pinned upon the 'contextual discontinuities' produced by repeated conquest and exile). Three thousand years later – a detour he never fully examined – Weber traced back the spirit of capitalism to these origins, which overcame the 'general incapacity and indisposition to depart from habituated paths'.[38]

Nevertheless, Weber cautioned the citizens of modernity to be 'constant in employing correctives against unthinking habit'.[39] In other

---

[33] Camic, 'The Matter of Habit', p. 1052.
[34] Emile Durkheim, *Professional Ethics and Civic Morals*, Glencoe, Ill., Free Press, 1958 (1898–1900).
[35] *Ibid.*, p. 1054.
[36] Max Weber, *Economy and Society*, Berkeley, Calif., University of California Press, 1978 (1922), p. 321.
[37] Camic, 'The Matter of Habit', p. 1063.
[38] Max Weber, *General Economic History*, Glencoe, Ill., Free Press, 1927 (1923), p. 355
[39] Donald L. Levine, 'Rationality and Freedom: Weber and Beyond', *Sociological Inquiry*, 51, 1981, 5–25, p. 20.

words, Weber did not see his four 'types of action', based upon different orientations, ceding place to one another seriatim as circumstances changed. Instead, traditional (habitual) and instrumental rationality were extreme types, neither mutually exclusive nor excluding the *Wertrationalität* or the charismatic. But, the *Zweckrationalität* became increasingly dominant in the slow, partial and differential process that was the progress of modernity. What he disavows *within modernity* is a strictly zero-sum relationship between habitual action and the reflexive deliberations entailed by the *Zweckrationalität*. This provides no justification for the *amalgamation* of the two in hybridization theories developed for globalized society a century later. All the same, it does capture nicely how the marker moves from predominantly habitual action to predominantly reflexive action when morphostasis *slowly tips* towards morphogenesis as structural and cultural differentiation engage in modernity.

However, human reflexivity was not entirely absent and could not be because it is socially indispensable in three ways: a reflexive 'sense of self' is necessary for the correct appropriation of rights and duties by those to whom they are ascribed, the self-monitoring of performance is necessarily a reflexive task, and reflexivity is crucial for bridging the gap between formal expectations and actual eventualities in the open social system. Nevertheless, what reflexivity does not and cannot do in traditional societies is to enable its members to re-envisage either the self or the social because they lack the ideational and organizational resources for doing so. This is why it is justifiable to use the term 'traditional societies'. It is so because the *co-existence of cultural and structural morphostasis together generated a high and lasting degree of* everyday *'contextual continuity' for the populations in question*: repetitive situations, stable expectations, and durable relations – and with them, habitual action.

> *Parity of importance between habit and reflexivity coincides with social formations which are simultaneously morphostatic and morphogenetic (i.e. situated towards the mid-point of the continuum)*

However, 'parity' is a summary term *covering different sections of the population*, rather than indicating 'hybridization' for all. 'Hybridization' is generally endorsed by those emphasizing the durability of the pre-reflexive period and the internalization of its influences – from significant others or more generally from the social background. The protagonists of hybridization are distinctive in withholding the power from subjects to override early socialization reflexively (or restricting it to the modification of socialized dispositions), thus derogating personal powers in favour of the social order. Importantly, such theorists show little inclination to discuss differences between those most proximately involved in morphogenetic social sectors, compared with those remaining embedded in morphostatic areas (rural), institutions (agriculture), and ideational preserves (folklore).

There are two fundamental ways in which the relation between habits and reflexivity can be conceptualized: one sees the two in tension and producing intra-personal struggles, whilst the other views reflexive, innovative action as built *upon* habitual dispositions. The first is antipathetic to 'hybridization'; the second endorses it. The former is hospitable to people's purposeful commitments, the latter is hostile. The one can accentuate macroscopic 'contextual discontinuity' as a spur to reflexivity; the other emphasizes minute quotidian continuities at the micro-level.

The first view is Peircian and is compressed into the following five points.[40] Firstly, Peirce is an advocate of our 'personal powers', especially those of our 'moral natures' which should result in the self-monitoring of our habits rather than their replication: 'you are well aware that the exercise of control over your own habits, if not the most important business in life, is at least very near to being so'.[41] Secondly, self-transformation comes about through the reflexive 'internal conversation' in which people seek to conform themselves to their ultimate concerns, ideals or commitments, arrived at intra-personally, 'by cherishing and tending them as I would the flowers in my garden'.[42] Thirdly, this involves a struggle on the part of the committed and innovative 'I' to overcome the inertia of the habitualized 'me' (or critical self), as Peirce pictures in his famous courtroom analogy where the advocate of change marshals his case against the deepest dispositions that have been developed biographically. Fourthly, imagination plays a major role in realizing our commitments through the 'power of preparatory meditation' because such 'musements' are prompted not only by obstacles impeding the routine accomplishment of courses of action: 'People who build castles in the air do not, for the most part accomplish much, it is true, but every man who does accomplish great things is given to building elaborate castles in the air'.[43] Fifthly, the

---

[40] See, Vincent M. Colapietro, *Perice's Approach to the Self: A Semioctic Perspective on Human Subjectivity*, Albany, N.Y., State University of New York Press, 1989, William H. Davis, *Peirce's Epistemology*, The Hague, Martinus Nijhoff, 1972 and Archer, *Structure, Agency and the Internal Conversation*, pp. 64–78.

[41] Cited in Davis, *Peirce's Epistemology*, p. 111.

[42] Charles S. Peirce, *Collected Papers of Charles Sanders Peirce*, vol. 6 (eds. Charles Hartshorne and Paul Weiss), Cambridge, Mass., Harvard University Press, 1958 (1935), p. 289.

[43] *Ibid.*, pp. 189 and 192.

more social variation and cultural variety *available* to ponder upon reflexively, which Colapietro calls 'booty', the greater the stimulus to innovative commitments: 'what most influences men to self-government is intense disgust with one kind of life and warm admiration for another'.[44]

This Peircian understanding, to which I have not done justice, allows for both irreducible personal powers and also for distinct social properties and powers, thus being compatible with realism's stratified ontology. Conversely, those who regard innovative or creative action as dependent upon habit have a 'flat' social ontology made up of a myriad of occurrent 'situations' (unlike Mead himself). Simultaneously, they also endorse a much more socially permeated concept of the person, hence their valorization of the pre-reflexive, with the quintessential expression of this outlook being Joas' *Creativity of Action*.[45] This insightful study has been noted for its greater affinities with Dewey and Mead, and its 'curious reluctance to assimilate the ideas of C. S. Peirce'.[46] In fact, it endorses none of the five points above. Again, I will over-compress by accentuating three issues.

Firstly, Joas holds creativity to be reliant upon the pre-reflexive because it is elicited by 'situations which call for solutions, and not as an unconstrained production of something new without any constitutive background in unreflected habits'.[47] Moreover, 'even acts of the utmost creativity assume the pre-existence of a bedrock of underlying routine actions and external conditions which are simply taken as given'.[48] This foreshadows the minimization of both personal and social properties and powers. Thus, in Joas' opposition to 'the tyranny of purposefulness' (whether normative or rational), he opposes both the presumption of goals prior to action and 'the actor's basic autonomy in the setting of goals': 'goal-setting does not take place by an act of the intellect *prior to* the actual action, but is instead the result of a reflection on aspirations and tendencies that are pre-reflexive and have *already always* been operative'.[49] Secondly, this is the fundamental stranglehold placed upon

44 Colapietro, *Peirce's Approach*, pp. 115–116. Colapietro maintains of Peirce: 'When I enter into the inner world, I take with me the booty from my exploits in the outer world, such things as my native language, any other languages I might know, a boundless number of visual forms, numerical systems and so on. The more booty I take to that secret hiding place, the more spacious that hiding place becomes...the domain of inwardness is not fixed in its limits; the power and wealth of signs that I borrow from others and create for myself determine the dimensions of my inwardness'. See also p. 111.
45 See Nick Crossley, *The Social Body: Habit, Identity, Desire*, London, Sage, 2001.
46 Erkki Kilpinen, 'Creativity is Coming', *Acta Sociologica*, 41, 1998, 173–179, p. 41.
47 Joas, *Creativity*, p. 129.   48 *Ibid.*, p. 197.
49 Thomas Burger, 'Review of *The Creativity of Action*', *Contemporary Sociology*, 27:1, 1998, 109 and Joas, *Creativity*, p. 158.

personal powers of self-commitment. It is intensified because the 'interactive situation is *constitutive* of goals and actions. It does not merely set limits to what may occur, it constantly and directly influences what does occur'.[50] Therefore, and at variance with Peirce, the autotelic process receives no examination. Thirdly, since the book and argument remain entirely at the situational level, macroscopic shifts and particularly the 'contextual discontinuities' that intensify with modernity are not admitted to have any impact on this seamless situational flow.[51]

In their very different ways, the founding fathers all accentuated that the transition to modernity constituted a huge growth in 'contextual discontinuity' manifested first amongst its prime movers. Whether the key transformation was conceptualized in terms of the transition from segmented to cooperative social organization, from feudalism to capitalism, or from pre-Reformation to post-Reformation, the common denominator was 'contextual discontinuity', represented by new forms of differentiation, dissimilarity, alienation, anomie and uncertainty. Correspondingly, those features that had been characteristic of traditional 'contextual continuity' – similarity, familiarity and solidarity – were presented as being progressively (if not irreversibly) undermined. As I have argued elsewhere, the slow and differential impacts of urbanization, industrialization and political participation were major prompts serving to extend the reflexivity of those groups in the vanguard of change and those whose support was solicited and mobilized, even if the very slowness of modernity allowed some contextual continuity and routinization to be re-established for others, for example, in urban working-class communities.[52]

Indeed, this very slowness of the modernization process and its differential impacts (on the urban and the rural, the political players and the populace, advanced and less advanced countries) meant that 'contextual discontinuity' and 'contextual continuity' co-existed cheek by jowl for different sections of any specific population at any particular time during the move through modernity. Nevertheless, the fact that ideational pluralism proliferated and recruited increased (sectional) support also precluded the re-establishment of old-style cultural morphostasis. No resumed reproduction of a traditional, systematized conspectus of ideas was possible in the face of sectionalized socio-cultural groupings. Similarly, the interaction of a growing variety of promotive interest groups,

---

[50] Nicos Mouzelis, 'Beyond the normative and the utilitarian', *British Journal of Sociology*, 49:3, 1998, 491–497, p. 492.
[51] Neil Gross, 'Review of *The Creativity of Action*', *Theory and Society*, 28, 1999, 335–342.
[52] Archer, *Making our Way*, pp. 317–330.

associated with newly differentiating institutions – each of which became articulate in its own defence and capable of detecting self-interest in the legitimatory claims of others – was sufficient to prevent any drift back to unquestioned structural morphostasis.

Increases in reflexivity depend upon morphogenesis

Swift change renders habitual guidelines to action of decreasing relevance or positively misleading. From the 1980s onwards, the synergy between multi-national production and information technology resulted in unprecedented morphogenesis, whose generative mechanism is for variety to spawn more variety. With it, the *situational logic of opportunity* began to emerge at both corporate and individual levels for the first time in human history, at variance with modernity's zero-sum 'situational logic of competition'. This is what Thévenot terms the 'imperative of innovation' and it constitutes the condition for 'the reflexive imperative'.[53] On the one hand, exercising personal reflexivity in order to make choices in uncharted territory means the previous guidelines, embedded in 'contextual continuity', are fast vanishing as they are becoming increasingly misleading. On the other hand, the prizes in work and employment start going to those who detect, manipulate and find applications for links between previously unrelated bits of knowledge – ones whose contingent complementarity could be exploited to advantage. The 'winners' become such by extruding their skills to match the fast shifting array of opportunities or making their own opportunities by innovating upon contingency. All of this fosters the 'reflexive imperative' because the old routine guidelines are no longer applicable and new ones cannot be forged because (even) nascent morphogenesis is inhospitable to routinization.

Increasingly, agents navigate by the compass of their own personal concerns. This growing reliance on their personal powers – whether deployed individually and relationally or collectively by promotive organizations – has as its counterparts the demise of the generalized other and the diminution of socialization as a quasi-unilateral process. Its corollary is that some of the better known theories from the 1990s are conceptually incapable of dealing with the consequences of nascent morphogenesis.

---

[53] Laurent Thévenot, *L'action au pluriel. Sociologie des régimes d'engagement*, Paris, La Découverte, 2006. Laurent Thévenot, 'Regimes of Engagement with the World and the Extension of Critique', paper presented to the Workshop on 'Pragmatism, Practice Theory and Social Change', Institute for Public Knowledge, New York University, September 13–14, 2008.

For example, whilst ever pragmatists insist upon the absence of 'pre-meditated action', this logically excludes 'prior personal commitments' functioning as navigational devices: if 'aspirations' were truly 'pre-reflexive' and '*always already* operative', there would be a misfit with new opportunities. Similarly, if those acknowledging 'individuation' simul-taneously derogate agential powers, as in the reflexive modernization thesis,[54] then they also disallow that 'the self-focussed individual is . . . in a position to take unavoidable decisions in a rational and responsible manner, that is, with reference to the possible consequences'.[55] He or she has had their personal compass confiscated by theoretical fiat.

Instead, it is maintained that extended reliance upon reflexivity to make and monitor agential commitments and a correspondingly selective rela-tionality (the two being mutually reinforcing) generates an agency of reflexive, evaluative engagement. This sociology of engagement, shared by the French 'pragmatic turn' and by my own position, although far from identical, stresses the growing reliance of agents on their per-sonal powers – whether deployed individually or collectively.[56] Its coun-terparts are an acknowledged demise of the generalized other and of socialization as a quasi-unilateral process. Evaluative engagement with the world, as the antithesis of Luhmann's 'self-despairing subject' and Habermas' 'utopianism' alike, finds its affinities in the work of Charles Taylor and Harry Frankfurt – that is, in the 'importance of what we care about'.[57]

In place of habitual guidelines, subjects become increasingly depen-dent upon their own personal concerns as their only guides to action. Reflexive deliberation is decreasingly escapable in order to endorse a course of action held likely to accomplish it; self-interrogation, self-monitoring and self-revision are now necessary given the ineluctability of autotelos (which is always developed relationally).

---

[54] Ulrich Beck, Anthony Giddens and Scott Lash, *Reflexive Modernization: Politics, Tradi-tion and Aesthetics in the Modern Social Order*, Cambridge, Polity, 1994. For a critique, see Archer, *Making our Way*, pp. 29–37.
[55] Ulrich Beck and Elizabeth Beck-Gernsheim, *Individualization*, London, Sage, 2002, p. 48.
[56] Andrea M. Maccarini, 'Verso una nuova sociologia europea. L'approcio morfogenetico tra analisi sociale e grande teoria', in Andrea M. Maccarini, Emmanuele Morandi and Riccardo Prandini (eds.), *Realismo Sociologico*, Genoa-Milan, Marietti, 2008.
[57] Andrea M. Maccarini and Riccardo Prandini, 'Human Reflexivity in Social Realism: Beyond the Modern Debate', in Margaret S. Archer (ed.), *Conversations about Reflexivity*, London, Routledge, 2010, pp. 77–107, Charles Taylor, *Sources of the Self. The Making of the Modern Identity*, Cambridge, Mass., Harvard University Press, 1989, pp. 27–43 and Harry Frankfurt, *The Importance of What We Care About*, Cambridge University Press, 1988, pp. 80–94.

Can realism and habit be run in double harness?

There are three reasons why critical realists do not, in principle, have good cause to be strong defenders of 'routine action'. Firstly, since social life in an open system is always at the mercy of contingencies so, by definition, people's responses cannot be entirely 'routinized'. Secondly, the co-existence and interplay of plural generative mechanisms often shapes the empirical situations encountered by subjects in unpredictable ways, thus requiring creative responses from them. Thirdly, realism's stratified social ontology includes a stratum of emergent personal properties and powers, which include the human capacity for innovative action.

Thus, it is unexpected to find Dave Elder-Vass, Steve Fleetwood and Andrew Sayer each mounting independent defences of 'routine action' and seeking to accommodate reflexivity to it.[58] All three articles tend to vaunt 'social conditioning' *over* subjects' degrees of freedom to produce non-determined, heterogeneous responses (not fully 'voluntaristic' ones, which no one is defending) through their reflexive practices. Reflexivity was first ventured to refine realism's vague account of how the process of 'social conditioning' actually works, by suggesting that people's reflexive deliberations constitute the *mediatory mechanism*. What is being counterposed by the above authors is the equivalent importance of *an alternative process of mediation*, namely 'habituation' – hence their attraction to Bourdieu.[59] But, because critical realists endorse a transformational or morphogenetic model of social action, involving change, innovation and creativity, their aim is to 'reconcile' *habitus* and reflexivity.

Hence, they also shun Bourdieu's most stringent French critic, Bernard Lahire and his attempt to replace the over-generalized

---

[58] Dave Elder-Vass, 'Reconciling Archer and Bourdieu', Steve Fleetwood, 'Structure, Institutions, Agency, Habit and Reflexive Deliberation', *Journal of Institutional Economics*, 4:2, 2008, 183–203, Andrew Sayer, *The Moral Significance of Class*, Cambridge University Press, 2005 and 'Review of *Making our Way through the World*', *Journal of Critical Realism*, 8:1, 2009, 113–123.

[59] Manicas is critical of any form of mediation between structure and agency being required and asks 'why postulate the existence of structure or culture as causally relevant if, to be causally effective, these must be mediated by social actors?' (*A Realist Philosophy of Social Science*, p. 72). Since the question is rhetorical, it is presumably held to be unanswerable. However, structure and culture could only be deemed causally irrelevant if what were being mediated was, in fact, invented then and there by actors whose own personal powers were entirely responsible for it. This 'ban' upon 'mediation' seems as untenable as holding that the wires bringing electricity into my house are entirely responsible for the working of my electrical appliances and that the existence of a national grid and electricity generators are causally irrelevant.

attribution of *habitus* to a collectivity by a precise specification of the *determinants* of subjectivity at the level of the individual.[60] As an explanatory programme in social psychology, this would deprive agency of all properties and powers other than malleability. Andrew Sayer dismisses this as 'demeaning reductionism' and the other two authors endorse the compromise he advocates: 'Yes we do monitor and mediate many social influences, but much still gets in below our radar'.[61] In other words, the social order is held partly to shape our subjectivity *internally*, rather than working as a wholly *external* feature encountered by people's independent *interiority* as, for example, in rational choice theory.

However, the complete independence of personal subjectivity from social objectivity is not what divides us here. Sayer never attributes this presumption to me and Fleetwood quotes a passage in which I explicitly deny it: 'Without nullifying the privacy of our inner lives, our sociality is there inside them because it is there inside us. Hence, the inner conversation cannot be portrayed as the fully independent activity of the isolated monad, who only takes cognisance of his external social context in the same way that he consults the weather.'[62] But, importantly, the passage reads on: 'Conversely, the internal conversation can too readily be colonized by the social, such that its causal powers are expropriated from the person and are reassigned to society'. In other words, the role I have assigned to reflexivity aims to strike a balance between construing everything that human beings are as a gift of society and modernity's monad, who is untouched by his social environment, as in the case of *homo economicus* and his kinfolk.[63]

Only by striking the right balance between personal, structural and cultural emergent powers is it possible to explain precisely what people do, rather than falling back upon correlations between group membership and action patterns, which are necessarily lacking in explanatory power. To account for variability as well as regularity in the courses of action taken by those similarly situated means acknowledging our singularity as *persons*, without denying that our sociality is essential for us to be recognizable as *human* persons.

---

[60] Bernard Lahire, *Portraits Sociologiques. Dispositions et variations individuelles*, Paris, Nathan, 2002 and 'From the Habitus to an Individual Heritage of Dispositions. Towards a Sociology at the Level of the Individual', *Poetics*, 31, 2003, 329–355.

[61] Sayer, 'Review', pp. 115 and 122.

[62] Fleetwood, 'Structure, Institutions, Agency', p. 195 and Archer, *Being Human*, p. 117.

[63] Rom Harré, 'A Person Is Not a Natural Object, but a Cultural Artefact', *Personal Being*, Oxford, Basil Blackwell, 1983, p. 20.

Three attempts to combine *habitus* and reflexivity

Empirical combination

There is a considerable difference in the amount of *theoretical adjustment* that those realists advocating a *combination* of *habitus* and reflexivity deem necessary for the two concepts to work in tandem. At one extreme, Fleetwood and Sayer largely advocate an empirical combination involving quite modest theoretical concessions from Bourdieu's thinking and my own.[64] On the one hand, both want me to be more generous in acknowledging the durable influences of socialization: that it imposes blinkers on the types of jobs that will be considered by those from lower class backgrounds and of female gender (Fleetwood); or (Sayer) that when novel occupational opportunities present themselves to the young adult – ones that did not exist in the parental generation – those from more privileged backgrounds exhibit 'precisely that sense of security, enterprise and entitlement that mark the middle-class habitus'.[65] Thus, both maintain that family socialization continues much as it did throughout most of the twentieth century.

This is an empirical question, which may be answered differently for particular groups in given locales even within Europe. However, there is evidence (discussed later) that socialization cannot be treated as a constant and, that especially for those now reaching adulthood, this process bears little resemblance to the practices continuing throughout most of the last century. In other words, Bourdieu may have been more or less right in practice for the period to which the bulk of his work relates (towards the mid-point of the morphostatic–morphogenetic continuum). What is debatable is if the socialized *habitus* continues to generate a goodness of fit between dispositionality and positionality during the last two decades. On the contrary, it can be argued that the young of the new millennium are no longer Bourdieu's people because they no longer live in Bourdieu's world.

Both Sayer and Fleetwood assign a greater role to reflexivity than did Bourdieu because they accept that people make choices and do so increasingly as the social order becomes more morphogenetic. Although the injection of reflexive deliberations would have the advantage of freeing Bourdieu's thought from charges of determinism, it is not clear that

---

[64] Fleetwood, 'Structure, Institutions, Agency' and Sayer, 'Review'.
[65] Sayer, 'Review', p. 123.

he would have accepted this olive branch.[66] Despite his 'late concessions', he persisted in maintaining that such choices as we did make were orchestrated by the hidden hand of *habitus*: 'this is a crucial proviso, it is *habitus* itself that commands this option. We can always say that individuals make choices, as long as we do not forget that they do not choose the principals [sic] of these choices'.[67]

Fleetwood's and Sayer's empirical case for combining *habitus* and reflexivity rests upon the prolongation of large tracts of routine action, even as morphogenesis engages. Thus, to Fleetwood: 'It does not follow that an open, morphogenetic system lacks routinized templates or established patterns, and/or moves too quickly for institutional rules to solidify and form habits with a degree of success . . . Some agents' intentions are non-deliberative, and the best explanation we have for such intentions is that they are rooted in habit.'[68] Similarly, Sayer maintains that 'habitus continues to loom large even in the midst of contextual discontinuity', to counteract my argument about the progressive de-routinization of life, which consigns *habitus* to more stable societies than our own, ones manifesting the 'contextual continuity' required for its acquisition. Thus, he continues:

Yet most children still have enough continuity in their relations and experiences to adjust to them – the familiar home, the dull routine of school, the daily reminders of their class and gender position. While there probably is an increase in contextual discontinuity there is still plenty of stability, and they could hardly become competent social actors if they did not develop a feel for familiar games.[69]

Thus, both Fleetwood and Sayer settle for an empirical *patrim et patrim* formula, which accepts that there is sufficient change to make some reflexive deliberation inescapable, but enough continuity for the formation of routinized responses still to be realistic and reproduced in large tracts of life. Empirical claims can only be adjudicated empirically. One graduate, when confronted with data presented in this book about children reared by four or more 'parents' by remarriage responded, 'Well, they're all middle class aren't they', which places a question mark over why similarity of class position is held automatically to trump differences in mother-tongue, country of origin, religion and politics in the process of socialization. This issue is taken up in the next chapter.

---

[66] Alexander Jeffrey, *Fin de Siècle Social Theory*, London, Verso, 1994.
[67] Bourdieu quoted in Löic Wacquant, 'Toward a Reflexive Sociology: a Workshop with Pierre Bourdieu', *Sociological Theory*, 7, 1989, 26–63.
[68] Fleetwood, 'Structure, Institutions, Agency', p. 198.   [69] Sayer, 'Review', p. 122.

Hybridizing habitus and reflexivity

'Hybridiziation' entails more than the basic empirical assumption that in some situations *habitus* governs action 'quasi-unconsciously', whilst in others resort is made to self-conscious reflexivity.[70] Specifically, it involves concept-stretching by advancing the notion of a 'reflexive habitus' in order to project Bourdieu's *dispositional* analysis forwards, despite contemporary *positional* transformations. In Sweetman's hybrid such societal changes are synonymous with those outlined in the theory of 'reflexive modernization', and his aim is to link them to the extended practice of reflexivity – now itself characterized as a new *habitus*:

> What is being suggested here is that, in conditions of late-, high-, or reflexive-modernity, endemic crises . . . lead to a more or less permanent disruption of social position, of a more or less constant disjunction between habitus and field. In this context reflexivity ceases to reflect a temporary lack of fit between habitus and field *but itself becomes habitual, and is thus incorporated into the habitus in the form of the flexible or reflexive habitus.*[71]

The compromise concept of a 'reflexive habitus' elides two concepts which Bourdieu consistently distinguished: the semi-unconscious dispositions constituting *habitus* and reflexivity as self-awareness of them. Moreover, what work does calling this a '*habitus*' do? Literally, it states that people now have a *disposition* to be reflexive about their circumstances and perhaps to be prepared for change rather than for stability. If so, 'preparedness' must be used transitively; one must be in a state of preparation for something determinate, otherwise this hybrid *habitus* cannot supply dispositional guidelines for action. Without these, the concept boils down to the statement that most people now *expect* to have to think about what to do in the novel situations they confront. True, but it is hard to see how calling this expectation a 'habitus' explains anything about either their deliberative processes or about what they do. In fact, given that for Bourdieu *habitus* underlined the pre-adaptation of people to circumstances and the 'semi-conscious', 'quasi-automatic' nature of its operations – all of which Sweetman accepts – it is difficult to think

---

[70] Matthew Adams, 'Hybridizing Habitus and Reflexivity: Towards an Understanding of Contemporary Identity', *Sociology*, 40:3, 2006, 511–528.

[71] Paul Sweetman, 'Twenty-first Century Dis-ease? Habitual Reflexivity or the Reflexive Habitus', *The Sociological Review*, 51:4, 2003, 528–549 (italics inserted). This quotation continues: 'To the extent that Bourdieu's 'non-reflexive' habitus depends upon relatively stable conditions and on 'lasting experience of social position', his analysis may thus be said to apply more to simple- or organised- modernity, where the comparative stability of people's social identities allowed for a sustained, coherent, and relatively secure relationship between habitus and field'.

of any concept less apposite for characterizing conscious deliberations about novel choices.

Sweetman maintains that 'certain forms of habitus may be *inherently* reflexive, and that the flexible or *reflexive* habitus may be both increasingly common and increasingly significant due to various social and cultural shifts'.[72] What does 'inherently' mean here, given that Bourdieu consistently held the formation of any *habitus* to be the result of socialization? What type of socialization can provide a preparation for the unpredictable and novel? This seems to be a contradiction in terms, unless it slides into vacuity – into something like the Boy Scouts' intransitive motto: 'Be Prepared!'

There are only two ways out of this impasse. One path is taken by Mouzelis who, consistent with Bourdieu, attempts to provide an answer in terms of a socialization that could result in the development of:

a reflexive disposition acquired not via crisis situations, but via a socialization focussing on the importance of "the inner life" or the necessity to "create one's own goals". For instance, growing up in a religious community which stresses meditation and inner contemplation can result in members of a community acquiring a type of *reflexive habitus* that is unrelated to contradictions between dispositions and positions.[73]

Although such experiences may indeed promote 'meta-reflexivity' (reflecting upon one's reflections), the mode of life that fosters 'apophatic' as opposed to 'cataphatic' reflexivity does not seem to be widespread in either Eastern or Western religious communities, much less to constitute a model for contemporary secular socialization outside them.[74]

The other path entails abandoning any claim that such a 'reflexive habitus' is acquired through socialization, but accepts that it is derived from the individual's own life experiences. The changes constituting 'reflexive modernization' are held to 'contribute towards a continual and pervasive reflexivity that itself becomes habitual, however paradoxical this notion may at first appear'.[75] But what does calling reflexivity 'habitual' add to noting that it is 'continual and pervasive', given that it cannot be the motor of habitual action – as the author agrees? When the concept is voided of all connection with courses of action, paradox gives way to contradiction. For example, Ostrow writes that there 'is no clear path

---

[72] *Ibid.*, p. 530.
[73] Nicos Mouzelis, 'Habitus and Reflexivity', in his *Modern and Postmodern Social Theorizing: Bridging the Divide*, Cambridge University Press, 2009, p. 135.
[74] Nicos Mouzelis, 'Self and Self-Other Reflexivity: The Apophatic Dimension', *European Journal of Social Theory*, 13, 2010, 271–284.
[75] Sweetman, 'Twenty-first Century Dis-ease?', p. 538.

from dispositions to conduct. What does exist is a protensional field, or perspective, that contextualizes all situations, setting the pre-objective framework for practice, without any express rules or codes that automatically and mechanically "tell" us what to do'.[76] What perspective could possibly 'contextualize all situations', especially unpredictable and unintended ones? Fatalism alone fits the bill, but presents us with the 'passive actors' who have resigned any governance over their own lives and is just as incompatible with Beck's notion of 'making a life of one's own', in a destructured social order, as it is with my own version of 'making one's way through the world', amidst morphogenetic re-structuring.

Ontological and theoretical reconciliation

The reconciliation Elder-Vass proposes entails a more radical theoretical revision in order to make *habitus* and reflexivity compatible.[77] The following stages are involved: (i) that Bourdieu's conception of the social order in general and agential powers in particular should be detached from 'central conflationism' and be linked to an emergentist ontology; (ii) that the influence accorded to reflexivity should be limited by confining it to subjects' modifications of their *habitus*.[78] Thus, Elder-Vass sees the main ontological 'adjustments' falling upon Bourdieu's work and the main theoretical ones on mine. If both are granted, he can then advance; (iii) his key claim that most of our actions are co-determined by *both* our *habitus* and our reflexive deliberations, on the basis of an 'emergentist theory of action'.[79]

In response to (i), this is argued to be an unwarranted interpretation of Bourdieu's own thought; to (ii) that it rests upon a widespread confusion between the kinds of knowledge required to play 'games' proficiently in the three orders of natural reality: the natural, the practical and the social; and to (iii) that it does not succeed in justifying the proposed 'reconciliation'. Of course, the author may wish to adduce this 'reconciliation' as his own theory, to be assessed on its merits, rather than as the progeny of a shotgun marriage.

---

[76] James Ostrow, 'Culture as a Fundamental Dimension of Experience: A Discussion of Pierre Bourdieu's Theory of Human Habitus', in Derek Robbins (ed.), *Pierre Bourdieu* vol. 1, Sage, London, 2000.

[77] For a revision that entirely favours *habitus* see Benjamin Dalton, 'Creativity, Habit, and the Social Products of Creative Action: Revising Joas, Incorporating Bourdieu', *Sociological Theory*, 22:4, 2004, 603–622.

[78] A term introduced to characterize theories where 'structure' and 'agency' are treated as inseparable because mutually constitutive. See Archer, *Culture and Agency*, chapter 4 and *Realist Social Theory*, chapter 4.

[79] Elder-Vass, 'Reconciling Archer and Bourdieu', p.335.

Can habitus, emergence and reflexivity live together? Elder-Vass is correct in maintaining that if structure, culture and agency are regarded as being mutually constitutive, this is incompatible with reflexivity because reflexive deliberations depend upon a clear object–subject distinction. Reflexivity is precluded by 'central conflation', where the properties and powers respective to 'structures' and to 'agents' are elided. As Mouzelis argues:

> It is only when the objective–subjective distinction is maintained that it is possible to deal in a theoretically congruent manner with cases where situated actors distance themselves from social structures relatively external to them in order to assess, more or less rationally, the degree of constraint and enablement these structures offer, the pros and cons, the chances of success or failure of different strategies, etc.[80]

Elder-Vass agrees and, as a well-established defender of emergent properties, protests that Bourdieu's phrase 'the internalization of externality' leading to his description of 'structured structures predisposed to function as structuring structures', is an 'ontological error' in that 'it fails to distinguish between a social structure and the consequences that it has for our mental states'.[81] Thus, it becomes crucial to distance Bourdieu and *habitus* from 'central conflation' if reflexivity is to be accommodated. The question is whether or not Bourdieu's thought can withstand 'adaptation' to an emergentist ontology. Specifically, can his theorizing in the *Logic of Practice* be so adapted – a text in which reflexivity is scarcely mentioned – but upon which Elder-Vass relies most. Although he is right to say that Bourdieu did not seem exercised by ontological *debates*, this does not mean he had no ontological *commitments*.

Ontological commitments contain judgements about the constituents (and non-constituents) of social reality and thus govern what kind of concepts may properly be countenanced. Certain concepts are precluded from appearing in explanations, just as atheists cannot attribute their well-being to divine providence. No explanation is acceptable to a theorist if it contains terms whose referents misconstrue social reality as they see it.[82] Bourdieu's ontological commitments are so strong in the *Logic of Practice* that, because of their forceful elisionism, they shut the door on emergence – leaving the concept and practice of reflexivity outside.

---

[80] Mouzelis, 'Habitus and Reflexivity', p. 138.
[81] Dave Elder-Vass, 'Emergence and the Realist Account of Cause', *Journal of Critical Realism*, 4, 2005, 315–38, Pierre Bourdieu, *The Logic of Practice*, Cambridge, Polity Press, 1990 (1980), p. 53 and Elder-Vass, 'Reconciling', p. 334.
[82] Margaret S. Archer, 'Social Theory and the Analysis of Society', in Tim May and Malcolm Williams, *Knowing the Social World*, Buckingham, Open University Press, 1998.

The strongest of Bourdieu's ontological convictions is forcefully expressed in the first sentence of his book: 'Of all the oppositions that artificially divide social science, the most fundamental, and the most ruinous, is the one that is set up between subjectivism and objectivism'.[83] At one extreme, the subjectivist phenomenology of daily life cannot exceed a *description* of lived experience and excludes inquiry into the objective conditions of its possibility. In brief, it cannot penetrate the 'ontological complicity' between *habitus* and habitat and move from lay epistemology to the 'world which determines it'.[84] At the other extreme, when academic social scientists pretend to 'objectivity', they occlude the necessarily *perspectival* nature of their epistemology, which places the inverted commas around their 'objective' accounts.[85]

Because there is no 'view from nowhere', the most that can be accomplished is akin to the Gadamerian 'fusion of horizons'.[86] For academic observers: 'There is *only* a perspective seeing, *only* a perspective 'knowing'; and the *more* eyes, different eyes, we use to observe one thing, the more complete will our 'concept' of this thing, our 'objectivity', be'.[87] There is no such criterion as the critical realists' 'judgemental rationality' to modify our ineluctable 'epistemic relativity'. The same epistemic barrier prevents the lay subjects from being or becoming 'pure visitors', capable of receiving or reporting 'unvarnished news' about the objective social contexts they inhabit: 'The 'subject' born of the world of objects does not arise as a subjectivity facing an objectivity: the objective universe is made up of objects which are the products of objectifying operations structured according to the same structures that the *habitus* applies to them'.[88] In consequence, ontology and epistemology are inextricably intertwined, for investigator and participant alike, thus rendering subjectivism and objectivism *inseparable* – the hallmark of central conflation, which is fundamentally hostile to the structural and cultural 'emergentism' to which Elder-Vass would 'reconcile' it.[89]

Beyond insistence upon *inseparability* and its correlate, the aim to 'transcend' the objective/subjective divide, there is also the centrality of *practice* shared with Giddens. But when we do turn to practice, it is equally inhospitable to construing lay subjects as acting for reasons, which are also causes of their actions.

[83] Bourdieu, *The Logic of Practice*, p. 25.
[84] Pierre Bourdieu and Löic Wacquant, *An Invitation to Reflexive Sociology*, Oxford, Polity Press, 1992, p. 20.
[85] Bourdieu, *The Logic of Practice*, p. 28.
[86] Thomas Nagel, *The View from Nowhere*, Oxford University Press, 1986.
[87] Bourdieu, *The Logic of Practice*, p. 28.   [88] *Ibid.*, pp. 76–77.
[89] Archer, *Realist Social Theory*, pp. 93–134.

For Bourdieu, the logic of practice 'flouts logical logic' because this 'fuzzy' logic 'understands only in order to act'.[90] This means responding to practical demands *in situ*, and such responses cannot be translated into the academic 'universes of discourse'. Thus, Elder-Vass appears to misinterpret Bourdieu's statement that: '[If] one fails to recognise any form of action other than rational action or mechanical reaction, it is impossible to understand the logic of all actions that are reasonable without being the product of a reasoned design, still less of rational calculation'.[91] This is interpreted as 'confirming . . . that he [Bourdieu] accepts that *some* actions are indeed the product of reasoned design'.[92] Not only does Bourdieu state the opposite above (the force of the word 'without'), but what is 'reasonable' is inscribed in *le sens pratique* and expressed in action, not in personal 'reasons' that can be articulated. Contextual embedding is all that *makes sense* to the subject of his/her actions: '[A]gents can adequately master the *modus operandi* that enables them to generate correctly formed ritual practices, only by making it work practically in a real situation, in relation to practical functions'.[93] Hence, *le sens pratique* is what Bourdieu opposes as 'reasonable' in contradistinction to personal designs (or reasons as causes).

However, *le sens pratique* 'excludes attention to itself'; the subject focuses upon 'knowing how', not 'knowing that' – or why.[94] It follows that the subject is incapable of reflexivity: 'Simply because he is questioned, *and questions himself*, about the reasons and the *raison d'être* of his practice, he cannot communicate the essential point, which is that the very nature of practice is that it excludes this question.'[95] The answer is buried too deep in the historical and practical genesis of both practices and the logic of practice for the subject to disinter them. In consequence, and in the present, such subjects do 'not react to "objective conditions" but to these conditions as apprehended through the socially constituted schemes that organize his perception'.[96] In many ways, Bourdieu never ceased to be an anthropologist and *le sens pratique* is close cousin to the Azande, so enmeshed in the strands of their own coherent culture as to be unable to question their own thinking and incapable of acquiring the requisite distance for being reflexive about their own doings.[97]

Are our actions co-determined by habitus and reflexivity? When Elder-Vass moves over to consider *theoretical* 'reconciliation' of the two

---

[90] Bourdieu, *The Logic of Practice*, p. 91.   [91] *Ibid.*, p. 91.
[92] Elder-Vass, 'Reconciling', p. 335.   [93] Bourdieu, *The Logic of Practice*, p. 90.
[94] *Ibid.*, p. 92.   [95] *Ibid.*, p. 91 (first italics added).   [96] *Ibid.*, p. 97.
[97] E. E. Evans-Pritchard, *Witchcraft, Oracles and Magic among the Azande*, Oxford University Press, 1937, p. 195.

views on the relationship of human causal powers to human action, it is the turn of the morphogenetic approach to be accommodating. In fact, this is no more amenable to the proposed theoretical 'adjustments' than Bourdieu would have been to ontological revision. Although Elder-Vass agrees 'that we human individuals do, as Archer claims, have emergent powers of our own', as far as reflexivity is concerned, this is reduced to half the story.[98] The reconciling of the two perspectives rests on Elder-Vass' *own* theory that 'many and perhaps most of our actions are co-determined by *both* our habitus and our reflexive determinations'.[99]

The reason for resisting 'co-determination' concerns the premise underlying Elder-Vass' 'theory of human action', that is, 'with the emergent roots of our power to *act*'.[100] This key premise is that 'action' and 'social action' are homogeneous. Colin Campbell has documented how the two have indeed become elided in sociological texts and thus provided unwarranted support for social imperialism.[101] The same premise is taken over directly from Bourdieu, to whom 'the feel for the game', embodied in *habitus*, is applied in an undifferentiated manner *across* the three orders of natural reality. However, this obliterates crucial ontological distinctions, discussed at length in *Being Human*, as underpinning the different types of knowledge that human subjects can develop in each order.[102] Bourdieu overrode these, in typical Meadian fashion, with his 'colonizing' assertion that: '[b]etween the child and the world, the whole group intervenes.'[103] This automatically renders all action as social action and gives *habitus* epistemological hegemony in every order of reality. Conversely, it will be maintained that our different relations with the three orders give rise to distinct and heterogeneous forms of knowledge, which entail very different amounts of reflexivity.

In scrutinizing Elder-Vass' key claim that 'most of our actions are co-determined by habitus and reflexivity' this seems to beg the sociological question. Co-determination means the influence of two factors upon a given outcome but varies between a 50/50 and a 99/1 per cent contribution, by either. My argument is that the proportional contributions of *habitus* and reflexivity vary systematically with the order of reality in question and are least determinate for the social order. If correct, this renders the 'reconciliation' formally feasible but empty in practice.

The following simple figure represents Elder-Vass' defence of the role of *habitus* in 'co-determining' action. It also serves to show that *two* issues are involved.

---

[98] Archer, *Making our Way*, p. 335.
[99] Elder-Vass, 'Reconciling', p. 335.   [100] *Ibid.*, p. 336.
[101] Colin Campbell, *The Myth of Social Action*, Cambridge University Press, 1996.
[102] Archer, *Being Human*.   [103] Bourdieu, *The Logic of Practice*, p. 76.

1. SOCIALIZATION

↓

2. EXPERIENCES

↓

3. DISPOSITIONS = *habitus* = 'feel for the game'

Firstly, are experiences the basis of human dispositions? This is crucial, because unless the move from (2) to (3) can be sustained, then the relevance of move (1) to (2) fails, and with it the purported influence of socialization falls. Secondly, can 'socialization' justifiably be regarded as a summary term governing the 'experiences' of groups, specifically social classes? This is an independent question from the first and will be examined in the next sub-section.

My general argument is that the types of knowledge acquired through experience of the three orders of reality are not homogeneous in kind and are emergent from different relations between the subject and each order, which *sui generis* permit or require variable degrees of reflexivity from subjects. This makes 'co-determination' an equally variable matter in terms of the proportional contributions made by dispositions and reflexivity to actions based on the three types of knowledge. Whereas Bourdieu applied *habitus* indifferently to all orders, I will maintain that acquiring 'a feel for the game' is a metaphor that does not work equally well across the whole of natural reality.

Figure 2.2 summarizes the argument advanced in *Being Human*.

In nature, the relational requisite for 'experience → disposition' (say, to swim) is simply the coordination of a body with an environment (a watery one in the case of floating). This emergent skill (swimming) hinges upon the relationship between our physiological potentialities/liabilities and the positive/negative feedback received from the water. Generically, our reflexivity is irrelevant to our 'floatability', or babies could not be launched into swimming pools when a few months old. Of course, some might wish to argue that they already had an embodied *habitus*, after nine months of experiencing a watery amniotic environment.

So let us change the example. On two occasions, Elder-Vass uses the activity of walking to exemplify 'embodied knowledge', employed as second nature in mundane activities such as going to the kitchen. Certainly it is, but why do we need to introduce a *habitus* in relation to walking? I hazard that none of us were taught or explicitly thought to incline our body weight forward when going uphill and the reverse for down an incline, we just found it easier that way. In other words, reflexivity does not enter into the acquisition of dispositions by trial and error learning, but neither does socialization. Moreover, it is impossible reflexively

	Natural Order	**Practical Order**	**Social Order**
Relationship	Object/Object	Subject/Object	Subject/Subject
Knowledge Type	Embodied	Practical	Discursive
Emergent From	Co-ordination	Compliance	Commitment
Importance of Reflexivity	Minimal	Moderate	Maximal

Figure 2.2 Types of knowledge and the three orders of natural reality

'to forget' embodied knowledge, such as how to swim; all we can do is to refuse to practise it. Certainly, we get 'rusty', but that has more to do with losing muscle tone than having lost the skill, which is literally beyond us. As concerns 'co-determination', the abilities represented by 'embodied knowledge' are a hundred per cent owing to experience; reflexivity does not come into the picture in the natural order. Of course, this analytic statement is rarely manifested empirically – that is one in which subjects are 'alone with nature' – but an instructor slowly deflating buoyancy aids does not actually teach anyone to float. Hence, the irony that where 'experience → dispositions' works best, this has nothing to do with socialization either!

In the practical order, tacit skills are emergent from the affordances and resistances presented by objects and the assimilation of and accommodation to them on the part of the subject. Activities such as competently playing tennis, a musical instrument, touch typing or driving all depend upon 'catching on' and, at more advanced levels (such as improvizing at jazz or manoeuvring an articulated lorry), upon acquiring a real 'feel for the game'. This is undoubtedly Bourdieu's territory, but the following statement shows him completely rejecting the 'co-determination' formula when discussing 'hexis' or bodily skills as permanent dispositions. 'The principles embodied in this way are placed beyond the grasp of consciousness, and hence cannot be touched by voluntary, deliberate transformation'.[104] Where 'practical knowledge' is concerned, I fully support Elder-Vass, because to acquire *virtuosity* as a tennis or piano player requires commitment, precisely in order to bring about 'deliberate transformation', and thus entails personal concerns and reflexive

---

[104] *Ibid.*, p. 93–94.

deliberations about the priority to accord sport or music in the constellation of skills defining personal identity.

To maintain that people, at any level of competence, can choose to improve a given skill seems uncontentious. Thus, Andrew Sayer accepts that much of playing tennis is getting used to making returns of service, for example, whose speed is estimated to exceed that of decision-making. But he comments, 'to be sure, she can't do a review and plan each time she hits a backhand, but she can go away and work on it if she finds she's been over-hitting it'.[105] Equally, Elder-Vass uses examples of 'hexis', frequently cited by Bourdieu: how we shape our mouths to speak or how we stand (in various situations) are generated by *habitus*, not by deliberation. Perhaps, but that does not preclude 'voluntary transformation'. Plenty of people (used to) take elocution lessons or (now) self-consciously change their accents.

Elder-Vass concludes that Bourdieu's *habitus* 'must be modified to show *how* we, as reflexive beings, are sometimes able to critically evaluate and thus modify our dispositions in the light of our experience, our reasoning capacities, and our value commitments'.[106] In that case, he sustains his argument for the 'co-determination of action' in the practical order. However, in the two orders of natural reality just touched upon, 'co-determination' did not maintain in the first, seemed appropriate in the second, and will be shown to vary dramatically *within* the social order. Hence, 'co-determination' does not even approximate to equal determination across the spectrum of natural reality.

Does Socialization generate shared experiences within social classes? To acquire 'a feel for the game' was used literally in relation to the practical order but it becomes a metaphor when applied to the discursive social order. How appropriate this trope is depends upon the historically changing state of the social world. However, it seems to me that Bourdieu almost elided 'a feel for the game' with a Wittgensteinian 'form of life' through the pervasiveness of his anthropological approach to later social configurations. After all, in the *Esquisse d'une théorie de la pratique*, where the concept of *le sens pratique* was first formulated, this was intimately intertwined with detailed ethnologies of the Kabyle.[107] The validity of projecting the metaphor forwards into modernity, onwards into high modernity and, perhaps, beyond that, is really what is at issue.

It is quite common for social theorists to note that the workability of Bourdieu's *habitus* is dependent both upon social stability and high

---

[105] Sayer, 'Review', p. 121.   [106] Elder-Vass, 'Reconciling', p. 345.
[107] Pierre Bourdieu, *Outline of a Theory of Practice*, Cambridge University Press, 1993 (1972).

social integration, reproducing 'contextual continuity' over time.[108] I will not repeat my own critique on these lines except to extract the precise connections that Bourdieu stipulates between 'class', 'experiences' and 'dispositions', all of which rely upon social stability and upon which Elder-Vass' argument also depends.[109] Firstly, 'class *habitus*' characterizes 'class practices' because all members of a class share '*indentical histories*': 'The practices of the members of the same group or, in a differentiated society, the same class, are always better harmonized than the agents know or wish ... The habitus is precisely this immanent law, *lex insita*, inscribed in bodies by identical histories'.[110]

Secondly, such homogeneous class biographies are constituted by a communality of 'experiences', themselves constitutive of shared collective 'dispositions':

> The *habitus*, a product of history, produces individual and collective practices – more history – in accordance with the schemes generated by history. It ensures the active presence of past experiences, which deposited in each organism in the form of schemes of perception, thought and action, tend to guarantee the "correctness" of practices and their constancy over time. This system of dispositions – a present past that tends to perpetuate itself into the future by reactivation in similarly structured practices ... is the principle of the continuity and regularity which objectivism sees in social practices without being able to account for it.[111]

Lastly, there is Bourdieu's own admission that this 'continuity and regularity' which was seen above as the outcome of *habitus* is also *the precondition of its operation*. This is because such reproductory practices work '*only to the extent that the structures within which they function are identical to or homologous with the objective structures of which they are the product*'.[112]

However, Elder-Vass does not buy into a history of the Western world characterized by the smooth reproduction of 'contextual continuity'. On the contrary, he accepts historical variability and accentuates that the greater its magnitude, the more reflexivity comes into play – 'most obviously when the set of existing dispositions does not provide decisive guidance' and this is also 'most obviously in situations which are not congruent with our previous experience. For example, when we adopt a new role, we may have to think carefully about *how* to perform it'.[113] He even maintains (a view shared by Lahire) that 'such situations are

---

[108] Craig Calhoun, 'Habitus, Field and Capital: the Question of Historical Specificity', in Craig Calhoun, Edward LiPuma and Moishe Postone (eds.), *Bourdieu: Critical Perspectives*, Cambridge, Polity Press, 1993, p. 82.
[109] Archer, *Making our Way*, pp. 38–48.   [110] Bourdieu, *The Logic of Practice*, p. 59.
[111] *Ibid.*, p. 54.   [112] *Ibid.*, p. 61 (italics added).
[113] Elder-Vass, 'Reconciling', pp. 341–342.

radically more frequent than Bourdieu seems to believe, and thus we are constantly presented with opportunities for reflexive review'.[114] That is precisely what allows a place for reflexivity. Nevertheless, for there *still* to be a place for *habitus*, Elder-Vass has to maintain (like Sayer and Fleetwood) that sufficient stability remains *despite* 'contextual incongruity' for *habitus* to be of continuing relevance.

Indeed, these are the terms of his proposed 'reconciliation'. Once this continuing relevance is accepted, 'then Archer's account of the development of personal identity and social identity can be seen as *an argument about the extent to which we are able to modify our habitus*'.[115] Yet, this is not acceptable, precisely because it is premised on the current durability of *habitus* as a guide to action. What is resisted is the argument that *habitus* is of continuing relevance in the wholly novel situation of 'contextual incongruity' today, already manifesting itself because of the intensification of morphogenesis. Increasingly, natal background and socialization practices no longer provide guidelines to action for the young members of any class, let alone ones tantamount to assuring reproduction of social position.

The impact of 'contextual incongruity' upon socialization will be taken up in the final section but to round off the argument with Elder-Vass, let me cite the kind of argument that leads me to reject his proposed 'reconciliation': 'personal identity, which seems to be a co-requisite of reflexive deliberation "comes only at maturity and is not attained by all". Hence at any one time some people will not yet have become reflexive, and others will never do so – leaving them, it would seem in the grip of their habitus'.[116] Leaving aside whether some will 'never do so', which I do not claim in the absence of the necessary evidence, the one case of 'near non-reflexivity' presented in *Structure, Agency and the Internal Conversation* was that of Jason.[117] This seventeen-year-old, who viewed himself more as a passive object than as an active subject, had been in the grip of both alcohol and drugs, whilst living on the streets since he was thirteen. But he was not in the grip of *habitus*. Kicked out of home by his parents, he had sought permission to live with either mother or father at their separate addresses but had been shunned. Far from having a *habitus* upon which to rely, he had tried to blot out his past in a haze of substance abuse. Four years later he had managed to get clean with huge determination and help from a programme for homeless young people. By means of his limited reflexivity, he sought an extremely routinized job

[114] Lahire, *Portraits* and Elder-Vass, 'Reconciling', p. 341.
[115] Elder-Vass, 'Reconciling', p. 344.   [116] *Ibid.*, p. 335.
[117] Archer, *Structure, Agency and the Internal Conversation*, pp. 333–341.

in retail – perhaps wanting precisely that stability which had never been his. Does 'co-determination' illuminate his human predicament by the reminder that, nevertheless, he could walk and talk?

Socialization isn't what it used to be

Neither Sayer nor Elder-Vass deny that social transformation simultaneously transforms the relevance of reflexive deliberation compared with that of routine action. This was the theme of the previous chapter and was summarized in the first section as the macroscopic historical shifts from 'contextual continuity', dominant in traditional societies, through the intensification of 'contextual discontinuity', gradually spreading with modernity itself, to the advent of 'contextual incongruity' in the last two decades of the twentieth century. This sequence was internally related to an increase in the scope and the range of reflexivity because of the growing number of novel situations encountered in the social order, where subjects could not rely upon routine action as guidelines to appropriate action.

Correspondingly, and especially over the last quarter of a century, socialization has been decreasingly able to 'prepare' for occupational and lifestyle opportunities that had not existed for the parental generation: for social skills that could not become embodied (stock-market trading or computer programming) or needed continuous upgrading, and readiness to relocate, retrain, and re-evaluate shifting *modi vivendi*. This new context surpasses the 'strictly limited generative capacity' of *habitus*, which is remote 'from the creation of unpredictable novelty' because it is restricted to 'the free production of all the thoughts, perceptions and actions *inherent in the particular conditions of its production – and only those*'.[118]

Furthermore, the family unit of socialization increasingly fails *normatively* as a transmitter of values that underpin the concerns adopted and endorsed by their children. Today, more and more families transmit mixed messages, which are themselves incongruous, and thus confront their children with the additional problem of normatively evaluating and arbitrating upon this mélange before they can crystallize their personal concerns.

Let us look briefly at one quite common example of parents actually intensifying the 'contextual incongruity' of their daughter because their attempted socialization sought to reap the advantages of new opportunities by following courses of action belonging to the second

---

[118] Bourdieu, *The Logic of Practice*, p. 55.

millennium.[119] As a South-East Asian student from a professional background who is taking her first degree in England, Han-Wing filters family socialization through her own personal concerns and what she herself finds congruent with them in her new Western context. Conversely, her parents seek to treat her as one of Bourdieu's *héritiers*, a recipient of their cultural and financial capital, used transactionally to secure their desired positional outcome – a daughter who will return home to practise as a qualified lawyer.

Han-Wing feels herself trapped between parental expectations and her own desire to explore her liberty: 'I come from a really conservative family . . . so they don't like me going out much. So when I came here, with the freedom, the new found freedom, that sort of thing – but then I have this guilty conscience – I'd be like, oh they don't want me doing this, they don't want me to be doing that – but I still do it.' She can disobey when 7,000 miles away but, when visiting home finds it irksome to account for her movements and be back early. She can also lie from a distance but not at close quarters: 'My parents have an important influence in my life . . . but I don't agree on many of the things they say, like religion for one. They really want me to go to church and all, but I don't believe in religion, so that's one thing. My mum calls me up and she's like 'Have you gone to church today?' and I lie, which is really bad, but every time I go to church I feel suffocated because I don't believe in it.'

The whole object of her studying in Britain was to become a lawyer, like her two brothers. Han-Wing has no idea yet what career she wishes to follow, but feels her parents only present her with a restricted list of options: 'Because back in [X] we have this thing about comparing the children and 'oh, my son's a doctor', 'well my daughter's a lawyer' and all that. It's different here, you still get it but it's different . . . Back there it's 'oh your daughter's a secretary' – not so good . . . If I wanted to be a wedding planner they'd probably be like, "What, we've spent so much for you to be a wedding planner!". They'd probably not be too happy. I feel I've disappointed them at home in so many things.' Yet, despite these interpersonal regrets, Han-Wing rejects a socialization that, to her, involves 'treating us like social objects'. Although not knowing what she wants to do, she feels that she must be free to respond to opportunities that are broader than 'doctor or lawyer' and that will entail getting away from home, probably to America. This attempt at social reproduction has actually generated 'contextual incongruity' for Han-Wing; parental

---

[119] All empirical statements in this sub-section are based upon my three-year longitudinal study, using in-depth interviews of the young people analysed in this book.

efforts to 'embed' her have had exactly the opposite effect – and they might well have lost their daughter.

Conclusion: turning the tables

There is a paradox about old-style reproduction that can be called 'working at staying put'. Approximately a quarter of the general population interviewed and a sixth of the student interviewees do embrace their natal context: dispositionally they are at one with it and positionally they wish to remain in it or return to it. Yet, today, routine action is no longer the basis upon which such subjects can achieve the 'contextual continuity' that they seek. Instead, most have to exercise their reflexivity to produce this outcome, which is not a default setting or fall-back position. Their motivation derives from finding their natal contexts satisfying, their means for realizing 'contextual continuity' turns upon identifying a sustainable position within the bounds of their backgrounds – and the modality for bringing the two together is 'communicative reflexivity'. This is reflexive deliberation, exercised as 'thought and talk' with interlocutors, who are also 'similars and familiars' and trusted to complete and confirm the subject's incohate internal conversations. It is only one of four modes of reflexivity regularly detected and it operates through a shared way of life to reinforce normative conventionalism amongst its practitioners.[120]

'Communicative reflexives' come from stable and geo-local backgrounds, where interpersonal relations are warm, convivial and lasting, with friendship networks including some of those with whom subjects grew up and went to school. Their natal context is unlike that of 'autonomous' and 'meta-reflexives', whose family backgrounds are usually ones of micro-'contextual discontinuity' and 'contextual incongruity' respectively as will be examined in Chapters 5 and 6. Such 'discontinuity' and 'incongruity' will both be seen to have deprived them of continuous, trusted interlocutors, to have thrown them back upon their own mental resources and generally to have done little to recommend perpetuating the natal context, compared with the alternative opportunities they personally encountered.

Could or should these be termed 'dispositions'? On the one hand, the answer is affirmative as concerns these different orientations towards the social order: the protection and prolongation of 'contextual continuity' versus the acceptance of 'discontinuity' and pursuit of personal concerns that augment it. These very different forms of social orientation are,

---

[120] Archer, *Structure, Agency and the Internal Conversation*, pp. 167–209.

indeed, *interior to subjects* and pre-dispose them towards equally different social trajectories. On the other hand, the answer is negative if 'dispositions' refer to the courses of action that are assumed to lead to these ends pre-reflexively, because in neither case does routine action any longer suffice. In other words, whether or not the influence of natal contexts – their 'continuity', 'discontinuity' or 'incongruity' – are regarded as *dispositional* influences accounting for the mode of reflexivity practised by different proportions of the population at any given time and at different points in history – no modality can now work as a *habitus*.

Both points are nicely illustrated by reference to the 'communicative reflexives'. Here, Fleetwood misses the point being made by and about a respondent called Angie, who followed her mother, aunt and many family friends into secretarial employment.[121] He argues that '[b]ecoming a welder never made it on to Angie's radar screen as a possible target for subsequent deliberation' because of the 'dead weight of (gendered) routines'.[122] This entails the shift from 'first-person' to 'third-person' authoritative interpretation, as was consistently Bourdieu's own procedure. But also, in pressing his conclusion about engendered routine action, he fails to note that neither did Angie settle down to a job in retail, reception or recruitment, to pick a few feminized and accessible alternatives. In order to maintain her 'contextual continuity' as closely as possible, she sought to do something much more demanding than the *reproduction* of her mother's social position, she wanted an exact *replication* of her occupational role and social circle. This is the extent of normative conventionalism induced by 'communicative reflexivity'.

Conversely, the next study (*Making our Way through the World*) showed how very non-routine was the maintenance of this 'continuity'. Job promotion, occupational relocation and even overtime were perceived as threats to an established and valued *modus vivendi*. By declining such advancement 'communicative reflexives' were active agents in monitoring and sustaining their own social *immobility*, making objective sacrifices in order to protect their main concern, which was invariably family well-being.[123]

However, as was outlined in Chapter 1, three reasons make the maintenance of 'communicative reflexivity' arduous and point to its likely diminution in the new millennium. Firstly, the 'costs' become manifestly steeper if opportunities are turned down whilst many others 'get ahead' by taking advantage of them. Secondly, 'staying as we are' is diminishingly possible: new skills must be acquired if jobs are to be kept, new

[121] *Ibid.*, pp. 170–176.   [122] Fleetwood, 'Structures, Institutions, Agency', p. 199.
[123] Archer, *Making our Way*, pp. 158–191.

technology mastered if everyday life is to go on, and new experiences weathered because they cannot be avoided. Thirdly, and most importantly, there will be a shrinking pool of 'similars and familiars' available as potential and durable interlocutors because many classmates, workmates, and neighbours will have embraced some element of their new opportunities or have had novelty thrust upon them. 'Communicative reflexivity' remains possible, but it has become considerably more 'costly' (in various currencies) and involves a great deal more effort to sustain. Above all, it has become a matter of active choice and personal ingenuity, bearing no resemblance to routine action (see Chapter 4).

If this diagnosis is correct, it also leads to a conclusion about Bourdieu's *habitus* and Elder-Vass' proposed 'reconciliation' between it and reflexivity. Bourdieu's *habitus*, entailing *both* social orientations (dispositions) *and* pre-reflexive templates for routine action (also dispositions) *effectively seems to presume* 'communicative reflexivity'. Because this mode entails 'talk' as well as 'thought', it is relatively easy to neglect the reflexive element. If this is the case, it places a date-stamp on Bourdieu's theorizing – despite his reference to '*transhistorical invariants*' – simply because times have changed.[124] With them, so have natal backgrounds, socialization practices, and ultimately, the social orientations of the majority and the deliberative nature of the courses of action they take. In other words, 'communicative reflexivity' flourishes most easily and appropriately when similarities are continuously distributed throughout the population – or stable classes within it – and similar situations are consistently encountered. This (Durkheimian) 'likeness', which is integral to 'contextual continuity', reconfirms the appositeness of conventional responses to them and, in turn, fosters social reproduction. The utility of the portmanteau term *habitus* peters out as the objective conditions for 'communicative reflexivity' undergo radical transformation – as is now the case.

---

[124] Wacquant, 'Toward a Reflexive Sociology', p. 36.

3 Reconceptualizing socialization as 'relational reflexivity'

The best known theories of socialization are firmly embedded in modernity. These can look back to earlier social formations, where their major premises are invariably found to be even better exemplified. What they cannot do, however, is to shed the lineaments of modernity without launching into utopianism. This is of no assistance in explaining how young people come to be the persons that they are once nascent morphogenesis has engaged. When deviation–amplifying processes (introducing novelty with increasing speed) begin to exceed the effects of negative feedback loops that restore morphostasis in the social order, time is up for the theoretical assumptions about socialization that were endorsed throughout the line of succession stretching from Durkheim to Mead, Parsons, Habermas and Beck.

Traditional theories of socialization

Durkheim's contrast between members of a 'segmented' versus those of a 'cooperative' society was the first full appreciation of the intimate linkage between progressive societal differentiation and growing personal individuation.[1] Nevertheless, he did not articulate a general theory of socialization associated with modernity and necessary to solve its macroscopic problems. This task fell to Mead who eschewed the macro-pathologies of modernity and focussed, instead, on the pivotal micro-role of socialization in dovetailing socio-functional differentiation with the individuation ineluctably associated with it. At its core, Mead introduced the concept of the 'generalized other' as an intrinsic part of the self without which we would have no conception of being 'selves'. This replaced Durkheim's diffuse notions about people coming to realize their

---

[1] Indeed, Jürgen Habermas acknowledges this as the bedrock of modern theories of socialization in his first sentence in 'Individuation through Socialization: George Herbert Mead's Theory of Subjectivity', in his *Postmetaphysical Thinking*', Oxford, Polity Press, 1992, p. 149.

interdependencies with others as the lynchpin of social re-integration within modernity. In turn, the workings of the 'generalized other' relied upon a mechanism acknowledged only in the American pragmatist tradition – stretching from William James, through Peirce and Dewey – namely reflexivity, as exercised through what Mead usually termed the 'inner conversation'. The role of reflexivity was abruptly severed by Parsons, never to be recovered within modernity's theories of social-ization. What was lost with the shedding of this key aspect of Mead's patrimony was his recognition that in the early Durkheimian 'segmented societies' members of the group were largely practitioners of habitual action, in contrast to what frees us from the iron hand of 'firmly organized habits', namely the reflexivity enabling people to become 'constructive conformers' to the novel requirements of modernity.[2]

In what follows, I will not provide a detailed exegesis, worthy of Mead's innovative contribution, but focus upon the last part of *Mind, Self and Society* alone because this is the main place where he looks forward and speculates about the self in a universal or globalizing society. This is examined simply to make three points.

(i)   To explain what part is played by the 'generalized other' in his account of socialization in later modernity.

(ii) To identify the structural and cultural assumptions upon which the tenability and workability of this concept rest, given how enduring these have proved for many of Mead's successors.

(iii) To show how the key concept of the 'generalized other' buckles when Mead himself contemplates universalistic impulses, global change and social justice developing within later modernity.

The reason for this brief excursion is simply an attempt to show that there is no place for the 'generalized other', or for the structural and cultural assumptions supporting it, when theorizing about 'socialization' in the new millennium. An alternative to it, based upon active human *engagement* with social reality, will be presented in the next section.[3]

The first two-thirds of *Mind, Self, and Society* is devoted to a sum-mary of Mead's early linguistic turn and introducing his two founda-tional propositions about the socialization of human beings: that 'out of

---

[2] '[T]he individual self is much more completely determined, with regard to his thinking and behaviour, by the general pattern of the organised social activity'. George Herbert Mead, *Mind, Self, and Society*, University of Chicago Press, 1934, pp. 124 and 221. The quotation in the text continues: 'It is this freedom, then, that is the prerequisite of reflection, and it is our social self-reflective conduct that gives this freedom to human individuals in their group life.' p. 124n.

[3] This was largely developed in Archer, *Being Human: The Problem of Agency*, Cambridge University Press, 2000.

language emerges the field of mind' and that 'the language process is essential for the development of the self'.[4] Language is what frees the human race from animal-like confinement to reflex action (stimulus-response). It enables a variety of courses of action to be held in mind, to be rationally reviewed, and the eventual response to be intelligently selected. Mead anticipates Habermas' universal pragmatics; all 'significant symbols' – constitutive of language – are such by evoking in the speaker the same response as in his listeners. But the symbols of communication have primacy in two senses. Firstly, they are indispensable to reflexivity itself, that is to inner conversation, because a 'person who is saying something is saying to himself what he says to others; otherwise he does not know what he is talking about'.[5] In other words, it is equally essential to internal and external conversation that the symbol should arouse the same reaction in one's self as it arouses in other people, otherwise 'self-talk' would deteriorate into what Wittgenstein dubbed 'idle conversation'. Secondly, the process of conceiving of oneself as a self also works from without to within: one has first to be a member of a linguistic 'community to be a self'.[6] In order to become both rational and reflexive – and thus to supersede the dictatorship of habit – each individual must become capable of being an object to themselves, otherwise the interlocution between subject and object that *is* the reflexive inner conversation cannot happen.

Mead posits that 'the gift to see ourselves as an object' is given by how others see us. Each 'enters his own experience as a self or individual, not directly or immediately, not by becoming a subject to himself, but only in so far as he first becomes an object to himself just as other individuals are objects to him or in his experience; and he becomes an object to himself only by taking the attitudes of other individuals towards himself within a social environment'.[7] These attitudes coalesce into the perceptions and judgements of the 'generalized other' and introduce the individual's self as a social object to himself enabling the reflexive

internal conversation of the individual with himself in terms of words and significant gestures – the conversation which constitutes the process or activity of thinking – is carried on by the individual from the standpoint of the 'generalized other' . . . [A]bstract concepts are concepts stated in terms of the entire social group or community; they are stated on the basis of the individual's consciousness of the attitudes of the generalized other toward them, as a result of his taking these attitudes of the generalized other and then responding to them.[8]

---

[4] Expanded in other works, especially, George Herbert Mead, *Philosophy of the Act*, University of Chicago Press, 1938. See Mead, *Mind, Self, and Society*, pp. 132–133, 135.
[5] Mead, *Mind, Self, and Society*, p. 147.   [6] *Ibid.*, p. 162.
[7] *Ibid.*, p. 138.   [8] *Ibid.*, p. 155–156, n8.

The social conditions of the generalized other

Despite the extremely sketchy manner in which Mead's account of social-ization has been presented, it can readily be seen that the pivotal role assigned to the 'generalized other' is dependent upon particular cultural and structural conditions pertaining in the social order if it is to work as specified. However, if states of affairs in both the cultural domain and the structural realm are variable rather than constant, then the tenability of this model of socialization as a universal one becomes questionable.

By drawing upon realism's stratified social ontology, we can explore what needs to be the case – both culturally and structurally – in order for people's experiences to be empirically as Mead described them. On that basis it is possible to evaluate whether or not the generative mechanisms (cultural and structural) were correctly detected at the time, have proved durable, and seem likely to endure. Only if all answers are positive is there the possibility (and nothing more than this because of the contingencies of life in an open system) that the same experiences could be the lot of successive generations of subjects. These conditions are schematized in Figure 3.1.

It seems almost definitional that if the 'generalized other' is capable of condensing society's behavioural requirements of its members, is able to project an evaluative overview of everyone as an object-self, and is susceptible of internalization as the individual conscience or *super ego*, that the *messages transmitted must be clear and consensual*. This is less and less the case today. Yet, if individuals are in receipt of mixed messages none of the above will hold and no one can have an unambiguous notion of acceptable or desirable social action.

High socio-cultural integration? For members of a social group to experience 'the receipt of consensual messages', Mead predicates their source – the 'generalized other' – on the existence of a state of high socio-cultural integration. This is necessarily the case, given his assertion that the 'attitude of the generalized other is the attitude *of the whole community*,' rather than merely the receipt of coherent messages from the family or significant others.[9] This is frequently repeated and is held to be a condition of the self: '[w]hat goes to make up the organized self is the organization of the attitudes which are *common to the group*. A person is a personality *because he belongs to a community*... The structure, then, on which the self is built is this response that *is common to all*, for one has to be a member of a community to be a self.'[10]

[9] *Ibid.*, p. 154 (italics added).   [10] *Ibid.*, p. 162 (italics added).

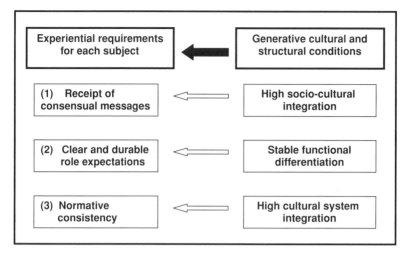

Figure 3.1 Conditions for the 'generalized other' to govern socialization in modernity

Socio-cultural integration is what is implied in everyday language when it is said that the ideas of X were influenced by those of Y; it is a causal matter of social interaction (including the use of power, mystification and manipulation).[11] The end result can be that symbols and their meanings are (become or remain) *either homogeneous or heterogeneous* at any given time and place. Writing in the United States in the first decades of the twentieth century, does Mead consider it to be homogeneity or heterogeneity that characterizes the 'community'? He accepted that a person may belong only to a small community, such as a gang or a clique, and remain inside it. In that case, '[t]he "organized other" present in ourselves is then a community of narrow diameter'.[12] Elsewhere, he allows that an individual may belong only to a section of a given social group or community, citing social classes, political parties, clubs and corporations as instances. What then about interclass and interparty antagonism, ideationally expressed? Moreover, can any of the above groups be presumed to possess the high socio-cultural consensus that would secure the generation and receipt of coherent messages? Such a presumption would fly in the face of historical fractionalism, factionalism and fissiparousness. Heterogeneity seems inescapable in the past and still more so in the

---

[11] The concept of the 'socio-cultural' level and the 'cultural system' level are worked out in detail in the preface and chapter 5 of Margaret S. Archer, *Culture and Agency*, Cambridge University Press, 1988.

[12] *Ibid.*, p. 265.

present. In that case, a given term cannot evoke the same resonance in 'me' as in all 'others' and vice versa, as seems increasingly to be the case today for concepts such as a 'global warming', 'Islamic terrorism' or 'the peace process' in different parts of the world.

Stable functional differentiation? What obviates this situation by ensuring that the 'generalized other' is the source of 'clear and durable role expectations' in the experience of the individual during progressive functional differentiation (as it was held to be by Durkheim, Parsons and Luhmann)? Distinguishing the usual three paradigmatic types of social differentiation – segmentary, stratified and functional[13] – Mead accentuated the integrative implications of the transition from the second to the third: '[t]he individual is not to be what he is in his specific caste or group set over against other groups, but his distinctions are to be distinctions of *functional difference which put him in relationship with others instead of separating him.*'[14] That these relationships are coherently and clearly dovetailed is what, in turn, makes the organized game the paradigm for societal activities.[15] The validity of this analogy is usually questioned because there is no certainty that organized social activities share either the constitutive or regulative rules of team games. Mead, however, like Durkheim before him and Parsons after him, simply assumes that functional differentiation and functional integration are closely coupled and applies the same organic analogy to both.[16] Indeed, he held cooperative integration to be more crucial than language per se because it is what anchors the *meaning* of clear role expectations transmitted by the 'generalized other' and experienced by members of the community.[17]

---

[13] Niklas Luhmann, *The Differentiation of Society*, New York, Columbia University Press, 1982.

[14] Mead, *Mind, Self, and Society*, p. 318 (italics added).

[15] *Ibid.*, 'The game has a logic, so that such an organization of the self is rendered possible: there is a definite end to be obtained; the actions of the different individuals are all related to each other with reference to that end so that they do not conflict.' pp. 158–159.

[16] 'The relation of individual organisms to the social whole of which they are members is analogous to the relation of individual cells of a multi-cellular organism to the organism as a whole', *ibid.*, p. 164n.

[17] '*back even of the process of discourse must lie co-operative activity.* The process of communication is . . . more universal then these different co-operative processes . . . But one must recognize that it is a medium for co-operative activities; there is not any field of thought as such which can simply go on by itself . . . *One must assume that sort of co-operative situation in order to reach what is called the "universe of discourse".* Such a universe of discourse is the medium for all these different social processes, and in that sense it is more universal than they; but it is not a process that, so to speak, runs by itself.' *Ibid.*, pp. 259–260 (italics added).

Although Habermas was later to reverse this argument, what did Mead, in his own day, make of the tendency of communities to expand because of the universalistic impulses fuelled materially through trade and ideationally through religion? In so far as these succeed, role expectations cannot remain durable, but what is it that ensures they remain clear?

In his endorsement of liberal economics (without any qualifying 'neo') and his optimism about international democracy, Mead showed himself to be a man of his times. He regarded capitalist expansion as a 'slow process of the integration of a society which binds people more and more closely together', correspondingly extending their communicative repertoire. Economic expansion is thus held to be 'the most *universal socializing factor in our whole modern society*' precisely because it extends the 'generalized other'.[18] How so? Through growing reliance upon money as the generalized medium of exchange: 'One cannot complete the process of bringing goods into a market except by developing means of communication. The language in which that is expressed is the language of money. The economic process goes right on tending to bring people closer together.'[19]

Yet during this upheaval (and the parallel one taking place in international relations), what is experientially lost are the clear and durable role expectations issuing from what Mead views as the nascent but unconsolidated 'generalized other'. This Mead accepts. There will be a period of conflict and hostility resulting in a fragmentation of some individual selves.[20] All that accounts for the equanimity of this genial writer is his unruffled Durkheimian confidence in the (re-)establishment of functional reintegration.[21] But what is causally responsible for this reintegration of the social order or of the individual personality? Here, Mead's thinking seems to lose its consistency. Whereas it was once the reference of each and all to the 'generalized other' that coordinated individual activities – in the same way that the Parsonian central value system was later to do – it is now a matter of the creativity of action on the part of individual members to develop their 'individual selves or personalities in such a way as adaptively to keep pace with such social reconstruction'.[22] However, the *adaptive consequences* of the uses to which they put such powers can only be secured by making certain assumptions about the nature of the cultural system upon which they draw, they do not underwrite 'clear and durable role expectations'.

---

[18] *Ibid.*, pp. 292, 296.   [19] *Ibid.*, p. 302.
[20] To Mead, that is to 'conflicts leading to cases of split personality when they are extreme and violent enough to be psychopathological'. *Ibid.*, p. 307.
[21] *Ibid.*, p. 310.   [22] *Ibid.*, pp. 309–310.

High cultural system integration Under circumstances of macroscopic social change, the 'intelligent reconstructions' upon which social reintegration depends imply a reversal of the conventional 'me' and the spontaneous 'I', a manoeuvre later repeated by Habermas.[23] However, what now binds the responses of the 'I' to the community, rather than it standing (up) for particularistic or sectional interests – ones that would undercut socio-cultural integration itself? Mead's solution is to insist that the creativity of action is itself communally tethered. Current conventions can be challenged only in the name of a 'higher sort of community, which in a certain sense out-votes the one we find . . . We can reform the order of things; we can insist on making the community standards better standards. We are not simply bound by the community . . . This is especially true in critical situations.'[24] But this appeal to the future can work only in terms of 'conventions which no longer have any meaning to a community' (in other words, socio-cultural integration is now admitted to be low) and on the assumption that what is being advocated somehow articulates or gives voice to 'a group of organized others that answers to one's own appeal – even if the appeal be made to posterity'.[25] Once again, and especially if this is how 'society gets ahead', why should such attempts at mobilization be firstly, disinterested, secondly, non-conflictual, and thirdly, reintegrative in their effects?[26] In any case, Mead clearly does not endorse the cultural system as a 'community of shared meanings' because if they were fully shared, they could not be bases of *innovative* appeals.

As creative or innovative appeals, these are by definition ones that are *not* currently salient at the socio-cultural level. Thus their source (since they are not invented *ex nihilo*) must be that of elements drawn and developed from the cultural system – from the entire corpus of ideas available in that particular social order. Yet, outside the evergreen 'myth of cultural integration', which I have criticized elsewhere, nothing assures the absence of logical contradictions at the cultural system level.[27] However, Mead – like so many others – avoids the threat of interested, conflictual and divisive results stemming from raids upon the cultural system for new sources of self-promotion or legitimation. He does so by *assuming* a high level of cultural system integration among the newly accentuated elements such that they can furnish a new source of normative consistency for the social order.

---

[23] Mead agrees that such innovative responses mean that in 'that case there is the attitude of the "I" as over against the "me"', ibid., p. 199.

[24] *Ibid.*, pp. 167–168.   [25] *Ibid.*, p. 199.   [26] *Ibid.*, p 168.

[27] Margaret S. Archer, 'The Myth of Cultural Integration', *British Journal of Sociology*, 36:3, 1985, 333–353.

What justifies this presumption? The answer he gives is that the appeals in question are made to *universal ideas* (religion and economics) which, because of their very universality cannot be countered by oppositional, contradictory or inconsistent notions.

Nevertheless, contradictions within the cultural system do rebound to undermine how he works out his key notion of adaptive ideational development as the source of social reintegration. Indeed, in the last pages of the book, Mead himself is highly equivocal about how far individuals can continue to take the roles of others once institutions – economies, religions, democracies – exceed a certain size. Thus, he accedes, 'the community may in its size transcend the social organization, may go beyond the social organization which makes such identification possible. The most striking illustration of that is the economic community. This includes everybody with whom one can trade in any circumstances, *but it represents a whole in which it would be next to impossible for all to enter into the attitudes of others*.'[28] Not only does the 'generalized other' cease to exist, constituting the 'me' and underwriting social integration, but its necessary anchorage in 'the community' has dragged loose. Thus, Mead rather wistfully concludes that one 'may say that the attainment of functional differentiation and social participation in the full degree *is a sort of ideal* which lies before the human community'.[29] It was not the reality even of early twentieth-century modernity.

Such utopianism was even more pronounced in Habermas' argument that the task of those whose 'I' now represents a 'post-conventional ego identity' was to re-animate the life world, previously regarded as itself being responsible for socialization.[30] Moreover, the identical 'appeal to posterity' was invoked and this 'future community' was regarded as validating the innovative-cum-restorative activities and attitudes of such advanced egos. Whatever else may be said about this manoeuvre, its effect is to exclude reflexivity from the conceptualization of socialization.[31] It

---

[28] *Ibid.*, pp. 326–327 (italics added).   [29] *Ibid.*, p. 326 (italics added).

[30] Habermas, 'Individuation through Socialization'. This post-conventional ego, '[c]an only assure itself of itself if it is able to return to itself from the perspective of others as their alter ego. But this time it does not return to itself as the alter ego from among its own concrete group (as the 'me'). It now comes upon itself as the alter ego of *all* others in every community – specifically as a free will in moral self-reflection and as a fully individuated being in existential self-reflection. Thus, the relationship between the "I" and the "me" *remains* the key even for an analysis of the socially imputed post-conventional ego-identity. But at this stage the relationship between the two is reversed', p. 187.

[31] Habermas' discussion of Mead's theory of communication as the foundation of social science scarcely mentions reflexivity (except for using it adjectivally). See Jürgen Habermas, *The Theory of Communicative Action*, Cambridge, Polity Press, 1989 (1981), chapter 1.

is impossible to conduct an internal conversation with posterity, except as a flight of pure imagination, and it is equally impossible for future generations to supply guidelines for how anyone should live his or her present life.

Three conclusions follow for the conceptualization of socialization in the tradition stretching from Mead to Habermas, which has only been cursorily sketched above. Each of them fuels the need to reconceptualize the process.

(a) The contextual conditions necessary for the subject's socialization to be governed by the generalized other (i.e. the receipt of consensual messages, clear and durable role expectations, and normative consistency) no longer maintain. On the contrary, by the late twentieth century each condition had become the obverse of the above. As nascent morphogenesis increasingly replaced morphostatic processes fostering social reproduction, especially from the 1980s onwards, 'sociocultural integration' declined precipitously; 'Stable functional differentation' ceded the way to novel variety in organizations, roles and occupations; and 'cultural system integration' plummeted as global connectivity increasingly exposed larger tracts of *both* ideational *complementarities and contradictions* to more and more of the world's population (see Chapter 1).

(b) Traditional conceptions of socialization no longer solve the original problem set by Durkheim, namely how to reconcile increasingly faster social differentiation – which can no longer be described as 'functional' – with the individuation that it not only continues to produce but does so more rapidly and intensively.

(c) As social change accelerates, socialization can no longer be credibly conceptualized as a largely passive process of 'internalization' because there is less and less to normalize, that is, to present as *being normal* and *normatively binding*. Correspondingly, the traditional agencies of socialization – the community (for Mead), the family (for Parsons), social class (for Bourdieu), or the life world (for Habermas) can no longer be conceived of as almost exclusively responsible for the process.

Reconceptualizing socialization as 'relational reflexivity'

In what follows the aim is to retrieve two elements from the preceding theorists and to recombine them in a form appropriate to the contextual transformations that increasingly characterize the social order of the new millennium. On the one hand, reflexivity is retrieved and redoubled in importance because in the relative absence of authoritative sources of normativity, young people are increasingly thrown back upon reflexively assessing how to realize their personal concerns in order to make their way through the world. On the other hand, their real relations with others also need retrieving as variable but powerful influences upon the equally variable outcomes that now constitute the lifelong socialization process. Otherwise, the entire concept risks drifting into an unacceptable monadism or slipping into Beck's portrayal of subjects' capricious and serial self-reinvention in a social context reduced to 'institutionalized individualism'.[32]

Instead, what I have termed 'relational reflexivity' is a reconceptualization that recombines these elements. In so doing, it provides traction upon how the main tasks confronting young and active agents are tackled, enabling them to make (i) personally meaningful (not instrumentally rational) choices from among the mixed messages they receive and (ii) to achieve some governance over the future trajectory of their own lives. Specifically, these tasks are:

(i) *The necessity of selection* that derives from the generative mechanism of morphogenesis for 'variety to stimulate more variety'. In the everyday life of the young this means more things to know, to do or to be – new occupations, new organizations and new relations. In short, these are new opportunities unknown and unavailable to their parental generation. However, there is no authoritative source of normativity recommending particular selections. The dramatic fall in social integration means that most family circles are themselves sources of mixed messages. Thus, the reflexive imperative is first encountered within the home. How the young deal with such messages is not a matter of lone inclinations but a product of the qualitative relations within their domestic environments.

(ii) *Shaping a life* is fundamentally a matter of dovetailing the personal 'concerns' that have been selected from the above *mélange* together with others adopted from outside the natal environment into a satisfying and sustainable *modus vivendi*. This includes the prioritization, accommodation, subordination and exclusion of those things that each and every (normal) person has identified as mattering most to them, because nothing guarantees their mutual compatibility. Once again, this is not a lone and arbitrary enterprise. The reflexive practical reasoning involved is shaped by the networks of relations within which it takes place because these profoundly affect what *does and can* satisfy the subject and be sustained by each of them.

---

[32] Ulrich Beck and Elizabeth Beck-Gernsheim, *Individualization*, London, Sage, 2002, p. 51f.

Socialization is reconceptualized as the process of tackling these two tasks. It is no longer reliant upon the three assumptions (Figure 3.1) undergirding the traditional conceptions, but rather presumes that their opposites characterize the social order. 'Relational reflexivity' re-tools the concept of socialization in response to the formative situations generated by an increasingly morphogenetic global society.

Relational goods in the family: their influence upon selection and reflexivity

This section combines the findings of my in-depth interviews for this study with Pierpaolo Donati's realist 'Relational Sociology'.[33] This Italian relational turn is quite distinct from 'relationalism', with its repudiation of emergence and endorsement of a flat ontology of 'transactions' alone.[34] In relational sociology, 'social relations' can never be reduced to 'interpersonal relations', which are non-emergent because all that is involved in the latter can be 'personalized' by downward reduction to the influences of A upon B and vice versa.[35] To Donati:

> The relation is made up of diverse components which can be further distinguished by *the effect of the ego on the other* (consistency in the behaviour of the ego towards others), *the effect of the other on the ego* (the responsiveness of a person to different *egos*), and the effect of their interaction (the behaviour that none of the actors 'brings' to the relation, but which results from their mutual conditioning of each other.) These effects can be observed and measured, given suitable methods. The first two effects can be analysed at the level of the individual, the third can only be examined by taking the relation as the unit of analysis.[36]

Instead, 'relations' are both the 'mediation' of prior structural and cultural conditioning and have emergent powers of causal consequence in their own right and of their own kind.

---

[33] See Pierpaolo Donati, *Introduzione alla sociologia relazionale*, Milan, Franco Angeli, 1983, especially chapter 1; and *Teoria relazionale della società*, Milan: Franco Angeli, 1991. See also, Pierpaolo Donati and Ivo Colozzi (eds.), *Il Paradigma Relazionale nelle Scienze Sociali: le prospettive sociologiche*, Bologna, Mulino, 2006.

[34] See Pierpaolo Donati, 'Engagement as a Social Relation: Getting out of Modernity', in Margaret Archer and Andrea Maccarini (eds.), *Engaging with the World: Agency, Institutions, Historical Formations* (forthcoming).

[35] A central strategy of methodological individualism from the beginning of its canon was to construe 'emergent properties' as the effects of 'other people', see J. W. N. Watkins, 'Methodological Individualism and Social Tendencies', in May Brodbeck (ed.), *Readings in the Philosophy of the Social Sciences*, New York, Macmillan, 1968, p. 271f. For a critique see Margaret S. Archer, *Realist Social Theory: The Morphogenetic Approach*, Cambridge University Press, 1995, pp. 33–46.

[36] Pierpaolo Donati, 'Observing and Thinking Relationally: the Premises of the Relational Theory of Society', in his *Relational Sociology: A New Paradigm for the Social Sciences*, London, Routledge, 2010, p. 126.

Because of this the relational approach can conceptualize *both* the emergence of 'relational goods' within any unit of social interaction and their opposites – 'relational evils' – thus helping to pinpoint how they contribute to the development of agents who foster morphogenesis versus morphostasis. Specifically, it forges the link between the types of familial 'relational goods/evils' received from the families of the subjects interviewed and their intensified reflexivity, as well as the form taken by it (the dominant mode tending to characterize their internal conversations at the point of leaving home).

Where the receipt of 'relational goods' is concerned, this has the generative tendency to create bonds and interdependencies at the empirical level amongst the persons involved that denote more than 'good interpersonal relations'. They indicate something in excess of a degree of warmth and some regularity of contact. That 'something' refers to emergent properties, namely 'internal goods' (such as love, reliance, caring and trust) that cannot be produced by aggregation and are *also* deemed highly worthwhile in themselves. As 'strong evaluators', the young subjects from such close families recognize the value of what their parents have generated – also enabling them to become part of the generative process because the family does not remain a couple plus a child, but widens the dyad into a triad (plus).[37] This recognition means respect for the relational goods produced and a concern for the preservation and prolongation of this worth that encourages a commitment to fostering the relationship itself. It spells endorsement of the family's *modus vivendi*, without preventing the subject from contemplating the odd tweak.

Such families (found to belong to the smallest sub-group amongst my university entrants) were the exceptions to the general transmission of 'mixed messages'. Instead, mother and father were portrayed as normatively consensual and these subjects uniformly wished their own future families to be 'much the same'. Hence, the necessity of selection had been drastically curtailed. It had been minimized, rather than entirely eliminated because the very experience of going to university confronted subjects with new experiences, often incongruent with the 'relational goods' to whose preservation they were committed. In general, members of this sub-group were not on the look-out for new items of experiential variety. On the contrary, their high valuation of their familial 'relational goods' acted as a filter, sifting friendships, social activities and leisure pursuits to ensure congruity with their families' normativity. In short,

---

[37] Charles Taylor, 'Self-Interpreting Animals', in his *Human Agency and Language*, Cambridge University Press, 1985, pp. 35–76.

these families did appear to work as consensual 'norm circles' *through* the emergent relational goods generated.[38]

Thus, the receipt of high 'relational goods' prior to university entry yielded a group of '*identifiers*' for whom the necessity of selection was minimized through decreasing the salience of new opportunities to them. In other words, the attractions of new opportunities were greatly reduced *by subjects turning their backs* upon morphogenetic novelty and variety and continuing to practise communicative reflexivity, exercised through 'thought and talk' with their similars and familiars.[39]

At the opposite extreme was a sub-group of the same small size whose experience was of 'relational harm' within their home backgrounds. The root causes included excessive maternal dependency or domination as well as coercion, antagonism and exploitation. In every case, the response to these relations by the young person was the repudiation of their home background as the source of their personal misery. Yet, equally uniformly, since the priority had been escape, it was accompanied by no clear notion of towards what; getting away was an end in itself. Here, necessary selectivity could not be handled purposefully, the need to make choices and to respond decisively to opportunities simply intensified their disorientation and distress. The need to survive predominated, meaning for some just trying to hold themselves together and for others taking expressive action whose consequences cumulatively intensified their difficulties. Not surprisingly, all '*rejecters*' scored as fractured reflexives.[40]

However, the majority of interviewees fell into the sub-groups termed the '*independents*' and the '*disengaged*'. The '*independents*' had experienced much less severe 'relational harm' than the rejecters but fell below the line of having received 'relational goods'. All started university as autonomous reflexives and one family feature was disproportionately concentrated amongst them: divorced parents, 'rocky relationships' and parents effectively living apart. Almost uniformly, relations were quite cordial with the parent(s) with whom the subject was still in contact, cordial but uninvolved. From their accounts, disruptive family dynamics had induced an early independence amongst these subjects who recognized the need to take responsibility for themselves and to avoid becoming responsible for the family situation or a particular parent. Nothing tied them to the 'mess other people had made' and the dissention they breathed was met by an assertion of their own individualism. As 'independents', with no

---

[38] Dave Elder-Vass, *The Causal Power of Social Structures: Emergence, Structure and Agency*, Cambridge University Press, 2010, pp. 122–127f.

[39] Archer, *Making our Way*, pp. 158–191.

[40] Scores refer to the 'internal conversation indicator' whose development is described in Archer, *Making our Way*, pp. 329–334.

desire to be bound, they were free both to select certain elements from their background, ones evaluated as worth retaining, but also to combine them with an unfazed examination of the opportunities on offer in the world beyond. Necessary selectivity had been their lot so far, but the prospect of making their own choices and their own lives was relished.

Finally, the largest group was the 'disengaged', who had experienced and appreciated family stability as a 'relational good' but one mitigated by parental tensions from which subjects withdrew. They manifested a critical detachment from their parents and dissociation from the *modus vivendi* in which they had been reared. Reviewing the dissensus characterizing their parents' way of life, these subjects' evaluation was that 'there must be better than this' and an avowed desire that their own would indeed be different. Distinctive of these meta-reflexives was that as teenagers they had already sought something better. Through their self-distancing they had found a 'cause' with which to identify. Even if this was inchoate and rudimentary, as was not invariably the case, they did not withdraw their adherence to it when at university. It was more a case of fine-tuning their 'vocation' and the fact that some of the new opportunities coming into view had to be selected for compatibility with their 'ultimate concern', which was already being drawn into service as an architectonic principle.

Figure 3.2 summarizes the influence of the quality of familial relational goods – a gradient from highly positive to extremely negative – on subjects' experiences of the necessity of selection whilst living at home. The minority sub-group of 'identifiers' were the only young people who could be said to approximate to the traditional image of socialization as internalizing both the normativity of their parents and identifying with the *modus vivendi* through which this was lived out. In other words, they dealt with the necessity of selection by trying to turn their backs on it and endorsing what had been given them. All of the other sub-groups had already encountered the necessity of selection in ways directly linked to their positions on the axis of familial relational goods/evils. Together they constituted the large majority and thus provided micro-representations (not Parsonian homologies) of the macro-historical change towards nascent morphogenesis in the social order.

For the overwhelming majority, the variable quality of their family relations and their active responses to them also meant that they displayed different orientations towards the necessity of selection: 'independents' being very open and ready to avail themselves of the situational logic of opportunity; the 'disengaged' already having made a preliminary identification of what they cared about most within the array of opportunities known to be available; and the 'rejecters' having escaped from negative

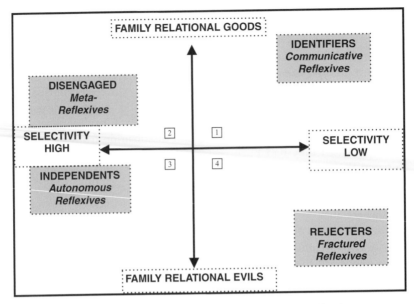

Figure 3.2 Family relational goods and necessary selection

family relations but being completely unprepared to face the necessity of selection purposefully.

However, their socialization remained far from complete because what had been accomplished so far consisted in the young giving selective approbation and disapprobation to various elements in their family backgrounds. Firstly, this alone does not reveal the importance they attached to seeking or shunning such elements. Secondly, it is not an exhaustive list of what these subjects also came to care about when they left home for university. Thirdly, and most importantly, it does not disclose the precise forms of engagement with the world that result from these different relational backgrounds. The sub-groups of 'identifiers', 'rejecters', 'independents' and the 'disengaged' are better regarded as clusters of subjects who bring a particular pre-disposition to the task of shaping their lives rather than revealing anything about this process itself or its outcomes in terms of different types of personal engagement.

Shaping a life and relational reflexivity

Apart from its 'over-social' nature, a great strength to retain from Mead – one immediately relinquished by Parsons – is that socialization was not conceptualized as a passive process. The very need for reflexive dialogue between the 'impulsive' 'I' and the 'me' (represented by the 'generalized other') allowed the subject her *active inclinations* and to battle internally for them, despite the fact that they were usually overruled by the 'me', as the 'voice' of community normativity.[41] However, even if such 'active inclinations' can be construed as 'pre-dispositions', what is required for their further specification, practical manifestation and, above all, their realization?

Shaping a life is the practical achievement of establishing a *modus vivendi* that is satisfying to and sustainable by the subject – at least *pro tem*. It calls upon much further reflexive deliberation, which is an expression of the reflexive imperative. But both our reflexive deliberations and their outcomes are closely associated with ongoing social relations that are developed (in this case) by subjects leaving home and going to university. None of this second task is understandable if socialization is simply regarded as 'internalization' and is confined to the young child rather than being completed *pro tem* by the young adult.

Our personal identities derive from our ultimate concerns, from what we care about most, together with our other concerns, which cannot be discarded but are accommodated to our prime commitment. As Frankfurt put the matter, our ultimate concerns are definitive of us in that what our commitments 'keep us from violating are not our duties or our obligations but ourselves' – this is precisely what I am calling our personal identities.[42]

A particular *modus vivendi* is forged by any given person through their reflexive 'internal conversation' and represented in what I have termed the DDD scheme of <'Discernment', 'Deliberation' and 'Dedication'>.[43] Through this fallible process, not only is personal identity shaped (I am the being with that specific constellation of concerns), but it is also the same process of internal dialogue that enables the subject to seek a *social identity* by attempting to occupy a social role(s) whose personification (they believe) would be expressive of *who they are*. With young subjects, it is not surprising that they are mainly preoccupied with *discernment* and *deliberation* because they are aware that they are still

---

[41] As Mead puts it, 'we are in possession of selves just in so far as we can and do take the attitudes of others towards ourselves and respond to those attitudes. We pat ourselves upon the back and in blind fury attack ourselves'. George Herbert Mead, 'The Genesis of the Self and Social Control', (1924–1925) in Andrew R. Reck, *Selected Writings: George Herbert Mead*, New York, Bobbs Merrill, 1964, p. 288. Equally strongly, '(s)ocial control is the expression of the "me" over against the expression of the "I". It sets the limits', *Mind, Self and Society*, p. 210.

[42] Harry G. Frankfurt, 'The Importance of what we care about', Cambridge University Press, 1988, p. 91.

[43] See Archer, *Being Human*, pp. 230–249.

learning about themselves, their world and the relations between them. Indeed, this is the reason why their time as undergraduates should be seen as part of socialization, as they deal with new information acquired on an almost daily basis. (This is what will be explored in Chapters 4–7 of the present book.) The fact that attending university and gaining a degree gives them better life chances than the rest of their age cohort does nothing whatsoever to show them how to live their lives. Only their reflexive deliberations can do this – fallibly but corrigibly.

Starting to shape a life – defining what matters to us

Relationally, each 'invitation' to a new experience produces a response from the subject, via the experiment taking place between them, one registered in terms of satisfaction or dissatisfaction (which may come close to reflex-rejection where fear or repugnance are concerned). What is of supreme importance, even though it may be misjudged, misevaluated and not be sustained, is the subject's discovery that a previously unknown experience '*matters* to me'. This is the beginning of practical reasoning about how one should live because it furnishes the potential raw materials, which may or may not be mutually compatible and thus have no guarantee of being retained. But what is meant by something 'mattering', as opposed to some first experiences being satisfying enough for anyone to welcome their repetition? Some are simultaneously recognized as trivial (such as regularly enjoying an ice-cream). What does it mean for a subject to discern that 'this is important to me?'

To care about something is the same as saying that 'something' is of concern or importance to someone, which is why the *discernment phase* is about identifying what does and does not matter to a subject. These are the elements from which our final ends (or 'ultimate concerns') are likely to become the keystone(s) upon which practical reasoning is based. However, young subjects will not yet have encountered or fully experienced some of the things that come to matter to them, although these can later be incorporated. *Discernment* is messy, incomplete and provisional for eighteen-year-olds. Nevertheless, what caring means remains constant, even if the 'list' of their concerns undergoes addition and deletion as well as accommodation and subordination.

To care is different from to want or to desire (i.e. from the Humean 'passions', which he held, as do current rational choice theorists, to be what moves us to action).[44] This is because we know that even some of our

[44] 'Reason alone can never be a motive to any action of the will . . . reason is and ought only to be the slave of the passions and can never pretend to any other office than to serve

strong feelings are inconsequential ('Please may I not have a 6am start') or undesirable ('I'm dying for a cigarette'). Nor does expressing our desires as preferences bring us any closer to understanding what it means to have a concern. For example, any student could produce a preference order for the modules they study each year, but this does not imply that they care about their course at all. Finally, to care is not the same as exercising moral judgement or high-mindedness because someone can have a deep concern for something that they themselves would not try to justify, at least publicly (for instance, the campus availability of illegal drugs). Consequently, there need be nothing laudable about our engagements.

To have a concern is a challenge to make a commitment, providing circumstances are propitious. If they are, an active commitment is a willing assent by a subject that what moves her to care is of real and (is believed to be) of enduring importance to her. In short, that concern is part of that subject's personal identity. It is simultaneously an affirmation of one kind of engagement with the world; things of no concern are the reverse. A student whose interest in car mechanics is important to him is literally engaged differently with his own vehicle (if competent, he is independent in maintaining it), with the students he knows and some he doesn't (the guy who can fix car problems), with fellow motorists (the helper not the helped) and with the garage and car trade (the one you don't overcharge). These instances of engagement are quite distinct from other forms of engaged action in which he *may also* participate, such as belonging to a car club, taking formal qualifications in motor mechanics, supporting the collective action of motoring organizations and so forth.

It follows that the mental activities involved in caring – making commitments that build our identities and affirm a particular engagement with the world – are all ones that entail reflexivity. As Frankfurt puts it:

[b]y its very nature, caring manifests and depends upon our distinctive [human] capacity to have thoughts, desires and attitudes that are *about* our own attitudes, desires and thoughts. In other words, it depends upon the fact that the human mind is *reflexive*... Creatures like ourselves are not limited to desires that move them to act. In addition they have the reflexive capacity to form desires regarding their own desires – that is, regarding both what they want to want, and what they want not to want.[45]

---

and obey them.' David Hume, *A Treatise on Human Nature*, Book II, Part III, Section 3, Harmondsworth, Penguin, 1969 (1739–1740). Margaret S. Archer, 'Homo economicus, Homo sociologicus and Homo sentiens' in Margaret S. Archer and Jonathan Q. Tritter (eds.), *Rational Choice Theory*, London, Routledge, 2000, pp. 36–56.

[45] Harry G. Frankfurt, *The Reasons of Love*, Princeton University Press, 2004, pp. 17–18.

In that case, to reconceptualize socialization as first entailing an active selection about what is and is not important for a subject, from the array of experiences that have come their way, is not only to endorse the active agent but one whose relations *with* the world also actively shape the kind of agency he or she seeks to exercise *in* the world.

Moreover, what anyone determines that they care about (or don't) involves a judgement about what they find worthwhile. It makes no sense to say, 'this is very important to me, but it's completely worthless'. However, this is not to maintain that subjects reflexively make an accurate assessment of the objective worth of their concerns. This would (illegitimately) impose the way the world is upon our knowledge about it and deliberations towards it. It would be one version of the 'ontic fallacy' which treats our epistemology as being a reflection of ontology, thus entailing equal and opposite defects from the 'epistemic fallacy': we are no more compelled to see and to know things as they are, when we can, than we are free to make what we will of any state of affairs.[46] That any of us may learn more at some later time is not in conflict with the fact that what we commit ourselves to caring about at a given time has to be deemed worthwhile in order for us to make it part of our identities.

The discernment phase is increasingly lifelong because as nascent morphogenesis grows exponentially, it means that more new opportunities become available sequentially.[47] Even the traditional *loci* of socialization, the home and the school, are better viewed as introduction bureaux rather than as induction agencies. In general, neither can be construed as consensual norm groups today; rather they are the sources of mixed messages and sometimes of messages that do not mix.

Hence, the role of social normativity in instilling conformity among the socialized is largely reversed; this becomes an elective matter of the norms to which subjects selectively subscribe by virtue of what they care about. Certainly, there were always historical instances of groups exempting themselves from a particular type of normative governance, such as the first waves of those to disassociate themselves from religious belief and thus from ecclesial normativity. However, with the proliferation of options and opportunities this becomes a more and more active and reflexive process, governed by the particular concerns that subjects adopt.

In other words, the position taken by normative regulation has been inverted, such that it is now the importance of what subjects care about

---

[46] See Andrew Collier, *Critical Realism*, London, Verso, 1994, pp. 76–85.
[47] In addition, the new variety being generated also increases the agents' potential for creative new combinations of compatible, but as yet unrelated items.

that determines with which organizations and with what kind of norma-tivity they will seek to work or be willing to support. Active agents expect to become active actors, who *personify* a role by investing something of themselves in it, thus acquiring a social identity expressive of their personal identities. However, occupational preferences are nearly always defined towards the end of the reflexive socialization process. This is an empirical finding but there are strong elements of necessity to it, the main one being that undergraduates need to have made considerable progress in defining their personal identities before they can begin to know what precise job descriptions would express and realize them. And to have done that, they must both have identified their main concerns and begun to align them *deliberatively*, which involves their projecting various scenar-ios within their internal conversation, involving several 'dummy' careers that they examine reflexively.

Discernment serves to highlight people's concerns without discrimi-nating between them. It can be seen as a logging-in process in which actual and potential items considered worthy of concern are registered for consideration. Sifting is necessarily incomplete because the contin-gent nature of experience means any given subject reviews a restricted set from the plenitude of concerns potentially available. Only those that have been logged-in constitute topics for further deliberation. Nevertheless, the 'list' of potential and available concerns remains open and hinders a young subject from speedily designing a *modus vivendi*.

The deliberation phase signals further recourse to reflexivity for the task of prioritizing, accommodating and subordinating a subject's var-ious concerns because these do not dovetail together automatically. This task played no part in the traditional model of socialization as the pas-sive internalization of a normative order, be it societal, regional, class, engendered and so forth. Not only could such normative systems, their associated role arrays and rule-sets, be presumed stable by virtue of mor-phostasis (although the presumption was usually exaggerated) but also be regarded as a system defining how the complex of roles and rules fitted together. Each specified who could do what, the order of prior-ity between role requirements and procedures for avoiding role conflict (for example, until the mid twentieth century in Britain women were required to resign from many professional and administrative posts upon marriage). In other words, the tasks of prioritization and accommodation were performed for the subject by the system. Now, this task, which St. Augustine called 'loving in due order', has to be shouldered reflexively by the subjects themselves.

The dedication phase remained 'unfinished business' for most under-graduates. The majority were still preoccupied with *discernment* and were

Defining and dovetailing one's	Developing concrete courses of action as	Establishing satisfying and sustainable
CONCERNS ▶▶▶	**PROJECTS** ▶▶▶	**PRACTICES**
(Internal goods)	(Micro-politics)	(*Modus vivendi*)

Figure 3.3 The reflexive pursuit of the good life

starting to confront *deliberation*, since issues of complementarity had begun to arise. Therefore, less than half were ready for the reflexive *dedication* involved in shaping a life, even *pro tem*. Those who did complete *dedication* by the time of graduating had determinate concerns, now consolidated into projects, whose realization they hoped could lead to the establishment of a satisfying and sustainable *modus vivendi* (as pictured in Figure 3.3).

If they are correct, then in one sense it can be said that the active process of socialization is provisionally complete. However, in the nascent morphogenetic social order, socialization must now be considered as lifelong learning, given the ineluctability of acquiring new skills, of undergoing novel experiences and encountering brand new opportunities.[48] Of course, lives can be reshaped and sometimes have to be, though not in the irrational and cavalier manner of serial self-reinvention presented by Beck, and not merely by proffering 'accountable biographies', as suggested by Habermas.[49] By definition, both of these deny any serious *engagement with the world on the part of the subject*. Instead, both accounts merely offer us *provisional* man and *pro tem* woman and have thrown in the sponge as far as shaping a life is concerned.

Yet this is of real concern to students, who at least want to make lasting commitments and are quite capable, for the most part, of projecting ten years ahead and describing the contours of the life they would then like to be leading. This means their undergraduate years will also be the time (for some) when the necessity of selection meets the need to shape a life. Why is this described as a 'need'? Because no one can simply continue adding to their list of concerns *ad infinitum* since they have insufficient time to attend to them all and would discover some conflict, generating

---

[48] Consider the age spread of those going online, which is now the case for 73 per cent of British households and means that internet skills, experiences and practices have broken the 'retirement barrier'.

[49] Ulrich Beck and Elizabeth Beck Gernsheim, *Individualization*, London, Sage, 2002. For a critique see Archer, *Making our Way*, pp. 32–37.

dissatisfaction (for example, it is almost impossible to be an avid gardener and to be travelling for six months of the year). Consequently, complementarity between concerns is sought and not as some abstract idea or strain towards consistency, but because it is desirable in itself. It is what protects that which matters to us most by ensuring it is well served and that concerns of lesser importance are not allowed to detract from it. This is why subjects (excepting the 'fractureds') actively though fallibly seek to dovetail their concerns.

The problem of configuring our concerns

There is a two-way relationship between selection and shaping. Inevitability we all have multiple concerns and these are the raw material out of which a life is shaped.[50] But to give it shape and to achieve the dovetailing involved usually means that concerns have to be modified, as well as subordinated or, in some cases, abandoned. The resulting difficulties prove common amongst undergraduates whose concerns are still quite fluid.

Only with the designation of an ultimate concern – or their articulation if subjects have more than one final end – can lesser concerns be accommodated in due order and the *modus vivendi* thus take shape. In turn, this ordering of concerns also specifies the precise kinds of engagement with the world endorsed by different subjects. In other words, the relative importance of what we care about is the door to that with which we will then become engaged, to greater or lesser degrees.

The prioritization of ultimate concern(s) is extremely difficult for many young subjects because the time at which they are necessarily deliberating about their careers – that will play a significant part in the social identities they assume – many are busy falling in love and are also considering their 'relationship' as a future part of their *modus vivendi*. What they have to resolve reflexively is *whether, how* and *in what combination* these two kinds of final ends can go forward together and accommodate other concerns, which may be subordinated without being repudiated.[51]

At this point, Frankfurt's counsels on love become too thin for two reasons. Firstly, he suggests that having plural loves (of a person, an institution, an ideal, one's work, etc.) is probable: 'However important

[50] In Archer, *Being Human*, I argued that we have three ineluctable concerns: with our 'physical well-being' in the natural order; our 'performative competence' in the practical order; and with our 'self-worth' in the social order. Chapter 6.

[51] This is an empirical statement about a common occurrence. There is no necessity to it. Some may experience no such dilemma, others may have a different one, and some may have no internal dispute about their ultimate concern.

to him a beloved [anything in parenthesis above] may be, it is unlikely to be the only thing that is important to him. It is unlikely, indeed to be the only thing that he loves. Thus there is ordinarily a strong possibility that disruptive conflict may arise between the lover's devotion to something that he loves and his concern for his other interests.'[52] The lover will suffer distress because serving one love will mean neglecting the requirements of the other. Here, Frankfurt gives a warning rather than a solution – love is risky, therefore exercise caution: 'They must try to avoid being caused to love what it would be undesirable for them to love.'[53] Yet this advice is impossible to follow, especially in relation to his two recurrent examples – love of a spouse and love of one's children. Prudential action would entail refraining from reproduction in the knowledge that this can lead to a conflict of interests, but to do so denies the fact that to one or both partners having children is crucial to *the expression* of their love. In that case, to refrain is contrary to loving wholeheartedly and it leaves at least one partner in distress.

Secondly, Frankfurt also accepts that however close the identification of a lover is with any of his loves, nevertheless, this is bound to be 'both inexact and less than totally comprehensive. His interests and those of his beloved can never be entirely the same; and it is improbable that they will even be wholly compatible'.[54] His general line of argument here is that we have no volitional option ('No choice in the matter') but to yield to the claims of love because 'the necessity with which love binds the will puts an end to indecisiveness concerning what to care about'.[55] This is not implausible, except in the case where the 'incompatibility' is *between two 'final ends' themselves*; for example, between the work the two people each believe they (will) love and the couple's belief that they (will continue to) love one another – a dilemma some of those interviewed were attempting to *live through*.[56] Where final ends are concerned, resolution cannot consist in repudiating one of them.

Frankfurt really does not tackle this problem, especially in his following observation: 'The fact that we have a variety of needs, and that we are therefore vulnerable to numerous kinds of harm, requires us to be more or less circumspect with regard to both love and work. We cannot permit ourselves to be altogether thoughtless or impulsive in selecting their objects.'[57] The subject is left without guidelines for discriminating

---

[52] Frankfurt, *The Reasons of Love*, p. 62.   [53] *Ibid.*   [54] *Ibid.*   [55] *Ibid.*, p. 65.

[56] Frankfurt effectively admits that for people in general 'useful work is among their final ends. They desire it for its own sake, since without it life is empty and vain.' Harry G. Frankfurt, 'On the Usefulness of Final Ends', in his *Necessity, Volition and Love*, Cambridge University Press, 1999, p. 91.

[57] Harry G. Frankfurt, 'On Caring', pp. 178–179. The quotation continues: 'one good reason in favour of a certain prospective object of love is simply that it is *possible* for

between their possibilities, beyond restraining their 'impulsiveness', and also with the unavoidable dilemma of how to combine 'love' and 'work'.

Yet more generally, the design of a *modus vivendi* seems to come to grief if two final ends are incompatible and constitute what some hold to be *incommensurables*.[58] This even prevents the establishment of an ordinal preference scale, thus precluding the dilemma from being solved by becoming rational actors. All the same, we seem to get by without resorting to arbitrary decisions about final ends. How is this possible?

Here, I want to draw upon Charles Taylor's Aristotelian suggestion and to flesh it out by considering what makes for sustainability over time. Taylor works on the intuition that a diversity of goods needs to be balanced with the unity of a life, at least as an aspiration, which is roughly what I have called 'dovetailing'. In other words, 'even if we see a plurality of final ends of equal rank, we still have to *live* them, that is, we have to design a life in which they can be integrated, in some proportions, since any life is finite and cannot admit of unlimited pursuit of any good. This sense of a life – or design or plan, if we want to emphasize our powers of leading here – is necessarily one. If this is our final end, there can only be one.'[59]

This suggests a way out of Frankfurt's gloomy conclusion that to engage in love's volitional commitments from which we cannot withdraw means that some of our concerns must be severely damaged and in a completely arbitrary manner because there can be no reason for selecting between final ends. Taylor's proposal also seems to gel with Lear's argument, which is of special importance here because he dwells upon the primacy of being connected to the world. This reflects exactly the same concern with *engagement* that I am pressing as necessary for making our way through the world as active agents:

Volitional unity is of course important to those who have achieved it, but, developmentally speaking, it is the last in a series of psychic configurations of staying wilfully connected to the world. From this point of view, what would be centrally important about volitional unity, even to the lover, would not be the unity of the will per se, but the types of connection to the world that that unity permitted.[60]

---

us to love it; and it follows similarly that one good reason in favour of undertaking a prospective type or task of productive activity is simply that it is *possible* for us to engage in it.'

[58] Ruth Chang (ed.), *Incommensurability, Incompatibility and Practical Reason*, Cambridge, Mass., Harvard University Press, 1997.

[59] Charles Taylor, 'Leading a Life', in Ruth Chang (ed.), *Incommensurability*, p. 183.

[60] Jonathan Lear, 'Love's Authority', in Sarah Buss and Lee Overton (eds.), *Contours of Agency*, Cambridge, Mass., MIT Press, 2002, p. 281.

Adducing a relational solution

The process of shaping a life is necessarily a matter of relations, but these are not approached relationally by most philosophers, even when they are dealing with careers or, more blatantly, with friendship, romance or parenthood. Instead, they are considered unilaterally, from the standpoint of a single lover. My argument will be that the social relations, within which the designation of ultimate concerns is enmeshed, are indispensable to explaining the life that is shaped. Taylor will be of considerable help here, but his approach will need supplementing by relational considerations.

The dilemma Taylor examines is how does our practical reasoning enable us to produce unity out of diversity? How can we define our (ultimate) 'life goods' from the 'constitutive goods' that make it up, if the latter themselves conflict? Specifically, how do we manage to reach non-arbitrary conclusions when deliberating between goods that are very different? This problem is bypassed in utilitarianism, since right action is that producing the greatest consequent utility, and in Kantianism, where it is action that proceeds from a maxim susceptible of universalization. It is also bypassed in traditional socialization theories because it is presumed to be solved in advance by virtue of the 'pre-packaged' coherence of what is internalized. (Thus Taylor comments: 'Habermas claims to be able to show that the standard of a discourse ethic is binding on us by showing how we are already committed to it in virtue of talking with each other the way we do. We can bypass altogether reflection on the good.'[61]) Instead, his own suggestion hinges upon the dilemma being 'not so much a matter of the relative importance of goods but of a sense of how they fit together in a whole life. In the end, what we are called upon to do is not just carry out isolated acts, each one being right, but to live a life, and that means to be and become a certain kind of human being.'[62]

Leading a life is both to have a bent towards moving in some direction and, as an active agent in one's own life, to exercise governance in guiding this movement to a certain degree. Taylor's insight is that 'insofar as we have some sense of our lives, of what we are trying to lead, we will be relating the different goods we seek not just in regard to their differential importance, *but also in the way they fit, or fail to fit, together in the unfolding of our lives*'.[63] What is at stake here is the dilemma – the fact that our concerns may not cohere with one another – but also the source of its solution (albeit fallible and *pro tem*). This lies in 'a sense of the complementarity and of how it may be threatened at some point by

---

[61] Taylor, 'Leading a Life', p. 174.   [62] *Ibid.*, p. 179.
[63] *Ibid.*, p. 180 (italics inserted).

the overwhelming of one side in the name of the other'.[64] However, this sense of complementarity itself is held to depend upon 'our sense of the shape of our lives, and how different goods fit together within it – their different places and times'.[65]

This is the problem as far as the young subjects investigated are concerned. For them, the completion of the *dedication* phase is seen as the last stage of their youthful socialization, but they have not reached it yet. For all of them it is work in progress. Therefore, Taylor's intuition that the 'diversity of goods needs to be balanced with the unity of life, at least as an inescapable aspiration' is one with which I agree for those who have reached 'maturity'.[66] But the difficulty for the undergraduates is that they lack precisely this crucial 'sense of unity'. Far from having achieved that meta-good, the 'sense of a life', this is exactly what they are struggling towards. Without it, they cannot have any corresponding 'sense of complementarity' with regard to the relative importance of diverse goods, such as their future 'career' and the future of their 'relationship'. Both are still relatively undefined and yet, as both continue to unfold, they will influence each other's definition. The sense of the life they wish to lead (even in aspiration) is inchoate, if it exists at all. Thus, it cannot arbitrate on their dilemmas, which may not even be perceived as such.

Hence, Taylor's conclusion that, 'this sense of a life – or design or plan . . . is necessarily one. If this is our final end, there can only be one' may ultimately be correct (as I believe it to be), but what is not accounted for is *how this comes about*. In seeking to understand the process involved, it is crucial not to see it as a lone individual accomplishment. This is the implication of much of the philosophical literature and may gain its force from the fact that the end result *must*, indeed, be a personal property in that only one person can have the internal, subjective sense of what gives unity to his or her own life. Nevertheless, the fact that this is *what* people end up with is not the same thing – or to be confused with – *how* they came by it. In fact, the achievement of that sense of what makes for unity in each of their lives (upon which the establishment of a *modus vivendi* is based), is *relationally* dependent. This is necessarily so because to have a concern entails a relationship and to have plural concerns involves plural relations. All the same, we should not relinquish Taylor's insight about 'complementarity', but rather rethink it in relational terms.

This means considering the reflexive and the relational in conjunction.[67] On the one hand, a subject's reflexivity is decisive for

---

[64] *Ibid.*, pp. 181–182.   [65] *Ibid.*, p. 183.   [66] *Ibid.*
[67] Much of the following discussion of relations and relationality is indebted to the work of Pierpaolo Donati, *Teoria Relazionale della Società*; 'Conclusioni e prospettive: la

which relations are relevant because it is she who has *discerned* what matters to her (although it has been stressed that she always does this in a particular context that is not of her making or choosing). Therefore, she too is responsible for her dilemma – the outcome of her *deliberation* which has concluded that two ultimate concerns are of importance to her. On the other hand, it does not follow that she alone – as a lone individual – determines the outcome as far as her final ends are concerned.[68] On the contrary, it is the relationships accompanying and surrounding her concerns that promote both the *subjective* sense of compatibility and *objectively* make concerns compatible, or the opposite. How do relational considerations help in answering the question Taylor has effectively posed: what does complementarity require, such that it can give rise to the 'sense of unity' of a life?

An answer is important because only when a subject has dovetailed her concerns can she move forward into the context of nascent morphogenesis and dedicate herself to a particular course of action as her response to the situational logic of opportunity. The difficulty for most students at the point of university entry (and usually aged eighteen) is that their concerns are fluid and often incomplete. In other words, they provide insufficient guidance for shaping a life. Whilst ever concerns can be displaced and replaced (without such shifts being prompted by dramatic contingencies), this indicates that *discernment and deliberation* are still ongoing and thus cannot provide the necessary traction for even being preoccupied about coherence amongst the components that the subject has started to flag up as important to her. This is where the majority of university entrants find themselves.

It is obvious that the eventual constituent concerns giving unity to a life must not be blatantly at odds with one another, such that it is volitionally impossible to serve both (wishing to remain a teetotaller and seeking to become a *sommelier*). Yet, something more than bald compatibility seems called for if the shape of a life is to prove durable and if it is to be more than one of several designs that 'on paper' might seem to yield the same 'life goods', to use Taylor's term. The 'constituent goods' endorsed also the need to be mutually reinforcing in a manner that requires further

sociologia relazionale come paradigma della società *dopo*-moderna', in his *Teoria Relazionale della Società: I concetti di base*, Milan, Franco Angeli, 2009; Pierpaolo Donati and Ivo Colozzi (eds.), *Il paradigma relazionale nelle scienze sociali: le prospettive sociologiche*, Bologna, Il Mulino, 2006.

[68] This strange and perverse assertion has been made repeatedly by Anthony King. For his latest repetition of it see, 'The Odd Couple: Margaret Archer, Anthony Giddens and British Social Theory', *British Journal of Sociology*, 61, 2010, 253–260.

clarification.[69] For instance, a concern to continue playing football during someone's career as an engineer appears neither complementary nor contradictory, but the two do not reinforce one another in any self-evident way. This is where introducing relations and relationality can assist with both of the problems posed above: how to shape a life non-arbitrarily and how to cope with having two final ends. This is because both relations and relationality generate emergent properties[70] whose effects exceed terms like 'reinforcement' or 'deterrent'.[71] They can make a life possible or impossible rather than simply being neutral towards it, as in the above example.

Illustrating the relational solution

Let me illustrate how the relations and relationality (relations between relations) of two couples A and B give answers to the issues Taylor raises concerning: (i) how plural final ends may or may not be combined into a 'unity of life' constitutive of a stable *modus vivendi*, and (ii) how complementarity between other concerns is or is not achieved and with what consequences for (i). The plural ends in question are two students' love for one another and their career commitments. Such concerns are chosen solely because of their empirical frequency of occurrence amongst undergraduates. Exactly the same points about relational enablement could be made about other 'beloveds': not only a person, but an institution, an ideal, or one's work – Frankfurt's illustrative list seems very well chosen.

I am going to introduce two extreme types to discuss the role of relations and relationality (relations between relations) in fostering *ceteris paribus* a stable and a non-stable *modus vivendi* respectively. These are not ideal types because they will immediately be illustrated by two real couples encountered in earlier investigations. All four people are about the same age now (mid-thirties), all are graduates, and both couples met whilst at university. In the first example the stable outcome hinges upon selection and shaping modifying each other, whilst the instability of the second rests upon the intransigence of selection towards shaping.

Figure 3.4 illustrates couple A, Ego and Alter, who are married and have been together for fifteen years. Their interpersonal relationship is

---

[69] Here I am talking only about non-trivial constituent concerns. Presumably any prospective life could find ways to accommodate continuing to eat ice-cream.

[70] Pierpaolo Donati, *Esplorare una galassia: il privato sociale come fenomeno emergente*, in Pierpaolo Donati and Ivo Colozzi (eds.), *Il privato sociale che emerge: realtà e dilemmi*, Bologna, Il Mulino, 2004, pp. 21–54.

[71] These could be reduced to the interpersonal influence of Ego on Alter and vice versa.

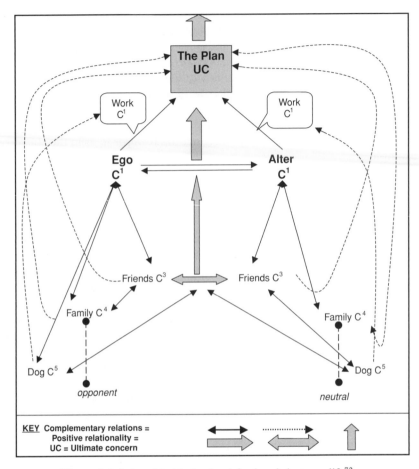

Figure 3.4 Aristotle's ideal: plural final ends but one life[72]

one of their ultimate concerns and their work is another (which is why both are labelled as C^1). Thus, according to Frankfurt, they should be experiencing volitional conflict between meeting these two final ends wholeheartedly. In fact, exactly the opposite is the case. How can this be? The answer is a relational version of Taylor's solution.

---

[72] Charles Taylor wryly comments: 'Some people have objected that Aristotle seems to fall into a confusion – or perhaps pulls a fast one on us – in the discussion of the supreme good in *Ethics* I, vii. He talks first as though there might be one, but there might be several such ends. Later he seems to slip into assuming that there is just one final aim.' 'Leading a Life', p. 183.

If we concentrate on the upper triangle constituted by Ego, Alter and both of their concerns about 'work' (labelled as $C^{1'}$ for both Ego and Alter since this is also an ultimate concern for each), Frankfurt's expectation of conflict is obviated by 'the plan' to which this couple have *dedicated* themselves as their conjoint ultimate concern. This act of dedication involved more than the simple consent of Ego and Alter to 'the plan', as if it had been put to them by a third party and each had independently assented to it. Instead, relations and relationality have come into play. Through their relations with each other over time, mutual trust has developed between them. Both are orientated towards this relational good that they have generated themselves, which exceeds both of them and which they conjointly seek to preserve and protect.[73] Thus, relations between relations now become important, specifically those between the couple and their future choices of work. Both are willing, because of their confidence in their personal relationship, to work together on a reciprocal basis. (In other words, they literally strive to bring about complementarity between their final ends.) They do this rather than hedging their bets, as it were, by choosing independent professions that dovetail fairly well in practice. The latter would mean that had their personal relationship broken down each would have their separate careers as their respective (but then only) ultimate concern.

'The plan' could not have been without the emergent relational goods involved. It would have been something different, namely a contract between the two parties, presumably with escape clauses if it did not meet specific expectations or with separate thresholds for the two signatories. Instead, their co-orientation towards the relational goods they had generated enabled this pair to sink all their assets in it and to invest themselves in making it work. Of course, this is no guarantee that it will, merely that they are both committed to doing their joint best to try to make a success of it. Their commitment to 'the plan' is the result of their emergent relations, which literally enabled both to count upon one another and thus volitionally to cede their professional independence in order to promote their common good.[74] Without their emergent relations

---

[73] This is what Donati terms 'relational reflexivity': '[s]uch reflexivity consists in orientating the subjects to the reality emergent from their interactions by their taking into consideration how this reality is able (by virtue of its own powers) to feed back onto the subjects (agents/actors) since it exceeds their individual as well as their aggregated personal powers.' This, of course, is what links explanation and understanding. Pierpaolo Donati, 'Preface' to his *Relational Sociology: A New Paradigm for the Social Sciences*, London, Routledge, 2010.

[74] Riccardo Prandini has an interesting and persuasive discussion about the emergence of joint-reflexivity in 'La soggettività ("anche" sociale) della famiglia: come osservare e quale significato attribuirle', *Anthropotes*, 22, n. 2, 2006, 315–332.

of trust, there could be no positive relationality vis à vis employment and, without relationality, there would have been no such plan, which is the shape of their joint lives.

Emergent trust is much more than a *feeling* of mutual confidence in one another, as in the popular saying 'He'll always be there for me' which carries the connotation of 'when things go badly wrong'. Instead, it is the building block upon which pro-active reciprocity enables projects to be accomplished that would not otherwise get off the ground because of their risky nature. This is what Beck's conception of the fickle agent discounts, thus leading to his exorbitation of risk. Yet, reciprocity reduces risk quite objectively. If Ego and Alter acted individualistically, then both would take out personal insurance – perhaps retaining a secure part-time job or keeping a 'rainy day' bank account. Both would thus withdraw resources from the plan (capabilities, time, commitment and finance), correspondingly reducing its chances of success.

Conversely, reciprocity maximizes their conjoint inputs. Ego sees Alter working hard for *them*, holding back nothing, and is stimulated to recip-rocate in like manner. In the process, two things happen. First, thanks to this developing 'we-ness', the plan has a better chance of succeed-ing (though without guarantees) because *their project* is now objectively better resourced, in a variety of currencies. Second, through reciprocity Ego and Alter have both made a more generous commitment of them-selves to it and, by relegating personal insurance to marginality, they have subjectively increased the complementarity of their joint concerns by co-endorsement of an architectonic principle that shapes their life as a couple.

However, other concerns and relationships are also involved. To keep Figure 3.4 simple, it has been assumed that the pair has the same kinds of further concerns, which is not necessarily the case. In turn, these too, generate relational goods, whose complementarity with the couple and 'the plan' enables it through *both* their direct relations (single arrows) *and* their relationality (solid arrows).

Single arrows indicate positive two-way approbation and support, that is, for example, Ego and Alter separately appreciate talking to their friends and receiving encouragement from them about the plan. How they recip-rocate to these friends is not incorporated in Figure 3.4. One element will be to make them beneficiaries – probably in some minor way – of the plan in action, as will be seen in what follows. Double, or thick arrows, indi-cate relationality. These occur, for instance, if and when Ego's and Alter's respective groups of friends coalesce to become *our friends*, meaning that when they are apart from the couple they themselves talk approvingly about the plan, rather than one set being enthusiastic whilst the other voices fear and reservations. Even if these two groups do not fully coalesce for whatever reason (geography, absence of other interests in common), they collectively support Ego and Alter by sending a consensual message of approbation. This exceeds the aggregate of their individual support, it enables Ego and Alter to believe (correctly) 'our friends are behind us', and it obviates their receipt of mixed messages – some cautionary and others enthusiastic – that could induce second thoughts in the couple, thus deflecting them from commitment to their goal. Equally, the bond itself between Ego and Alter strengthens in its 'we-ness' if neither are taken aside by individual friends for a warning about how the one is exerting a dangerous influence on the other or for a counselling about reserve that would be hostile to the couple's generous reciprocity and complementarity of concerns.

Faithful readers may recall our Ego and Alter – Leo and Annie – from previous books.[75] Leo's ultimate concern for mountaineering went back to his school days when he summited his first of the 'big seven', but he went to university no clearer about his career beyond wanting 'life in a fleece'. Annie listed 'career' as her prime concern, had a love of the natural order and for travel, but was even less clear in her first year about what kind of employment to pursue. Early in their second year they became a couple through that famous university experience, the field trip. They are now in their eleventh season of running mountaineering courses in the French Alps as a joint business, with joint assets and a flexible division of labour.

Focussing on the centre of Figure 3.4, before they graduated Leo and Annie had already co-designed their plan for operating a residential centre for adventure holidays: venue undetermined, roles unspecified and capital wanting. Their own relationship, a final end for both, generated trust and confidence, cemented by a fairly dramatic episode in the far north of Russia during their second long vacation. Because of the value attached by both to their emergent relational goods as a couple, Leo could willingly incorporate Annie's gap year experience of adventure holidays and catering for teenagers, and Annie began to climb seriously, abandoning the idea of ever wearing anything other than a fleece. Out of this mutual adjustment of their ultimate concerns, their project was born as 'our plan'. This was *dedication* to one another and to what they would do together, spelling the compatibility of their two final ends that shaped one life for them. Dedication was needed because as 'independents' from their families they had not only to concretize but also to capitalize 'the plan'. After three years of holding down four uncongenial jobs between

---

[75] See especially, *Making our Way*, p. 59.

them, they were engaged – the rings symbolically being their only personal expenditure – and sufficient savings banked to start their company in the French Alps on a shoestring.

Moving to the wider circles denoting other concerns of the couple, two aspects of relationality gradually came into play. Firstly, their assorted university friends became winnowed out, until those who remained had at least some interest in climbing or living in the Alps. To these were added the most diverse group of French guides and British residents, all hankering after the same lifestyle. Friendship had become selective and self-selected; the success of the plan – bolder than that of any of the friends' who merely gravitated to the same town to spend their leave or to acquire a chalet – made them a group of compatible concelebrants with Leo and Annie (now married): taking an interest, lending a hand, a vehicle or an apartment, and thus stabilizing the venture.

Secondly, quite cordial relations had been maintained with their families. From the start, their joint-venture had been a litmus test for both sets of parents, with Leo's father being dismissive ('they'll never succeed') and Annie's mother feeling rather thrown by the foreignness of it all. The two parents who were 'retained' represented the 'familial supporters' club' – their relation with the couple producing its own relational goods: delight, respect and being able to go there and share in some of the plan. This is nearly the end of this Aristotelian vignette, except that their last concern (C^5) should not be omitted – the dog. Leo and Annie had grown up with dogs, the supporting parent on both sides was 'doggie', and their friends loved the local pup who became a huge mountain dog. But, to complete this *modus vivendi*, so did many of the clients. The dog now almost earns his dinner by special requests for canine company when snow-shoeing.

What I have been describing, Elder-Vass terms a 'proximate norm group', that is those sharing a belief or disposition whose emergent effect is to strengthen commitment to it throughout the group itself.[76] Elder-Vass confines his discussion to the synchronic effects of 'group membership' but, by introducing the relational history of this informal group's formation, it has also been supplemented by the necessary diachronic account of how this group came into being.[77]

As already emphasized, Leo and Annie are an extreme type whose reciprocal relations as a couple and whose relations with others generate

---

[76] Dave Elder-Vass, *The Causal Powers of Social Structures: Emergence, Structure, Agency*, Cambridge University Press, 2010, chapter 6.

[77] Donati employs three time registers, the 'interactional', the 'relational' and the 'symbolic' of which the 'relational' is important here, although the other two play a part: see Pierpaolo Donati, 'Studi interdisciplinari sulla famiglia', n. 13, Milan, Vita e Pensiero, 1994, pp. 61–80.

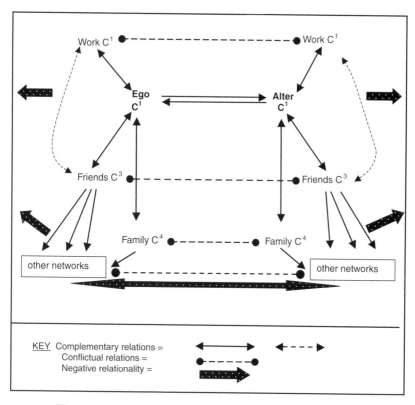

Figure 3.5 Frankfurt's revenge: 'a man cannot serve two masters'

further relationalities whose consequences are to bond their project more securely and to intensify the couple's commitment to it. In other words, this is both an interpretative and explanatory account of the successful establishment of a *modus vivendi*, which is stable barring the contingencies of life in an open system. Let us now introduce couple B, who represent the opposite polar extreme, and see how they fare in relation to entertaining two independent final ends whilst attempting to shape a life together. This will serve to illustrate relational conflict and negative relationality whose consequences preclude the establishment of a *modus vivendi* at all (Figure 3.5).

In the case of couple B, Ego and Alter are similar to Couple A in only two respects: their relationship with one another is a final end and work is also an ultimate concern for each of them. However, in Figure 3.5 their personal relationship is shown as sandwiched between four other sets of relations that have been filtered and stabilized through their second ultimate concern (work) and their subordinate concerns (friends and family). Although 'work' is a final end for each of the pair, neither have yet arrived at a choice of career. Why can they not define their future employment in a manner that is complementary to their personal relationship, instead of in a way that becomes detrimental to it? Fundamentally, this is because all their other relations militate against a positive outcome, meaning compatible careers.

Working downwards from the couple in Figure 3.5, they have segregated friendship groups that not only fail to overlap but also feel some animosity towards one another. Their friends are important to both Ego and Alter, who engage in separate activities with their respective groups. In turn, each friendship group interlocks with other networks of friends whose values and commitments are even more disparate from and negative towards their opposite numbers. Furthermore, the couple's respective families (their C^4s) have been pictured as having affinities with the friendship group of either their son or daughter. Thus, a lower triangle of relationality has developed whose emergent effect is to draw the couple further apart as the result of the intensified antagonism that surrounds the pair from others who matter to them. If they wish to retain their friends and families, Ego and Alter do so at the price of receiving a constant stream of criticism of their partner, of the company that each keeps, and of their social backgrounds.

In turn, friends and family are also important sources of information and encouragement when making decisions about future careers. Here, if we look at the extreme left- and right-hand sides of Figure 3.5, it can be seen that two further triangles of relationality are created over time, when Ego chooses a very different career from Alter. Soon, Ego makes new friends through her work, whom it is assumed are congenial to her original friendship group, which had promoted this particular career in the first place (and are also acceptable to her family). The same is the case for Alter. At this point, the couple also comes to realize that their different forms of employment not only have nothing in common, but actually confront them with conflicting requirements (working hours and relocation). Not only are Frankfurt's forebodings about the misery resulting from pursuing two final ends realized, but also the durability of Ego and Alter as a couple is now completely dependent upon their interpersonal love surviving in the sea of hostility that surrounds it, for nothing else bonds them together.

Couple B also met at university, though as doctoral students from different faculties. Darya is from a well-educated and relatively affluent Eastern European family, whilst Mustafa is from a Muslim family, some of whom are illiterate, of North African origins but now living in the suburbs of Paris. Their meeting on campus was entirely circumstantial, a result of the two starting to talk whilst using a campus facility. Although they quickly became a couple, they did not co-habit but continued to live with their respective friends in rented accommodation. Mustafa's routine scarcely changed: working late hours in the science laboratory, taking a break during the day to play team games with his male friends in the gym, and unwinding with the same friends after work and around midnight. This friendship group was predominantly Muslim, orientated towards obtaining well-paid jobs in corporate research, and much given to boasting about their female conquests. Darya continued to live with two or three young women, also from Eastern Europe and also working on PhDs, and became more and more dedicated to an academic career in which all her three housemates eventually succeeded. The two friendship groups thus represented mutually exclusive and conflicting norm circles, which pre-dated Darya and Mustafa as a couple and were to post-date them too.

Almost two years later, the couple decided to marry and Darya insisted on an Orthodox wedding back home. Her parents put a brave face on it and hosted the usual lavish ceremony, probably hoping with Darya that since the marriage entailed Mustafa's baptism, his acceptance of Christianity would help to cement their relationship and to distance him from his friendship network. Conversely, the newlyweds' attempted visit to Mustafa's parents resulted in abuse and a refusal to meet his new wife. In short, the segregation of their respective friends and family was intensifying rather than attenuating and becoming more overtly conflictual.

On their return to England Mustafa, who was a year ahead with his PhD, successfully defended his thesis and promptly obtained exactly the corporate research post that he had originally wanted. There seems to have been little consultation between the couple on this matter, little if any reciprocity, and little sharing of its benefits. Darya found herself living on the outskirts of London, knowing no one, finishing her own thesis, and constantly phoning her old roommates for support, by now having learned of Mustafa's repeated infidelities.

When Mustafa had the opportunity of a posting abroad, he accepted on the understanding that the couple would re-unite once Darya had her PhD. She returned to university, resumed living with her old friends and began making applications for academic jobs, regardless of their geographical location. In this she was encouraged by her friends and their wider circle. Moreover, as they learned of Mustafa's serial unfaithfulness, their unanimous advice was that she should cut her losses, divorce him and make a new life for herself. Relations had now become polarized and

Mustafa kept up with his family and friends, one of whom intensified antagonism by holding a party to celebrate his 100th 'conquest'. Since relationality was pulling them further apart and their own relations were deteriorating, Darya seriously contemplated a last attempt to create their own relational goods by having a child. Her friends immediately weighed in to advise that this would become a relational evil, leaving her as an unemployed single mother. Her own mother flew in for a couple of months and was reluctantly of the same view. Darya procrastinated, but when she found unexpected satisfaction in her employment by a London charity – intended to be a stop-gap but soon offering her promotion and a career track – this represented the final centrifugal pressure and completed her triangle of negative relationality on the left-hand side of the diagram. The divorce swiftly followed, along with the 'I told you so's' from the left and the right. Perhaps this did reflect a lay understanding that the couple's chances of shaping a life together had always been remote.[78]

Conclusion

Contemporary socialization is not viewed as a passive process, partly because the messages received from 'socializers' are increasingly 'mixed' rather than those traditionally held to stem from consensual 'norm circles' in the past. Therefore, the reflexive imperative is confronted in the form of the necessity of selection, requiring an active 'socializant' who is a 'strong evaluator' about his or her concerns. Partly, too, this is because – in the context made up of their subsequent social relations – all agents have *to work at establishing complementarity* between these concerns. Their relations are not a static environmental background – like unchanging wallpaper – against which self-contained 'individuals' engage in reflexive 'decisionism'. Relations and relationality may both result in modification (shedding conflicting concerns and incongruent elements) and in novelty (elaborating innovations representing a higher order of complementarity than had been envisaged), in order to arrive at a *unity of life* capable of yielding a satisfying but also sustainable *modus vivendi*.

---

[78] See Jean-Claude Kaufmann, *La Trame Conjugale: Analyse du Couple par son Linge*, Paris, Nathan, 1992. Part 3 on 'adjustments and contradictions between the couple' contains some interesting case histories.

4   Communicative reflexivity and its decline

This chapter deals with the decline of 'contextual continuity' as nascent morphogenesis engages and with how the reflexive imperative correspondingly makes 'communicative reflexivity' more difficult to sustain. Why does this matter? It matters because in the past the communicatives were the only group whose responses to their social circumstances were socially reproductive in their effects and integrative in their consequences. Thus, this chapter emphasizes the shrinkage of 'Bourdieu's people' as the world Bourdieu knew changes. At the same time, it helps to account for modernity's growing deficit in social solidarity, or what some politicians have called the 'broken society'.[1]

The undergraduate subjects whose interviews will be examined, neither desire nor regularly obtain a rough parity of social position with their parents. Rather, what they seek is an intergenerational *replication* of their familial relationships, which nascent morphogenesis makes increasingly difficult to accomplish. In turn, their communicative reflexivity is of little assistance with the necessity of selection or with shaping their lives.

Why the reflexive imperative cannot be avoided

As these subjects encounter 'contextual incongruity' in everyday ways, the last thing they can rely upon in order to duplicate the source of the relational goods they received whilst growing up is 'habitual action'.[2] Instead, to achieve some approximation to replication – as the most that can be accomplished – involves strenuous work on the part of those concerned. This has to be deliberative in kind because of the novel paradox that *reproduction now entails innovative action*. What requires reflexive deliberation is the design of a *modus vivendi* whose satisfactions and

---

[1] David Cameron during the 2010 British General Election.
[2] Margaret S. Archer, 'Routine, Reflexivity and Realism', *Sociological Theory*, 28:3, 2010, 272–303.

sustainability are subjectively sufficient for the communicative reflexives and thus encourage them to continue to practise this as their dominant mode of reflexivity. As on a moving floor, you do not stay put by standing still and the simple solution of walking backwards is not an option.[3]

Standing still is not a course of action open to those who in one sense or another have chosen to go to university. Even if they have acquiesced to enrolment without great enthusiasm – as is the case for some of those to be examined – they immediately had to engage in deliberative activities: which university, what course, where is it situated, although this decision-making is not a lone – let alone – task for this sub-group. Since interviewees had taken this decision before the present study begins, it is impossible to know what proportion of those similarly placed, but equally qualified for entry, actually declined the option of university education. That some did is indubitable from respondents' descriptions of various qualified school friends who remained at home, though none claim them to have been the majority.

Entry to university (in Britain) necessarily introduces quotidian 'contextual discontinuities' through living away from home, amongst multicultural strangers, and having to establish new mundane practices of shopping, eating and doing the laundry. Today it is much more than this. It represents an exposure to 'contextual incongruity' because those with different views and experiences, if not living in the next room, will be sitting in the same seminar; because of the numerous university societies badgering them to participate; and because of the options for travel, work experience and future careers encountered through university. In other words, they are all confronted with the necessity of selection and, much as this sub-group seeks to retain continuity with their natal contexts, this must be part of the active enterprise of shaping a life because it cannot be a matter of passive reproduction. It follows that the group of 'identifiers' described in Chapter 3, that is those in receipt of high family relational goods and who are not voracious for new experiences, nevertheless cannot avoid the reflexive imperative. This is the case for three main reasons.

Firstly, they have to work out reflexively how they are going to maintain these relational goods, that is, what are they going to do to sustain contact with their families, as the prime concern listed by all in this sub-group upon entry and throughout their three years as undergraduates.

---

[3] See Margaret S. Archer, *Making our Way through the World: Human Reflexivity and Social Mobility*, Cambridge University Press, 2007, chapter 4: 'Communicative reflexives: working at staying put', pp. 158–191.

Secondly, since the 'identifiers' are communicative reflexives who need interlocutors to confirm and complete their internal conversations, who is going to fulfil this day to day, if not necessarily face to face, role?[4] It will prove essential to eschew their own elision of 'friends and family' as their ultimate concern and to focus, instead, upon the *relations between the two*. An interlocutor needs to be a 'similar and familiar' in order to enter into the subject's deliberations and decision making. Yet, 'familiarity' can be exaggerated in the hothouse of university accommodation and shared seminars and 'similarity' must, at best, be an approximation as no new university friends will have shared the minutiae of one another's backgrounds. Thus, the 'identifiers' become reflexive about friendship itself – above all as concerns the development of trust as the fundamental requirement of an interlocutor.[5]

Thirdly, the consideration of a future career, as a constituent of shaping a life, cannot be evaded. It follows that reflexive deliberation is also ineluctable, minimally to confirm a subject's first inclination, about which he or she will now learn more, moderately because other options will become known to them, and maximally because they have to work at compatibility and assure themselves that the *modus vivendi* they project is indeed one through which they can realize their inchoate personal identities and acquire social identities that personify them.[6]

It is these three areas of extended reflexivity – about family, friendship and work – that will be examined in this chapter. Because the precise and proximate social relations in which any person is enmeshed are seen as both the prime mediating (and mutational influence) upon how they develop and sustain a particular mode of reflexivity, the account will be relational. Specifically, it will focus upon the quantity and, more importantly, the quality of the relational matrix from which – according to their own accounts – they entered university. The aim here is to answer the question, what was (and perhaps needed to be) the case in their home background relations for them to start university as communicative reflexives? The second question concerns what needs to be the case in relationships *between* friends, family and work for this mode to be sustained and result in maintaining 'micro-contextual continuity'.

---

[4] For an introduction to this modality see Margaret S. Archer, *Structure, Agency and the Internal Conversation*, Cambridge University Press, 2003, chapter 6: 'Communicative reflexives', pp. 167–209.

[5] Contra Barbara A. Misztal, *Trust in Modern Societies*, Cambridge, Polity Press, 1996, pp. 2–3, trust is seen here as an emergent relational property rather than as the pre-requisite for friendship. Specifically, the development of trust pre-dates and is a predicate of adopting an interlocutor.

[6] Martin Hollis, *The Cunning of Reason*, Cambridge University Press, 1988.

Introducing the natal 'identifiers'

Communicative reflexives or 'identifiers', the two being identical for those interviewed, are a small minority of those entering university, constituting 13.5 per cent of those reading sociology that year (see the Methodological appendix). By the final year, this had shrunk to 9.4 per cent, making it the smallest of any of the four dominant modes of reflexivity practised.[7] This sub-group is a net loser of practitioners: most remain constant for the three years but seven of the original seventeen had changed their dominant mode of internal conversation by the time they graduated. The numbers are small but do serve to show that unlike every other modality, *communicative reflexivity does not make new recruits*. The question is therefore about the relational dynamics of retaining this reflexive mode versus those resulting in the opposite outcome.

From the data it is evident that the conditions making for reflexivity through 'thought and talk' have already exerted their influence before the age of eighteen. To some extent it is possible to reconstruct the factors responsible from interviewees' narratives (as in Chapter 3) but they fall short of supplying a full relational analysis because presented from the subject's perspective alone. The temptation to conclude that no one can be a communicative unless brought up in the appropriate natal context is too sweeping to be warranted by the data, although it is a strong hypothesis well worth testing by a research design starting earlier in life and focussing upon the density and intensity of family relations. What the data do support is the characterization of a very distinctive matrix of relations which pertained (at least) immediately prior to entering university as a communicative reflexive, as registered on ICONI.[8]

In any case, there is one caveat to the previous paragraph. Upon entry, there was a small number (12) who could not be assigned to a dominant mode.[9] After interview, these turned out to be a category previously

---

[7] This figure is less than half of the 21 per cent of respondents found among the population of Coventry residents, in a sample stratified by age, gender and socio-economic status. See Archer, *Making our Way through the World*, p. 335. However, length of education was correlated with the practice of autonomous and meta-reflexive modes, as is probably reflected in the percentage difference for communicative reflexives in the two populations.

[8] The 'Internal Conversation Indicator'; for its construction see the Methodological appendix of *Making our Way through the World*.

[9] This is artefactual because everyone could have been assigned to the mode upon which they scored highest on ICONI and no one scored zero for any of the four modes. However, a score of over the median (4.00) on the seven-point Likert scales used was required plus a difference of at least one point from the nearest other score to assign subjects to a dominant mode. Those termed 'underdeveloped' reflexives represented twelve students (9.5 per cent of those entering). This had reduced to five (3.9 per cent) in the final year.

encountered, the 'underdeveloped reflexives', termed such because they engaged in a minority of the ten mental activities held to be constituents of internal conversation.[10] Underdevelopment – to which we will return in Chapter 7 – could resolve into the practice of any other mode or could remain as such until after graduation. Two such cases were found amongst the volunteers for interview whose background relational matrices were indistinguishable from those of the communicatives. Both students were strong 'identifiers' and in years 2 and 3 each registered as practitioners of the communicative mode. They will be examined as part of this sub-group of interviewees, which also includes one 'leaver' and one who underwent fractured reflexivity for nearly two years.[11]

Thus far, the use of those volunteering to be interviewed has been kind in the diversity it produced, but its generosity ran out where sex was concerned. All six interviewed in depth were female. Given that women outnumbered men by four to one in the entry population and that the seventeen who registered as communicative reflexives is composed of two young men and fifteen young women, the all-female nature of these interviewees was unsurprising.[12] In any case, cross-tabulating gender with dominant mode of reflexivity produced no statistically significant results for the entry cohort in any of their three years as undergraduates.[13]

Is going to university an exciting opportunity?

Compared with fifty years ago when four per cent of the age cohort gained entry to university, the fact that this is nearly ten times greater today has taken some of the shine off gaining a place. Simultaneously, this expansion also meant that many entrants are the first in their families to attend university and constitutes a new opportunity available to those from more modest social backgrounds. Was this seized upon with excitement by this sub-group because it promised a broader horizon of new possibilities – of itself and through graduation? To introduce the cast, all six members will initially be considered together. What we find is

---

[10] See Archer, *Structure, Agency and the Internal Conversation*, pp. 333–341. The ten mental activities are planning, rehearsing, mulling-over, deciding, re-living, prioritizing, imagining, clarifying, imaginary conversations and budgeting. P. 161. See chapter 1, p. 13 in this volume.

[11] The case of fractured reflexivity will be examined in Chapter 7.

[12] Females 80.2 per cent and males 19.8 per cent (valid N = 126) in the October of entry.

[13] P-values for chi-squared tests: Year 1, p = 0.348; Year 2, p = 0.189; Year 3, p = 0.656. The same absence of statistical significance was found for the Coventry stratified sample. See Archer, *Making our Way through the World*, pp. 96–97. Probably this runs counter to the expectations of most people, myself included.

a manifest lack of enthusiasm, blending personal uncertainty and some-times apprehension with a countervailing desire to make their parents or a parent proud of them, this being just as marked in those from the more privileged social backgrounds. Indeed, the involvement of parents, either as direct interlocutors whose advice was sought, or as imagined participants in internal conversations, or as final ends whose appro-bation was desired, is striking in this sub-group. Neither the decision to apply nor that to enter was taken autonomously. What also distin-guished the six communicatives from others was that not one subject had taken a gap year and thus had only school or college experiences upon which to draw. In turn, this meant that all had been enmeshed in unbroken 'micro-contextual continuity' during the run up to university entry.

Let us look at the two *non*-middle-class students from this sub-group of six. Emily's father is a builder, her mother a teaching assistant, and neither of her older sisters went to university. On the one hand, staying in the south-eastern town in which she was born 'was quite attractive because I'm close to my family and I had a nice little secure group of friends – but even if I went back now it wouldn't be like that because a lot of them have gone to university'. On the other hand,

I applied to Warwick and my second choice was X University, a lot closer to home. And the reason why I did this was because I knew it might make my parents proud and because I'd get a better degree at the end of the day. I do make decisions based on what other people think. I tend to go for what is right rather than what I want to do.

Her final comment is surprising because it indicates the closeness of her extended family as a unit: 'It was touch and go whether I'd come this year because my nan had had a fall and broken her hip and she was quite ill.' My own internal comment – and there is plenty of time to exercise (and gag) one's own reflexivity when interviewing – was to wonder why that would have affected Emily's higher education. This was salutary because presumptions about the prevalence or pre-eminence of the nuclear family have to be abandoned where some in this sub-group are concerned.

Coming from a similar socio-economic background (her mother a saleswoman and father a service technician), Jill has two brothers, such larger than average families being the norm in this sub-group. Her solu-tion to ambivalence about enrolling for university was solved by the unique decision to live at home for her three undergraduate years. As she says, 'I wasn't ready to leave home'; she felt too insecure and staying also lessened the economic burden. Again there is benign but non-directional supportiveness, particularly from her mother and, in Jill's case, pride from her extended family.

If I didn't want to have gone to university that would have been fine [by her parents], but if I wanted to go to university, which I did, that was great too . . . They're pleased, yeah. Certainly I know my granddad was pleased . . . I think he's happy because both his daughters, that's my mum and my aunt, they just went straight into work, whereas my granddad did a sort of part-time degree.

Within this sub-group there are cases of school leavers seeking to please or propitiate their parents, but also of close families working effectively but with self-restraint to see their children into and through a degree course. The next two students are from Irish backgrounds and quite well off, both of whom presented problems in different ways. Maura, the youngest of five siblings (her mother is a retired nurse and her father the managing director of a construction company) had her confidence dented by a false start at another university whose Design course turned out to be overly mathematical for her. Maura had attended an 'all girls Catholic grammar school. From year 7 it's drummed into you – "and when you go to university" – so for me it wasn't really a decision in a way.' She duly went but had left before Christmas. Then,

for me it was do I get a job or do I go to university? . . . it was a lot of asking people's opinions because I didn't want to make the same mistake again . . . I obviously consulted my two sisters . . . one was at university at the time, though she's graduated now . . . I went back to my school – I had a good relationship with my sixth form teachers and they were like 'you have to go back, you worked so hard for your A levels', and were really encouraging . . . All my friends had gone to university as well, so they were all for me going.

What followed was a concerted rescue operation, with the school being pro-active, her parents supportive but restrained, and others weighing in on the side of trying again on a different course.

Sinead could have repeated a similar scenario of opting for what she had been successful in at school. However, her mother (a solicitor) and father (a dentist) successfully worked at procrastination. Looking back, Sinead says:

In school I was never really, you know, the top of my class and I was never really the sportiest. I wasn't really that confident either. When I was in primary school we did a lot of drama and I used to love it and used to get the lead roles and kind of liked that position of being on stage . . . and then in my secondary school I did loads of drama exams and did well and felt good about doing it.

Far from throwing cold water on Sinead's aim of going to drama school, her mother promised that they would look into RADA [Royal Academy of Dramatic Art] later, a promise that was kept. 'But it was always sort of university first, get a sort of secure degree, so that if you try the drama thing you'll always have something to fall back on.'

So far, no enthusiasm for new opportunities or extended horizons has been expressed by the four interviewees introduced. This continues to be the case with the remaining two subjects who entered Warwick as 'undeveloped' reflexives but who registered as communicatives by year two and maintained this as their dominant mode in their final year. Both put social reasons first in their choice of universities and tended to use the academic default setting for their choice of courses.

The first thing that cannot help striking one about Ruth is her smallness, with feet that scarcely touch the ground when sitting on an office chair. Because she is small and wears no make-up it is tempting to regard her as 'childlike' and assimilate this to her 'underdeveloped' reflexivity. She turns out to have a high level of musical proficiency on three instruments and to have been teaching twelve pupils at home during the preceding year, but she is adamant that music must be kept as her hobby. Instead, Ruth keeps her options open: 'at least with this [sociology], you can pretty much go into anything'. True, but the same goes for many disciplines, so why read sociology? Ruth answers by elimination from the three subjects she had taken at A level: maths at degree level would be too difficult, French entailed a year abroad which she didn't want, leaving sociology as her default choice.

Kirsty, again from a privileged background (her father a finance director and her mother a college lecturer), is one of four siblings and her brother was attending a plate glass university in the North. She calls herself indecisive and left the choice between her two offers of places until the last day. On what basis did she come to decide upon Warwick?

Well the other place was LSE and when I looked round it I wasn't so keen and it's an inner-city location rather than a campus and it looked more friendly here, more inviting and I think that tipped it for me in the end. I discussed it a lot with my parents and they said 'Just do what feels right for you'. They didn't want to influence my decision in case I blamed them for it later. I discussed it with my sociology teacher at college and one of my friends who had applied to LSE as well. I discussed it with a lot of people because it's a big decision.

Kirsty is open about finding prioritization difficult: 'my teacher was like "Go for LSE", but I kind of prioritized the social – I am going to go and make friends – and I don't know if that should have been my priority, but that's what tipped it in the end and I'm glad it did'.

There have been many attitudes and characteristics common to these six young women at point of entry: diffidence, uncertainty, indecisiveness and a lack of self-confidence. It is important to dispose of any suspicion that these are a group of weak students, i.e. ones with good reason to be diffident. Quite apart from their A level grades being higher than required, all six eventually graduated with upper second class honours. What is much more important is something that all lacked. Not one came up to university with a clear personal 'project' in mind, be it vocational, a deep interest in the discipline, commitment to some ancillary 'cause', or even to the serious enterprise of having a good time. It follows that they provide no basis upon which one can even guess what they are likely to do as undergraduates or upon graduation. Certainly they cannot behave as rational actors because they endorse no ends to which instrumental rationality can serve as the means. In other words, there is no knowing how they will respond to the necessity of selection, let alone how they will progress towards shaping their lives. Both of these are held to be highly dependent upon the use of reflexivity in order to exercise some governance over their own lives, as opposed to passive people to whom things just happen.

The first two studies in this triad have shown that the courses of action, deliberatively defined through subjects' internal conversations, are very different according to the dominant mode of reflexivity practised and produce distinctively different outcomes.[14] Therefore, the crucial piece of missing information is that there is no way of knowing if these young women can or will sustain their communicative reflexivity throughout the course and graduate with it operating as their dominant mode. Hence, this longitudinal study was necessary in order to cover a crucial transitional stage, given the variety of new opportunities confronting these subjects over the three years of their degree. Nevertheless, it has already been seen that their motivation comes from their proximate social relations rather than the 'pull' of the blue yonder.

Upon what does maintaining communicative reflexivity depend?

Historically (in Chapter 1) and biographically (in *Making our Way through the World*), the answer given was 'contextual continuity'. In addition, this has to be a context in which subjects could realize their 'ultimate concerns' through developing a *modus vivendi* expressive of them. Given this theoretical and empirical backcloth, the making of a communicative reflexive and the maintenance of this mode will be examined separately.

---

[14] Archer, *Structure, Agency and the Internal Conversation* and *Making our Way through the World*.

Firstly, the interview data will be interrogated in order to discover what relational communalities these students shared in their natal backgrounds that were connected to their entering university as communicative reflexives. Of course, this is quite different from specifying either the necessary or sufficient conditions for communicative reflexivity. For example, it has already been noted that the subjects in question came from larger than average sized families. However, since the 'mother–daughter' bond assumed considerable significance for several in this group, the existence of siblings in the plural may play neither a necessary nor a contingent part. Moreover, it is quite possible that the development of the dominant communicative mode amongst the six subjects is over-determined and that some relations can actually substitute for others.

Secondly, and in order to explore some of these unknowns, changes in and disruptions of this initial relational matrix will be tracked as the subjects proceed through their undergraduate careers in an attempt to identify the most important relations for the *maintenance* of communicative reflexivity and the incursion of those most hostile to it. As has already been seen (in Chapter 3), 'identifiers' are those who have received valued relational goods from their families. Since their receipt was face to face in a stable natal context, the generic questions to answer are whether and how these goods can be sustained at a distance and if they can weather the 'contextual incongruity' represented by the university experience.

'Identifiers' and family relations

In order to tackle these two questions I am going to begin by presenting a composite picture of their relational matrix as derived from the six students' accounts recoded several weeks after entering university. This is not an ideal type because there is no one-sided accentuation of particular relationships, nor is it an average type, since the relations that feature are not the common denominator of the sub-group. It is best regarded as an extreme type because the generosity of its linkages is not shared by all. Nevertheless, it is quite real and taken from Maura's description of her natal and ongoing context. We will work 'downwards' to others with less all-embracing natal backgrounds. In Figure 4.1, all arrows represent positive relationships, some of which generated emergent relational goods and some of whose relations with other relations constituted 'relationality' (second order relational goods). The diagram has been kept uncluttered and many more interrelationships could have been added. The visual impression of the subject being encircled is intentional.

Early in the first interview, Maura provides a vignette of her family and natal community, which is both descriptive and evaluative. This also

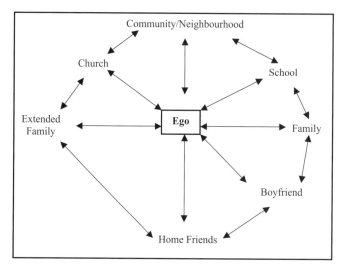

Figure 4.1 The relational matrix of the communicative reflexive (extreme type)

serves to confirm that she is an 'identifier' who would eventually like a family of her own to have much the same characteristics:

We live in London in an Irish community and my mum and dad are known for having two daughters at good universities, healthy grandchildren and older kids who have done well for themselves. I know my parents are proud of their children and that's an issue I would like to have and I'd like to have a large family as well – I like being in the Irish community at home. I went to a Catholic school, all my friends are like me, they've got Irish parents and we always go to the Irish pubs at home and mix in with Irish people. That's something that I really like and would like to continue. Even though I was born in London – I think me and my family are always going to be Irish.

This family and community seem to be an intertwined but dispersed resource whose component elements are mutually reinforcing. Maura's interlocutors are her younger sister, described as her 'best friend', and her older one, who is 'like a second mother figure'. These relationships are reciprocal as they discuss their own problems with her. With her parents, Maura tends to accentuate the father–daughter relationship, with dad popping up regularly over the three years as a gentle and generous figure not wanting her to get overstressed, providing her with a car and financing her way through university. Nevertheless, he does not appear to be an interlocutor, although there is reciprocity, because Maura regards establishing her career as important so that she can be in a position to take care of both parents.

Her proximate family appears to work as a resource that can be mobilized when needed, as has been seen when Maura quit her first university course. Spearheaded by her English teacher, who knew her mother and father as well as having taught her sister, the re-application to university was quickly made, but owed much to a depth of relational reinforcement that lay behind these personal initiatives. The school was a Catholic selective girls' grammar school, served by the local church that was attended by her parents and many of her extended family: 'My parents are quite strong Catholics, they go to Mass every Sunday and with the Irish, the Catholic thing it's a social thing as well, a community thing.' So we circle around the upper half of Maura's home context and its reinforcing relationality. As far as the lower half is concerned, her friends are shared with her sister, which has reduced the (remote) likelihood of losing contact with them whilst at university; her current boyfriend is from home and known to her parents; when any friend has a twenty-first birthday party, 'her mum and dad's friends will go because it's part of the Irish thing and there'll be an Irish band and I'll know everyone's parents – it's *Eastenders* basically'.

The research design precluded a proper exploration of the relations making for this contextual continuity since they are all filtered through Maura's perceptions. It would have been useful to know, for example, if her father's gentleness was typical of his relations (it sounds not from his relationships with her brothers who work in his company) or was shown towards Maura in particular. Equally, her mother remains rather a cipher as to the dynamics of mobilization and who initiates them. Nevertheless, Maura's account seems to point to an enduring enmeshing in her natal context which is as deep as it is contrary to the Beck–Bauman stereotype of 'individualization' and 'disembedding' in late modernity.[15]

Consonant with her account is Maura's preference for becoming 'a good member of the local community. The people around you are the most important. I admire people that are known internationally, but it's not me.' How far she acts to further this ambition of an 'identifier' and what countervailing influences assail it will be taken up when other members of the sub-group have introduced their own home backgrounds.

Living at home throughout her time as an undergraduate, Jill can be expected to have remained the one most enmeshed in her natal context. This is the case even though her home life lacks the density of Maura's. Again her parental relationships appear affable but undemanding. Although Jill attributes her general values to osmosis from her

---

[15] Ulrich Beck and Elizabeth Beck-Gernsheim, *Individualization*, London, Sage, 2002. Zygmunt Bauman, 'Foreword', in Beck and Beck-Gernsheim, *Individualization*, p. xvi.

parents, what she accentuates (concern for the community) and what she attenuates (early marriage and no career), she accounts for by the differences of 'life today'. Nevertheless, Jill is 'very happy to get married and have lots of children, but I think that's going to be much later for me . . . just so I can experience the world of work and why I want to do that sort of work, what I'd get out of it, give all that a go'. Yet, we will see that her occupational inclinations were fostered by home contacts, just as was her (now) serious relationship with her boyfriend. Moreover, Jill, along with others in this sub-group, contemplates giving up work when she has children: 'I'd be happy to, I'd love that, I think it's important. It's something my mum did for me and it's something I'd like to be able to do for my kids . . . that's definitely a value of my mother's that's rubbed off on me.'

There are two subjects whose practice of communicative reflexivity turns, instead, upon close mother–daughter relationships supported by a weaker network of relations than characterized Maura's home context. Ruth has a particularly intense bond with her mother, which is the crucial relationship upon which her ties to home pivot. Extended family members only have brief walk-on roles as uncles and aunts doing their duty at Christmas and on birthdays. Perhaps the fact that her parents moved to Wales after they married, yet neither are Welsh, goes some way towards accounting for the absence of any reference to organizations and activities outside the family. However, whilst Maura's background generated broad trust and reliance, but simultaneously diffused the intensity of her relationship with interlocutors, Ruth's relation with her mother is highly emotional:

We're really close – I think I'm a lot closer to my mum than a lot of my friends are to their mums. I'm quite affectionate, I always want cuddles and stuff and I think my friends aren't like that at all, but I really do miss her when I'm at uni. I think we're quite similar because she's sensitive as well, like me. If I'm watching anything like films or soaps and a mum dies it really touches me. I think, if that was my mum and I can really feel for those people and I just get really upset . . . My grandma died over Easter and my dad was upset and I was thinking if that was my mum I just couldn't deal with that because I'm just so close to her.

Although fond of her father there is not the same closeness because both of them are quite opinionated. Ruth believes, 'it's to do with the sociology as well because you learn about quite a lot stuff to do with race and gay people and he's quite different in his views so we do clash'. Although mother is 'quite laid back about stuff like that' and basically of Ruth's opinion, she assumes the role of domestic peacemaker and sustains good relations with her husband.

Her mother reciprocates this intensity and tells Ruth how difficult it was to be so far away from her own mother when, as newlyweds, they moved to Wales – and she still phones her every evening. During Ruth's second year, her mother visited relatives in Canada and her grandmother 'has been ringing me every day while my mum's on holiday because we both miss talking to her. [Normally] I call my mum every day and my mum calls her every day, so we're calling each other every day to make up for it.' Both send Ruth regular 'little packages', symbolic gifts to show they care and indicating that their relationship is fully reciprocal. It seems as though Ruth's mother is also duplicating her own ongoing relationship with her mother very successfully with her daughter.

The one addition to these close intergenerational relationships comes from her mother's work as a childminder. Since Ruth was two years old, 'there've always been children in the house, so I've just grown up with loads of children and babies and I just love them. I can't wait to have my own baby.' Meanwhile, Ruth has been writing essays and a dissertation about breastfeeding and motherhood but, 'never having been passionate about jobs', she wants to replicate her own family immediately and not ten years down the line:

I've got this image that by twenty-four or twenty-five I'd like to be married and sort of at twenty-seven start to have children. I'm twenty now. My mum was married to my dad when she was nineteen and they're still together now, so I feel like time's running out! My friends are like 'You're mad', they don't want to get married until they're in their thirties, some of them don't even want children, but I'm like oh that's what I want though.

Ruth seeks not reproduction but strict replication and she continues: 'oh, I've got to have a girl, I don't care how many girls I have, I've just got to have a girl . . . I think because I'm so close with my mum, I want that relationship with my daughter I suppose.'

Subtract the emotional intensity of Ruth's key relationship and add twenty years of successful Irish migration to Maura's family and that approximates to Sinead's relational context at home. On the one hand, she is closer to her mother than she is to her father and their relationship is 'really good, we share a lot of things, it's good fun as well . . . she's really chilled out so we can talk about a lot'. Instead of emotionality there is trust (mother cannot harbour an ulterior motive unlike friends), approval of her taste (having acquired the classic fashion tips from Gran who used to own a department store in Ireland) and a willingness to promote Sinead's interest in drama ever since this first surfaced through school.

Much more needs to be known about mother and father's own relationship, but as far as their daughter is concerned, they appear to be playing 'good cop and bad cop', with mother more receptive to Sinead's enthusiasm for the stage and father promoting a degree in law and a lucrative professional career. Although they compromise over her studying sociology, they have successfully collaborated in heading her off drama school until 'afterwards'. Exactly the same routine is played out when Sinead wants a gap year after graduation. Her parents jointly threatened no funding but eventually capitulated, perhaps in the hope that dreams of RADA would recede altogether. Their concerted messages prevailed.

On the other hand, these successful and young professional parents – twenty years younger than Maura's – display all the signs of the progressive integration of the Irish in Britain, which spells a diminution of the institutional cluster in Figure 4.1.[16] They live in 'leafy suburbs', attend secular private schools and their Catholicism has attenuated to rites of passage. As Sinead puts it, 'I don't really have any religious ideas. I mean we're an Irish family so Catholic ... I did my First Communion, Confirmation, that kind of thing ... but I don't think they [my parents] really believe it ... My Grandma, she was really religious, so we had to be really religious then, when she came over'. Thus, Sinead's attachment to her family context hangs entirely on the strength and durability of her interpersonal relations with her parents.

What of those who have neither the dense community network of relations like Maura, nor the pronounced mother–daughter bond of those just examined? Emily has neither density nor intensity bonding her to the home background she was uncertain about leaving for university. The tension between the two decisions continues in her first year:

> I just keep thinking the same thing. I think 'Oh I could be at home will all my family, earning money' or 'Well in the long run it will be worth it' – you kind of have to keep telling yourself that. It depends on what kind of day you have had as well. Sometimes, if I've had a hard day I'll sit in my room and think 'Is this the right thing?' Or I'll have a really good day and think 'Yeah, I'm really glad I made the decision to come to university'.

When these doubts were at their peak, Emily kept them from her parents 'because I wouldn't want to worry my mum and dad', a consideration on her part that deprived her of her usual interlocutors and pushed her towards the boundary of fracturing.[17]

---

[16] M. P. Hornsby-Smith, *Roman Catholics in England: Studies in Social Structure since the Second World War*, Cambridge University Press, 1987.

[17] Some of her distressed statements are very close to the fractured mode of internal conversation. For example, 'So it's kind of looking for a way out of a situation, but often

Emily tries to bring her two worlds together even though, as the first in the family to be at university, some of her requests for confirmation and completion of her internal conversations must be foreign territory for her parents, such as being consulted about her choice between assessment or examination. But, once she has explained, 'they're happy to [do it] and I trust their opinion as well'. She describes her mother, father and sister as being 'rocks' when she was revising for her exams at home and, by her third year they are very excited about Emily's graduation (and worrying about what to wear) but their role now seems to be a nurturing one: 'Oh they're so proud, bless them. They put up with a very stressed me over Easter, when I had my dissertation and my essays to write, and they just were very patient with me. They were "Oh I wish we could help", and I was "No, you can't", but everything I needed they provided me with.'

At point of entry, Kirsty seems to be closely identified with her quite affluent nuclear family; there is little mention of extended family members or of external involvements, perhaps because they have only lived on the South Coast for two years. She is an unhesitating 'identifier' and 'replicator': 'I'd love to be like my family now. I think we've got a really strong family bond and I'd like that to be reflected in my future family. I think it would be the perfect family.' I ask what she considers generates this bond and she responds:

I think the fact that my parents are very close and always have been, that really helps. I've got an older brother and two much younger sisters and we get on really well because of the age difference. As a family we make sure we prioritize time for the family and spend time together – sometimes when I'm at home I feel bad if I'm out with friends.

However, no single family member is her interlocutor: 'career things I will always talk to my dad about, my mum sort of more personal things . . . but, I don't know, they're probably not the first people I'd speak to now . . . because it's not quite the same as discussing it face to face with someone.' As she develops into a fully-fledged communicative reflexive, she needs her interlocutors to hand, particularly as the frequency of her 'I don't knows' persists as a residue of her under-developed reflexivity at the start of university.

These accounts of family relations have followed a gradient from Maura's dense and geo-local community, through various instances of interpersonal intensity within stable families, to the last case where Kirsty's family context literally shifted from under her as her father's

not finding one and just going through the same old cycle again, just going round and round.' Her first recorded ICONI score falls just above the cut-off point for 'fractured reflexivity'.

occupation involved a move to Belgium in her final year. Despite their differences these are all, with one exception, 'success stories'. That is, the natal context itself as a relational matrix, rather than only as a supplier of interlocutors, appears to have provided conditions propitious to the practice of communicative reflexivity as the dominant mode of internal conversation and engendered the desire among these 'identifiers' to replicate the most salient features of their own families.

Nevertheless, if this aspiration is considered as a long-term project, there are numbers of potentially reinforcing and countervailing relational factors that need to be introduced in order to explain the variety of outcomes. Specifically, as far as the necessity of selection is concerned, we need to examine the whole area of friendship: boyfriends from the natal context or from university, participation in campus activities and home friends in relation to university friends. Moreover, the relationality between family, friendship and career planning has to be introduced to account for progress – or lack of it – towards the shaping of a life.

The hard work of staying close

Even when their worth is fully acknowledged, there is nothing automatic about sustaining the relational goods that have been generated in the past between a subject and members of her family. On the contrary, if the relationships involved diminish or cease, so does their production of emergent relational goods. The latter cannot be parcelled out and taken away (except as memories), any more than a footballer can make off with 'his share' of the team's prowess. Yet, the relationships must change, if not in kind then at least in expression, simply because the student is no longer living at home (with a single exception). Thus, the first impact of the reflexive imperative is that these subjects must deliberate about the practical means of staying close. As communicative reflexives, whose interlocutors mostly now live over a hundred miles away, the desire to maintain these relations is strong, as will be shown.[18] In other words, the 'identifiers' have to devise ways and means of sustaining the familial bond, despite the effort and expense involved and in the face of new counter-claims for their time and attention. The *leitmotif* of what follows is that maintaining close relations at a distance is hard work, undertaken reflexively and with effects for reflexivity.

---

[18] As is typical for the cohort of entrants, amongst whom (129 valid cases) 10.9 per cent live in towns surrounding the university, 13.2 per cent live within 50 miles, 22.5 per cent within 100 miles, 44.2 per cent live elsewhere in the UK and 9.3 per cent come from overseas.

Significantly, the first illustration of these difficulties is the break-up with the 'home boyfriend'. All six split up during the first term and their litany of grievances is standardized; 'he' is uniformly presented as having been 'too possessive' in relation to their new activities and too routine in his expectations about the same old round of pubs and clubs when they did meet. Thus, Emily talks of the boyfriend she had been with since she was fifteen: 'I wasn't able to be myself because things I would have done, he would have been like "What are you doing that for?" and he'd make me feel bad for it.' This is another facet of the encounter with 'contextual incongruity' because it is the subject's occupancy of a new context that interrupts practices that could otherwise have solidified into habitual action.

Although some had agonized beforehand about leaving him 'behind', there are also suggestions that refusing a university place for his sake would have left them behind by not enabling them to explore their new opportunities. As Kirsty sums up the situation: 'If I'd stayed in X with him I'd probably be working as a receptionist or childminder or something now . . . I just wouldn't be trying to aim for the same things.' Resolving her dilemma had been facilitated by the antipathy that had always existed between her professional parents and her boyfriend the barman, and was now cemented by her change of attitude towards him. However, for most of the others their break-ups represented the loss of one reason to return home regularly, a loosening of one tie that bound them to their backgrounds.

Apart from Jill, who continues to live at home, all of the others return regularly for most of the vacations and usually for at least a couple of weekends during term time, a frequency greater than that of any other sub-group. Maura, who is attached to her whole extended Irish community, rather than closely bonded to a particular person, is the one who makes most use of visiting, but she had a car from the start and has only to drive to North London. Thus, in her third year, with a crowd of friends, a happy house and a roaring social life ('[in the evenings] we never come on to campus anymore – the beer's too expensive'), she also says 'I'm the sort of person who has to go home every two weeks . . . It is difficult living with your friends!' The last is said with cheerful irony and Maura is equally casual about the readiness with which she attracts a series of boyfriends at home.

Whilst all follow the pattern of regularly returning to home base, four of them make special efforts to retain contact by phoning, texting and electronic messaging, which had sometimes involved teaching family members how to email. Emily's comment illustrates the constancy of this contact with her parents and sisters and shows how closely this is reciprocated: 'I am very close to both of them [parents]. I speak to them every night pretty much on the phone. And my dad texted me the other night just to say "Hope you are not getting wet" because it was raining. And my sister texted me this morning just to ask me something and they email.' This to and fro does not wane and Ruth, who continues to receive her little presents through the post, tells that in her final year she still remains 'really close' to her mother, so much so that during weekends on campus 'I speak to her sort of three times a day, sometimes just when I'm bored and doing work and stuff. That's kind of my relief I guess, talking to my mum. Yeah, I speak to her every evening without fail and I sometimes text as well in the day.'

However, now that such contact has to be voluntarily initiated, rather than 'just happening' around the house, Ruth puts her finger on one constraint limiting complete communicativity, the felt need to spare the interlocutor from distress: 'Well sometimes it's difficult when Mum's at home and I'm here. If I'm upset about something I prefer not to talk to her because she gets upset when I'm upset, so then I'll go to one of my friends up here about that.' This is also the first hint that friends made at university can become alternative interlocutors. All of this implies a new reflexive deliberation, largely uncalled for when living in the home context, and the reflexive learning of new coping strategies.

Another variant, in the absence of trust having developed with new friends, is self-censorship. Sinead is fully aware that self-editing is needed: each passing difficulty may well have passed for her overnight, but mother is found worrying on days later about the same ephemeral episode. Without trustworthy friends, the only solution is to 'bottle it all up'. In other words, however close the relationship and however sensitively communication is handled, retaining contact imposes its own reflexive imperative, one that precludes the unrestrained flow of communicative reflexivity and necessarily nudges the subject towards the practice of some autonomous deliberation.

However, what of those who find maintaining contact even more difficult? By the start of her second year, Kirsty is ready to admit that

when I first started university, I'd go home for the holidays and find it really difficult to be around them all the time, I don't know, quite claustrophobic, being used to being on your own and independent and then going back. But now we've sort of got a different relationship. It's sort of more like a friendship, rather than reliant, you know, like a parent–child relationship, so I think I'm still as close to them in some senses, but in a different way.

Yet, part of this difference is that Kirsty would go to her university friends rather than her family with her problems, making the interesting comment that this is 'because they know, well they don't know me better but because they spend more time with me now'. Newly shared activities with new people are a novel form of 'similarity and familiarity' which may point either to a change of interlocutors or to the addition of *confidantes*. By her final year, Kirsty's balance sheet on maintaining contact reads: 'I don't see them so much, but now when I see them it's so much nicer.' Nevertheless, she does count the 240-mile round trip to visit home and is apprehensive about her own ability to cross over to Belgium on a regular basis once the family has relocated. In addition, this will mean that her original context of 'family' and 'home friends' are no longer co-existent, and hence the ties are loosening independently of her volition.

Although another daily communicator with her family and regular in her visits home, Emily became immediately and uncomfortably aware of contextual incongruity during her first weeks at Warwick. This is 'because I am sort of different. I can hear myself being different when I go back [home] at the weekends without even meaning to. And looking at my parents and my friends and having to stop myself from judging them. But I realized I was doing it so I kind of thought no, what are you doing, you can't think like that – it's a scary thought.' Yet this holding back and self-monitoring is not the free play of communicative reflexivity. Nor does it appear to work satisfactorily because eighteen months later she says of her parents:

I have to admit I can still be a bit like horrible and act as if I'm superior to them just because I'm at university, but I don't mean to and I think they know I don't mean to really. It's a bit weird, there's a bit of a transition period. When I go home, the first few days I really notice it but as soon as I get back into my old way of life and spend time with them . . . I just accept it and I adore my mum and dad so I wouldn't change that really. Just sometimes, the transition . . .

By not making comparisons, Emily partitions rather than shapes her life. She tells me (and herself) 'so I'm quite happy to spend half the year here and half the year there', but that is necessarily temporary and I wonder if Emily herself is temporizing with this split-level living until closer to the end of her course.

In other words, is she postponing the resolution of her lived experience of class conflict? There are three reasons for suspecting that this partitioning might end with her family being partitioned off. Firstly, Emily is another who begins to employ her university friends as interlocutors, confiding matters intentionally kept from her parents: 'I don't tell them everything . . . not like I tell my best friends.' Secondly, she does not receive full reciprocity, at least from her extended family, further discouraging the free flow of communicativity. Emily regularly took her laptop home to show her mother ('who loves hearing all about it') photos of her friends and their doings. But an episode in her final year shows some cracks in the possibility of full contextual intimacy: 'on my twenty-first I had a party in [near the university] and me and my housemates were dressed up as Playboy Bunnies and with these little hotpants on and stuff. And my mum and dad know what I'm like and they're used to it, but my aunty, my mum's sister has never had children and she was like, "Oh, you going out like that!"'. Sometimes, partitioning simply does not work.

Thirdly, and equally importantly, Emily is one of the only two who became involved in various campus activities, joining many societies, playing a lot of sport, becoming an officer of the lifesaving club and following the Warwick scheme for gaining teaching practice. 'In the second year I just realized all these opportunities are there.' This is how Emily saw them and grasped them. Only Ruth was somewhat similar in using her musical skills to join the big band with which she travelled extensively and joining the ski trip although, in both cases, the attraction was 'the very good social side.'

From year to year, all of the others express regrets for not having become involved in anything and voice their intentions about participating 'next year' – one that never comes. As far as the necessity of selection is concerned, their collective choice is a negative one, to turn down the new experiences that Emily sees as opportunities. This appears to be both a product of their communicative reflexivity and also a preserver of it. On the one hand, their many weekends away and the time devoted to maintaining home contact detracts and deflects from experimenting with new activities. On the other hand, nearly every member of this sub-group volunteers that she is a 'people person', becomes absorbed by her new friends and keeping up with her old ones, prefers to do things in a group of 'similars and familiars', and generally sees the ready array of possible university activities as something she should make an effort to try but never does because her interpersonal relations always make it inconvenient. Thus, their highest common denominator in terms of participating in university offerings is 'going to the gym', which is doubtless good for their physical well-being but does nothing to stretch their horizons.

Given the wide range of performative competence with which members of the sub-group came up to university – in music, drama, sport and languages – this poses a key question as to why only Sinead seriously seeks to *continue and develop* her skills (in this case acting). The answer lies in the fact that although all of us have to show some concern for each order of natural reality – nature, practice and the social order – we each have leeway to prioritize in which we invest ourselves most.[19] The importance of what the communicative reflexives care about is undoubtedly invested in the social order and specifically revolves around the demands and distractions of friendship.[20] Until we have examined the import of friends, old and new, it will be impossible to go further in understanding the trajectories of their relations with their natal contexts whilst they are undergraduates.

Home friends versus university friends

The familiar phrase 'friends and family', popularized by British Telecom for discount phone rates, may have led one of Joanna Trollope's characters to assert that 'friends are the new family'.[21] However, if we attempt to express this notion propositionally, there are at least two options and they assert very different and incompatible things. On the one hand, the claim may be that friendship has come to *substitute* for the family, either as a further stage in the progressive loss of family 'functions' and their assumption by other bodies or as a feature of late or second-wave modernity and its vaunted 'individualization'. On the other hand, the claim may be that, with the prolongation of 'youth', friendship takes over the baton and acts as a *supplement* to the family, as in everyday references to 'youth culture' and 'peer pressure'. However, there appears to be no consensus as to whether the latter are *complementary* with the family or not. Yet if friendships are divergent from familial standards, what started out as the *supplementary* thesis becomes grist to the mill of the *substitution* argument.

These rather dated arguments serve to highlight the central issue here, namely whether or not friends are *continuous and complementary with subjects' natal backgrounds* or are at variance with them. In the latter case, the influence of friends would be antipathetic to the 'identifiers'' goal of familial replication. In other words, this section is concerned with relationality between 'home friends' and 'university friends'. Friendship matters to all, but how it matters is closely bound up with subjects' dominant mode of reflexivity and vice versa. For communicative reflexives,

---

[19] Each order is associated with a concern that cannot be entirely repudiated but rather has to be accommodated; the natural order is linked to our physical well-being, the practical to our performative competence and the social to our sense of self-worth. See Margaret S. Archer, *Being Human: the Problem of Agency*, Cambridge University Press, 2000, pp. 193–221.

[20] Harry G. Frankfurt, *The Importance of What We Care About*, Cambridge University Press, 1988, chapter 7.

[21] Joanna Trollope, *Second Honeymoon*, London, Black Swan, 2007, p. 48.

the empirical tendency is for them to work hard at sustaining their 'home friends' despite the fact that they all acquire new friends at university. From the relational perspective,[22] it is crucial to avoid eliding 'friends and family' (as so many students themselves conflate them when listing their main concerns in life) given that the aim is to understand the role of friendship in sustaining relations with the natal context – or its reverse – and the part it plays in shaping a life.[23]

Although almost everyone needs friends, friendship itself signifies different types of relationship serving distinctive ends, illustrated in Figure 4.2 for practitioners of the four dominant modes of reflexivity.

Friendship can be conceptualized on a continuum running from the uni-faceted (as in 'my tennis friend', someone with whom the game is regularly played but with whom nothing significant is shared beyond it) to the multi-faceted, where the friendship covers a plurality of dimensions. The communicative reflexive seeks the multiplex friendship provided by 'similars and familiars', people who can understand and enter into the subject's concerns and preoccupations to such an extent that they can complete and confirm their friend's tentative thoughts by their talk together.

Kirsty captures this needy side of friendship for the communicative: 'I think I'm probably worse than a lot of people in terms of right and wrong, I'm a bit more of a wavy line in terms of that . . . I think it's really

---

[22] Pierpaolo Donati, *Teoria Relazionale della Società*, Milan, Franco Angeli, 1991; 'Conclusioni e prospettive: la sociologia relazionale come paradigma della società *dopo-moderna*', in his *Teoria Relazionale della Società: I concetti di base*, Milan, Franco Angeli; Pierpaolo Donati and Ivo Colozzi (eds.), *Il paradigma relazionale nelle scienze sociali: le prospettive sociologiche*, Bologna, Il Mulino, 2006.

[23] Each year the population was invited to list their three main concerns in life in their own words. Every time a number amalgamated 'family and friends' into a single concern. In each data set over the three years, more than 75 per cent listed an interpersonal concern as their most important in life and less than 5 per cent failed to mention one at all. Data on the first (prime or ultimate) concern listed by the students (in January 2005) found 30 per cent citing this to be their 'family', under their own definitions. Figures for frequency of mention amongst respondents' three main concerns at that date were: 'family' 15.7 per cent, 'family and friends' 10.5 per cent and 'friends' 17.5 per cent. When the student population is compared with the Coventry group of 16–24-year-olds investigated in Archer, *Making our Way*, the percentage listing 'family' as their first concern was higher at 53 per cent. However, the age groups are not identical and the student population was disproportionately middle class compared with the Coventry group stratified into four socio-economic groupings. Among the students, 72.3 per cent had fathers working in or who used to work in managerial and professional occupations and 52 per cent had mothers whose work had the same occupational status. See Margaret S. Archer, 'Family Concerns and Inter-generational Solidarity', in Mary Ann Glendon (ed.), *Intergenerational Solidarity, Welfare and Human Ecology*, Vatican Press, 2004, pp. 122–152. Recall also the role played by the friends of Couple A and Couple B in supporting or helping to scupper their life projects in Chapter 3.

Dominant Mode of Reflexivity	Home Friends	Bases of New Friendships
Communicative Reflexives	Retention	Commonalities
Autonomous Reflexives	Selection	Interest-based
Meta-Reflexives	Rejection	Value-based
Fractured Reflexives	Absence	Dependency

Figure 4.2 Modes of reflexivity and friendship patterns

important to have a big network of support and friends, people you can go to ... I mean for the fun ... but also you need some other sort of perspective on things.' Ruth stresses the other side, that such friendship requires reciprocity when she tells of an ex-friend who ceaselessly unburdened herself about her boyfriend: 'I think I was really disappointed that I just felt used ... she'd just be talking about him all the time and she'd never sort of ask how I was or what I was up to. She was very self-centred and so I think people like that they're not, you know, true friends.' Extensive sharing plus generous reciprocity is the formula for what the communicative reflexive seeks from those she will call her friends.

Since all students form new friendships at university yet (almost all) have home friends at point of entry, they again confront the reflexive imperative. They have to deliberate in which of these groups they will invest most of themselves. They may well not see it in these terms, they may only become aware of it when met by reproach or a realization of differences, they may experiment with compartmentalization or combination, but they ineluctably confront the necessity of selection in acting: with whom do they spend most time, who do they phone, for whom do they make efforts and, above all, to whom do they turn as interlocutors? Effectively, they are answering the question 'In whom do I place my trust' and to answer it is a reflexive task.

There are three basic options for all subjects: they can (1) give priority to home friends, (2) seek to maintain their two friendship groups or (3) opt for their university friends. Option (1) is most propitious to 'identifiers' remaining as such and succeeding in their aim of replication because the relationality between 'home friends' and 'family background' will tend to be positively reinforcing. Nevertheless, such friendships can be fraught because home friends do not remain completely unchanged and even if they do, they may subsequently be perceived differently by the subject. Option (2) is at the mercy of how the two groups gel and, if they do not, the subject may reluctantly find herself living out one of the other forms of prioritization.

To an even greater extent, Option (3) necessarily introduces differences into friendship relations because new friends cannot be 'similars' let alone 'familiars' in the way home friends are: usually with shared biographies, a common fund of local references, some intertwining with significant others in the same background, and a commonwealth of mutual knowledge. Therefore, university friends will invariably be a source of new variety and, it follows that, if 'familiarity' grows between them, then the subject's identification with her natal background is likely to diminish though not be discarded. This does not mean that she will cease to be a communicative reflexive, but opting for her university friends (wholly or in part) spells a change of interlocutors, which implies some shift away from or tension with the normativity of her familial background. These theoretical expectations, derived from the earlier two studies, map interestingly onto the lived experiences of these young communicative reflexives. Significantly, sub-group members take up only the first two of the above options. In fact, they divide two to four in favour of Option (1) and Option (2).

Of those who opt for their home friends, Jill is the most readily understandable because she is still living there. She has not spent much more time on campus than academically necessary but she does have university friends of whom she says: 'I have made a few good friends – whether I will keep in contact with them or not is debatable.' Conversely, 'my closest friends are the girls that I've known since I was three or four, and at primary school and secondary school, whom I'm still in contact with. There's about six or seven of them, so that's my close friendship group and I'm very happy with that'. Most of these home peers are moving ahead in their careers ('not just jobs'), have no plans to leave the area and are further cemented by their ability to assimilate one another's boyfriends into the group – including Jill's own partner whom she met through a home friend. Her case is straightforward, propitious to remaining in the ambit of her natal context and involving little deliberation. Much the same holds for Maura, who also takes up Option (1) after some ambivalence in her first year.

Despite her avowed sociability that plunged her into university friendships immediately after entry, Maura tells of her 'awakening' on her twenty-first birthday (in the second year): 'twelve of my friends from home came up [to Warwick], and that's when I thought I've got a really good group of friends there because obviously that meant quite a lot. So, that's when I started thinking I've got to stop taking my friends at home for granted.' She describes her home friends as being 'pretty much like me', meaning easy talkers and ready mixers, but she had also been taking stock reflexively:

When you first come up to uni you've made a new group of friends and for a while, I mean I've got to admit I probably valued them a lot more than my friends at home, but now the table's completely turned because . . . you come to uni for three years and then you go back home and I'll probably live in London. When I go back home my friends are still going to be there, people at uni, you'll keep in contact with a select few . . . But that's reality, you can't have millions of friends.

The remainder of subjects are all hoping that they can keep up with their two sets of friends. Before turning to the relationality between these friendship groups themselves and between them and the students' families, there are two points to stress. Firstly, not one of these communicative reflexives has elected to go down the path of Option (3), by selecting university friends over home friends and thus loosening ties with their natal contexts in this important respect. Secondly, as just seen, Jill and Maura have turned their backs on university friends as future interlocutors and have re-endorsed home influences, thus strengthening the bond with their natal contexts. Conversely, Kirsty, Sinead, Ruth and Emily are – knowingly or unknowingly – sustaining a higher potential for dissonance, for receiving contradictory advice and for being pulled in different directions in the future by the two sets of friends they want to retain.

The three main points are set out by Kirsty and all of them entail reflexive deliberation. Firstly, as a communicative reflexive, she recognizes her ongoing dependence on interlocutors: 'I'm really bad at keeping things to myself, I'm like as soon as I've got an issue, I have to talk to someone about it.' Secondly, although she does keep up with home and school friends, she is aware that some of these are whittling themselves out as partners for 'thought and talk': 'one of them, it's a bit strange, because she didn't go to college or university and she's had a boyfriend now for six years and she's been renting a house for ages, so my life and her life are completely different.' Thus, she retains those from home whose experiences have tracked her own, now feels closer to her university housemates ('because I see them all the time'), and uses them as her interlocutors in preference to her parents. Thirdly, Kirsty highlights her awareness of the (potential) relational tension between friends and family because her parents pointed out 'that I put my friends before my family'. However, compatibility is probably greater now that her friendships are concentrated upon graduates in both groups, rather than embracing the South Coast clubbers.

Because of her absorption with her university boyfriend for eighteen months, Sinead's main friends on campus came from the Drama Society and precipitated the end of this relationship in year two as her boyfriend resented the time she spent in rehearsals. Then the Society took a play to the Edinburgh festival and Sinead, who thoroughly appreciated the fun and intensity of interaction also took rapid and reflexive stock of her fellow actors in the role of 'friends' and concluded 'I don't know if I could hang around with thespians for the rest of my life because they are really kinky and I'm not really like them at all. They're really kind of, overly dramatic and the thing is they try and be different and slightly dramatic yet by doing that they're all the same, like you can spot a thespian from a mile off.' Sinead self-consciously decided that their 'friendship' finished with the play. Thus, in her final year she developed a new set of university friends from those on her course and with whom she shared a house.

Having now assumed a certain reflexive awareness towards this theme, she also observes the cliquishness on campus and how this becomes intensified as small groups move into shared accommodation and the gossiping increases in proportion to proximity. She becomes rather sardonic about university friendships:

what everyone thinks when they go to uni – they're always told 'Oh I found the best friends of my life there'. So in the first week, you expect to meet your best friends and you forget how hard it is because say you've been at school, some people are in the same school from the age of four with the same friends, you forget how hard it is then to go out and start new friendships again. And who do you trust and not trust?

Her own internal conversational answer to this is one that reinforces her mother – daughter bond: 'I trust my mum more than I trust my friends, because, with your friends they can be really, really nice but you're never sure if they have an ulterior motive or why they are giving you this advice for that reason, especially with friends at uni'. Thus, Sinead retains her mother as her prime interlocutor.

On the other hand, from this perspective she makes an unexpected discovery:

it's strange because from being at university and not being with my friends at home, we've got closer as well. It's really strange – a lot of us drifted apart but then a small number of us have kind of kept in contact. We might ring each other a few times during term ... just a quick update ... but then when we meet up at

Easter or the summer or at Christmas, it's like we've never been apart. We go out to the same places at home and, yeah it's really nice keeping that.

Yet, this is not an unambiguous endorsement of 'home friends':

they'll go straight into working in the city, living in a kind of nice house, hanging around with the same sort of people they went to school with, when they go on holiday they'll always go to a really nice hotel ... there's so much more to life, there're so many like other societies and other groups of people, who it would just be so unfortunate to miss.

Thus, Sinead keeps up with both groups of friends but reflexively appreciates the limitations of each and the different directions in which they point: 'sex and the city' or the African experience, courtesy of a course friend's father and his company.

Importantly, Ruth put her finger on the relational incompatibility between her two groups of friends and her own future self, thus registering the necessity of selection but without having yet brought herself to make it. On the one hand, as her travels with the big band have shown, she does respond to the situational logic of opportunity and it rebounds on her friendship pattern:

I think your friends change when you come to university. I'm still in contact with my friends from home ... I do meet up with them when I go home but it's very different because you do change as a person I think and they change and you don't always change in the same way ... and you feel you don't know them anymore ... I do feel closer to my friends up here than I do with some of my friends at home ... you expect more from life in going to university and some just work in the same old jobs – it does give you more opportunities.

On the other hand, since she clings to her ideal of replication Ruth also persists in the belief that, after she has responded to the challenge of a year's voluntary work in Africa, she can reinsert herself in her home friendship group: 'I hope that we can all still be like a big group of friends like we were ... and I think it will go back to how it was. Obviously you do make new friends and you do grow apart, but I think that with everyone coming back home then you know hopefully it should be back to – they will be your main friends again.' Her willingness to live *pro tem* with this manifest contradiction is indicative of her reluctance to shape a life reflexively, like Sinead, for neither is indifferent to the novel opportunities to which their university friends have introduced them.

This is intensified in Emily's case and we already have seen that she has become expert at partitioning her undergraduate life into spending half the year at university and half at home with entirely different people whom she does not attempt to mix. This is paralleled by growing very close to her university friends, with whom she lives and plans to go on living with in London after graduation for a couple of years, as a kind of experiential sabbatical with similarities to Ruth and Sinead's plans for an African adventure. At the same time, she has maintained a largish group of home friends despite being fully aware of how they differ from her university friends:

The people at Warwick are very good at talking . . . they're not people who just kind of pass life by, whereas a couple of my friends from home are more – one of them . . . she can chat for hours about fashion and what you're going to wear that evening, anything like that. But she's not quite that good at having the same kind of conversation you'd have with someone here about the election or things like that. I didn't know young people existed like the people at Warwick so I just took it for granted that that everyone just chatted about their hair and their make-up whereas now I find it difficult sometimes going home and sitting in a pub having conversations about who wore what last night.

All the same, Emily keeps up with both groups. This is symbolized by her two twenty-first birthday parties, one near the university and the other at home. We have already heard about the former and how its Playboy theme shocked her aunt. The second, in complete contrast, saw 'all the girls' back home going out to dinner after having bought one another 'a really special necklace – like each one is slightly different but they're all kind of gold and diamonds, just so it's something to keep for when we're older, we're all still very close, but . . . ' But are these gifts mementos of good times past or the pledge of an enduring bond? Emily herself does not know: she describes the home group spreading out, herself (when in London) included, but cannot bring herself to see this as a self-selected break.

What emerges in turning to career planning is the impact exerted by the relationality just discussed. On the one hand, there is the relative ease with which selection of their future profession is confronted by the two (Jill and Maura) who plumped for Option (1), which generated congruent relations between 'home friends' and 'family background'. Conversely, the four seeking to maintain incongruent relations between 'friends and friends' and 'friends and family' had the greatest difficulties in career choice because their two groups of friends and their families have become sources of mixed messages. Since interlocutors can now come from three sources, their 'confirmation and completion' of communicative reflexivity will be different and divergent. The effect of this incompatibility serves – to varying degrees – to immobilize the subject and prevent progress towards her shaping a life.

Career planning and the difficulties of shaping a life

To make a commitment to a future career, even if this is not the subject's ultimate concern and although it can later be revised, is a big step forward in shaping a life. In particular, this is because the type of occupation chosen serves (provisionally) to seal continuity with the natal context or to signal rupture with it. Even the provisional choice of work continuous with that context may foster new ties rebinding subjects to the familial background. Specifically, it will be at work that they are now most likely to find a partner (only Jill is in a serious relationship when they graduate) and be in a position to carry out their project of 'having a family much like their own', with an increased probability that this will be lived out in continuity and continuous contact with their backgrounds.

Correspondingly, choice of career is much more problematic for some than others because it not only presents them with the necessity of selection of their future work but also a real choice between continued pursuit of their initial 'replicatory' project or responding to the new opportunities with which they have been confronted at university. Obviously, taking such decisions – despite their being corrigible – places heavy demands upon their reflexivity. Under their own descriptions, they are making a commitment about what kind of life they want to lead: one continuous with their natal context or one that spells engagement with activities, people and places that wend away from it.

This is where the relational matrices with which they entered university and the agential modifications that they have introduced into them as undergraduates exert their influence in terms of 'relationality', that is, where relations between relations manifestly come into play. They do so not as determinants but because, even if they are dense and congruent influences, they nonetheless require an active agent who endorses them by selecting a career complementary to them. If they constitute incongruent complexes, the necessity of selection is literally a choice of future engagement, not pre-figured by the subject's background. Instead, it is effectively a choice between accepting or rejecting continuous engagement with it. The receipt of mixed messages places an enormous strain upon communicative reflexivity, which is a mode of deliberation that is much better suited to following the lead of consensual interlocutors and being guided by relational normative conventions.

At the point of graduation, these six subjects are enmeshed, to different degrees, in their background contexts and the distinctive forms of relations to have emerged over their three years as undergraduates.[24] Let us first examine Maura and Jill, the two who have remained most closely bonded to their natal contexts and whose agential preferences for 'home friends' over 'university friends' have reinforced these ties and produced positive relationality between them. If they succeed, they will then represent the communicative version of Couple A at the end of Chapter 3. The emergent influence of relationality means that what is germane to the outcome is not reducible to the aggregate influence of independent, interpersonal influences, but that the relational matrix *qua matrix* packs an extra punch through operating with normative consensus. This is the case for these two subjects but not for the others, because the careers Maura and Jill now envisage are complementary with this matrix.

Jill, living at home, has been drawn into few university activities, remained close to her home friends and met her boyfriend – now a medical student in London with whom she is in a serious relationship – through them. From the start of her degree she has been thinking about a career in the overlapping areas of social, youth or community work. So immersed has she been in family, friends and activities at home that in her final year she comments: 'I probably didn't get that much out of the whole social scene of uni but I think coming to university – it was always for me to get the degree, so I can go on to the sorts of work that I'd like to go on to, so, not making that many close contacts at uni, hasn't really bothered me too much.' In other words, Jill knew roughly where she was going in terms of employment from the start, took a rather instrumental attitude towards her degree, which protected her from encountering countervailing attractions or a friendship group at variance with her original intentions. In short, the effect of relationality served to insulate Jill against the full brunt of the situational logic of opportunity.

She has already had work experience in a local organization for adults with learning difficulties, thanks to a (home) friend's mother who is head of human resources. It was so positive that she would now like to work for a similar agency, and has thus found a career complementary with her natal context that she also believes would contribute towards a satisfying and sustaining *modus vivendi*. Her boyfriend closes this circle of mutually reinforcing relations. Jill met him at the birthday party of a friend whose parents were friendly with his parents. He is as close if not closer to his

---

[24] This has to remain a crude statement or 'more or less' from the point of view of the subject. Since other participants in these relationships were not interviewed, nothing can be said about the quality of relations in themselves.

parents as Jill is to her own, shares the same values of service to the community with her and has become Jill's interlocutor.

Having made her 'selections', she is already addressing the practicalities of shaping a life: planning to stay at home and save, whilst gaining more work experience for a couple of years, before joining her boyfriend in London who will still have two years to go before qualifying. Of this move, Jill, the pattern communicative reflexive, says significantly 'you've got to stretch your wings and see what's out there'. The reflexive imperative does not let up even for one who has evaded the siren call of opportunity thus far. Moreover, as the member of this sub-group most 'successful' in realizing her replicatory aims, it is clear that this will not result in either exact replication or even reproduction. As the professional wife of a doctor, she will have become socially mobile and will also have to accept the prospect of geographical mobility.[25]

The same reinforcing relationality also surrounded Maura, who cooperated with it through her preference for 'home friends' and her frequent visits. She also had help from home with work placements, first through her sister and then in a commercial law firm through 'a woman my mum plays golf with'. However, she had reservations about a career in law from the start, even though this was her second start and her father had tried to discourage her from joint honours with law. Her reserve came from the realization that becoming a solicitor might be difficult to combine with having her own family – her replicatory aim. Negative selection is at work and was reinforced by equally negative experiences of her vacation placements in a family law firm, whose cases were found 'too distressing', and in the commercial law firm, where she encountered 'snobby comments' about her joint degree. Thus, at the end of her second year she changed to straight sociology. Admitting to having made two mistakes was clearly quite painful, but both were rejected along with the occupational opportunities they represented.

Although Maura gained a good degree, she had endorsed no new opportunity that would reorientate her life course. Thereafter, she seems to shed the burden of reflexively shaping her own life, preferring to reinsert herself into the matrix of her home background: 'as soon as I'd done the work experience I decided I'd quite like to go into a bank, both my sisters work for banks . . . So I wouldn't be surprised if I did end up in a bank too.' Once Maura has reached this conclusion, everything else seems to slot into place: 'It's easy, I'll go back home, live in London, live at home, save up money and get a mortgage'. Her father will help her to

---

[25] They will marry in a year's time when Jill is 25 (personal communication 8 June 2010).

do the house up as he had done for her sister and Maura will rejoin the London Irish community that she had never really left.

The four others (Kirsty, Sinead, Ruth and Emily) have weakened the consensual nature of the relationality impinging upon them, largely through their friendship choices and the opportunities of which they had availed themselves as undergraduates. Now, all four show that they are not immune to the attractions of career opportunities that are at variance with their initial replicatory projects and ones that would lead to disjunctions with their family backgrounds. Their shared problem is that they cannot reflexively define any course of action that would generate *complementarity* between the work projects they contemplate and their natal contexts. Because of this incongruity they cannot commit to shaping a life around the opportunity to which they are attracted. The reflexive imperative confronts them with this dilemma and the response is to back away from the lure of the alternative future they had contemplated for themselves, but if and only if actively assisted by family and friends who are also consensual – as was the case for Kirsty alone.

It is significant that work and employment are not among Kirsty's three main listed concerns in life (friends, family and finances) because it indicates that it is her career that will be subordinated to fit in. She wants the London experience:

just to be in a big city and that. I think you expect there to be more opportunities – just to live for a couple of years. I don't think I'd like to raise a family in London but, maybe on the outskirts. I'd rather be with a friend. I think it could be quite scary, but a lot of people I know from here [Warwick] are planning on moving to London after university.

Interestingly, the career she has in mind is mentioned last, implying that her life-style preferences – ones to be shared with her university friends – take priority. When she does talk about taking a short course with the London School of Journalism, following her brief experience of writing pop music reviews for the student paper, it is also to say that she is rather afraid of the competition and that her alternative is 'to live at home and just like get [journalistic] experience'.

By her third year, this latter option is off the agenda because her family is busy relocating abroad. Without their support, she considers that career to be too financially insecure and recognizes that she cannot move with them and begin journalism in French. Thus, she has accepted a post in accountancy, despite its lesser attractions:

I never used to want to do it because my dad does accountancy and I always thought it was just really boring, but I sort of looked into it a bit more because a lot of my friends are doing graduate schemes in accountancy and just talking to them instead of writing it off straight away, I sort of found out that it can be quite diverse, it can be quite interesting.

Given this consensus between her networks of significant relationships, Kirsty complied and Dad immediately supplied the contact details. She was accepted by a firm just outside London, where she will be working with a university friend, and living with another friend from Warwick and her brother.

Since pursuing journalism had become increasingly incongruous with Kirsty's other more highly ranked concerns, it was exchanged for accountancy, which was much more compatible. Importantly, she exercised her 'thought and talk' with both her university friends and her father, and then bowed to the conjoint influence of their positively reinforcing relationality. Valuing the bond with both family and friends over the lonely enterprise of an uncertain career in journalism, she opted for a shape of life reflecting these priorities and whose design was mediated by these congruent relationships.

Sinead's attachment to drama was of much longer duration, although again it is not listed among her three prime concerns. In her second year the pull of this opportunity seems strong: 'just touring with a drama company and going places and meeting different people, I think that would be ideal because then you get to see so much of . . . different places, experience new things . . . '. This ideal is tarnished by meeting a professional actress whose marriage had broken down because of her touring and whose son had been at boarding school from as early as possible, which obviously clashed with Sinead's aim to have a family much like her own. Also, as we have seen, Sinead's intense experience of the Edinburgh Fringe had not endeared the thespians to her.

Now in her third year, although she does not overtly rescind her theatre project, she thinks that 'probably from the people I've been hanging out with, I've just changed my ideals. I would have loved to have worked in London, working for like PR or a Media company, sharing a house with the girls . . . and living that sort of cosmopolitan lifestyle . . . and then luckily meeting a nice guy'. Instead, she has persuaded her (reluctant) parents to support a gap year in Africa 'doing the humanitarian thing'. It is as if her parents accept that these opportunities have to be sampled before being dropped in favour of the 'nice guy' and perhaps they are right. Sinead has not made much progress towards shaping a life, but her last words echo a theme reiterated from the beginning: 'I would quite like a family inevitably . . . and to kind of have dinner parties and that kind of stuff and . . . to bring them up in kind of a really, really nice happy home.' Once again, in her attempt to strike out for a new horizon, Sinead's communicative reflexivity was of little assistance because her interlocutors were not consensual, resulting in a drift towards agential passivity expressed through procrastination.

Passivity about a career has always been marked with Ruth and seems to be part of the communicative reflexives' uniform avowal of their inability to engage in long-term planning. Once again, work and employment do not feature among her three main concerns during her time as an undergraduate. In her first year she mentions the possibility of teaching, but the main attraction is working with young children and thus edging closer to the passion shared with her mother for babies. By year two, she admits 'well I just don't know what else I'm going to do, so maybe I should do that [teaching]'. Vacation work experience with her local Health Authority only contributed to Ruth's conviction that she detests office work of any kind and would shun it. Yet the problem is that the necessity of selection cannot be approached by the *via negativa*, because the situational logic of opportunity means there are simply too many options to deal with by elimination.

In her final year, Ruth is totally pre-occupied with a trip to Africa as a volunteer worker in a children's home that she will take with two friends after graduation. This plan brings into play negative relationality between her university based friends, equally keen to go, and her mother and extended family members, who do all they can to discourage it on grounds of safety. For the first time, rough words are reported with her mother: 'at the end of the day I'm twenty-one, I said, and you know I'm going to do what I want to do, so you can either support me [or not] because I'm going to go anyway'. Mother capitulated, perhaps afraid of the gulf now opening up between them, and possibly reassured by Ruth's insistence that she will 'come home' afterwards. Even about this Ruth vacillates, sometimes saying 'who knows', she may stay and work in Africa. At other times she voices a clear intention to return and try to gain work experience from home for the remainder of the year, but the way in which she describes this shows the same passivity and uncertainty as encountered with the previous subject: 'I really need to just to look into it, so I think maybe do a play scheme or something like that, that's one thing, but I don't know, I just need to look into it really and see what opportunities there are out there.'

If that is what transpires, then Ruth's primary bond (her mother–daughter relationship) will continue to anchor her, but not give her orientation in the face of 'contextual incongruity'. What Ruth has realized is that, as a graduate, she simply cannot replicate her mother's *modus vivendi*:

Well I would love to work with babies but I really don't know in what context because it's so difficult because I don't want to be a childminder or anything like that, but I don't really, like I don't know – maybe look into charities, you know, there are various sorts of baby charities around but, I don't know, I just sort of well, you know, I've sort of thought about it and think well I don't really know how I would go about doing that.

This has been reproduced verbatim because the repetitive 'don't knows' help to show the limitations of communicative reflexivity when the chief interlocutor – in this case her mother – is (experientially) incapable of completing and confirming Ruth's 'thought and talk', especially when it conveys only extreme uncertainty. In consequence, what she said a little earlier about seeing 'what opportunities there are out there' is much more akin to the passive agent 'waiting for things to happen to her'.[26] Such relationally induced passivity is not a stance from which 'contextual incongruity' can be tackled or a life be shaped.

The suspension of communicative reflexivity

What has been highlighted through examining the last two subjects is an intensification of negative relationality between 'friends and family' and its correspondingly negative effects on the workings of communicative reflexivity as a means for designing courses of action to realize subjects' concerns. This is because a mixture of incongruent interlocutors and relational influences generate mixed messages, which by definition cannot provide clear guidelines to action. Since these subjects resist the necessity of selection between their relational networks ('friends and family') that would enable the subject to move on to shaping a life, then complementarity cannot be re-established. Instead, they come to resemble Couple B in Chapter 3. Specifically, they succumb increasingly to agential passivity as this relational incompatibility intensifies, illustrated by their most frequent responses: 'I don't know' and 'We'll see'. In other words, circumstances will decide, rather than their assuming any governance over their own life courses. In relinquishing that responsibility, they increasingly become passive agents to whom 'things happen.[27]

Because they refuse to choose – since they are relationally attached to both groups and their corresponding interlocutors – communicative reflexivity fails to work for them and their ultimate response is to

---

[26] 'Passive agents' are defined as those whose subjectivity performs no mediatory role in relation to their objective circumstances, permitting no intentional relationship between self and society.

[27] Martin Hollis, *Models of Man: Philosophical Thoughts on Social Action*, Cambridge University Press, 1977.

abandon the practice of reflexivity. (The alternative, namely to shift to a different mode of reflexivity, may result later but from the data available it does not happen immediately even if it does happen eventually.) Instead, incongruity exacerbates passivity and results in a retreat from reflexivity in so far as possible and for a period impossible to ascertain here. This is best exemplified by Emily in her final year, when her strategy of compartmentalization (living half of the time at home and half at university) is brought to an end because on graduation she can no longer live her life in two halves. Minimally she has to live somewhere and to do something. Yet communicative reflexivity cannot assist her, given the incongruity between the two ways in which her 'thought and talk' is completed. Consequently, in her final year, Emily does not clear the threshold used throughout this study to assign any subject to the practice of a dominant mode of reflexivity. Her lack of relational complementarity ultimately results in her becoming an 'impeded reflexive', as manifested in her difficulties over career choice.[28]

Emily had chosen her degree course in history and sociology 'because I knew doing a National Curriculum subject, history, I'd have the opportunity to go into teaching if I wanted to.' Her mother works as a teaching assistant and several members of her extended family are teachers, but already upon entry she is reflexively aware that 'there are so many jobs to do and because you don't know what exists you go for the more conventional ones.' By her second year, although she has not abandoned teaching and allied trades, she describes herself as 'still undecided' but is now attracted to

a London job, you know, Marketing or PR or something like that. I know it's very different because part of me thinks maybe for a few years I'd like to do something like that in the city and then go on to teaching afterwards . . . but then I don't want to go into teaching because it's easy . . . I don't want to go into it just for the convenience.

No one in her family has any experience of the type of city job she is envisaging, but being at university has made Emily confront a new range of opportunities: 'It's made me aware that there's more out there than I would have found out, there's more beyond your home, your town. There's a big world out there and it's not unusual these days to work in different countries or travel with your job. There are so many different careers and lifestyles out there when you finish.' And Emily is responsive to this.

---

[28] As first encountered in Archer, *Structure, Agency and the Internal Conversation* and considered to be a form of fractured reflexivity, pp. 305–313.

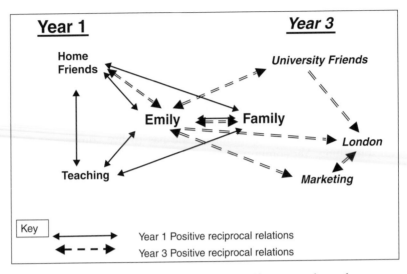

Figure 4.3 Emily's inability to shape a life as an undergraduate

By her third year, Emily has now transferred her compartmentaliz-ing strategy to her future career and, indeed, her future life. She has completed the Warwick Teaching Certificate but 'I feel that I need to experience something else first, get some life experience, otherwise I've just been straight through education and I haven't really seen anything else and I want to see what's out there a bit more.[29] And then I can probably imagine myself going quite easily into teaching and, probably in ten years' time maybe when I've got a husband . . . but at the moment I don't really want to spend my time in a school with the older ladies that are teaching.' Instead, she first wants the London experience with her university friends: 'you know, the busy, hustley lifestyle really and I love living with my friends and so I want to do that for a couple more years'. Yet, although she again mentions marketing, this is not a clear career project: 'It's so different and it's so new and unexplored to me that I don't really have any, I haven't really got any ideas in my mind what it's going to be like, so I'm just going to see what happens and see how I feel.' Her three-year trajectory is illustrated in Figure 4.3.

This is the passivity. She has kept faith with her family background, prepared for the career compatible with it, but has postponed making a commitment to it. On the other hand, she cannot resist following her university friends to the bright lights but, beyond the lifestyle, she has no

[29] The Warwick Teaching Certificate is for undergraduates: giving teaching practice and earning a small exemption on the Post-Graduate Certificate in Education (PGCE).

idea where it will lead and resists deliberating about this by designating it as 'temporary'. Emily is temporizing, because she cannot bring herself to choose between 'family and friends', she cannot deliberate about shaping her life but rather lives emotively (something she calls 'being selfish'), which paradoxically is to have renounced self-governance.

As a working-class girl, she had refused to be cowed by 'all the amazing things' fellow students had done, but rather saw them as opportunities that she could emulate and did by going skiing and discovering Easyjet. The situational logic of opportunity was both irresistible and manageable through compartmentalizing her undergraduate career, but now it is not and her response is revealing:

I absolutely don't want to leave [Warwick], I absolutely love it, I love everything about it, I love the place, I love the people, I love what I've got out of it . . . I've made loads of friends, a lot of whom will be in London next year, so I'm hoping to keep in contact with all of them . . . I've done so many new things, I've found out about so many opportunities that I would never even have known were available before, and like everything now seems do-able, whereas before – I never realized how easy they were and it's made me so aware that you can do whatever you want, like, you know, within reason you can see whatever you want, go wherever you want, everything's accessible – and yeah, I absolutely love it. And, umm, the negative point is I'll have to leave.

Leaving means Emily putting aside compartmentalization and having to come down on one side or another. This is a form of engagement that she cannot bring herself to make, given the incongruent messages received from her two sets of relational networks and their interlocutors.

Conclusion

This chapter has sought to show how communicative reflexivity is ill-fitted to the nascent morphogenetic social order because it does not enable its practitioners to deal readily with the reflexive imperative. In drawing this conclusion, it should be clear that this does not refer to some abstract lack of fit or to functional non-adaptation. Instead, it is argued that the 'thought and talk' mode of exercising reflexivity depends upon a continuity of and complementarity between the interlocutors used but, when such is the case then it is conducive to normative conventionalism. However, no form of conventional normativity can cope with the necessity of selection other than by a simple rejection of the new opportunities on offer, yet many of the young subjects examined are attracted by the new options available to them. Moreover, without a mode of reflexivity that facilitates making such selections they cannot progress towards shaping a life and establishing a *modus vivendi*.

In Chapter 1 it was maintained that the generic condition for the predominance of communicative reflexivity was 'contextual continuity'. Thanks to this first longitudinal study undertaken on reflexivity, it is possible to be more precise about which aspects of the context need to be continuous in order to foster and nurture the communicative mode. All of these highlight *relational elements in subjects' background contexts*, ones that must not be incongruous with other relationships formed after leaving home if the practice of communicative reflexivity is to persist and to provide guidelines to the courses of action to be taken. In short, *this mode of reflexivity is relationally formed and needs to be relationally sustained.* What has been found is that the conditions of formation and of maintenance are being seriously undermined and together they spell the future diminution if not demise of communicative reflexivity. This argument can be summarized in the following points.

Firstly, dominant communicative reflexivity is found only amongst those termed 'identifiers' with their natal contexts in Chapter 3 (Figure 3.3). This means those who were in receipt of high relational goods from their family backgrounds (including networks extending into the natal locale) *and* who subjectively valued these goods so highly that they wished to replicate them in their own lives and families-to-be – which all interviewees examined in this chapter projected and wanted. The key relational good as far as communicative reflexivity is concerned was the generation of sufficient trust and mutual concern for some family member to become an interlocutor upon whom the subject could rely to complete and confirm the distinctive reflexive practice of 'thought and talk'. Although the subjects examined all came from stable two-parent families (no divorce, separation or re-marriage), the salience of the mother–daughter bond in several cases does not logically preclude the generation of the same quality of relational goods by a single parent. What does militate against the production of the requisite quality of relational goods in the future is the decreasing amount of time that either or both parents are spending with their children today, since shared experience, common reference points and literal co-existence are the elements required from the natal context in order to generate them.

Secondly, and accentuated by the British practice of attending university away from home (see footnote 21), communicative reflexivity is potentially threatened by the formation of new friendships. In following the six young practitioners through a brief but crucial tract of their lives, it appeared that negative relationality emerged between their familial contexts and the friendships formed during their period as undergraduates, especially if one or more of these friends assumed the role of interlocutor(s). There is nothing inevitable about the emergence of negative relationality, indeed, two subjects (Jill and Maura) avoided it by continuing to value their 'home friends' over their 'university friends'. For both, communicative reflexivity remained in good working order by filtering out their susceptibility to novel opportunities and thus preventing any discordant expansion of their horizons.

Thirdly, when it did arise, negative relationality had serious and deleterious consequences for the working of communicative reflexivity as an effective guide to action. Quite simply, it meant that subjects were confronted with 'mixed messages' as they consulted their incongruent interlocutors for 'confirmation and completion' of their internal conversations. In effect, they had imported the societal incongruity between home background (its preparation and expectations) and the proliferating array of opportunities into their own life worlds as micro-versions of 'contextual incongruity'. As the recipients of 'mixed messages', their communicative reflexivity became an obstacle that inhibited their response to the necessity of selection and therefore to shaping a life. The obvious solution to being pulled in two different directions through their 'thought and talk', namely to reject family relationships in favour of the one(s) newly acquired, was (as yet) undertaken by no one. Because these relational goods are precious, owing to the time required to build them, the reciprocity involved and the amount of self-investment entailed by the adoption of an interlocutor, they are not readily shed.

Fourthly, when communicative reflexivity continues to be practised with incongruent interlocutors, the result is progressively to immobilize the subject who is caught in the cross-current. Instead of their distinctive form of internal conversation being their guide to action, they decline the responsibility of active agency and resort to passivity. In going with the proximate flow, in awarding themselves time out, in discounting the next year or decade with a promissory note to return to their replicatory project 'afterwards', they decline to take any governance of their own lives and become people to whom things happen. In the worst-case scenario, their reflexivity itself is compromised and as 'impeded reflexives' they can neither determinedly seek to replicate what they consider of worth from their backgrounds nor take advantage of the situational logic of opportunity.

In brief, communicative reflexivity does not adequately equip subjects to confront the reflexive imperative and the nascent morphogenetic order from which it derives, thus explaining the shrinking ranks of its practitioners among undergraduates and fostering expectations of their further shrinkage as morphogenesis becomes increasingly unbound.

5   Autonomous reflexivity: the new spirit of social enterprise

The autonomous reflexives are subjects who both seize the situational logic of opportunity and, already as undergraduates, are deliberating about occupational outlets for themselves. Their aspirations constitute a new mediatory mechanism that is registering an impact on corporate recruitment and multi-national practice. On the one hand, the attraction to most of being able to fund an 'expensive lifestyle' partly accounts for why they are forthcoming as applicants, even from a discipline like sociology. On the other hand, all of these subjects have well-articulated social concerns that cannot be attributed to their exposure to the social sciences, since most already displayed them at point of entry.[1] Obviously, the effects of self-selection should not be underestimated for the subjects interviewed. Nevertheless, since sociologists are a small minority of such applicants, their presence cannot explain the complicated self-presentational pavane currently danced by representatives of multi-national capital: their veneer of environmental concern, *pro bono* initiatives for the underprivileged and projects for improving the immediate surroundings of their enterprises. Presenting the caring face of the corporation is probably more of a response to collective action and critique but a crucial consequence is continuing to keep a new generation of applicants coming forward. Autonomous reflexives, deliberating according to instrumental rationality, are those who replenish the cadres of *homo economicus* and the new administrative ranks of *homo sociologicus*. As the source of new recruits, further and sometimes cosmetic concessions can be made to their tender spots.

However, as active agents, these new applicants and recruits also have their own agendas. None of those interviewed was considering more than five to ten years of multi-national corporate employment. What they sought were the high earnings that would establish them – as debt-free, as home owners, as high livers from the start – on which foundations they

---

[1] No association was found between students' dominant mode of reflexivity and whether or not sociology had been studied during secondary education.

could then respond to the evergreen attraction to autonomous subjects of starting their own self-employed enterprises. If the buzz of current corporatism was certainly no disincentive, the old pull of being in sole control retained its past vigour.

As far as their relational origins are concerned, this new generation of autonomous reflexives remained the converse of the communicative subjects in every way. In part, the attenuation of communicative reflexivity can be attributed to the atrophy of the stable semi-nuclear family and with it, the attrition of the relational goods that it generated. Although all the parental marriages examined in the previous chapter had proved lasting, even there geo-locality was on the wane but pockets of it were still found (as with Maura and the London Irish community); the significance of the grandparental generation was sometimes important but far from general; working wives had become a normal expectation but already this enabled some of them to personify values at variance with those of the *pater familias*. In part, all of these changes stem from parental responses to the new 'logic of opportunity'. Despite their children being 'identifiers' and 'replicators', it seemed extremely unlikely that these young subjects could project familial replication into their own generation.

However, when the family circumstances of the autonomous reflexives are pictured as being the antithesis of the communicatives (see Figure 3.2), this is *not simply* to highlight major statistical divergences. The families of this small group of autonomous interviewees show a vastly greater amount of geographical mobility on an intercontinental scale and their tendency to divorce, separate and live apart is in marked contrast. Nevertheless, it is emergent relations within the familial group that are regarded in this study as crucial for explaining the making of one form of reflexivity rather than another. Most likely, the quantitative statistics and the qualitative absence of relational goods would be found to be positively associated in a large-scale empirical study, but my point is to explore the causal mechanisms involved rather than to track empiricist indicators of them.[2]

To be precise, these young autonomous reflexives entering university had familial backgrounds that reflected the *absence of relational goods* rather than the *presence of relational evils* (which was the lot of the fractured reflexives), although 'absence' was always tinged with negativity for these autonomous subjects. Relational goods and evils are both emergent from the nature of parental relations. To highlight their 'absence' is to emphasize that, regardless of the tenuously lasting nature of their marriages

---

[2] This involves both 'explanation' and 'understanding', rather than viewing these as antinomies.

(in the majority of cases), these parents are not 'couples'. For emergent goods or evils to be generated, both parents need to be oriented towards their relationship and its products (good or bad), whose preservation (or exacerbation) is crucial to the courses of action undertaken by both partners, including actions towards their children. 'Absence' stands for the lack of such an orientation on the part of the two adults. From the standpoint of their children, this means that autonomous subjects are parented by *two individuals rather than by a couple*.

In everyday terms, each parent is more preoccupied with himself and herself (often, but not invariably, with their careers) than concerned with self-investment in the family relationship and its well-being, which would make each a beneficiary of its emergent goods as indivisible common goods. From the point of view of their children, this implies they have to engage with two separate (if not separated) people, at least whilst they live at home. There is nothing to ensure the two parents have shared values or even work reciprocally to further each other's concerns within the family. In short, such parents are purveyors of mixed messages – or messages that don't mix – meaning that 'contextual incongruity' is encountered *within the family* by their children, where they confront the necessity of selection much earlier than the subjects examined so far. Although the present concern is with their offspring, it is important to recall that many of these parents are in their early to mid-forties and thus their own relationships were contracted and developed in the last twenty years, when nascent morphogenesis was also beginning to present them with the situational logic of opportunity and to which the two parents had often responded differently.

For the children there are three consequences that have a direct bearing upon their making as autonomous reflexives. Firstly, what is pivotal is that all of these young people had *independence thrust upon them*, such that they could be called 'enforced independents' even whilst living at home. Circumstances vary, but common exemplifications are children assuming domestic responsibilities that are usually associated with adult roles and certainly taking charge of their own personal and practical needs. Not infrequently, this extended to providing support for one parent or intermittently for both, thus seeking to compensate for the interpersonal deficiencies in the parental relationship. They phoned home to check that everyone was all right rather than to reassure their parent(s) that they were. It is no surprise that these subjects appeared considerably more mature than their fellow undergraduates, unenthralled by life in the hall (more restrictive than they were used to), under-whelmed by campus life (treated as an *à la carte menu*) and not ready to bestow friendship on those whose main recommendation was mere proximity.

Secondly, this was reinforced in nearly all cases by the fact that these subjects had taken gap years, had travelled and worked as well as having had the 'amazing experiences' that certain other entrants found intimidating. Their parents had chosen and changed their own lifestyles (often out of synchrony with their partner) and their children were no strangers to observing such selections. Thus, their response to the *necessity of selection was to go out to meet it* rather than to await its exigencies. As soon as the school door closed, it was as if they had completed the terms of the childhood contract and adulthood spelt 'their turn' to experience what they would. In the course of that year, all shed their frail local bonds and defined themselves as 'global citizens'. At most, what remained of any geo-local attachment reduced to generalities such as 'preferring rural living' or 'a lasting liking for London'.

Thirdly, these young autonomous reflexives were distinctive in the relatively low value that they attached to the social order. Certainly half contracted what they hoped were lasting relationships, but the others appeared in no hurry and gave the impression of considering the university a rather small pond for partnering. Significantly, every member of this group had *a deep self-investment in the practical order* – in music, languages, competitive sports, car mechanics, cookery and property development. For most, in their independence at home, such interests had already been discovered and honed. Although some were put on hold at university, for the greater part they were continued and other practical interests added to them. This proved important for their friendship patterns, which were interest-led, and for the use they made of university activities – the autonomous reflexives proving one of the two most intense user groups of all entrants.

Although a bright group (two of the interviewees gaining first-class degrees), all eventually concluded that the attractions of academic life were not for them. It would be too facile an elision to suggest that their concern for the practical order acted as the deterrent – although there is something in this – because the attractions of, say, international banking or corporate marketing passed the test of practical utility. It is to establish these connections and the interconnections between the three points made above, that the subjects' own reasons-as-causes for action must be scrutinized more closely.

Family lives: receiving 'mixed messages' and responding to them

In one way or another, for these subjects disruptive family dynamics meant a complete absence of familial relational goods. Its generic consequence was that all four interviewees were in receipt of 'mixed messages' from *within* the family, stemming directly from their respective parents. The obvious implication was that the possibility of becoming 'identifiers' and would-be 'replicators' was simply not on offer to them. Either their parents had split up over their differences, were preoccupied with renegotiating their own relationships or had engaged in commitments that distanced themselves from their offspring. This group of students had been strangers to 'contextual continuity' from the start. None had normative consensus as part of their natal backgrounds but were presented with necessary of selection as a normal ingredient of their life worlds whilst growing up. All were confronted with the need to shape a life as an everyday occurrence, evidenced by their parents' doings and struggles, and all absorbed the lesson that this was a personal responsibility to be undertaken without a template.

This is well illustrated by Adam, and amongst these interviewees his circumstances are not as extreme as they first appear. He is the son of a Swedish mother and English father, was born and brought up in the Caribbean until the age of thirteen when the parents and their three children moved to an old university town in England. His biography graphically exemplifies how impossible it was for these two people to socialize Adam in a manner that extended stable and consensual expectations towards any aspect of his future, partly because his parents were busy renegotiating a new *modus vivendi* of their own during his early teens. Although all of the following comes from Adam's perception of their relationship, it appears that his parents had substantial normative differences from the beginning and were held together by mutual tolerance and their individual entrepreneurial pursuits in Barbados.

Dad, who was 'laid-back and cool, having seen it all' on the Berkeley campus, had put student revolt behind him and was successfully running his own business in computer management on the island. Mum, herself raised there, had been brought up as a Muslim, thanks to her stepfather, and her half-siblings intensified in Islamic orthodoxy as they grew older, without this leading to a complete break in extended family relations. Significantly, because it intentionally excluded Adam, Swedish – his mother's first language – was withheld as pointless for him to learn although it was acquired by his mother's female siblings and used as a 'code' by the Islamic side of the family to exclude others. On top of this, they are a white family living on a black island, though not part of the 'ex-pat' community. To complete the recipe, Adam is a young boy, excelling at school, at ease with his Caribbean friends, but starting to feel that he was 'different', a difference he was to recognize at puberty as being gay.

For the parents, the move to England – though mother would have preferred America – seems to have signalled a transformation of their concerns and an equally radical change in their *modus vivendi*. Father exchanged the high earnings from his company for the intrinsic satisfaction he gained from school-teaching. At first, mother continued to enjoy corporate life in advertising but, before Adam left school, had become entirely disillusioned and insisted on working only 'for charity, she wouldn't work for anyone else because she just sees it as going to the fat cats'. In other words, it does not appear that his parents were a couple who together underwent a conversion of their values and the social identities expressive of them. Rather, father led and mother gradually came to endorse his repudiation of market capitalism.

Meanwhile, Adam was now installed in a comprehensive school, where the standards were dire in comparison to his Caribbean grammar school: 'I honestly thought I'd come to the ghetto! I distanced myself because the boys didn't care . . . I used my intelligence as a route out of there in a sense.' What else could he do but, by distancing himself, try reflexively to evaluate these normative incongruities cross-cutting his everyday life? In terms of guidelines, his dilemma could not be solved by selectively siding with one of his parents. On the one hand, his father's newly found job satisfaction in teaching conflicted with Adam's own negative experiences of English schooling, besides his equally negative assessment that dad now worked for 'peanuts'. On the other hand, mother's work for a charity shop would have brought home more peanuts. Although she became more relaxed about her strict Muslim upbringing, Adam was still aware that the Islamic tradition, at least in the hands of his (London-based) aunts and cousins, considered being gay the 'ultimate sin'. Although his parents were 'not exactly thrilled' when Adam announced his gayness, they began conniving to keep his homosexuality from the Islamic side of the family and managed to make a joke about this secrecy.

Adam voices the following types of independent comments about his own normativity: 'I'd like to think that lots of my values are self-defined'; 'within the law, there are no rules really defined for what we can do'; 'the bigger picture is always the target' and, significantly, 'when we lived in the Caribbean, I had to sort of evaluate a lot of things and at quite a young age'. What he had to evaluate was a normative smorgasbord.

His reflexive resolution of these mixed messages was by 'picking and mixing' from this disparate array of 'socializing' experiences. Achieving this synthesis was promoted by the fact that, despite all these dilemmas, the family appears to have sustained good, if not close, interpersonal relationships. From both his father's and his mother's pasts he assimilated the desirability of corporate and financial success. Ironically, this seems to have entailed a rejection of the newly found parental values of community service and opposition to capitalism. Yet, it is a nuanced rejection because he himself was contemplating doing voluntary work at weekends in the future and his gap year was partly spent in a school withdrawal unit where he appreciated the intrinsic satisfaction of helping kids through their problems. These are the sources of Adam's syncretism, which I have termed 'social entrepreneurship'.

In sum, Adam's family background had provided sufficient diffuse cultural capital for him to meet academic standards without stress. Just as importantly, both parents offered financial capital to support him through post-graduate courses, further training and house purchase, if he desired. What they had not and could not have provided were consensual normative guidelines. Instead, they effectively presented him with the necessity of selection as something entailing much more than simple career choice.

What Adam assimilated from his synthesis of these diverse strands was, above all, a confident cosmopolitan outlook: 'I don't really blend in anywhere to be honest, which I think is quite a good thing. If you don't blend in anywhere that means you can blend in everywhere.' He continues in the same vein: 'I think that's the main element that you make a life for yourself where you are.' Adam has rightly diagnosed that he must establish his own *modus vivendi* on the basis of his personal concerns and reflexive deliberations – and do so autonomously. There will be nothing quasi-automatic about what career he follows, what language or country he adopts and how he lives life as a gay man. Reflexive self-management will be required every step of the way. To represent Adam as just another statistic of educational success, attributable to a middle-class background, is to miss most of the point and all of the process.

Riccardo is a copybook illustration of enforced independence. He has an Italian father, his mother is from New Zealand and the extended family is globally dispersed. Riccardo's parental background shares many themes with that of Adam, though with more emphasis upon his independence training because his mother and father have lived on separate continents since he was five – without divorcing but with what he describes as a 'rocky relationship'. His father, too, underwent a change of direction and, having worked for an Italian car distributor in England for thirty years he then moved to East Africa and set up his own media company. Riccardo regards this as 'quite a strange move', perhaps implying that he was not party to all the details. 'Dad's been away now for sixteen years this summer so . . . I haven't really had a father figure as such and then with my brother going to university and spending time abroad as part of his degree, it left me and my mum, on our own.'

Given that his elder brother was away and that they were 'not exceptionally close', it fell to Riccardo to support his mother after she had cancer, recovered and resumed work. They got on well, but without the close bonding encountered amongst some of the communicatives. In consequence, Riccardo is fully accustomed to taking domestic responsibility: 'my dad used to sort out most things. He had a secretary who probably did most of it when I was younger. So I've sort of had to be the managing director and the secretary of the house, but I've enjoyed that.'

Since no more than two family members ever seem to be found together, Riccardo provides the cement for the unit. In fact, he seems to take more responsibility for his parents than they do for him. He took a couple of weeks off university to visit his father in Africa: 'I hadn't seen him for well over a year, things between him and my mum were a bit rocky, relationships were strained and he had no one out there to talk to, and I'd just had a few conversations on the phone that felt bad.' Although they had useful discussions about his father retiring soon, these sound to have been unilateral because 'my dad doesn't understand the [university] world I'm in'. Riccardo sums up the consequences of these family relationships: 'I've not necessarily chosen to take responsibility for myself, but I've had to in so many ways, and it's the way I work best now.'

He demonstrated this during his gap year, spent selling parts for a car distributor and learning all he could about mechanics: 'I like responsibility. I don't like being told what to do. Well, when it's necessary to be told what to do then I'll go and do it, but I like to take responsibility for my own actions.' His self-confidence ('I feel if I really wanted to get something, I could get it'), good self-organization, decisiveness and preference for being in control of his own activities are the fruits of his independence training and the making of an autonomous reflexive.

Already he seems to have drawn up a balance sheet about his future involvement with his family. On the one hand, he rings his mother a couple of times a week saying: 'It's important to keep up this relationship, because my mum hasn't got my dad there as a companion.' He is compassionate, recognizing that 'it's been very tough on Mum – I appreciate that a lot and she's done a fantastic job'. On the other hand, he has no intention of returning home and resuming his role as family mainstay after university: 'I've always had to take responsibility for myself and I enjoy it and I'm really enjoying the idea of moving out and sort of cutting the apron strings. That's not to say that I resent my mum in any way at all, but it's time for me to move on and it's time for her to move on as well.'

What has he assimilated from this fragile family unit? Perhaps, mainly from his own role as go-between, a recognition of the need for non-judgemental human empathy and for behaving 'decently', which was very influential for his university relationships – including being in no hurry to contemplate the first step towards having his own partner. Secondly, coming from a family that 'has never really struggled', he is not averse to free enterprise but, since he wants to be in control and father is in control of his company, there must be questions about how content he would be with a junior post in a multi-national. Thirdly, Riccardo has a social conscience. In part, this stems from living in what he terms a 'quite rough' area of London and from his mother's values; in part, from his approval of his father's charity work for the UN in Africa, 'which is something I'd like to take up myself in whatever way I can as I grow older'; and in part, from his own experiences: 'basically Africa's done a lot to make me appreciate that I am very lucky, beyond lucky, massively fortunate to sit here and wear a pair of Levi jeans and wear a nice pair of trainers'. Of course, he is another 'global citizen'.

Enforced independence does appear to play a very significant role in the making of an autonomous reflexive and the absence of familial relational goods contributes to being independent through the lack of ties other than those of interpersonal relations – freely sustained but carefully monitored lest they become constrainingly binding. However, if Riccardo took something from the general values of both parents and synthesized them through his own experiences, Evan is much more parsimonious. This can be attributed to the polarization of his parents, one that entailed none of Riccardo's appreciation of the best of both 'sides' or his leaving home having synthesized significant elements from each.

Evan (whose mother is a civil servant and father an electrical retail manager) says that 'it's only a very small section of my family that's very important to me', meaning his mother and to a lesser extent his sister. After a lot of tensions, his parents divorced when he was five and some of the bitterness about his broken home remains to this day: 'There are some painful memories of early childhood, or just childhood as a whole really, in relation to my parents and their separation. I try not to dwell on it because it's something that as a child I dwelt on for a very, very long time. Although it's been quite important in shaping who I am now, it's something I try to move away from.' His mother he considered a 'good friend' and the origin of many of his values. His father is a source not only of resentment because of his 'lack of conscientiousness', but also a negative reference point, someone whose own *modus vivendi* – centring on a treadmill of work and television – is one from which Evan entirely dissociates himself.

He views his upbringing as a form of independence training:

it's not as though [working] Mum neglected us in any way but, out of necessity, we were forced to fend for ourselves a bit and we were always encouraged to earn our own money to pay our own way, and so from the age of fifteen I had my own job and . . . my own money and I've learnt to really like the independence I've been encouraged to have . . . I mean I think Mum may have inadvertently made [my sister] and myself very independent . . . but it's been enormously beneficial to us.

Part of what Evan now places on the positive side of the balance sheet are not simply domestic skills and personal budgeting but also his influential work experience and the gap year he earned for himself on the other side of the world. Mother promoted his travelling, urging him 'to seize the opportunities that weren't really there for her' after leaving school at sixteen. These 'lonely planet' travels did open up a new world of opportunities, which he came to university ready to explore.

What Evan was bitter about, as he admits,

was not so much the fact that my parents had divorced but the fact that my dad . . . I don't think he wanted to take us on. He remarried a really nice woman with two kids of her own, and he never really made time for me and my sister on our own. It was always, we were one big happy family and yet that was never the case . . . I do wish my dad hadn't neglected us and I'm quite sure that if I ever have children, which I'm fairly sure I will, that I never, ever do that. Whatever happens with the respective partners I would never, never let the kids have the impression that I don't care about them or that I'm just spending time with them as a token gesture, because that is how it felt.

Evan is not regretful about the divorce itself, which 'benefited all concerned', but by these signs of his father's lack of caring. In turn, his parents became polarized into two separate individuals representing very different values and, thus, the source of mixed messages.

In Evan's view, his own values owe vastly more to his mother's influence, with his father's often working as a negative point of reference:

the standards I live by and the values I have are a lot of hers and my desire to achieve in life and fulfil my ability are again my mum . . . she's an ardent reader and a very clever woman and she's always wished that she could have gone on to college or university and has always been really proud of the fact that I'm doing it and wants me to do really well with it. That's one of the big things that drive me on.

Conversely, Evan rejects his father's platitudes about 'the harder you work now the less hard you'll have to work for the rest of your life', and identifies more closely with the maternal uncle who made time for Evan and his sister and conveyed the importance of taking 'responsibility for other people', even if they are not your own children.

Sadly, Evan has lost his early closeness to his sister amidst these tensions: 'she has always been more conventional and she's very consumption oriented. She's far more like my dad than my mum. It's quite like polarization in our family I suppose.' Having dropped out of university but then made a good career with high earnings, she loves shopping, sophisticated restaurants and wine bars, but Evan calls this 'a life that I don't see the pleasure in'. He prefers his solitary music which had been, he reflects 'a way of expressing myself and getting it out of me and kind of reaching some form of not so much closure, but almost an escape from your thoughts, a relief from them'. These and his passionate love of nature and rural living, attributed to walking in the countryside with his mother, constitute the remainder of his family heritage.

His mother is the only friend mentioned from his time at home. She promoted his travels, seconded his interest in the environment (though she could not take an active part in the developing-world relief projects that attracted Evan in Latin America) and continued to do so when he began his degree in politics and sociology. With her he had experienced a close and reciprocal relationship: 'I get on really well with Mum and talk to her about anything and everything. I always turn to her when things are bad and I'm always there for her when she needs support. At the same time, being so far apart, our relationship when I'm at university is limited to a phone call... there's just a set pattern of questions that you exchange.' Mother remains 'a friend' and Evan recognizes that his independence is rather rough on her, alone in the house now with only the cats for company but, he concludes, like Riccardo, 'it's sadly how life is and I can't ultimately take responsibility for that'.

In presenting this group of interviewees, Noémia (Mia) has been left until last because her upbringing is the most extreme instance of radical disembedding and yet is a mode of living that is becoming increasingly common. She is one of two daughters of a Portuguese diplomat, whose family have been part of his travelling entourage. They moved from Portugal to the United States when she was three and then to Spain, where her father was posted nine years later: 'we were brought up not thinking we were in one place or meant to stay in one place'. On the one hand, this lack of any stable geographical context meant that she had to confront 'contextual incongruity' as a way of life: 'I've never actually been settled anywhere, it's always been once you get to April/May kind of asking your parents where are we going next year – are we staying or are we going – so if I move somewhere else I don't think I'd be very upset.'

On the other hand, she became technically well equipped for living in globalized society: fluent in three languages and passable in a fourth, holding the International Baccalaureate and educated in the US and at an international school in Spain.

When it came to choice of university, she first had to decide in which country to study and could do so only with the help of her international high school teachers: 'That was kind of a hard choice, because once you have so many choices you get very confused I think.' In other words, Mia had to deal with the situational logic of opportunity very early and the confusion was understandable because she could think solely in terms of current advantages and disadvantages rather than about the realization of her unestablished priorities. She contemplated returning to the US because it was most familiar and continuous with her schooling in English, but knew she would be alone there; she was also drawn to Portugal to discover her 'home' country, but recognized she would have a difficult start, because of its unfamiliarity. Significantly, Spain did not feature as a possibility, despite the fact that she could have remained with her family, because the Iberian educational system was viewed as inferior on the international scale. In other words, it was accepted by all concerned that this was a decision to be taken on instrumental rational grounds, ones that presumed Mia's status as an 'enforced independent'. At school 'they kind of give you the information to do your own decision-making' and she accepted the advantages of enrolling in England, despite the fact that 'I will have to go away, I will miss my parents and things like that'.

Her last sentence is important in indicating both her acceptance of independence and also her acquiescence to the dictates of instrumental rationality. This is underscored by the fact that in the preceding year her mother had undergone a liver transplant and prolonged hospitalization. Mia is undoubtedly concerned about mother's health and makes trips to Madrid if there are any signs of deterioration. Nevertheless, she herself accepts the collateral emotional costs attending rational instrumental action. In her own words, 'I tend to adapt myself better to situations as opposed to trying to change things that I've done but that you can't change.'

Mia's parents have confronted her with the mixed messages emanating from her shifting contexts, but what role have they themselves played? Mainly that of being a fixed point in her moving world or, in Parsonian terms, they constitute a tension management unit: 'We were brought up and taught and we learned to live with each other in the world as opposed to a certain setting.' On the plus side, family members get on well and represent a constancy and stability that Mia values:

my family is very, very important, especially since I've always been far away. I've always been closest to my direct family, my mother and father because they were always the ones – they've always been with me around the crazy background and my sister as well. My sister's now studying in Portugal and my parents are in Madrid, so we're all a bit divided but I still speak to them every day, we're very close even though we've never been physically close . . . They are a big part of keeping me sane.

On the minus side, all members acknowledge that this interpersonal closeness – at a distance – will never entail living in close proximity, in the present or in the future. Mia clearly misses having any 'kind of home base': 'I'd like to go to Portugal and stay there for a year or two, I think, or maybe more. I haven't lived there in a long time and I think it would be good to settle down and not to live out of a suitcase for a while.' Note that she does not think of Madrid and recognizes that she does not really belong in Portugal, so she speaks of it rather as awarding herself a sabbatical in which to discover her home country. This absence is something she chalks up as a deficit in her upbringing, for she says: 'I think that I will get to the point where I will choose something that will help me settle down and look for somewhere to fit in rather than just having that broad sense of global citizenship.'

Nevertheless, Mia recognizes the lack of any stable geographical context in her background as her strength and expects to move around and to work in an international setting. Instead of repining about her rootless inheritance, she acknowledges that: 'the fact that I speak so many languages and have the opportunity to come and study here in the UK has given me many more opportunities than I would have had if I had only lived in one place. And I think opportunities are good in that they give you so many choices.' Undoubtedly, her parents have been responsible for her international outlook but, out of the many futures open to her, one has to be made and that can only be through her own independent deliberations. This is the impact of the reflexive imperative, but 'enforced independence' is a good training school for making one's own decisions – autonomously.

Friendships and relationships: sources of diversion or deflection?

Friendship relations also generate their own emergent properties whose powers – as was seen in Chapter 4 – are capable of deflecting previously established action tendencies and through them the subsequent life course. The question is whether or not autonomous reflexives are equally susceptible to these influences. All relationships entail the confluence of two powers: those that the singular subjects involved bring to them and those emerging from being-in-relation, which may significantly modify the former. Clearly, those attributes – expectations, needs and desires – with which subjects enter any new social relationships have themselves been relationally shaped in prior contexts, the most important at this stage in their lives being those examined in the previous section.

Two features are marked amongst these young autonomous reflexives. Firstly, as a sub-group they are quite distinct from the communicative reflexives. For none of them are the friendships developed at university matters of the highest priority, for none are they of great interpersonal intensity and for none would dependency in friendship be anything but repugnant. On the contrary, rather than the face-to-face bonding, characteristic of communicative reflexives, the friendships formed by autonomous subjects are mediated through their well-developed practical interests and often confined to them. In other words, autonomous reflexives sustain a plurality of uni-faceted friendship networks, linked to different activities and valued largely because they promote these common pursuits and enhance their enjoyment. Indeed, developing multi-faceted friends – as in housemates – can be extremely problematic to them.

Secondly, within the autonomous group, there is a very radical difference between their controlled and controlling approach to friendship and their involvement in 'serious relationships', if any. The latter can neither be uni-faceted nor easily subordinated to some other governing interest, although the interests important to subjects play a large role in their formation. Not only do partnerships require self-investment by the subject, but also the relational goods that are generated by the couple determine what kind of couple they become. The process of becoming a couple, meaning that both parties are committed to the well-being of their relationship, does not have symmetrical effects upon the two. In consequence, this will be shown to be where autonomous subjects come willingly to compromise over the shaping of their lives, to the extent that some may be deflected from the earlier selections that they had believed would be immediately and directly expressed in the next stage of their life courses – most particularly in their career choices.

The group of four interviewees divides into two pairs in these respects: whilst one pair simply regards their friendships as pleasant forms of diversion, the other becomes markedly 'deflected' by the partnerships they begin as undergraduates. Although the latter do not cede their autonomous reflexivity, what is now factored into their internal conversations and also marks their out-workings means that the courses of action they undertake are different from those they would have imagined endorsing prior to becoming part of a couple. Riccardo and Mia constitute the first pair, Adam and Evan the second.

Riccardo goes straight to the point: in the first year 'I didn't really have any good friends' at university, because 'they were so sort of "schooly", there just wasn't really anyone that I could connect with.' Instead, he pursued his practical interests, especially in cars and planned to do a car mechanics course over the summer. In addition, he was a major user of university facilities, continuing to enjoy and give instruction in canoeing and kayaking, as he had done as a sixth former, following up on First Aid and St. John's Ambulance training, and playing rugby and football. However, he was crystal clear that it was the game that mattered: 'We were quite a good team, but what puts me off about here is the social side. It scares me a bit to tell the truth, especially after seeing some of those initiation rites... I like to have a game but I don't really want to get caught up in being labelled a rugby boy, so I gave that one a miss.' Riccardo's new venture was to become Chair of the Staff Student Liaison Committee, which launched him on an undergraduate career of representative functions. Residing on campus after having had the free run of London was 'claustrophobic': 'my relationships in my hall were not fantastic, not because they were bad people, simply because I didn't have the same interests as them. They were into very different hobbies, different pastimes and I got on with them fine but I couldn't go out with them.'

This interest-dominated pattern continues throughout his three years. During this time he never had a long-term relationship, with most of his dating lasting no longer than three to four months: 'the way I see it is there's plenty of time. I think some people really feel that need for security, especially in quite a closed environment here. Some really want that companionship, but I don't feel I need it... There's plenty of time for that.' Instead, his university activities intensified and he became a students' union officer, a faculty representative and a member of the Undergraduate Board of Studies, positions which his instrumental rationality indicated were not irrelevant to enhancing his 'portfolio of skills'. He continued with his sporting life but distanced himself from its 'social side': 'I don't like to be structured, [with people] saying you have to go into training, and then you're in with this group and that means you have to go out with them on this certain night and drink pints out of your shoe and god knows what else.'

Instead, his enduring relationship with the car continued and he acquired one from his own holiday savings, which had repercussions for his friendships. On the one hand, he made interest-based – but again uni-faceted – friends for whom he undertook cheap repairs on campus.

On the other hand, his new wheels meant that he could 'get out of the Warwick "bubble", which does get on top of me sometimes, so having the opportunity to get into the car and go home or go to another university and visit friends is something I've really valued'. Comparing this 'bubble' with his early life in London, he says, significantly, 'my anonymity is quite important'. By this he means 'just not having to deal with people when you don't want to and it seems that's something very difficult to get away from here.' Again, in the second year, his verdict is: 'I do prefer to devote my free time to improving the practical things I'm interested in.'

Daily life improved immensely during his last two years of house-sharing in Leamington Spa and, importantly, provided the setting for Riccardo to develop another practical interest – in cooking, or to be precise, in exploring a 'fusion cuisine' by combining ideas and ingredients from the recipes of his globally dispersed family. Typically for an autonomous reflexive, this is honed and becomes competitive, with Riccardo getting into the final of a TV 'chef of the year' show, which was not irrelevant to his shaping of a life.

His housemates include an old school friend plus three others, which serves to define for him where his friendship lies. Although he tried to play 'the good guy' in his second year, undertaking the cleaning and then organizing it and being sympathetic to those pouring out their troubles, he becomes annoyed by their endless rehearsal of their woes. When he breaks his shoulder in a football game and has his arm in a sling for weeks, their lack of help prompts his full recognition that 'my social life is at home'. He has kept up with many of his public school friends from London, some of whom he has known for fourteen years, and concludes that what has been built up over that period cannot be replaced by sudden and ephemeral relations at university.

Apart from the fact that Mia's pre-university friends are spread all over the world rather than being an hour away, like some of Riccardo's, their friendship patterns are similar in formal respects. Although he had encountered a few snide comments about his Italian surname, having being raised in Britain the ethnocentricism ended there. Conversely, Mia meets with unfriendliness because of her American accent and rejection increases when she tries to explain: 'I find a lot of English students, they're not kind of resentful, but they don't necessarily like it if I say I'm Portuguese, but I've lived in Spain, I've lived in America, I've done this, I've done that. They tend to keep you at a distance.' Increasingly she finds that her friends are also from abroad – a girl from her own school in Madrid and a boy from another international school – and she discovers that there are many Portuguese students around in her second year.

Since languages are Mia's main practical interest, she was instrumental in starting up the Portuguese-speaking society. This seems to have alerted her to other university activities: she became involved in the Politics Society, One World Week,[3] and 'Jail Break', a fundraiser for charity which gives competitors thirty-six hours to travel as far as they can without spending a penny on transport. Because of this, she preferred to live on campus: 'there are always interesting things to do, there are always societies'.

However, many of the international friends she made through these activities would either return home or go to other countries through the Erasmus programme. Mia reckons that 'the friend hunt might have to begin again' in her third year. One of those departing as an Erasmus student is her current boyfriend but she does not seem distressed, given her lifelong experience of comings and goings. Instead, she puts herself forward as the coordinator of the One World Week events, no sinecure in her final year: 'but it will be good, it's a really fun group, all foreigners – interestingly enough there are really few English people that participate in it or care about One World Week.' Thus, Mia will not graduate with a cluster of close friends and those with whom she may remain in contact will be fellow 'internationals' like herself. In other words, her university friends will not have deflected her career plans in the least, whilst her interest-driven involvement in students' union activities that have been her main diversion from work have only served to intensify her 'global citizenship'.

At any stage in life, becoming a couple also stands in a two-way relationship with other groups that are important to the two subjects involved. This is what was accentuated in Chapter 3, with particular emphasis upon how the family and friendship networks jointly and separately evaluated the partnership and acted in positive or negative ways towards it, as was illustrated by Couple A and Couple B. However, as far as friendship is concerned, that presumes a relatively well-established group of friends who pre-exist the relationship between the couple and are retained by them. Part of the social dynamics of the couple is the extent to which these prior networks are adopted as 'our friends', remain 'segregated' or are 'shed'. This cannot be fully examined in these cases because the relationship between the couple is itself still in formation. Therefore, the focus will be upon the other directional influence, namely how the development of a serious relationship (which may or may not prove enduring) filters friendship with others. This filtering is particularly important at

---

[3] This is the students' union's biggest annual event, which features every continent and has a huge range of activities of various kinds.

university – the time for making new friends – and the earlier it occurs the more important its effect tends to be.

In the last pair of subjects examined, this situation did not arise because neither Riccardo not Mia were in any way deflected from the life courses they projected for themselves from entry to university until graduation from it. Certainly, their aims had become more precise over the three years, but their friendships had also remained much as they were prior to university and their growing clarification of their futures owed little to new campus-based friends. It was the interests of this pair that directed the activities in which they participated and thus reinforced the initial proclivities of these two autonomous reflexives and the autonomous nature of their reflexivity. Turning to Evan and Adam, the reverse is the case because the earliness with which both entered into serious relationships appears to have deflected both by reshaping their original intentions.

Evan met his girlfriend after only four months at university and the deepening of their relationship over the rest of their undergraduate careers appears to have worked to the exclusion of other activities and the acquisition of new friends. Evan began university as a rather solitary person, in the sense that he gained most satisfaction from three interests that required little sociability from others for their enjoyment: music, the countryside and travel. Music he admits 'well it's my passion, I didn't want to study it and it doesn't have to be channelled towards getting somewhere with it. To me, the majority of music that actually gets somewhere, in terms of making money, is just awful.' Instead, what he seems to relish is exploring ideas – 'metaphors for the social world' in lone creativity. The same theme permeates his love of the countryside: 'I like being able to escape from the world. What I value most is being able to get in my car and drive to the coast and go for a walk and just be away from everything... being alone with it feels quite magical in a way.' Similarly, as he reflects back over his Peruvian travels, 'not to have shared it with anyone, but to have been entirely alone in that place would just have been really amazing'.

His relationship with Amy has had an impact on all of these interests, despite the fact that they enjoy similar things. By year two he admits, 'I don't really consider playing music as a big part of my life anymore and it's something I'm aware of and kind of sad about... I used to find music really good, as a vent almost... but in terms of self-expression it's not really a medium I use anymore.' This is something he regrets in his final year and resolves to go back to 'later'. However, his own explanation for its interruption is that 'I don't get a lot of time to myself and, particularly when it comes to my music which I still neglect – and I am not pleased that I have done so – but I just don't really have much free time to play with, and when I do, I don't want to use the word "consumed", but it's taken up by my relationship with Amy.'

However, as far as the countryside is concerned, Evan does not miss his solitude: 'I feel as comfortable with her as when I'm on my own, which is something that really astounded me. I kind of realized it over a couple of holidays where we were apart.' Walking had begun with his mother as companion and is now continued with Amy. Long vacations have been spent walking and travelling as far as cash allowed. Despite her fear of flying, which had previously confined her own travels to Europe, she wants to see the world and Evan declares, 'I'm certainly going to encourage her to see it with me'. Thus, with the exception of music, Evan's interests do not appear to have changed significantly.

Neither does his friendship pattern. Not being gregarious and 'liking [his] personal space', he did not enjoy living in halls and says ironically, 'it's a great thing that you meet so many people, but you also have to endure so many people'. He has not participated in any clubs or societies, beyond buying tickets for specific events, and says quite revealingly that these 'are brilliant for people that want an added social dimension to their life, but when you don't feel like that because you've got one, then there's just no need'. That could be read as a commentary upon Mia, whereas Evan is more like Riccardo in having come to value a couple of his school friends more highly, especially one who dropped out of university to enrol in agricultural college on a course in outdoor education and activities: 'that just says it all about university, you really learn a lot about yourself and what you value'.

He expects to stay in contact with only 'a small group, but I've never been one for having massive groups of friends because I like to feel that I really know them, rather than just people I go to the pub with'. On the other hand, he continues: 'but having a girlfriend I've been aware has also meant that my socializing has been kind of narrowed. It's just a big part of my life and has been over the last two years, so although it hasn't stopped me meeting people, I think I haven't followed up on friendships in the same way I would have done.' Given his selectiveness in developing friendships with only those who share the same interests, it seems likely that his relationship with Amy has reduced their number rather than changed their kind. Exactly the opposite is the case for Adam. Equally, Evan and Amy appear to approach necessary selection in ways that are highly compatible with one another. In so far as one can judge an emergent 'we-ness' may be forming on a reciprocal basis.[4] The question is

---

[4] Given that respondents were volunteers from the foundation course in sociology, this study keeps encountering its own limitations, especially the absence of the perspective of the other in these lasting relationships. Although it would have been possible to invite

whether or not this reciprocity can be successfully extended into shaping a life together. Halfway through his course, Evan is already aware that his 'choices are going to be kind of, not dictated, but certainly influenced by what she ends up doing'. Exactly the same is true for Adam.

Adam does not throw himself into the experiences offered by campus activities ('this is my weak point'), partly because many are not particularly new to him, partly because he is a hard worker ('I'm here to do my degree') and partly because the student lifestyle is not very appealing ('I'll buy my prawns and caviar...but then, equally, I won't go out five nights a week...so I don't cut back on things that I enjoy'). Thus, he settles for using the gym and supplementing his income by working some hours in the campus' most upmarket retail outlet. He is comfortable about declaring himself to be gay, but has nothing to do with the gay organization on campus given his belief that gay activism as opposed to being actively gay might damage his career prospects. In this he displays his instrumental rationality: 'I'm not involved in the [campus society for lesbians, gays and bisexuals] because to put that on my CV might count against me.' Adam also shows an acute awareness of the need to work towards complementarity in a serious relationship, even before he has one. Thus, shortly after entering university, he talks about the partnership he desires and what their relation should ideally mean for both: 'I think long-term relationships are much healthier...and I think that person becomes part of you, a part of your priorities. So, essentially you become a unit that has the same priorities, rather than being individuals with priorities that conflict and contrast.'

Eighteen months later, Adam has been in a relationship for over a year (with a student following a humanities course) during which he has also spent time *deliberating* about the complementarity and conflict between his final ends and started to adjust his other relations accordingly. In fact, his preoccupation with gay life permeates all his other relations, activities, friendships and even the choices he makes within his degree course.

Firstly, his sexual orientation is serving to filter out his friendships. To begin with, he reflects, 'when you get to this stage in your life, you sort of narrow down your friends don't you because you really can't stay in contact with all of them and then you make friends that you don't really want to keep and you let them drift'. Other interviewees voice much the same sentiments, regardless of their sexuality, but Adam goes on to detail that he has retained two friends from home, one who is also gay,

these partners for interview, I regarded this as an undue intrusion in their private lives and was further deterred by the ephemeral nature of many student relationships. Quite often, it was only when the subject was about to graduate that it was justifiable to regard their relationship as 'lasting', by which stage it was too late, given the constraints of final examinations.

and describes his two valued university friends who are, like him, then bent on academic careers: 'one in the year above me and then one in the year above that...it's quite odd that they are both gay as well. It's odd because there're millions of students at Warwick – it's a conspiracy.' Well, not really. Given he later describes his partnership as 'the overriding element' this appears to be the sieve that weeded out incongruent friends and only let through compatible ones.

Secondly, Adam is already showing signs that their relationship is becoming his one final end and the architectonic principle governing his response to the necessity of selection. His new-found gay contentment is spilling over to influence all his relations, including that to his degree. This is reflected in the choice of options he makes in the second year and in his plans for his third year dissertation, 'Being gay in the Caribbean', bringing together his early upbringing, enduring love of the islands and islanders, with what he perceives as their homophobia. Is he seeking to become a gay man whose expertise is about gay lifestyles?

Finally, Adam and his partner are on a steep learning curve, at first surprised that the university acknowledges them as a couple in the allocation of accommodation, then irritated to learn about hospital limitations on visiting rights for gay couples, and finally challenged by legislation on civil unions then going through Parliament. The latter has a direct and enabling consequence for shaping a life: 'the fact that that option is there is also an incentive and it means that therefore you can be more stable and you can make long-term plans because it means that you're allowed to make those plans'.

He is aware that this increasing absorption with the various dimensions of gay culture meant that his tendency to filter out friendships with other than gay men had intensified during his final year: 'at uni, because you're so small a minority – it's all a minority sort of mentality isn't it...the religions stick together, the nationalities stick together, homosexuals stick together.' Accepting this, he wants to differentiate within it relationally and very firmly. Thus, he talks at length about his and his partner's repugnance for gay men's obsession with money:

We've noticed one thing, when introduced to an archetypal friend of a friend, the first thing he said to us was "oh yeah you know, I've got a sixty-grand job, forty-grand car, twenty-grand bonus, and it's kind of like "What was your name again?"... Gay men haven't got the kids and stuff going for them, you know how you sort of assert yourself with your family so, now it's "look how much money I've got" and "look how good I look" and "how young I look". And it's image and it's money and of course the two go together because you can spend money on your image...it's very sort of shallow.

Adam reassures himself with the diagnosis that this is mostly true of single people 'because the relationship isn't there'. Given that it is for them, and both are committed to it, he believes they can avoid 'the association of sexuality with money that echoes into everyday life . . . we want money but we're not sort of going to lose ourselves over it'.

He is aware that in shaping their lives together, they have to determine what kind of gay lifestyle they will adopt. Thus to Adam and, it seems his partner, their relationship is to be pivotal in their *modus vivendi*, but this requires a reflexive decision about what social form this relationship will take. Adam is suitably ironic about the 'literature around the whole gay marriage thing – that a gay couple who have married would be more accepted than a gay couple who have not. But, then, the flip side is that the fact that, well, you're not really a gay couple if you're married because part of being gay is that you cannot get married, it's about sort of being different.' Consequently, having discussed this with both Adam's middle-class parents and his partner's working-class parents, all of whom have come through as supportive, they decide upon a civil union in four years' time, in full awareness that you cannot 'take a carbon copy and sort of typex out the dress and just add on a suit and think it's almost a gay marriage'. Adam reflects that 'it's nice that as a couple we've got both family networks to use, so family is definitely still there as a support network.' The hope is that having gone through the ceremony, 'people will accept it as something a bit more' – a bit more stable, definitely monogamous, but they will not mimic heterosexuals.

What then about the relatively new possibility for gay couples to adopt? Is this an impossible question for a twenty-two-year old to answer? Adam has reflexively addressed this issue of future relations and reports the couple to be seriously undecided. What they do contemplate, as a practical contribution they could make, instead of engaging in gay activism, is to foster teenagers thrown out of home for their sexual orientation/activities. By working hard, staying together and, in those respects 'conforming', his hope is that 'people will know us and be like, "oh, they're gay but they're completely normal"'. Obviously he is being ironic, but one cannot live entirely in the ironic mode and he remarks that there will be people to whom 'even the word normal is offensive' in relation to a gay couple. They will pass as clean-cut individuals, as successful young professionals and, to that extent, be both legitimated by but also legitimate the legislation on civil unions. Nevertheless, in what will the 'normality' of their *modus vivendi* consist, given there are no constitutive or regulative rules and norms for the 'gay couple'? Indeed, the project of fostering teenagers of their own orientation may encounter even more dubiety from their neighbours (about 'leading them astray') than adoption (about 'bringing them up oddly'). How is normativity elaborated in the gay couple *qua* couple? For the time being the shape of life that Adam contemplates is that of creating a good, gay role model in the surrounding residential area-to-be. In this project for elaborating norms by example, is Adam prepared for the rebuffs and exclusion that could be encountered and, even more pertinently, is his partner (about whom so little is known here) ready to accept the costs of pioneering, retreating and reformulating? Can they establish a stable, satisfying and reciprocal *modus vivendi*? Certainly, Adam rightly accepts that 'being in a relationship, you know, it's work', but can they work out a complementarity between their careers as the first step towards it?

Careers: the new spirit of social enterprise

The need to select a career, or at least a first post, not only entails exploring the range of appealing opportunities and then narrowing these down to a shortlist of options, but also dovetailing these with the subject's other concerns to reflexively produce a *modus vivendi*, subjectively deemed satisfactory and sustainable. Since autonomous reflexives pronounce themselves to be decisive and well organized, *ceteris paribus* they should make faster headway with the necessity of selection than other groups. This may indeed be the case and two exemplars of it – Riccardo and Mia – will be examined first. However, this pair of subjects is distinctive in having neither a friendship network nor a serious relationship to take into consideration in moving towards completion of the <Discernment – Deliberation – Dedication> scheme. For the two who have entered into serious relationships – Evan and Adam – their task is more complicated because they are already embroiled in trying to shape a life such that their careers and partnerships are complementary rather than representing a conflict between two final ends. Not only is this a more complex and demanding undertaking than simply accomplishing necessary selection, but it may also entail a return to and revision of a provisional, deliberative and selective decision that for the subject alone could have invited his or her *dedication*. As will be seen, these relational dynamics have the power to derail or seriously modify quite well-developed career plans.

However, whether or not subjects press ahead with their career projects or revise them, what is of equal interest is their conception of the ideal appointment and the *desiderata* associated with it. What is distinctive about the autonomous reflexives is that this is the only group whose members (with one exception) are uncritically enthusiastic about employment in corporate enterprise or (inter)governmental bureaucracy. As such, they represent the new cadres for the market and the state, but are significantly different from their predecessors. They are at pains to stress that the rapacious practices of multi-national companies have been transformed (often demonizing McDonald's as the unregenerate exemplar of past bad practice) and to accentuate the *pro bono* works of international organizations and finance. Behind this perception, the stubborn fact remains that within this group are found those most concerned to achieve earnings capable of sustaining an expensive lifestyle, those who find excitement in this type of working environment (compared with academia, which they universally reject) and who have willingly exposed themselves to the stringent competition for entry. Success is then rewarded by attractive incentives to new entrants (the instant visit to New York) and throughout the recruitment process there is a carefully managed process of self-presentation on the part of the company.

Nevertheless, these young subjects are far from lacking in a public service ethic and one task will be to understand how they see this being realized within multi-national for-profit organizations. In other words, their first-person accounts are necessary rather than simply being written off in the third person for their gullibility. Moreover, by taking them seriously new dynamics can be discerned within corporate life, ones that increase its complexity *through* the induction of such recruits who do not endorse the unbridled profit-motive but believe in 'corporate social responsibility'. As such, the entry of autonomous reflexives, especially these undergraduate sociologists who are not masters of mainstream economics, points to an adaptive life-support strategy that protects the main institutions of late modernity despite the advent of nascent morhogenesis.

In addition, these autonomous subjects must be credited with active agency in another respect: they have their own personal agendas. Corporate life is not something to which they have 'sold their souls', if only because it is rarely seen as more than a lucrative staging post for a maximum of ten years. Of course, these interviewees are fallible and may be found unable to resist climbing higher up these greasy poles. Nevertheless, in the ineluctable process of shaping a life, one of their considerations is that the job for life is disappearing and that their other interests can later find full expression. They may be wrong, contingency may intervene, but such expectations must be given their due since what we are trying to understand is their personal motivation – what enters into their reflexive deliberations – when these undergraduates select this option. The four interviewees will be presented in the two pairs – those who are not in a serious relationship and those who are (becoming) couples – as described in the previous section. The former, who confront the necessity of selection alone in making their career decisions, have simpler trajectories because shaping their lives as a whole has been placed in abeyance until after this (not insignificant) first career move has been made.

Riccardo represents an uncomplicated instance of the new spirit of social enterprise amongst the autonomous reflexives. Like every other interviewee in the first year, he had no clear career plans, the difference being that within the first few weeks he says 'I doubt I'll go in for something hugely related to sociology in terms of social work or something, and I do prefer to devote my time to improving those practical things I'm interested in', an opinion he never alters. Instead, the two possibilities he ventures are related to his practical interests: management and sales in the car trade (building upon his positive gap year experience) or joining the police force (which ties into the St. John's Ambulance certificate he is pursuing). Although in relation to both he accentuates 'public service', 'assuming responsibility' and 'making a difference', his approach is instrumentally rational and he quickly moves on to talk, for example, about the fast-track scheme for graduates in the police and the hierarchy for promotion that it opens up. Nevertheless, his social concern is genuine because the next year he applies to become a voluntary community support officer for Warwickshire, yet a 'police special' earns no material benefits and few other than intrinsic ones.

At the same time, the fact that he mentions a management position with a large car retailer shows that he is not averse to corporate life. It is likely that he is signalling something quite other by 'making a difference' than the meta-reflexives' humanitarian meaning. This interpretation is reinforced when he says: 'I'd never like to be doing something that people were protesting against, like an oil company . . . but if you're advising people on the interior design of their new home or something, I think even in that way you're still making a difference to someone, because that's important to them.' In other words, the difference to be made is defined by other people's subjective evaluations more than his own values.

Year two is the fulcrum for Riccardo's immediate future career. From reading about the effects of the Iraq War on oil prices, he became sufficiently interested in banking to apply for summer internships and is remarkably successful, being made offers by both Goldman Sachs and the Deutsche Bundesbank. Having A-level maths was clearly advantageous in the tests, but he thinks that his discussing the relevance of political, economic and social factors, rather than purely financial considerations, was what impressed at interview. Riccardo is unreservedly delighted by the Goldman Sachs offer ('possibly this summer is the beginning of the

rest of my life'), both his parents are proud and he 'found it very stimu-
lating, very exciting, very dynamic, people rushing around on one of the
trading floors. It was somewhere I could definitely picture myself in the
future.'

When asked to specify the attractions more closely, Riccardo detailed
two, the first being an honest admission: 'I think the money for me is
quite a large factor in it' along with the big plus of working in central
London. Secondly, he was impressed by the Bank's projects

for helping the community and building diversity – people at the interviews saying
that on a Thursday afternoon you're told that tomorrow you have the day off and
you're helping to develop a playground in some very, very under-privileged part
of east London and that sort of awareness of having such a huge amount of money
as a company and it being important to allocate part of it to those less fortunate
was very honourable and something that would be important to me.

He hopes that the internship will lead to a job offer and hence considers
that the police is something he will 'now downgrade to a spare time
thing'. Equally, although his passion for car mechanics remains, this has
also ceased to be a vocational project and become a leisure prospect:
'whether I'm working a hundred hours a week as a banker, I'm still going
to want to fiddle about with cars at the weekend'.

Perhaps this should be a time of uncertainty for Riccardo, for a ten-
week vacation internship is not a permanent job offer. In explaining his
confidence, he also reveals his instrumental rationality:

the Deutsche Bank, when I sent them my email explaining why I wasn't taking
them on phoned me and said is there anything we can do to change your mind
and then the lady said: 'well if things don't work out with Goldman's then by all
means please reapply'. So the worst-case scenario is Goldman's say they're not
interested, I can always just turn it a bit and say it didn't work out at Goldman's
and I'd be much more inclined to work for you. So, hopefully it's a win–win
situation.

In his buoyancy, he readily admits, too, that his heavy involvement with
the Undergraduate Board of Studies had been 'a useful experience for
conducting myself in an appropriate manner in a boardroom with university officials, for job interviews and having the confidence to speak
in quite an intimidating atmosphere.' Had this students' union activity
merely been a means to this end? It seems not, because in his final year
he does voluntary work for the university in raising bursaries for potential students from poorer backgrounds. Undoubtedly, he wants to excel
himself, but is also serious about improving the opportunities of others.
Five years later, we have become more familiar with this outlook if the
Coalition government's 'big society' is taken at face value.

Early in his final year, he is made and accepts a full-time offer from Goldman Sachs and is excited by the promise of an immediate trip to New York. When I question him quite closely about his evaluation of their social initiatives, his reply is ambiguous:

well, what we actually ended up doing, with having so many of us, we donned Wellingtons and we cleaned the Thames for a day, just clearing the banks. It wasn't massively effective I don't think – it was more a tool for them to see how people worked out of the office and how they got on with each other, but I really enjoyed it and I think later you get a lot more choice as to what you do – I mean painting schools or helping kids.

I press further and ask if this was simply shop-window dressing and am told 'what appeals to me is the company ethos towards it, it's not like a sideline you know, wave the card and say "we do this". It is a genuine commitment from what I've seen to reinvesting back in the communities that they work in. That's quite important for me, I wouldn't really be able to work for a McDonald's.'

Riccardo admits to the attractions of the money, the glamour, the excitement of working on the high wire, but he believes that without authentic social reinvestment policies, he wouldn't want to be in banking. As a Goldman Sachs' ambassador to Warwick for those taking up internships the next summer, he is undoubtedly spreading the message but he is also living it out with his charitable endeavours for the university, as a different kind of corporation: 'Money's quite important to me but I also believe in a sort of redistribution of wealth as well, sort of charity-wise doing things to support people'. We will find that Evan could not disagree more with this charitable approach. In other words, there is no uniformity amongst autonomous reflexives in their new-found aim of injecting a social conscience into the institutions of modernity.

Keen as Riccardo is about his future in banking, he respects the reflexive imperative and feels he should keep another option open. Thus, the second string to his bow is his desire to open his own restaurant. This has the familiar attraction for autonomous reflexives of 'being the one in managerial control' and the more novel appeal of its 'social aspect of contact with the public'. However, 'if in two years' time I find that I really love banking and I'm moving on upwards, then fantastic, I hope in many ways that does happen'. Since these 'two years' took us to the height of the financial crisis, perhaps it is as well that Riccardo is responsive to the situational logic of opportunity.

The noteworthy point is that Riccardo had given undivided priority to realizing his first concern – success at work – uncomplicated by considerations about shaping a life, which had been shelved until later. Exactly the same is true for Mia. Given her parental background, it would be deceptively easy to read the outcome of her undergraduate years as simple social reproduction effected by familial social capital. However, that would be to miss out on the internal reflexive process and the need to respond to the situational logic of opportunity, which was vastly different from in her diplomat father's younger days. In fact, Mia spends her time at Warwick addressing the necessity of selection, both seeking out and then narrowing down her options.

This is a well-known problem for her. It began at school through taking the International Baccalaureate and proving equally good at biological sciences and social science: 'I think I've always had a great deal of options – there are too many things I would want to study'. She resolved this through her greater interest in 'anything to do with international relations, something to do with the world at large', and plumped for her politics and sociology degree. When I raise the possibility of working for a UN agency, Mia agrees 'I've been brought up in that sort of environment, like when I was in New York my parents had friends that worked for the UN'. However, she expresses more interest in international research and, surprisingly, adds: 'I think now is the time to see new things that you can do that you didn't expect to find'. In other words, those are new openings to which she has not already been introduced by her family.

The only career about which she has been negative is academia for – despite eventually graduating with a first-class degree – she believes she lacks the creativity for lone research, finds difficulty in maintaining the focus and drawing the threads together. Moreover, she wants 'to make a difference in some people's lives', to which she sees theoretical research making no direct contribution. Mia can get no further in her first year than expressing an interest in 'investigative research' within a company or research team: 'I would tend to take a humanistic approach to everything, but I do tend to be very practical'.

Over the next two years Mia gradually narrows down her selection whilst pursuing direct knowledge of new opportunities by attempting to gain an internship in the EU civil service. Although this is 'virtually impossible to get into, I think 7,000 applicants for 600 places', she knows people who have had them and the attraction is being able to nominate three departments in which to gain work experience. She has chosen the European Commission over returning to Portugal, despite her desire to discover her home country and be with her sister and large extended family, 'because [paid] Portuguese internships do have a sort of slave driving motif, but if you're unpaid they might just make you do photocopying all day'. Mia also declined a job offer from a friend who had been in Warwick and returned to Portugal to establish an organization to overcome gender discrimination in primary schools. This would have offered the practical usefulness she wants and relocated her where she would most like to be. She has also chosen it over the College of Europe, which her uncle attended, because she was unsure of the modules for which to enrol in terms of their relevance.

In sum, Mia is prepared to undertake end-on internships, 'jumping around' as she puts it, to discover precisely what kind of policy research best suits her. As she reiterates, 'I have a lot of choices, but I'm not quite sure yet'. She thinks this may be the social committee within the Commission because this conforms both to her self-assessment and desire for useful public service: 'I always thought of myself as a much more practical person and I think if I'm working with people and kind of for people, I'll be much more satisfied or gratified.' Mia has successfully narrowed down her options, but will not finalize her choice until she has had hands-on experience. Finally, I ask if the EU's reputation for bureaucratic regulation and volume of paperwork is not a deterrent and her reply is: 'Yes, it does worry me. I think this is why I really need to go and try and do it, but I think I might actually enjoy that to some extent – practical in the sense that it's actually creating something. I might actually enjoy being behind a desk with lots of paperwork!'

It is significant Riccardo and Mia, as autonomous reflexives with a sense of public service, believe they can realize these goals within existing international financial and European bureaucratic institutions. In other words, the market and state institutions of late modernity appeal to them, implying that the opportunities for autonomous subjects are morphing in a manner compatible with their modified aspirations. Clearly, the recruitment of such candidates is unproblematic since the competitiveness in gaining entry has been underlined. Moreover, not only do they legitimate these institutional developments by simply participating in them, they also become agents for information and proselytism.

Mia has repeatedly made reference to the experience of her family and friendship network, whose occupational reproduction she has declined, but in so doing she has added a new outlet to the repertoire of recommendations that younger members of her international circle will consult as serious possibilities and about which they will have access to insider knowledge. Riccardo has gone even further by assuming the role of ambassador for international finance on campus. Effectively he has become part of the recruitment team for Goldman Sachs before even becoming a permanent employee! This can be seen as quite a canny move on the part of the bank because he will speak (in his third year) as an independent student who is giving an objective assessment of his ten-week experience as an intern. He will do so, not as someone from the business school, but as a sociologist presenting this opportunity to an extended category of potential applicants. Significantly, in Chapter 7, we will meet Yasmin who became a member of Riccardo's seminar on internships and followed him into Goldman Sachs.

In turning to Evan and Adam, the interest is twofold. Do they share this pursuit of a career in the market and bureaucracy of late modernity with the pair just discussed? Does the fact that each is in a serious partnership serve to modify the single-mindedness of their career planning, since both are dealing *simultaneously* with the necessity of selection and their first attempts at shaping their lives?

Evan gives a categorical answer to the first question, illustrating the diversity of autonomous reflexives, particularly since their values have begun to exceed the competitive logic of modernity and have also extended the range of employment opportunities that are correspondingly entertained by them. He could not be more direct: 'although I need to start earning some money, I don't want to go and work for any of the financial organizations that wander around Warwick trying to entice students in with their offers of high salaries. I can't think of anything worse to be honest.' This comes directly from reflecting on his own experience of working part-time in a high-street bank before entering university:

just being at that level and seeing how unethical it is – no, it's not something I want to do. I had problems with the management at that age because I wasn't very willing to force mortgages and loans upon the old dears that frequented the branch . . . they don't need these foisted on them and I found it so exasperating being expected to say "would you like a credit card with your twenty pounds?". You know they don't want it and you also know it's perhaps quite dangerous for them to have it. We have such a spiralling debt crisis at the moment and it's because of these unethical practices, so the last thing I want to do is that.

This he said in the same year that Riccardo was acting as Goldman Sachs' ambassador on campus.

In the first year (before he has entered a relationship) Evan can be no clearer about his future career than saying: 'I'd like a job that gives me some scope for creativity and enables me to create things that will benefit or educate people or enable people to understand things . . . I'd like to do something that enables me to create in a way rather than just push paper.' Thus, it seems as though Mia's preference would be no more congenial to him. Is this a modest way in which a first-year student hints that he is attracted to academic life? Certainly not, as he is quite explicit the following year, despite having received encouragement from his teachers and eventually graduating with a first-class degree:

I'm quite a bookworm and I do enjoy studying but I don't really feel that I'm cut out for a career in academia. I find I'm quite driven with it, but I do find the lack of a result quite frustrating... If I was going to pursue a career in it I would be asking to be funded, expecting to read these various people and then discuss their thoughts. I wouldn't be producing any result other than literature of which there is already quite an abundance.

Evan wants a combination of creative thinking and practical results in the outside world rather than remaining within the enclosure of academia, which to him is 'a bubble that takes over everything'.

By the second year he has become much more decisive and begun narrowing down his *desiderata* for a satisfying career that would ideally combine work and long-haul travel or, at least, allow plenty of time for travelling. Thus he surprises both of us by pronouncing in favour of secondary school teaching: 'I'd genuinely consider it, which I never thought I'd find myself saying'. He is frank that this is influenced by his partnership and the need for the two of them to select complementary careers: 'I have no desire to part with Amy at any time in the future and thus my choices are going to be – not dictated – but certainly influenced by what she ends up doing.' It is important to note that his commitment to them as a couple *precedes* his reflexive dedication to a career, but is the same true of her, such that their decisions will be conjoint and compatible? It seems that Amy has concluded her own career deliberations earlier and without recognition of the reciprocity involved in being a couple. At least, that is what I derive from Evan's very forthright statement: 'I've been forced into thinking long term by my partner. She loves her books, she's an academic through and through and so she's looking forward to doing a Master's degree. Because she's applying in September, I've been forced, confronted with it and challenged with things I would have perhaps put off.'

By the start of his final year and having already gained some teaching experience, Evan immediately enrolled for a Postgraduate Certificate in Education (PGCE). Does this mean he has rescinded his prior aim of working in the developing world because of his relationship? This he denies: 'it remains a commitment in terms of the work I'm looking to do'. Initially, he appears to deal with this issue by mental postponement, as have other autonomous reflexives who envisaged staying in their first type of employment for a limited period: 'going into teaching it's something I do with the idea of stepping out of later on... I wouldn't like to spend the rest of my life in it because there's so much out there and I really want to try other things.' However, this is not another and perhaps pious hope about 'later on' because Evan has thought through a strategy, recognizing that 'there's a lot of opportunity to combine the two in teaching – reaching those places and working in aid projects at the same time'. Again, is this project a rationalization in the light of his relationship?

It is certainly consonant with the latter, but Evan has other reasons for endorsing it: he needs to be earning quickly, he requires the qualification and he wants some classroom experience and responsibility in school because he envisages implementing his project under his own steam rather than under the auspices of a charity. He has two evaluative reservations about charitable interventions: that 'they're almost patronizing in their approaches' and 'often, they're just mopping up the symptoms rather than addressing the roots of the problem'. As he puts it, 'I'm very much of the independent school' and thus, independently, he wants to 'give people the chance to help themselves, I think that's hugely important in developing countries through, for example, encouraging them to bring derelict land into cultivation and thus to evade exploitation by the multi-nationals'. Hence, he concludes: 'Teaching was a profession I chose because it gave me flexibility and scope so that I can ensure that I can move around with it' even though he is aware that he will doubtless soon find plenty to malign about professional practices.

In articulating this project, he displays the independence typical of autonomous reflexives and he fully acknowledges his instrumental rationality: 'trying to do things for future benefit – instrumental rationality and all that, permeates my thinking, it has to happen . . . it just dominates the world – the idea of means and ends, calculations and rational choice logic, you know, costs and benefits'. Moreover, he frankly admits that he also applies this in his relationship with Amy, since he has enrolled for his PGCE in Exeter (preferring the curriculum) whilst she will begin her postgraduate study in York: 'I wanted to do what's best for me even though I'm fully aware that it will put a bit of a strain on a relationship that's been very intimate over the last two years due to our sheer proximity, but I have no doubts, I'm confident that it will be fine because we're close – it should work out, no problem at all.'

This is Evan's view and we don't know Amy's. From his standpoint he has made a considerable contribution to their future together by accepting to become a teacher, to work in the UK for a few years in order to gain experience (whilst she finishes her PhD?) and to join her in York after this year spent apart. However, has he fully taken her longer-term perspective into account? As he discusses Amy's (short-term) career concerns, these focus exclusively on her PhD. She will be working on medieval literature and Evan says, 'she absolutely loves it . . . she'll be excellent at it, she'll really excel at it'. Yet, if she does, will she be ready to leave British academia to work overseas with Evan? This would be a possible career move for her – though not the easiest or perhaps the most advantageous given her specialism – but it is one that would be compatible with the realization of Evan's own concerns. Their future as a couple partly hinges upon Evan's project not being frustrated and his future career not reducing to a lower-status teaching job than that of his partner, if she becomes a successful academic, or yielding diminishing satisfaction for him if he remains in this country. Yet, Amy's specialism does not travel readily. Therefore, the next stages of Evan's trajectory – both interpersonal and in relation to his work concerns – turn entirely upon the willingness and success of the two in shaping a life together.

A similar and growing preoccupation with establishing complementarity between his career and his partnership is the case for Adam who tries to work his way towards Charles Taylor's 'unity of life' over his undergraduate years. Central to this quest for an eventual *modus vivendi* was the development of one particular relationship that he gradually promoted to being his ultimate concern (his one final end). Correspondingly, he actively monitored other relations, including his own reflexive relationship to his future career, in order that they complemented rather than contradicted the shape of life that he sought to establish as satisfying and, to the best of his (fallible) judgement, to render sustainable. Helpfully, for presenting how he tackles this, each of Adam's three years approximates to a particular phase of the DDD scheme, and these are given as his 'first-person account' of his own reflexive consideration of his concerns *in terms of his relations* – as he *sees* them, *evaluates* them and *acts* towards them.

His first year represents the *discernment* of a confident and articulate nineteen-year-old, who has begun to 'pick and mix' from the array of mixed messages derived from his culturally diverse and geographically mobile family background plus his own biographical experiences. He enrolled for sociology rather than law (for which he can later do a conversion course) largely out of respect for the situational logic of opportunity: 'I think people always want to have lots of options'. Simultaneously, he acknowledges the necessity of selection because to him 'thinking about the fourth year is in fact thinking about the next ten or twenty years.' At this time, his degree is listed as his prime concern. He has not completed, but has made a start on binding selection by logging in three career options for further scrutiny: postgraduate study, teacher training or a law conversion course. Planning is mandatory to Adam at this point: 'I'd like to know what I'll be doing at the end of my three-year degree; I want to know where I'll be living in the future. It's not necessary that this has to happen, but if you have a list of options, even if in the end you choose option number three, you've still attained your goal.'

He will use instrumental rationality in his planning, as is typical of autonomous reflexives: 'to plan is about how I think it's going to benefit me in the long run'. Further information will be acquired 'when I can see some sort of benefit other than just purely knowing a bit more about it'. Thus, in his first year his reflexive deliberations are confined to himself and he makes no reference to relational considerations. Indeed, he goes further: 'I think that for someone who's going to be single, it's either job or family. For me I think I'd rather have the job, the career and the lifestyle and be completely selfish rather than having to worry about kids.' Nevertheless, he volunteers an anecdote that reveals he is far from resistant to promoting the importance of relationships. He was working on a school essay at home, when visited by a young school mate who had ridden round to show him her new pony. Instead of annoyance at the interruption he recalls that 'I was perfectly willing to sacrifice the homework to form a new social bond'. This was to be the leitmotif of his next two years at university.

Eighteen months later, Adam has been in a relationship for over a year, which he has also spent *deliberating* about the complementarity and conflict between his final ends. He has also begun to adjust his friendship relations accordingly, as was seen in the previous section. His major tension is between his future career and his partnership, even though he has the insight to recognize that pursuing different careers is preferable for him and his partner, 'because I'm quite competitive – it's perhaps down to power . . . I think about things a lot because I want to make sure I have the upper hand'. This attitude eroded as he began to realize and re-evaluate what being in a relationship implied if he and his partner were to become a couple.

At the same time, his interest in sociology intensified, he had 'cut down on other [career] options', was talking to his tutor about the ways and means of taking an MA and then a PhD, and had set his sights on gaining a first-class degree, having concluded that upper seconds are 'standard issue'. Simultaneously, Adam and his partner were both confronted by the new possibility of a civil union. How does this prospect for their relationship – which now does include a civil union – impact upon Adam's career project? That it does, he is becoming aware: 'Because I'm in a long-term relationship . . . I think it probably makes a difference. I think that probably links into what you're doing with your degree.' Objectively, there is no *prima facie* incompatibility about Adam becoming an academic and his partner pursuing a career in corporate accountancy, beyond clashes of geographical location, as for all other dual career couples.

However, Adam is already showing signs that their relationship is becoming his one final end and that everything else should be subordinated to it, his career included. Clearly, his new-found gay contentment is starting to operate as an architectonic principle and is beginning to order and reorder all his relations, precisely in order to shape his nascent *modus vivendi*. For example, he now rules out a return to the Caribbean because of the difficulties of living there as gay men. In his own words: 'there's more at stake and therefore you have to sort of work harder on the things that matter but, obviously, there are more things that matter right now'.

The last interview, taking place a month before he graduated from university, has a leitmotif of *dedication* that Adam almost voices as his motto: 'me and [my partner] are focussing our lives around us, again it's to do with priorities'. This means that his own career is no longer 'competing' as a final end but has dropped to second place in his concerns. It is not surprising that having written his dissertation on the topic planned, he feels rather surfeited with 'gay sub-cultures' and 'needed a break' rather than going on to write a PhD on a similar theme. Instead, he has applied unsuccessfully to eleven graduate schemes in sales and marketing largely 'because my mum did advertising for years and I quite like the whole thing about thinking outside the box'. He was usually let down by his maths, despite his partner trying to coach him, and received the generic message that he 'lacked experience' and 'business awareness'.

What is significant is the type of companies he targeted, ones specializing in either 'cosmetics or cocktails', believing that he could promote 'things like beauty products and alcohol, because they actually relate directly to my biography... something that is important to you or that relates to you as a person'. Adam voiced no great interest in such work but dwelt rather upon the relevance of his background knowledge: 'I know quite a lot about the cosmetic round and stuff, probably because, I mean it's not your sexuality, but you know how to use a product.' In other words, not only has he demoted his career as a concern but is also trying to tie it in with his gay lifestyle, unlike his partner.

The couple are moving to London, where his partner's job is based, but Adam admits that he recently made the following laconic entry in his diary: 'in a few months' time get a job'. Whilst this turns out to mean gaining work experience that supplies 'corporate awareness' before re-applying to international corporations, he also admits that if he enjoys a post he might remain in it for several years. Moreover, instead of narrowing down his future career he now introduces the idea of becoming a graduate estate agent and also reverts to the notion of teaching. What has happened to all that first-year ambition and desire for an extravagant lifestyle? It has taken a back seat to his personal relationship, his partner having landed the position he sought in corporate accountancy:

> it is quite an anxious situation but the comfort is the fact that my partner's got a job with X so financially, I won't have to work . . . because his salary's quite good in corporate tax . . . so it could be that we arrive in London and then I'll find a job once we're there. So, I've got to the running joke that I'm going to sit at home, go to the gym and like, you know, just be a housewife. But, obviously I'll get a job because what's the point of having a degree?

Doubtless he will, if only because he thinks he would suffer from 'cabin fever' without one.

However, it seems likely that it will be his work that is accommodated to his partner's. Given that the latter has both coached and encouraged Adam to re-apply for graduate schemes, there is nothing to indicate that he seeks the subordination of Adam's career or that he would not prefer an egalitarian relationship between two successful young professionals. Conversely, Adam seems caught in an undergraduate time trap. When I ask him how he sees life, if all goes well, ten years later on he says: 'basically it's see where it goes, but I think as it stands sort of just lift us up, take us to London, put us down and replace degree with job and the rest you know'. On the contrary, I could not even guess.

What has emerged from the contrast between Riccardo and Mia, on the one hand, and Evan and Adam, on the other, is that autonomous reflexives appear to advance unproblematically as single people, whose fundamental individualism is unimpeded as they select their careers. Perhaps for this group, Riccardo is correct that there should be 'no hurry' in forming serious relationships. Perhaps he is right *qua* autonomous reflexive to separate the two tasks, tackling the necessity of selection first and postponing the shaping of a life until one's career is established. Right, that is, unless the career can be 'our career' as with Couple A in Chapter 3. Otherwise, autonomous reflexives do not appear adept at dealing with the plural final ends that are inescapable if and when they seek to become a couple. When they attempt to counter their individualism by subordinating their own goals, they seem to do so unilaterally, without establishing what kind of reciprocity the other entertains or would welcome. They prefer to make assumptions and presumptions in an individualistic manner that may find them later disillusioned. The autonomous reflexive seems better fitted to a relationship between two individuals than seeking to be a couple generating relational goods. The former was their experience in their own families and also was the dominant pattern of modernity.

Conclusion: the future of autonomous reflexivity

The old European leaders of the world economy are now residual manufacturers, increasingly reliant on their financial services to generate GDP and on their public services to provide employment. Given that shift, what is the motivational attraction for young graduates to join the financial or public service sectors? Since entry to them in Europe is extremely competitive, what can be distilled from this chapter about the motives of young autonomous reflexives, their origins and outlooks, which lead them to form the bulk of these applicants? More speculatively, what does this indicate about the future of autonomous reflexivity itself and its dialectical relationship with the institutional structure of late modernity in the future?

Firstly, their family relationships and also the relations they themselves contract appear to make two important contributions to the likely durability of autonomous reflexivity as a significant mode of practice. In other words, there are reasons to believe that the pool of willing recruits to graduate positions in financial services and public administration will not start to dry up but will tend to augment.

On the one hand, this is because the making of current young autonomous reflexives has been traced back to their positions as 'enforced independents' because of their parents' own changeable, fragile or broken relationships. These natal backgrounds supplied neither relational goods nor normative consensus, and the independence induced in their offspring was immediately deployed to sieve parental values and lifestyles for what was deemed worthy of retention. Given the increasing rates of divorce, separation and re-partnering together with relatively novel arrangements such as 'living apart but together', Europe appears to guarantee a continuing output, if not growth, of 'enforced independents' in the coming decades.

On the other hand, it is because some of these young autonomous reflexives appear more concerned to establish their careers first and not to be distracted from the pursuit of this goal by friendship or serious relationships, which coincides with the European tendency to marry later.[5] These appeared to be the readiest recruits to internships in both public bureaucracy and financial services. Others who contracted partnerships during their undergraduate years were distracted but seemingly undeterred from the same type of career destination. In other words, late modernity does not appear about to suffer from a crisis in recruitment

[5] Data is available for marriage alone. Civil unions are too new for trends to be discernable and, obviously, there are no records of lasting partnerships.

because of a shortage of autonomous reflexives – if only because of the 'rocky' state of marriage itself.

Secondly, such recruits are both the cause and the effect of the shift away from market brutalism and state authoritarianism in the last two decades of the twentieth century. Prior to the mid-eighties and nineties, Donati had analysed the manifestations of the opposition between market and state as the oscillation between '*lib*' and '*lab*' politics.[6] Polity directed 'lib' changes favoured market competition whilst 'lab' egalitarianism fosters wealth redistribution in the interests of social justice and stability. It was precisely because of this alternation that most of the social institutions of late modernity had staggered on in Europe from the end of the Second World War. The occupational outlets of previous generations of autonomous reflexives were in either the market or the state, precisely because both were predicated upon the *individualism* that is highly consonant with autonomous subjects.[7]

Until the 1980s 'lib' politics continued to give unabashed support to neo-liberal economics, going beyond the taming of the trade unions to accepting the growth of multi-national corporations and deregulated foreign exchange dealings by the banks. Moreover, the market model was also upheld as without equal for delivering efficiency in such crucial institutions as education, health care and the social services. But efficiency is not value free; within 'lib' thinking, it depends upon competition and choice. Above all, it results from the foundational concept of the subject as *homo economicus* on which neo-liberalism is grounded: we are all held to be bargain hunters seeking to maximize our individual preferences in the various institutional markets, such as health or education. We are customers or clients out for the best deal and thus are in competition with other parents or sick people for a school place or a hospital bed. In 'lib' politics we are presumed to be – or encouraged and induced to become – *homo economicus* and the autonomous reflexive is his exemplar of rational man who pilots his way through the world on the basis of instrumental rationality.[8]

'Lab' politics continued to rely upon state intervention, increasingly under the guise of its 'more acceptable face', namely bureaucratic regulation in the name of fairness. In a pre-recession 'affluent society',

[6] Pierpaolo Donati, *Introduzione alla sociologia relazionale*, Milan, FrancoAngeli, 1983 (6th edn 2002) and *Teoria relazionale della società*, Milan FrancoAngeli, 1991.

[7] Margaret S. Archer, 'The Current Crisis: Consequences of the Four Key Principles of Social Doctrine', in José T. Raga and Mary A. Glendon (eds.), *Crisis in the Global Economy – Re-planning the Journey*, Vatican City Press, 2011.

[8] Margaret S. Archer, *Making our Way through the World*, Cambridge University Press, 2007.

'excellence for all' became the new clarion call and 'stakeholders' and 'shareholders' the new versions of citizens. Yet, 'excellence' was not a value free term either because it was defined by the government's own 'performance indicators'. Given the growing deficit in social solidarity, few traditional professional groups resisted their imposition. Indeed, since funding depended upon 'performance', many autonomous reflexives found an appeal in these new managerial positions executing national regulations. As occupants of closely prescribed roles, policed by annual reviews, they became *homo sociologicus*, the executors of role expectations now known as 'human resources', but with considerable individual powers within component institutions.

When political centrism intensified in the last decades of the twentieth century, European politics shifted to produce the first 'lib'/'lab' governments, generated through compromise and concession, and with little effective dissent except from some regional nationalists and nascent 'greens'.[9] Of particular interest to sociologists was Anthony Giddens' *The Third Way*, although it was not unique in its attempt to 'transcend' right/left politics by a compromise between market capitalism and democratic socialism.[10]

However, what has not often been signalled is its continuity with the individualism of both 'lib' and 'lab' political philosophies as underlined above. Of course this is called 'the new individualism', and immediately embraces Ulrich Beck's model of the self-constituted individual.[11] From this perspective, the recent shedding of tradition merely ends in a further compromise between self-expressive autonomy and necessary contractual obligations. Today's autonomous reflexives are children of the Third Way, of the lib/lab game now being played out in collaboration, conciliation and coalition between state and market. As causes, the new social concern of young autonomous reflexives is a distant echo of old 'lab' preoccupations, whilst their financial interests resonate with traditional 'lib' thinking. These young subjects, like their 'lib/lab' political leaders have melded the two together in what I have termed the 'new spirit of social enterprise'. They manifest variations, even among this tiny group of interviewees, with Evan situated closer to the 'lab' pole and Riccardo closer to the 'lib' pole, as is also the case for many in what remains of party politics. Nevertheless, the overriding tendency was for the 'social'

---

[9] Maurice Duverger, 'The Eternal Morass: French Centrism', in Mattei Dogan and Richard Rose (eds.), *European Politics*, London, Macmillan, 1971.

[10] Anthony Giddens, *The Third Way*, Oxford, Polity Press, 1998. The divide between right and left politics is tenaciously defended by Noberto Bobbio, *Right and Left*, Cambridge, Polity Press, 1996.

[11] Giddens, *The Third Way*, p. 35ff and p. 36.

and the 'enterprise' components to be held together in their own versions of a *via media* – their personalized but still individualistic Third Ways.

In turn, these young autonomous reflexives staff and support both sets of institutions – those of the market and of the state as represented by financial services and public services – encouraging them to continue morphing in mutual compatibility and coalition. In consequence, both increasingly present the career opportunities they offer as ones giving equally strong endorsement to the combination of social entrepreneurship and social regulation. The amalgam termed 'social enterprise' was initially prompted by social movements and brokered between failing political parties and non-productive economic corporations rather than by the aggregate expectations of their new recruits. Nevertheless, as representatives of the new corporate social responsibility and of the new-found social conscience of regulatory administration start to take themselves seriously – despite some enduring bad faith – new appointments will be made accordingly. Thus, the autonomous reflexives find a ready home and feel thoroughly at home in these institutions of late modernity.

This compatibility means that autonomous reflexives will not fade away and, indeed, their ranks may grow at the expense of the communicative reflexives. In the immediate future they will provide aggregate support for the institutions that embody the new spirit of social enterprise in Europe, hence delaying the emergence of morphogenesis unbound and continuing to obscure the lineaments of any fully morphogenetic society.

6   Meta-reflexives: critics of market and state

Meta-reflexivity is the dominant mode of internal deliberation intimately associated with nascent morphogenesis. During the transitional period, which straddles the start of the new millennium, this mode of internal conversation is poised to overtake the practice of autonomous reflexivity induced by modernity and complementary to both its situational logic of competition and the institutional hegemony of market and state. Such is the thesis advanced in the present chapter and illustrated with reference to the life histories of subjects interviewed. To defend it involves a convincing demonstration of *how* meta-reflexivity is fostered by the situational logic of opportunity and *that* responses to it are positive towards the further unbinding of morphogenesis and negative towards buttressing the institutional complex of modernity.

Such a defence has to reveal the processes responsible because otherwise the thesis would remain merely a Weberian claim about elective affinity. Thus, as in each of the four empirically based chapters of the present book, it is necessary to identify the distinctive natal relationships that constitute the generative mechanism of this particular reflexive mode even though their effects can and often will be overridden by countervailing influences. It is inadequate – because empiricist – simply to show that meta-reflexives constituted the largest proportion of the student intake examined, representing 38.9 per cent at point of entry, even if any claim could be made that these particular entrants are representative of their age cohort – as is obviously not the case.[1]

Only slightly more persuasive is the finding that this sub-group largely succeeds in retaining its members and is also a net recruiter, with the proportion of its practitioners rising marginally (to 40 per cent) by the end of their second year as undergraduates. Although the sheer volume

---

[1] Because it was established on the same basis (using ICONI and in-depth interviews conducted by the same interviewer) this figure of 38.9 per cent can be compared with the 22.7 per cent found for the all-age, stratified sample of Coventry residents in Margaret S. Archer, *Making our Way through the World*, Cambridge University Press, 2007.

of meta-reflexives present as well as the ability of this mode to retain its practitioners and to add to them may be indicative of the growing importance of this modality amongst the young and educated, it may equally reflect self-selection amongst those electing to study sociology or be restricted to those entering university at that time.[2]

It follows that providing any substantiation for the bold opening theses falls squarely upon the qualitative interview data. This will carry more conviction the better it succeeds in identifying the processes operative in the natal relational backgrounds that have prime responsibility for the initial proclivity towards meta-reflexivity. However, before plunging into biographical analysis it is vital to convey the phenomenological feel of becoming a tyro meta-reflexive and how this differs from the kinds of reflexive practice examined in the two preceding chapters and the one to follow. The key to its experiential core is that *far from the social order being internalized or normalized, it is peculiarly problematized* for those who come to practise meta-reflexivity. It is this that makes them particularly open to the situational logic of opportunity and it stems directly from the particularities of their relational experiences in the family.

These young subjects have effectively been precipitated into the necessity of selection early in life because their selective and critical faculties have been unintentionally honed by their family lives. Whilst still at school they evidence interests and activities that represent proto-commitments, ones that are later refined rather than being retracted. In other words, they come to university with 'vocations' in the making, meaning that such subjects use their undergraduate years more than most others for shaping their lives. Furthermore, what I have termed their proto-commitments are also early exercises in social critique. There is (almost) nothing that they seek to replicate from their natal backgrounds and there is nothing at all, amongst the opportunities open to them, that they seize upon because it can be an opening to objective social advantage in the future. This distinguishes them respectively from the communicative and autonomous reflexives.

Unlike the communicative reflexives, these subjects are aliens to normative conventionalism. As such, they are the antithesis of those (examined in Chapter 4) who wanted to live up to contextual expectations, meaning that one of their frequent anxieties about entering university regardless of their class origins was not knowing what was expected of an

---

[2] Please consult the Methodological appendix for directly comparable work on entrants to other disciplines in faculties other than sociology. It seems self-evident that university entrants after the spending cuts and increases in tuition fees announced in 2010 are likely to be significantly different in socio-economic terms, which will be manifested first amongst the cohorts entering in 2011or 2012.

undergraduate. On the contrary, when entering university young meta-reflexives declared themselves to be immune to group pressure and indifferent to group expectations, whether these stemmed from the natal background or the student collectivity. Part of their difficulty with the social order is that they would like to proclaim themselves to be individualists, yet are uneasy and queasy about endorsing individualism. Epistemologically they are not yet able to articulate why exactly they shy away from full-blooded individualism but are inchoately aware that the causes to which they are drawn are inimical to it – as all come to recognize during the course of their degree.

Underpinning these attitudes is the fact that they are 'loners' rather than individualists. To understand the origins of this distinctive social orientation, developed prior to university entry, it is necessary to explore why their family relations had produced disengagement in these young subjects, one which temporarily hampered their sociality without fundamentally crippling it. *Qua* loners, they are clear about what they do not want, which is any personal version of social reproduction. Thus, a major consequence of their critical disengagement from their natal backgrounds is their adoption of an *exploratory outlook* towards the social.

They approach the social order interrogatively rather than through a repertoire of internalized responses that have already divided up the social world into what should be shunned and what sought. Certainly, they do shun many attitudes and activities that lie (uncomfortably) close to many family practices and proclivities, although they may adopt and accentuate a particular strand encountered in the home background. However, it is crucial to emphasize that it is *familial relations* rather than the outlooks of the particular parents that are the root causes of subjects' disengagement. This is evidenced by the fact that all young meta-reflexives want their own imagined families to be distinctively different in this key respect.

Correspondingly, their quest is for 'difference' rather than for the 'similarity' and 'familiarity' after which the communicatives crave and also need in order to exercise this type of internal conversation as their dominant mode of reflexivity. It follows that their openness to new experiences, their search for otherness and responsiveness to new variety is what draws meta-reflexives towards the situational logic of opportunity from the beginning. What they make of it in terms of shaping a life during their undergraduate careers forms the end towards which this chapter tends.

Ultimately, the contextual incongruity experienced by young meta-reflexives is something that they welcome and even accentuate at times. It is not only that for them, in common with their undergraduate peers who are autonomous reflexives, their natal background has been a place transmitting mixed messages. It is also that dissatisfaction with the familial *modus vivendi* leads these young subjects to distance themselves from it and therefore to be readily attracted to alternative ways of life. The incongruence of such alternatives with key elements of the parental context serves to crystallize their disengagement from it. Nevertheless, it is not the case that 'anything different goes' or 'the more different the better'. Young meta-reflexives are exercising critical detachment. Not only are such judgements necessarily and negatively evaluative of the parental relationships experienced at home, but also the form of incongruence to be embraced must be positively (though fallibly) evaluated in its own right. This is because these subjects seek a 'cause' through whose service they believe they will lead better lives than their domestic role models.

Being on the lookout for a *vocation* in the social order is what sets the meta-reflexives firmly apart from their autonomous counterparts. As was seen in the previous chapter, the latter had independence thrust upon them as the practical consequence of family breakdown: divorce, separation or 'rocky relationships'. They managed their own daily living, sometimes supported one or both parents and often took generous responsibility for domestic affairs. Yet none of the above implied critical detachment. When they drew a line beyond which their sense of dutiful responsibility would not go, this was to assert an individualism that paralleled exactly what their two parents had claimed for themselves. In fact, it was precisely what had prevented the latter from forming a couple, i.e. partners generating relational goods together. However, that did nothing to preclude their children from selecting and syncretizing various elements from the *modus vivendi* presented by either or both parents. Although their home life was deemed – to different degrees – to be sub-optimal, the autonomous subjects were remarkable for not being judgemental except in the one case of an acrimonious divorce. Indeed, the careers they elected fell within the same spectrum as those of their parents (in the present or the past) and were generally approved by them. In other words, the last response found amongst the autonomous subjects was 'a plague on both of your houses' and 'may my own be different in its most important respects'. They too distanced themselves, but as fellow individualists laying claim to their own individualism. Their independence was circumstantially induced by family fragility or actual breakdown, rather than being based upon critical detachment founded upon negative evaluation. Indeed, one crucially important difference between these two sub-groups was that the parents of meta-reflexives all maintained stable relationships, meaning that durability and security were their relational gift to their children.[3] Critical detachment is therefore quite different in kind from enforced independence.

In addition, we have seen how the practical order was the great resort of young autonomous subjects. Certainly, there is no contradiction involved between a career based on refining practical skills and it being regarded as a vocation. In *Being Human* (2000) I argued that this was precisely the case for dedicated musicians, athletes and craft workers. Nevertheless, such a vocational orientation is not characteristic of the autonomous interviewees if only because most believed that they would remain in the career they selected for only a limited period, until certain material targets had been attained. This is neither the stuff from which vocations are made – nor meta-reflexives. None of those who entered university as practitioners of meta-reflexivity had anything other than recreational interests in the practical order. For them, self-investment was reserved for the social order. In other words, the 'causes' to which they were drawn and the vocations to which these eventually led were deeply social and relational in kind, producing what Sayer terms 'internal' rather than 'external' goods.[4] These were the interviewees who protested their indifference to a career enabling them to enjoy an expensive lifestyle, or to experience status acclaim, or to exercise significant amounts of power.

Thus, young meta-reflexives represent a paradox in several respects. They are 'loners' who seek to devote themselves to social relations; they are people for whom the most proximate social institution – their own family – is one from whose social bonds they seek to distance themselves; in short, they are critically detached from that part of the social order they know best yet dedicated to re-ordering the social through their vocational endeavours.

It seems useful to unpack such apparent paradoxes into their component elements because it is these that have to be understood and explained by reference to the family biographies shared by subjects entering university as meta-reflexives. Specifically, it is necessary to gain explanatory purchase upon the following four questions.

(a) What effect does the transmission of mixed messages by two parents who have nonetheless achieved a stable and durable relationship have upon their offspring? This constitutes a lasting exposure to parental dissention whilst children are growing up but, nevertheless, the latter are simultaneously beneficiaries of one relational good, namely

---

[3] As Halina (introduced later in this chapter) puts it, 'I think I'm really lucky to have had two parents who stuck together . . . because I learned different things from both my parents'.

[4] Andrew Sayer, *The Moral Significance of Class*, Cambridge University Press, 2005, chapter 5.

the stability of the domestic context. How do these two opposed influences play out in shaping meta-reflexivity amongst the children?

(b) Why do the young meta-reflexives become 'loners', often branding themselves as deficient in social skills but at the same time fiercely individuated and insistent upon being the authors of their own values? In what sense is the stable family that is *not* a consensual 'norm circle' also the cradle of individuation?

(c) What accounts for the young meta-reflexives already having aligned themselves with a 'cause' and being active in pursuing it whilst still at school? How have they encountered this otherness in which they invest themselves much earlier than their peers and despite most not having had a gap year in which to expand their horizons?

(d) Why are the meta-reflexives the only sub-group that does not list 'my family' among its three main concerns in life? After all, we have seen how pervasive is this concern amongst all others in the same under-graduate cohort, among Coventry residents in the previous study and even amidst some of the fractured reflexives (in the following chapter), who were in receipt of severely negative relational family goods. In short, what accounts for 'dissatisfaction' resulting in radical 'disengagement'?

Family tensions and meta-reflexivity

When all those attending the foundation course were first administered ICONI, after a month at university, Halina, the daughter of a Polish mother who works as an interpreter and a father who was a telecommunications officer, voluntarily annotated her completed form with the following details. This unsolicited comment provides a useful means of coming to grips with the questions posed above as well as already highlighting the salience of family 'unity' to the meta-reflexive interviewees. There are five statements in this quotation, as enumerated in brackets, that broadly summarize how members of this sub-group relate to their respective families.

(1) Everyone is very argumentative and wants to have the last word, so there are lots of arguments. (2) But, we're also quick to forget and put it behind us. (3) However, I don't feel like going home from university. I wanted to live away while at university to get my freedom and space. (4) When I have my own family, I do want to do a lot of things differently. (5) But I do appreciate how much my parents have taught and given me.

Domestic dissention is the case for all three interviewees who began university as established meta-reflexives – although the issues that proved most contentious differed. So, too, did parental methods of handling the potential for overt conflict, which would have threatened the stability of the family unit to which they all appeared committed. The first statement also characterizes the family relationships of the fourth interviewee (allowing for his special circumstances as an adopted child), who first registered as a meta-reflexive in his second year. Exploring tensions and tension management within these stable family units provides a handle upon how these subjects became 'loners' – a term they volunteer themselves – inside their own homes. One relevant difference to note compared with the parents of autonomous reflexives is that none of the mothers and fathers to be discussed could be described as front line workers for either state or market. Thus, the nature of their differences did not revolve around support for versus opposition to the great Leviathans of modernity.

For Kate (her mother a nursing assistant for those with learning difficulties and her father an American-born IT technician employed by an insurance firm) the domestic bone of contention was politics and the tension-management strategy consisted in limiting the voicing of divisive political opinions. What she says below illustrates the source of tension and the means her parents adopted for containing it:

> My mum's a bit of a Thatcherite... my dad's slightly more left-wing than my mum is I'd say. I've got a lot of family in America from my dad's side and we went across there... They're very patriotic, Republican voters, it's that kind of mentality that they have. I was advised by my mum before we got there not to talk politics because it would just cause an argument and a confrontation that wasn't necessary. So I avoided that. I could have got into some very big arguments.

Kate declares that 'politics is where my passion is' (she changed to a politics degree after her first year) and also describes herself as a 'news junky' who switches on her computer as soon as she wakes up and depends on her daily reading of the *Guardian* and *Independent*. At the end of her degree she still recalls with horror that summer of US censorship: 'the only news coverage we had over there was American news and I absolutely hated it because I had no idea – we didn't have the Internet either – so I just didn't know what was going on in the world. I like to be informed about things, I like to be knowledgeable about things so I can talk to people about them.'

Yet forming your own opinions but not talking about them is precisely the marital formula used for maintaining domestic peace. Although Kate knows that her parents are both 'pretty hostile to New Labour', she remembers asking my mother who she voted for in an election. I was maybe about eleven or twelve, and she wouldn't tell me who she'd voted for because she didn't want to influence who I voted for in the future... when I was younger my parents were always very much like 'you make your own decisions about things and you form your own beliefs and we're not going to force you or encourage you into a particular political view or anything like that.'

This reflects a self-conscious martial pact between the spouses in an attempt to restrict the collateral damage inflicted on their three children by their own irresolvable differences.

Hence, Kate was induced to become a loner within her own family circle, forming her own opinions but not exacerbating domestic tensions by being vociferous about them – a quietude that was reinforced by growing up in a small rural village with few age peers. Unsurprisingly, she considers her (more progressive) political convictions to be of her own making and is resistant to any suggestion that her humanitarian concerns derive even indirectly from her parents. She availed herself of the obvious external outlet, namely her secondary school, where she recalls: 'I used to be quite active. I remember organizing a demonstration against the Iraq war when I was in the sixth form. Only about twelve people came along but it got into the local newspaper' and thus received a frosty reception from the Head and a veiled caution against repetition.

Kate had thus developed her 'passion', but both her family and school conveyed the same message: neither institution would allow her the freedom to express it. This is the making of an ideational loner. On the one hand, Kate's natal background was responsible for muzzling that about which she cared most. On the other hand, imposition of the marital concordat did result in interpersonal relations remaining amicable within her family. What seems to have happened is that Kate had picked up on the forbidden field of political dissention both parents had declared taboo because of its potentially divisive effects. However, in developing her own outlook on politics she knew it must remain without expression in her natal environment. Once Kate found her political voice at university, she also knew that returning home meant encountering this embargo. Small wonder that on finding no such constraints at university she ceased to be a frequent visitor home, her family never featured on her annual list of concerns and her parents did not figure among the relationships she dwelt upon during her three years of interviews.

From day to day Kate's family operated as a largely self-contained nuclear unit and neither friends nor colleagues from the home neighbourhood are ever mentioned as crossing the doorstep. Much the same is the case for Neville and Halina, with the former living quite close to London but the extended family being in Devon, whilst the latter had a fund of Polish relatives on her mother's side who remained in Warsaw and are visited occasionally. Thus, the relational factors contributing to the development of meta-reflexivity again seem confined to dynamics operative within the nuclear family.

Of the three founder members of the meta-reflexives, Halina is the most forthcoming and analytical about the impact of family relations upon her when living at home. She has clearly dwelt upon this in many internal conversations (described as being continuous) and arrived at her own diagnosis of their effects during successive tracts of her childhood. Retrospectively, Halina scrutinized her own reaction formation and analysed the dynamics resulting in the vocation to which she was already actively committed prior to university. Significantly, the dominance of her meta-reflexivity is the most marked of all four interviewees and may be proportionate to the extreme manifestations of dissention within her extremely stable family unit.[5]

Brought up in London with a Polish mother and English father and speaking both languages, Halina is critical of their self-imposed isolation and increasingly intolerant of their overt differences in outlook:

I live with my mum, my dad, my brother and my grandma, my dad's mum. My family is quite argumentative and there's quite a lot of tension at home ... My dad's got quite a bit of a temper and both of my parents want to have the last say and always want to be right. I don't think it's natural actually the amount of arguing that goes on in my family. I mean I was used to it from a young age ... You know, voices will be raised and shouting will go on, but my grandma gets really upset. My mum gets angry for my grandma being upset, whereas for dad it's "If I can't have it out with my family in my own house, where can I?" ... Sometimes when I go home it does stress me out, just the atmosphere, and I was so used to it I didn't realize.

The main bones of contention were partly religious, partly nuanced political issues, partly Polish versus English conventionalism and, at least in some part, two personalities neither of whom would concede dominance to the other.

Given these ingredients Halina undoubtedly received mixed messages, often explicitly directed at her. To begin with, her mother remained a practising Catholic once in England and Halina was baptized, had her first communion and was confirmed, influences that were intensified by attending Polish school on Saturdays where the Polish priest was

---

[5] Kate recorded quite a high score for the practice of autonomous reflexivity and Ryan was remarkable as the only student registering the highest possible scores for both autonomous and meta-reflexivity on entry, becoming an unambiguous member of this sub-group only in his second year.

doctrinally strict. This doubly marginal position – belonging to a minority faith and being partly foreign – was rendered more ambiguous by the multi-ethnic primary school she attended and was sometimes dissonant with what she describes as her father's 'old fashioned values': 'My dad's an atheist, although he was brought up Church of England, and he's got very strong moral values. He would call anything such as bunking your train fare very wrong. It's always about where you cross the boundaries. Most people wouldn't be that bothered about using the photocopier at work for something else but he would.' Bombarded by these differences, Halina admits in her first year that 'sometimes I don't always know on certain issues where I stand'. By her final undergraduate year she states: 'I have developed my own values, so I don't agree with what the Catholic Church says about everything, especially things like homosexuality and contraception.' She still believes and she still prays but squares this particular circle by maintaining that 'it's not about God, it's about yourself and how you behave towards others in society' and supports this with her historic picture of Jesus-the-radical.

Equally, each parent tried to impose particular values and practices upon their daughter, which Halina found hard to resist. For example, she recalls, 'my dad's quite opinionated and he has some weird ideas, like he thinks, for example, that it's really silly that women want to wear make-up and high heels – he'd put that forward really, really strongly and I didn't want him to look down on me. So then I was the one who's not wearing the make-up and felt embarrassed about even buying teenage magazines.' Equally, her mother's 'healthy eating regime', justified by Halina's childhood eczema (which does not fully account for it being applied to her brother), was of an intensity that created incongruities with her first friends:

My mum's . . . really worried about health and we weren't allowed to eat all sorts of things with additives when we were kids. It made it quite difficult socially, because when I went to parties I didn't enjoy them because I felt self-conscious. All my friends were eating sweets and crisps and I wanted to be part of the group and join in. But it was always, 'Do I eat this and betray my mum?' and 'I know it's bad for me and she's really right' or 'Do I do what my friends do?'

These two examples both had serious and lasting impacts. In seeking to satisfy her father's anti-femininity ('because I really looked up to my dad'), Halina usually adopts the casually sporty style. This imposed androgyny meant she came to wonder if she had bisexual tendencies when she experienced schoolgirl 'crushes' on older girls, despite all her relationships being with males. Equally, as far as her mother's eating regime was concerned, Halina eventually compromised because she became sure that 'being stressed and miserable can impact on your health as much as additives . . . these kinds of things can lead to eating disorders. I mean, it's actually surprising that I haven't got one because I was so worried.'

Halina tried hard to propitiate both parents: 'most kids look up to their friends more than their parents, but it took me a long time to get to that stage . . . to actually be able to challenge my parents and think "well, they can have their opinions but I can also do my own thing"'. Nevertheless, the problem intrinsic to mixed messages remained, namely that it was impossible to satisfy both parents simultaneously because of their lack of normative consensus. In her own words, she cannot agree with her parents on everything 'because they don't agree with each other on everything'.

Disengagement from her family was long and painful, entailing a growing dissatisfaction with her parents' respective expectations, as described above. However, Halina tried to exemplify the one set of norms that her parents held in common – their environmental concerns – although she took this to extremes that provoked their own discontents: 'I think because my family are quite green I did things like that even when I was little . . . I used to run after people and say you should have put that litter in the bin, don't drop it on the ground . . . By the time I was in the juniors I had a book called *Fifty things kids can do to save the earth.*' The playground response depressed her, it did not increase her popularity and seemed to herald her difficulties with the social order that dogged her into university.

What she provides as the storyline of growing up is that of a loner, something she attributes to the influence of both parents, to their not working together as a couple and to their own social isolation:

I find that I'm a bit different, well, I've never really fitted in with any group. I used to get bullied because I'm an individual and reluctant to fit in with a group for the sake of fitting in and compromising everything. When I was little I found it quite hard to make friends. I'm different but I taught myself to be more like other people. It just took me longer to learn social skills.

This problem threads through Halina's schooldays. From nursery school she can 'remember just going around playing on my own and I didn't really know how to make friends within a group but I didn't really feel the need for it'. At primary school, 'I was more likely to want to boss kids around than to fit in. And that didn't do me any favours because it only doubled the number of people not liking me.' Halina got by through enjoying boisterous games but this no longer worked after junior level:

When I went to secondary school you can't just play with your friends anymore, you've got to be able to talk to them all the time and I found that difficult. I thought 'Wow, all the kids are going to be like me', but they weren't. I thought that all of a sudden they'd all be into the environment and all be completely different, but they were still just kids and sort of moulded round the capitalist system, like materialistic and into fashion.

Discomfort with being a loner prompted Halina to recognize that because of her parental background it took her 'a much longer time to learn social skills and I think I'm still learning', though from people outside the family. Simultaneously, she accepts that 'I'm not really like anyone else': internally idiosyncratic and externally the eternal outsider. She is aware that alienating as many of her experiences have been this has equipped her with critical detachment to form her own views and sustain them against pressure to conform: 'I'm not that influenced by groups of people, even when I'm in a crowd. I was never in a mainstream crowd but even when I'm in a group, whatever group of people, I'm still myself'. Significantly, this is equally the case for the Greenpeace group with which she became increasingly involved whilst still at home: 'even with the Green Party I might not necessarily agree with all their policies, I will still have a critical view on stuff, I will still be a slight outsider so I'm never just one of a crowd'. This distancing runs from a refusal to use drugs, unlike the hippy-ish and alternative members of her local Greenpeace group, to doggedly attempting to insert opposition to genetic modification of food more prominently on their collective agenda.

The corollary is that Halina engages in a great deal of internal conversation to clarify her own opinions, often confounding others who assume, for example, that because of her environmental concerns she will automatically support animal rights, whereas she refuses to give more than a highly qualified assent. Although throughout her teens she had her mother's backing on the issue of genetic modification and her father was generically 'green', Halina maintains that her own views are not the lowest common denominator of parental consensus because they were sharpened as much by the books she read and the speakers she encountered whilst at school. From these resources she made her personal commitment, became an engaged activist and, in short, identified her ultimate concern. She has been actively campaigning since she was sixteen and on the day of her last interview was standing as a 'paper candidate' in the General Election. As she talks about the environmentalist 'cause' she had embraced, Halina says: 'I don't know if that's my calling, but that's what I'm really passionate about and I'd like to do something about it in the future'.

Neville, whose mother is an infant school classroom assistant and his father a legal auditor in an insurance firm, is circumspect about his family, no member of which is given a speaking part throughout the interviews. Because he, like Kate and Halina, is a rare visitor home, it is tempting to conclude that his natal background has become of minor importance to him. However, and like them, his consideration in insisting that he must cost them nothing after his first degree belies unconcern. His role as a loner whilst living at home calls for explanation but is hampered by the paucity of references to his early years.

He does produce one memory from before he was three, which may have initiated his enduring inward turn:

When my sister was born things were a bit up in the air. My mum's a twin and my sister was also a twin, but my brother was stillborn and my sister was premature and they weren't too sure. I remember spending a lot of time with my great aunt around then and it had been weeks since seeing my mum and missing my mum and wondering what was going on. I remember the first time I met my sister, and, after that it's just patchy – I think I was a rather quiet child.

On such a slender basis it would be unjustifiable to picture a family in lasting grief and its withdrawn first child. Nevertheless, Neville's mother was Catholic and may have mourned the loss of one of her children, whilst his father was 'not really religious'. Neville was brought up in the faith, attended Catholic schools and admits when young to having been bogged down in self-reproach until he 'suddenly realized this isn't helping you, look at it from a different perspective. That's what I try and do with everything.' Religion was the source of contention in this family and from these mixed messages he elaborated his own idiosyncratic notion in which

as long as you feel spiritually – no religious connotation – fulfilled then I don't think anything else much matters . . . by spirituality I mean the buzz you get when not being selfish. I just think it's important not to put yourself first. As long as I felt fulfilled and that I was improving someone or helping someone that would be it. So, spiritual fulfilment is that you get a rush from these things.

Neville seems to have grown up as a loner, manifesting this at school by his lateral takes on essay topics, whose good marks conventionally confirmed his unconventionality. Teachers recognized his analytical ability and rewarded it, but Neville again turned this inward: 'I work best when I'm analysing things basically, and a lot of that I do within myself – I kind of see it as a way of enabling me to grow as a person.' Much of this can be summarized as learning from his own experiences, followed up by self-monitoring. This he feels is 'a way that will allow me to become the kind of person I'm capable of being. I know not everyone works like that but it's the way I work.'

This may sound narcissistic until it is juxtaposed with Neville's social uneasiness and its consequences, which he readily admits derive from his own conduct: 'most of the complexities in my relationships stem from myself.' Mulling this over out loud he concludes: 'I think it's just my mind is the only one I understand and it's the same for anyone else. So the best ideas for me are going to come from myself. I do find it quite difficult to listen to what other people are saying because I know what will work for me and they might not.' This he justifies further by saying: 'I don't think there's anything more important than to be happy with who you are because until you're comfortable with yourself, how can you be comfortable with anyone else?' Moreover, his desire to be of service to others is something in which he has been actively engaged from his school involvement with the Catholic Association for Overseas Development (CAFOD) projects for the developing world, to his undergraduate donations to similar charities and his first glimmerings at university about his future social engagement, which hover around the alleviation of marginality: 'I don't really believe there's anything beyond that. That's the least you can do for someone else, to try and make something better for someone else is what I want to do, even if it's just one person. If you can't do that then what's the point really?'

If Halina is the subject whose practice of meta-reflexivity is most dominant, Ryan is a mature student who on entry gained the highest possible scores for both autonomous and meta-reflexivity and only assimilated himself to the latter group during his second year.[6] In the making of Ryan as a meta-reflexive, interest turns on how far his natal background generated the same pattern of disengagement, distancing and critical detachment by virtue of its relational dissention as has been found for the three students examined so far. Conversely, was there anything of the 'enforced independence', characteristic of the autonomous reflexives, which pertained in his case?

In fact, strong elements of both were present in his biography of familial relations. On the one hand, Ryan was adopted and it appears that he experienced both the objective and subjective effects of this very different kind of 'enforced independence' within his adoptive family. On the other hand, tensions within this adoptive family resulted in a divorce before he was two and also accompanied his adopted mother's re-marriage when he was seven. However, this second union did generate the relational

---

[6] He was therefore recorded as 'unclassifiable' in the first year.

good – that of stability and durability – which was the main patrimony of the meta-reflexive sub-group.

Consequences of both elements reverberated through his life before entering university, persisted during his undergraduate career and reached a crescendo when he had to face (re)shaping his life by choosing a career at the end of his degree. Although his meta-reflexivity predominated and served to harness the perennial attraction self-employment holds for autonomous subjects towards a 'cause' or vocation, much of this must be attributed to relational factors within his own marriage and family rather than to influences of his natal background.

Ryan's adoptive mother worked in hospital administration and his step-father was a tool maker with his own business. He left school at sixteen to spend eight years as a sheet metal worker and then a similar period until he was thirty-two employed by a van manufacturer. He met his wife-to-be as a school leaver and the couple had two children, one of whom became disabled following a severe illness in early childhood.

Early in the first interview, when asked whether or not his internal conversations entailed much reliving of past events, Ryan agreed that he often did 'go back and reassess things'. Significantly, he immediately attributed this mental activity to his adoption: 'you always ask, ask, ask and you always wonder, so I think that maybe the way I am is because of that situation'. Specifically, what troubles him is not the generic questioning about what might have been but the unnecessary barrier of silence imposed between his birth family and his adoptive family. Hence, he ruminated aloud: 'there's been recent government legislation on adoption and they're putting children with extended family members, but I think that should have been a practice that was practised for ever'. Had it been, Ryan believes that he would not have experienced such a persistent feeling of detachment from his adoptive context, one arising 'because you don't know where you come from or belong to or what your history is. I mean my history was tacitly my adopted family's history, but obviously there is something besides that which you don't know.'

Reflecting on his childhood, what he describes is a sense of detachment tantamount to being a 'loner' in his adoptive context:

In retrospect I was never part of a kind of cohesive family unit or history. I remember as a young child we would go and visit our nan most weekends and there would be like a family gathering and talk about past histories and you never really totally slotted into that. The more they talked the more you were aware that you . . . were always just a little bit different. I've always been a little bit different from birth it seems. I suppose taking a step like going to university or taking myself out of that comfort zone, it's just continuing what I've already done and how I felt.

In other words, Ryan continuously sensed himself to be something of an outsider within this family. Yet he was prepared to re-endorse his position as a 'loner' by starting a degree as a mature student knowing that he would not have much in common with younger undergraduates. By corollary, he would not settle for the partial satisfactions provided by his adoptive family or a well-paid job whose benefits he could not embrace wholeheartedly. As he sees it, his adopted status has made him 'a little bit more unique' and given him the capacity for critical evaluation of and detachment from the social settings in which he has found himself.

However, Ryan's disengagement was augmented by tensions within the family he had involuntarily entered. In particular, there was political division between what he describes as the 'conservative background' represented by his nuclear family and the active socialism of his extended family: 'my mother was conservative yet my granddad and uncles were union shop stewards, were hard-on socialists. I can remember there'd be political discussions and it kind of opened my eyes. I've probably had my feet in both camps from being fourteen or fifteen to the present.' That this was of lasting importance is shown when Ryan joined the Socialist Workers' Party for a year at university, not because he felt drawn towards it but in order 'to understand their take on things'. In other words, the factor prompting his disengagement also promoted his attitude of inquiry.

Although Ryan consistently defines himself as working class, protesting that he will remain such even when in a middle-class career, he has distanced himself from the political engagements of both the nuclear and extended parts of his adoptive family by turning his back on party politics: 'I'm pretty much disenchanted with politics per se at the moment. I'm one of those people who would rather not vote. I get pretty upset when people say you've got to vote... I say if you listen to the people who didn't vote that's where the real message is... My voice is saying a lot more by not voting.' What it is saying is that 'a lot of what's wrong with society today you can trace back to this ideology of the individual, especially as regards consumerism', which is promoted by all the current political parties. Conversely, Ryan characterizes his own values as being 'traditional and family oriented without a doubt' and he attributes these to the influence of his adoptive grandmother, 'the kind of matriarch of the family.'

Since he did not enter university as a meta-reflexive it is unsurprising that he had not identified a vocation and can go no further than saying: 'I know what it's like to wake up every morning thinking I don't want to go to work. I want to get up in the morning and think "oh, I'm looking forward to this".' In seeking to make this dream concrete Ryan wants it to promote the well-being of his own family in line with his grandmother's values and his own anti-individualism. At the same time, if Ryan does have a consuming interest, it is in collecting art deco furniture and smaller items, love and knowledge of whose style he has cultivated for himself but collecting was also a practice into which he was inducted by his mother and stepfather: 'I've been brought up in a house full of antiques and we always went to antique fairs and I suppose it developed from that.' What will be of particular interest as his meta-reflexivity comes to dominate is how as an undergraduate he weaves together these two strands he has retained from his adoptive background as he confronts the (re)shaping of a life for his own family in the future.

Meta-reflexives and the challenge of friendship

Although family relationships have resulted in this sub-group entering university as 'loners', this is not a way of life with which they are comfortable or wish to perpetuate. On the contrary, most are avid for new experiences and new people with whom to share them. However, they are not ready to settle for the first people to hand and take scant advantage of the random allocation of those who have been assigned to the same hall of residence on arrival at university. They are friendly with their co-residents but these relationships do not mature into important or lasting friendships. Similarly, those who plunge themselves into university activities are experimenting and will withdraw if they learn that these are not a source of like-minded people. Furthermore, if their involvements embrace organizations, such as the students' union, these are strictly *ad experimentum* and display none of the 'careerism' of the autonomous subjects with their instrumental rational approach to building up their CVs.

Instead, these subjects are interest-directed as is reflected in the durable friendships they eventually form. Since their interests are developing and clarifying over their three years as undergraduates, it is not surprising to discover a general pattern of attenuation in their home friends as they share less and less in common. This proves to be the case even for friends from the natal background who do support the same 'cause' but are felt not to have moved on in their thinking.

Simultaneously, because meta-reflexives are the most work-focussed students of all the sub-groups interviewed, their friendship patterns overlap much more with those taking the same modules and seminars. Often, these young subjects will be disappointed at the unwillingness of their classmates to be sufficiently involved in the issues covered and especially at their reluctance to participate in seminar discussions. To the meta-reflexives their studies are neither a means to an end nor an unavoidable trial standing between them and obtaining a degree. They choose their options with care and in accordance with their interests, they integrate course material into the development of their own thinking and they frequently refer to the effects that their engagement with particular materials or ideas have had upon them. Hermeneutically, what they cannot understand is that not all are like them and their friends are self-selected from those who are equally involved. It follows that it is the meta-reflexives alone who seriously entertain academic careers even if this is not the path they finally take. Education is not seen by them as an obstacle course to be negotiated in order to obtain credentials (which is largely the communicatives' view) nor is it to be milked for its potential to open doors to lucrative careers in the market or the state (which is how autonomous subjects tend to regard it). Instead, it is an end in itself and friendships are formed amongst those with similar outlooks.

These friendship patterns will be examined for our four subjects, with particular attention being given to two sets of questions. Firstly, since all have been characterized as 'loners', disengaged from their home backgrounds and returning relatively infrequently, do they tend to shed pre-university friends more readily than other sub-groups? How do they fare in overcoming their unsociable sociality as undergraduates? What influence is exerted on their friendships by the proto-commitments that they have already made to a 'cause'? In other words, because these subjects tend to have confronted the necessity of selection earlier than their peers, do the choices they have made serve to filter the friendships they form? Secondly, and in common with the other sub-groups, the formation of a serious personal relationship can exert a decisive influence for meta-reflexives upon both their friendship patterns and future careers. Thus, does the formation of a durable relationship serve to moderate or to accentuate the wholehearted vocational commitment of these young subjects if and when they begin to tackle the shaping of a life together? In becoming a couple, do they resemble more closely Couple A or Couple B from Chapter 3?

Two of the interviewees – Halina and Neville – graduated without having formed a personal relationship that could affect what they did upon leaving university. Therefore, they can only be examined in relation to the first question. Of the other two, Ryan was already married at point of entry and Kate met her partner-to-be a few weeks after the start of her enrolment. This pair of interviewees can thus shed some light on the second question as well.

Despite obvious personality differences – Halina is outgoing and uninhibitedly informative whereas Neville is guarded and cautious in his self-revelations – neither has entered university with a large group of home friends and both experienced difficulties in forming new friendships. In their very different ways, both found it hard to overcome the 'loner' role they had assumed in their natal backgrounds. For each, their coursework remained an important pre-occupation and, though they both graduated with good degrees, neither felt that academic success came to them without effort. The commitment of both to hard work served to moderate the space that friendship was allowed to occupy in their undergraduate lives. Beyond that, their main common denominators are that friendships are formed on the basis of their concerns and the former are not allowed to deflect them from the latter and from seizing opportunities to realize them.

In the preceding section it was seen that Halina regarded her background as responsible for leaving her deficient in social skills. Two themes come to dominate her university career in this respect: she developed a longing for friendship and a close relationship, but in both regards was entirely interest-driven and would experiment but not deviate. In addition, she was not reconciled to being alone – in part because she very much wants to have her own family – but she became highly reflexive about being over precipitous and less and less compromising about her *desiderata* for a partner.

Halina had split up with her boyfriend before coming to university. She says she had

self-consciously thought 'Don't get involved with anybody'...Now I'm thinking that I'm at university, there are lots of people around and just because I get on with a particular guy doesn't mean I'm going to go out with him straight away. I'll get to know lots of people and then decide or I'll be stuck with one person and I won't even have the opportunity to get to know other people.

Despite throwing herself into a variety of university activities (including roller hockey and women's football) and having the usual openings in her hall of residence, neither generated friendship or partnership. As she reflects on her first year:

maybe I was too individualistic in a way and tried to join lots of societies and do too much but I didn't have the chance to get really into any of them or to really get to know the people from any of them. I didn't make friends very easily, I suppose because I'm quite strong-minded and I'll do my own thing – so I'd cook vegetarian food for myself, I'd buy my own food on my own, I'd cook for myself and then I wouldn't even be having dinner with a group of people. And you know an absolutely integral part of community and society is eating dinner together. So I'd be doing a lot of things on my own. There were twenty-nine people in my kitchen and I didn't really click with any of them, then I met someone...

She had a very brief fling, probably out of loneliness, which was short-lived because 'we didn't have that much in common. I think we didn't share the same ideals and that was the main problem.'

By her second year Halina says: 'I do now really have the need to have friends and to have people around. I'm at the stage where I'm really fed up with being single.' From this, she tries reflexively to draw the conclusion that 'you really have to accept people as they are' and to learn the lesson from her father that she will end up lonely if she allows her interests to rule as his did:

he doesn't have that many friends. I mean he's not the kind of person who will go out to the pub and have a drink. He's got his own interests and he'd rather pursue them. He's interested in talking to people if they've got the same interests too, but he's not at all into going out socially with his work colleagues because if they don't have much in common then he just gets really bored and frustrated, but I don't want to be like that because I don't think my parents have a social life.

In an attempt to practise these insights Halina started playing women's football and socializing with the group afterwards. However, she concludes, 'that's one crowd I don't really feel that comfortable hanging around, they're just out to have a good time and drink loads and go really crazy and I feel quite uncomfortable'.

Thus, despite her good advice to herself, Halina finds that she gravitates towards those who share her environmental interests. Her best friend is a twenty-seven-year-old graduate, living close to the university and whom Halina had met at a conference about genetic modification. Although they do quite a lot together, this friend has a boyfriend and sometimes wants to be alone with him. Hence Halina tries various other activities – mountain biking and First Aid – but is drawn back into organizing 'Environment Week' on campus and starts playing a bigger role in a student organization called 'People and Planet': 'I've definitely got more in common with the Planet people than I have with the girls who play football.' Thus her ultimate environmental concerns are again serving to filter her potential friendships. Nevertheless, she wonders whether the Planet people do count as friends: 'I still don't feel like I've got to know them really well because a lot of time we're doing campaigning. I haven't had time to get to know them on a social level and I sometimes wonder how important I am as a friend or am I just another hand to help out?'

By the end of year two Halina thinks she has progressed socially relative to her first year but reflects: 'I thought I was strong and fine on my own and would wait for the right person and all that, but it can actually be quite lonely'. She begins to build castles in the air about developing a relationship with a fellow campaigner who seems to be free of attachments. These fantasies – as they turn out to be when she tells him her feelings – reveal the extent to which even this much wanted relationship is conceptualized as subordinate to her ultimate concern:

I mean he is quite radical as well but he's just managed to land this really steady job [as a London lawyer], but he stands for everything that I stand for and we have the most fantastic conversations till five in the morning. If I was lucky enough to get into a situation like that, with someone who had a good salary coming in, then I could focus more on the campaigning, the radical side of things, without having to worry about the financial situation.

By her third year Halina has done some self-learning and come to the conclusion that 'it's taken me a long time to realize that you don't always have to join societies or clubs in order to do something productive. Sometimes just chilling out with a group of people and having a few drinks you can have some amazing conversations and get to know people and good things can happen.' They are doing now because she has acknowledged that she has to give time to friendship and is living with her two closest friends from 'People and Planet'. Yet, not only is her selection of close friends interest-led, but since she is also work-driven she has constant difficulties in making room for them as the following anecdote reveals:

there have actually been times when I went out and I knew I had an essay hanging over me and everyone would be on the dance floor and I'd be dancing and I'd just suddenly start thinking about what I'd got to do and so I was not into it. I'd sort of be moving my body but my mind could be somewhere else and they'd be like 'are you OK?' and I'd be like, 'oh I'm not enjoying this anymore, I'm just going home'.

Sociability remains something she values but Halina has to drill herself into meeting the demands of friendship.

Nevertheless, she has not become more reliant upon her Greenpeace friends at home but, instead, is more critical of them. As she puts it,

you've just got to let things go and move on and I feel I'm moving on. My Greenpeace group seems stuck in a bit of a rut. A lot of them are quite alternative and they don't have steady jobs because that's not what they value most . . . there's a lot of drinking and cannabis smoking and I can just see the way that it has affected those people and it's made them really apathetic and really not moving forward.

Thus, for example, she is irritated with the long-running soap opera about the unrequited love of one member, just as she is dismissive about her older friend and her unsuitable partner. In other words, Halina is in the process of dropping her home friends, despite their having shared interests in the same social movement.

Although at the end of her second year she has a relationship with a German student, and despite her gratitude to him for being very supportive when her father was tragically killed, she recognizes that this is unlikely to be a permanent partnership because 'we have got different values'. She will not compromise on this even though she remains as dedicated as ever to having a family before she is thirty – and that, to her, means children whose father is part of their lives. Equally, although she thinks and cares more about her natal family after her father's death, she does not return home much more frequently because she is mentally moving on and to much further away, as will be seen. Her basic message is that nothing will deflect her from following her vocation and the university friendships she has developed are wholly compatible with it. Moreover, the 'apathy' of her remaining home friends will not prove contagious because the bonds are weakening between them since she has become critical of their lifestyle.

One of the major differences between Halina and Neville where friendship is concerned is that the former has an organized network of fellow campaigners to whom she can and does turn in her loneliness. In fact, Halina is one of the few subjects to illustrate how a person's ultimate concern can link up to a social movement and result in more than an aggregate outcome. Neville has no such network and in consequence remains almost unchanged as the 'loner' who entered university. His motto seems to be one that he voiced in his second year: 'I've come for the work, so why not do it? I categorically am not going to look back after three years and say "oh, I could have done better". I do not want to be in that position, so I will not let myself be in that position.' Even during its advent, nascent morphogenetic society can be a very lonely place. As was seen in Chapter 4, geo-local bonds are fragile and take a great deal of subjective commitment and objective effort to sustain. When a subject like Neville has neither and, on the contrary, seeks to shed his background contacts, it follows that his relationship to the social order largely reduces to those human relations that are mediated through work.

As has already been seen, Neville achieved his first academic rewards at college where his lateral thinking gained approbation from his teachers, which he relished: 'throughout pre-GCSE I had teachers telling me you're doing work to GCSE standard; at GCSE they were saying you're working to an A-level standard, then at A-level you've got teachers saying this is far beyond anything you're going to get marked for.' Prior to such praise he conveys that his school career was rather undistinguished and he is not one who would have compensated for this on the sports field.

His ultimate concern for work began there and seems to have simply carried over to university where it fills his days. During weekends he does paid and 'easy retail work' in a record store in order not to be a financial burden on his parents. This attitude is shared with other meta-reflexives who, having distanced themselves from home, all voice the same moral obligation to take as little monetary help as possible from their parents and none at all once they have graduated. It is as if their freedom to pursue their own concerns and realize their differences cannot be subsidized.

Neville's early concern for academic achievement also spelt a desire to sever contact with those from his secondary school once he had entered college: 'the problem you've got with schools at the end of the day is that you've had five years maturing with the same people and I guess because those people have seen your worst sides and formed their own cliques, you know people make judgements.' The implication is that these 'judgements' were negative towards Neville. Thus, he says that, 'when I got to college I made a conscious effort to break with the constant bickering, just constant bitching in the friendship group I was in at school. I just made a conscious effort to break with the people I'd been stuck with at school.'

As he puts it, 'I'm one of those to lose my roots quite easily'. He seems fully aware of his own pattern of shedding unwanted relationships, one that persists throughout his undergraduate career: 'I mean, you keep hold of what you want to keep hold of but I'm not one to carry around much in-flight baggage essentially, because you stop knowing people . . . I know a couple who regret the friends that they've lost, but I never do.' Therefore, it is unsurprising that he derived nothing from the ready-made conviviality of the hall of residence in which he spent his first year. This is typical of meta-reflexives – with the exception of Kate who temporarily welcomed the contrast with her isolated village background. Neville, however, is the most analytical and least intra-punitive about failing to make friendships from amongst his co-residents: 'whilst they're the closest to your situation that may not be mentally or emotionally. Living under the same roof as people means it can be a lot harder to be open with them than with people who aren't in the immediate vicinity.' In other words, Neville wants to choose his friends, a choice which is not guaranteed by proximity and he cannot be inveigled into intimacy by physical closeness.

Indeed, he is aware that with a very few exceptions his aim is to cut connections with his home friends:

I have to be honest and there are some people who I wouldn't mind loosing as friends . . . as I get older I've got less time to keep in touch with people. If someone gets in touch with me, I'll get back in touch with them, but normally it will be like 'I'm too busy, I'll catch up with you at Easter or in the summer'.

However, we have already seen that he goes back for only a few days a year and these are largely spent writing essays. He is adamant that he will not be the one to maintain friendships from home and the only exception is a young man (classed amongst his 'best mates') who is suffering from clinical depression: 'I've been spending a lot of time talking with him and he appreciates me being analytical . . . it's working and he's getting through it. He's thanked me for being there, that's all I need – well, I don't even need that. He's a mate and I'll be there for him.' What Neville conveys is that he prefers the role of the giver rather than the receiver.

Does this carry over to his university friendships and do these expand as home friends retract? His pattern remains a sparse one and his closest friends, one male and one female, are housemates with intellectual interests in common. During his three years as an undergraduate there is no mention of dating, let alone a relationship, and a family does not appear in his projected 'ideal life' ten years later on. The shared house is in Coventry, a place he singularly dislikes, and it is clear that the company of his 'closest friends' is no compensation: 'It's one of those places that's very uninspiring and quite often if I wanted to work I'd have to drag myself into the library and just sit there till it closes. Because I know that if I go home, I will just look out of the window and think "this is rubbish". It's one of those places that's kind of sapping without you even realizing it.'

This is a pattern of neither giving nor receiving but of a 'loner' who remains one, since none of those at all close to him appear in need of his attention. Thus, he remains single-minded about his ultimate concern, his academic work, and lives up to his own statement: 'I don't mind what I walk away with from here so long as I feel I've got the most out of my degree.' Of course, he does mind as will be seen when we come to his career. However, his work-orientation is so dominant that it precludes anything but the sparest and barest acknowledgement of friendship. Thus, Neville has not invested anything of himself in friendship that could possibly deflect him from his ultimate concern. Simultaneously, by shedding his old network without acquiring a new one, he also has no one to stimulate or to encourage him. That meta-reflexives are strongly autogenic about their final ends is indubitable, but whether they can be so self-sufficient seems more doubtful; Neville says 'yes' to this where Halina has said 'no'.

Clearly, those who have or who form personal relationships are also amongst the 'nays', that is, Kate and Ryan. When Kate discusses her three main concerns in life at the start of her course, namely 'university work', 'friends', and her 'boyfriend', she is very decisive about their order of importance: 'I think you've just got to be able to put your foot down and just sort of prioritize. So it would be more important if it came down to it to do university work than to go out with friends, and it would be more important to maintain a relationship with friends than to maintain a "relationship".' Although this will modify over the three years, what remains unchanging is Kate's engagement with her course (having changed to straight politics in year two), which is integral to her search to articulate her own moral and political philosophy – being attracted to feminism, consequentialism and utilitarianism in turn.

Having been a 'loner' at home she initially welcomes the ready-made group of potential friends she finds in her hall of residence: 'I'm used to living in this small village and not really having people around . . . it was nice on a social level just to have people around me, not having to catch a bus to go and see people.' Although she remains friendly with a few of them, by her second year her friendships 'tend to be with people whom I've met in the seminars this year' and with whom informal discussions continue in the coffee bar on the theme just tackled: 'We'll sit and talk about the international relations stuff and discuss the different theories, so that's been quite good'. These students gravitate towards one another because of their intellectual involvement, whilst Kate finds her course group a whole too passive and unengaged:

It's been a bit of a disappointment in a way. You have this idea of university as us all sitting there having debates and discussions and it hasn't really been like that . . . it's like trying to squeeze blood from a stone to actually get people to put ideas forward about things . . . I tend to get better discussions outside of seminars than I do in them.

Increasingly important among these are her lengthy exchanges with her boyfriend who, although a natural scientist, is 'very into philosophy so we tend to get some good discussions going about political philosophy and ethics and that kind of thing'.

As far as her home friends are concerned, Kate admits 'I only really stay in contact with a few people – I've noticed them falling away'. Since she sees these friends forming strata of different importance to her, it is only those in the top tier with whom she tries to stay in touch. Yet, their meetings are not very satisfactory: 'you're asking someone what their experience of university is like and it's different to the Warwick experience and it's almost like you're talking past each other'. Increasingly, this space is being filled by her boyfriend who also serves to reduce her participation in university activities, leaving her with less time for the music society and for being a member of the union council, which she gave up during her second year. Thus, it appears they are developing a serious and multi-faceted relationship that is the focus of both her intellectual concerns and of her relaxation.

Moreover, in the third year her boyfriend Chris' friends from his department have also become her friends, thus binding them closer together. They met soon after Kate came to university and in her first year we have seen that he occupied third place in her list of concerns. By year two he has moved into second place and by her final year he heads her list. This rank order is directly paralleled by the extent of Chris' influence over her attitudes and aspirations. Thus, at the start of her course Kate emphasizes how well her three concerns dovetail together: 'my boyfriend gets on with my friends and I'm balancing university life with seeing him and being with my friends. So I think at the moment it's working out pretty well and there haven't been any major conflicts.' Just as her degree work comes first, so does her future career when she thinks ahead. Kate is unsure if she wants children at all, but certain that if she does they must post-date the consolidation of her professional life and not be detrimental to it. All of this was to alter quite radically prior to her graduation.

The second year was the fulcrum and she is aware that many of her shifts in attitude stem directly from her talks with Chris, as she illustrates from her abandonment of feminism: 'through discussions with him and thinking about myself I realized that I wasn't [a feminist] because for me a feminist is somebody who places gender inequalities and differences as the most important thing in society'. For the same reason, whereas 'last year I would have identified myself as being left-wing, not socialist or Marxist but left-wing, now I'd say I'm a much more classic liberal, more centrist'. In turn, Kate jibs at contemplating what she would do if pursuing her career entailed her going abroad for a year or two: 'it's something I have been thinking about – if it came down to a choice between him and my career, what would I do? At the moment I'm not too sure and it's something I'm trying not to think about because it may not be a decision that I have to make.'

By her final year she has brought herself to confront this possibility alongside further attitudinal shifts following their ongoing discussions. For example, Kate's political centricism has intensified and she now considers that her views are closest to those of the Liberal Democrats. On the other hand, as a couple they have reached a humanitarian pact that they will give 10 per cent of their future income to charities like

Oxfam, hoping to help the poorest in Africa rather than the homeless in Britain. Attitudinally they appear to have reached a rapprochement, but how does this affect the future they now envisage together? Fundamentally, it sounds more like a compromise than a conjoint and concerted plan:

my boyfriend and I have talked about this and he said "Well what if you were offered two jobs, one at the other end of the country that you know you would really enjoy and another that maybe you wouldn't enjoy so much but that was closer?" And I said I'd probably go for the one that was closer because it's all very well and good to have this amazing job that you absolutely adore from nine to five but then you go home to an empty house with someone that you love at the other end of the country, then that's not going to make you happy in general. Fair enough because he said if he wasn't with me he could go wherever he liked to do his PhD. He could go to America or Australia or Japan and he would have more options available to him if he was on his own, but he wouldn't be as happy. So, it's all a question of balancing and I'm hoping they'll sort of merge together and if it comes to a time where one or both of us has to make a decision then we'll make that decision together.

Being or becoming a couple affects the shaping of their lives together in response to the opportunities available. If compromise and concession characterized Kate and Chris, the mutual elastication of their careers and the tentative evolution of a joint 'plan' was the case for Ryan and Vickie. The relative isolation of this last subject meant that his marital relationship and his wife's extended family played a larger role than friendship in supporting the development and direction taken by the couple's eventual plan.

One of the factors first prompting Ryan to enrol on an access course was his wife being made redundant from a job she hated as a computer operator. 'She was at a kind of crossroads' and Ryan encouraged her to take stock and change direction. This resulted in Vickie enrolling on an access course and from there to a university degree in disability nursing; for Ryan, 'that's where the process started'. In other words, although he remained in his monotonous job for another couple of years in order to support the family, there is clear evidence of collaborative decision-making between the couple. This was to colour the rest of his account and to direct it away from the lone self-determination of the autonomous reflexive: 'obviously I could see that my wife had the opportunity and it was a good opportunity for me as well'. Equally, for Ryan the knowledge that his son, though bright, would always require some physical care was also 'a major factor in why I actually had to do something'. Although these considerations did not eliminate the conflict Ryan was to experience between his autonomous and his meta-reflexive inclinations, it was to weigh in on the latter side and to transform the subsequent narrative into one about (re)shaping life as a family.

In fact, the desire to reshape a different life together was a self-conscious motive. Retrospectively, Ryan reveals: 'me and my wife were actually going through difficulties at the time and split up for a couple of months as well. And I think if things were going to get back on track again it was not going to be how it was previously.' That was undoubtedly the case since both were to emerge several years later with degrees, with transformed aspirations and new opportunities. The question was, could they pursue them in tandem or would their elasticized ambitions become a new reason for their relationship to break down or merely to stagger on for the sake of their children, especially their son with special needs?

One of the many reasons why Ryan quit factory work was that he did not find the friendship of his workmates compensated for the monotony of the job:

it's okay when you build up a relationship with the chaps you're working with but even in that kind of environment that can only go so far – kind of work related – it doesn't seem to go much further. Don't get me wrong, I've always been interested in football and that was a major topic of conversation. But I've always had a deep interest in politics and sometimes it's hard to initiate a conversation like that. On a Monday morning it was about football results and who was offside. The most theory you probably got round to was offside theory, which is all good and well but there's only so much you can talk about that.

Even in his first year Ryan had largely lost track of these workmates unless he occasionally popped into his local pub. Maintaining this network was of no concern to him: 'People are always asking me "what are you planning to do?" In one way, it's not what I'm going to do, it's what I've already done – I've made that break.'

However, Ryan did not find it easy to form a new friendship group on campus, even allowing for the fact that he was returning home at the end of the day whilst the younger students were free to socialize. Like others in this sub-group, he is annoyed by the general lack of engagement of students in seminars and absence of intellectual stimulus. He wonders if his involvement would have been easier

if I'd gone to another institution, another university that's probably not as middle class as this and has a few more working-class people of the same age and background, would I have been better in that environment? I do feel disappointed that I haven't become more involved in events. I would have loved to go to some of the [outside] lectures but it's just been difficult. I would have been there on my own and I would have felt uncomfortable going there I think, but I would have really loved it.

By the second year, his main friend was a mature female student who had also entered by an 'unorthodox' route, whom he found intelligent and approachable and ready to discuss lectures in the bar afterwards. Ryan was particularly disappointed when she left for personal reasons because, in his view, 'we were the same kind of people to be honest'. Those intense but informal discussions were what he hoped for: 'That's what I really wanted from university – I naively thought university would be like that, but it's not; everyone is kind of getting their qualifications to go into banking and such like.' His closest friend is also a mature, married man, who Ryan is always trying to convert to his latest academic enthusiasm whilst 'slowly working on him', meaning Ryan is bluntly telling his friend 'You can't keep working on this managerial stuff for the rest of your life, you've got to think of something else to do now. It can't be all about money and your next house.'

Thus he has shed most of his friends from before university, but not gained a network from either campus activities or his course. After the euphoria of enrolment and the challenge of his first year, Ryan found the second year rather flat but sought to explore his own intellectual interests through his choice of modules, essays and plans for his dissertation. Significantly, it was his brother-in-law for whom he worked on a summer job, who first sparked his interest in the Roma and his best work was produced on this marginalized group. What this points to is that in his relative social isolation he was increasingly thrown back on the resources of his family and marriage. Especially whilst Ryan was enjoying his discussions with Kelly, the mature student who withdrew, he reflected rather sadly on their absence between himself and his wife:

I think a problem with our relationship is that we don't really talk. It's frustrating that we don't talk about each other's work or get involved in each other's doings . . . Whereas Vickie's interested on a superficial level in what I'm doing, it's never really – that's why I just love talking to people every time I get the chance. Kelly was brilliant for me because we could have deep discussions. And I love to do so but I've never really had that kind of relationship with my wife anyway. We're both going through the same processes together and have got a bit of understanding. It's okay on that level, but it would be nice to go home and carry on a chat with her.

However, three factors help to bond this family more closely together. Firstly, both he and Vickie have their son's special needs in mind and both have a growing awareness of the paucity of local provisions, which they are drawn towards rectifying. By the end of that year, Ryan says, 'I can see myself doing something like mentoring or community-based work or helping people with educational difficulties and I think my wife will end up doing something like that as well.' Secondly, he has started buying fashion and décor products from the mid twentieth century at car boot sales and selling them on ebay. Although this consuming hobby is to create a conflict about his future career, it also serves to draw him and Vickie closer together and she is fully supportive of his weekend trading. Thirdly, this new shared interest is further cemented as Ryan becomes deeply involved with a cousin living nearby who is a heroin user but does not find methodone plus inactivity a formula that helps him to quit. Ryan admits, 'I've got a bit of a mission to get him out of it' and begins dreaming of giving him a new start working in an expanded antiques business. Again his wife is in favour but although the family has re-bonded, it also seems that this couple may go forward together but in two different directions, fuelled respectively by Ryan's meta- and autonomous reflexive concerns. Alternatively, can this conflict be resolved by the pair elaborating a concerted plan?

Meta-reflexives: careers, commitments and seizing opportunities

Whether single or in a partnership, all members of this sub-group have to reach a decision about their career paths after university, even though these are later revisable. For none of them is this simply a matter of matching their ultimate concerns upon entry with an appropriate pro-fession on exit: their concerns themselves have both crystallized but also mutated to different degrees; the subjects have learned a great deal more about the avenues available for their expression; and each has formed or developed social relationships that influence what advantage they will take of the opportunities of which they have become aware.

Unlike the individualistic autonomous reflexives, it is not that those in durable relationships are necessarily the ones to curtail their commit-ments by compromising with their partners. Being in a couple may have this effect but it can also supply the confidence to respond more openly to opportunity and the spur to create new opportunities by pooling the variety furnished by the two partners.

Nevertheless, it is the case that the pair of subjects who not only began university as 'loners' but also graduated without a dense friendship network capable of deflecting them were those whose eventual careers remained closest to their ultimate concerns upon entry. We have seen that both Neville and Halina persisted in being interest-led throughout their undergraduate years, that both were better at shedding old friends than acquiring new ones, and that those to whom they were drawn were like-minded people sharing similar concerns. Therefore, despite the exi-gencies they confronted, their trajectories are rather smooth learning curves about the opportunities for realizing their concerns – to which they gave enthusiastic responses.

During his first weeks as an undergraduate, Neville declared: 'after I finish university I would like to spend a year out travelling, or possibly doing volunteer work. Then after that I might choose to do teacher training because ultimately I feel that I want to go into a career where I feel I'm making a difference to someone. That's my ultimate goal.' Teaching to him is a vocation 'because whatever you do will have a lasting effect on the people that you teach and if you're not committed to that then you shouldn't be in it.' And vocational dedication takes precedence over all other considerations about the future: 'I would like to be making a difference to someone and that's it really. I don't want to be saying "I'd like to live in a house so big and be married and have x children".' All the same, he is not ready to make that particular commitment then as he recognizes that he is insufficiently knowledgeable about the array of options open to him.

Thus, in his second year he declares, 'yes, teaching's still in the frame, but there's lots of different things this year and I find I want to get a full picture of what's available to me.' He is typical of the meta-reflexives in being more influenced than other students by his degree course and integrating those parts he finds most interesting into his career planning, which in his case was a course on 'migration'. This alerted him to the pos- sibility of working in migration services and he correspondingly explored career openings in the Foreign and Commonwealth Office. Even on its website, this struck him as overly 'based in a kind of economic and polit- ical rhetoric and to lack a bit of the interpersonal stuff that I'm looking for,' but he still decided to explore their open day. His verdict was: 'it's not something that I want to be part of. I don't want to be where I'm sta- tioned, sitting there going "yes, but I have to protect British interests so you can't do this" ... but we do want your investment.' In this comment he first hints at his rejection of both the state and the market. Having decided that this was not a door for him to go through, his response to the perceived absence of institutionalized openings is significant: 'I think it would be difficult to justify your existence if you didn't create oppor- tunity where there would be none without your being there ... I know it's a very personal belief, but I don't think I'd be happy if I didn't create opportunities.' What is striking is not that he actually does so but that he is the first of all the interviewees to articulate this outlook.

Although Neville refuses to be instrumentally rational about his assessed work and follows his interests rather than the curriculum, he receives positive feedback on his assessments and does creditably in his second-year examinations. Consequently, he enters his third year with enhanced self-confidence and announces: 'I'm doing migration studies as an MA next year, down in X, which is a bit of a change of direction but I didn't know such a thing existed last year, so I applied and got a conditional offer.' Thus, his hard work, from which he has not been deflected by a busy social life, had resulted in an elastication of his expectations and he had learned about an opportunity that was previously unknown but was readily seized as soon as discovered.

What he will make of it Neville is uncertain because unsure for whom he would subsequently wish to work. On the one hand, he believes that his future employment should be with an international charity because 'I see little outside of charitable organizations that will make a difference at the current moment – the global economics that has emerged since the Second World War has got no intention of levelling out the playing field at all.' On the other hand, he considers that the best-known charities spend far too much on advertising, a commercialization that Neville holds ethically undermines them. Moreover, in the face of institutions such as the IMF, he considers there is little that voluntary organizations can do without the power of the state behind them, which will never be the case because 'people are always going to be paying more in tax than they are to charitable causes.'

Thus, he hopes to follow up his MA with a PhD, but is quite aware that this is going to culminate in a dilemma between continuing as an academic (and thus upgrading his initial attraction towards teaching to a higher level) or seeking a hands-on post dealing with migration issues in, most likely, the United Nations Development Programme. In his view, 'I've yet got to decide because I don't know how much difference there is to be made.' In the case of UN agencies, he says that 'I don't think there's a lot at the moment. I think you could just end up pen pushing, whereas in academia at least you have the opportunity to try and make a difference to more people than you would sitting in an office somewhere trawling through paperwork, which is not for me.'

At the start of her course in sociology and social policy, Halina admits to uncertainty about her future career: 'I've got vague notions, I know what I'm interested in but it's hard to get jobs to do those things or I don't know what jobs could materialize from them'. However, as a thorough meta-reflexive she projects mental scenarios of possible outcomes: 'it's like playing things out in my mind and thinking what could happen if I went down this path.' From the concerns she has already developed and the values underpinning them, it is easier for her to eliminate possibilities than to endorse them. Thus, she can say categorically that she would 'have a problem working for a really big company that I knew was destroying the environment.' Equally, although she used to want to go into teaching, 'certain things have put me off, one of them is the whole bureaucracy nowadays, just the amount of tests and exams that young children have to go through, all these regulations that just get ridiculous and take the fun out of learning'. Halina has already rejected working in the market and to a lesser extent the state.

The latter was honed during a year in which she worked for the street care department of her local council, when university entry was delayed by her last-minute change of course. During that time, her ultimate concern was a source of critique and of unilateral action. To Halina, the council 'didn't care about environmental issues very much, whereas I kept thinking how this could be reformed, how the council could do a better job towards the environment.' She noted the contradiction in local government that whilst street care would get residents to pay for the disposal of furniture, the housing department was simultaneously crying out for it for those being rehoused and Halina began to ask phone inquirers to consider charitable outlets for quality items: 'that wasn't part of my job. That was more of a vocation and using my beliefs – that I should be doing my job properly, not properly from the council's point of view, but it didn't feel right having all this stuff going to landfill when it could be recycled.'

Halina does not dismiss such forms of local action, and continues to champion environmental activities at all levels throughout her course and at this stage she does not rule it out for her own future. Thus she ruminates: 'I want something that can make a difference, even if it's on a small scale. I've just got all these vague notions about something to do with making a difference, either socially or environmentally. It's not easy to get something, but maybe even in local government, helping a small area to be more green or to make social improvements – I don't know.'

During her second year, in which her activism has been seen to continue and her selection of options was in line with her interests, her concern increased for 'the big picture' about the politics of climate change. Halina struggled to clarify whether she could make an impact were she to work for a government department or would find her commitment compromised and decided she needed to acquire more knowledge through experiencing internships over the summer. She applied for one in the department of bio-conventions, but had increasing reservations about committing herself to this as a career: 'I'm not sure if that's what I want to do because it would just be putting through the government's strategy and working for them and I'm always the one who sits back and thinks "hang on, I want to be able to criticize everything.' This she failed to obtain, but still wanted an experiential basis upon which to evaluate the pros and cons of working from inside government agencies.

Halina thus put in for another internship with the Department of Work and Pensions and began to work on carers' allowances before this summer placement was abruptly truncated by her father's death. Although she immediately returned home, she had been in post sufficiently long to resolve her own dilemma:

if I'd been working for them I would have just accepted it because at the end of the day when you work for someone like that you're part of the system and you just think 'well, yes, it would be lovely if they could earn more but we haven't the money to give them'. Whereas if you're an activist on the outside, you think 'well why can't the government allocate more money, why are they spending all this on the arms trade instead of on carers?' But you can't change it and this means you can probably make more of a difference from outside than from within.

She has answered her own question and will no more contemplate working for state services than for corporate enterprise. Yet determining on an 'outside' role confronts her with another problem because 'there are not many jobs going as campaign officers'.

Returning to university after the funeral, Halina was far from being unmoved but reflects:

I've come to realize, you've got to make the best of the situation you're in and . . . if there's something you can't change, like a death in the family, then you've just got to try to make the best of the life you have. I miss my dad . . . but you've just got to get on with things and, at the end of the day the way you experience life is all about your attitude.

Her tribute to him is to make the most of the opportunity tantalizingly almost within her grasp. She actively sought out openings on the Internet and discovered that Greenpeace offered unpaid internships in Washington. When she pursued the matter Halina was made an offer because, she was told, 'I had so much prior experience'.

She had found an 'alternative' opening and had also successfully explored an international agency organizing volunteer projects in Latin America. The latter will give her three months in Ecuador working on rainforest conservation and then she will move to Washington to take up the Greenpeace internship. This will position Halina favourably for one of the few full-time posts as a project leader, but she remains adamant that 'all I can do is be part of the movement for change'. Having partly grasped and partly made her opportunity for working outside the market and the state she has also become fully convinced that civil society is crucial to social transformation 'because it's actually showing what people care about and they're doing it not because they get paid but because they're passionate about it'.

As in every biography, contingency plays its part and in Halina's her father's death was unpredictable. Moreover, given her unchanging wish for a family, the trajectory could also have ended otherwise. It is contingent whether such a relationship eventuates or not and also what consequences transpire if it does. The latter can only be explained by the dynamics of the relationship between the two people involved. Kate, who began university with aspirations that are not so very different from Halina's, is a subject whose partnership is responsible for these gradually reducing in kind and in scope. That this is not necessarily the case will be illustrated by Ryan and his wife, whose marital relations work in precisely the opposite direction.

Kate, too, sees her future career as a vocation: 'I don't see a job as just a means to get money, it's got to be more important than that or you're not going to get any satisfaction out of it.' To her, 'that satisfaction will come from benefiting other people, that's something I feel quite strongly about'. At some stage she would like to take an MA but, during her first year, she says:

my dream job would be working for the UN. That's something that I would be interested in, working for an international organization or a non-governmental organization. It's very idealistic but I want to do something that's going to help people and that's going to try and change things for the better. Probably something like the Human Rights Commission because that's something I feel very strongly about.

Her characterization of this career as a 'dream' shows her awareness of the uncertainties about obtaining it.

After she changed her degree to straight politics, Kate became even more interested in this kind of work through absorption in her course on International Relations. Like the other meta-reflexive subjects, employment in a multi-national enterprise, accountancy, consultancy or banking is something she rejected out of hand and never wavered about. However, during her second year she shared Halina's dilemma about working inside the state in relation to compromising one's values and being unable to promote policy change. The desirability of being employed by an NGO is that 'you're kind of influencing the system without being a part of it, so you're not being constrained by it but you are still being able to influence it and actually make a difference'. Conversely, she is attracted to 'work for a foreign policy think tank, or for the civil service, or in diplomacy'. Yet Kate sees these careers as entailing much the same constraints and collusion that Halina had highlighted:

The only problem I'd maybe have with that was being part of the government, having to take the line the government takes. It kind of precludes your own views and your own beliefs to a certain extent. It doesn't mean that you can't have them but you have to be a bit more quiet about them and toe the line – this is what they want me to say, this is the position the government has and you have to follow that.

However, as the year goes by we have already seen how Kate's relationship with Chris is serving to moderate her political views and it is no
surprise that she comes to endorse the 'insider' position and has applied
for the civil service fast track, although she still hopes to make an impact
on policy. By the end of the year, she is beginning to worry about the
implications of separation that even this option would entail, although
she says firmly: 'I'll cross that bridge when I come to it. If it comes
to the time when I'm having to decide whether I want to do this civil
service thing that will take me abroad for eighteen months, I'll consider
the implications of that for the relationship if it's still there.' Yet more
robustly, she finishes the interview by affirming that 'at the end of the
day I have my destiny in my own hands'. This may be the case for the
partnerships between independent individuals that were encountered in
Chapter 5 amongst the parents of autonomous reflexives, but can it be
the case for a meta-reflexive?

In her final year, Kate tries to square this circle. On the one hand, she
admits that the nature of her social concern has modified considerably.
As far as the most oppressed are concerned, 'I suppose it's weakened,
maybe. I've always been very concerned with social justice, with the suffering of people, not just directly around me but in a more global sense
and maybe I don't feel as strongly about that as I used to do.' On the
other hand, her rejection of modernity's Leviathans seems firm: 'At the
moment the sort of things I'm interested in are in the realm of government corruption and collusion with the industrial multi-nationals like
BP and Shell . . . especially in America, the collusion between the energy
companies and the government.' However, it is significant that her con-
demnation is directed or deflected towards the US because she is now
applying for fast-track entry to the civil service, to become a parliamen-
tary assistant and for a position as a graduate intelligence analyst with
GCHQ.[7]

Kate freely admits that the attraction of such work is that it would
satisfy her political interests whilst absolving her of political responsibility,
a compromise formula she has evolved through discussions with her
boyfriend:

I mean in the intelligence work, I wouldn't be the person making the decisions,
I'd just be providing the data and information. Because me and my boyfriend
have had discussions like this about science . . . and I've always maintained that
knowledge itself and information is neutral, it's what you do with the information
that makes it moral or immoral. So, in the GCHQ job I feel I'd be providing

---

[7] Government Communications Headquarters (the central agency gathering and analysing
intelligence).

information and what people chose to do with that information is in their hands and I have no responsibility for that. . . . I was a bit dubious about the diplomatic corps because that would be kind of the government tells you this and that's what you communicate, whereas working in the actual civil service, they're an entirely neutral group for it's the government that makes the actual decisions.

Yet her formula is fuzzy because she still wants policy influence without assuming political responsibility and she oscillates between opting for a career that 'actually has an effect rather than just being some sort of cog in a giant wheel'.

The opportunities to which Kate will respond have contracted as her relationship has become her prime concern. She now concedes that 'so long as I don't wake up in the morning resenting the fact that I have to go to work and as long as I got on with the people I work with then I'd be content with that.' Chris will proceed to an MA, and, he hopes to a PhD. They plan to live together in Warwick when he becomes a post-graduate, meaning that Kate has ceased to consider working for an NGO or any appointment involving time posted overseas. In fact she now wants her employment to be within commutable distance and her attitude towards having a family has reversed as 'we've sort of talked about kids names.' Kate and Chris seem to be a partnership without a plan: compromise and convenience have curtailed the response of both to the opportunities that each once considered because their relationship has resulted in clipping each other's wings rather than designing a flight path together.

Ryan and Vickie illustrate the opposite outcome, namely how a couple can extend one another's horizons and create new opportunities for themselves and their family by exploiting the synergy between their respective concerns and career projects. As has been seen, this was a lengthy process in which the establishment of compatibility began to be elaborated only when Ryan was about to graduate and seemed to have found a solution to the competition for domination between his autonomous and meta-reflexive tendencies. These had effectively pulled him in different directions from the start of his degree. On the one hand, he stressed that his complete absence of control in factory work was crucial to his re-entry to education: 'it was a major factor in my life not to have control and to have no say in what or where you are going to go', a grievance frequently expressed by autonomous reflexives and possibly exacerbated by his step-father's self-employment. On the other hand, from the start he emphasized the archetypical goal of the meta-reflexive to make a difference that improved the lives of others: 'I can't really think of anything apart from that as rewarding'.

In his first year he was clearly unsure how these two *desiderata* can coincide in a concrete career and merely mentioned 'research work, although what research work entails I don't know'. A year later and now a clear meta-reflexive who has developed an interest in sociology of education, he foresaw

community-based work, education-based work, but not, you know, mainstream – maybe working with kids who are pretty much how I used to be, those that are marginalized, hence my interest in the Roma, or those that find it a little bit more difficult in society to get a foot up. What it is I'm going to be doing in that area I don't know yet, but without a shadow of a doubt I think I will be doing something like that.

Moreover, Vickie is moving on complementary lines with her placement in a residential care home. If their combined response to opportunity had rested there, it only wanted in precision to represent the (re)shaping of the life of this couple, one mutually compatible for the partners and complementing their family's needs.

However, more than a 'shadow of a doubt' was introduced by Ryan's foray into buying and selling antiques, which re-animated his autonomous proclivity and, as he underscores, 'I've always imagined me getting enjoyment out of working if it was for myself and I've experimented with that a little bit. So if worst came to worst and I struggled to find my ideal career, there's something else I could develop as well.' This is an opportunity he has made for himself, has learned the knack of how to present objects on ebay with the appropriate photographs and descriptions and is making money. This could be seen as an incipient threat to the (re)shaped life that seemed to be forming above. However, Ryan refuses to view his trading as thrusting entrepreneurialism: 'at the moment I'm doing it for myself and, even if I got big I'd be doing it for my family. And if it got bigger still I'd be doing it for the community because it's those in the community that I'd employ.'

Nevertheless, in his final year he had more of a struggle with himself than anticipated and found himself back in the thick of the 'discernment' phase, rather than clinching his 'dedication'. It was precipitated by the couple receiving two career openings: Vickie's to become Deputy Manager of the residential home and Ryan's being offered a place on the MA in Social Work. His response was 'I'd say I'm 80 per cent sure . . . I've accepted it anyway so it's an option there if I want to take it'. This would seem to gel nicely with his wife's new opportunity and confirms their initial plan for conjoint community involvement. He sees that the MA could lead into working with fostering and adoption, and not only does this reverberate with his 'vested interest' in this issue, reflect the fascination with it fuelled by a module he is following on narrative life history but it also represents 'a vocation' to him. Ryan took this module knowing it would give him 'the opportunity to look at adoption and get into it a bit more and it's paid dividends. It's opened my eyes, so I thought "well that is interesting, I would like to do that" and along came the MA course and I thought, "ideal timing let's go for it".' The impact was indubitable because he also determined to locate his birth parents and his wife was fully in favour.

Matters were complicated because throughout his last year he has been stockpiling antiques without having the time to sell or the space to store them, although his knowledge of the overseas market had grown considerably. So, too, has his commitment to employing his cousin and keeping him off drugs, thus Ryan says: 'that's why I'm 80 per cent certain about my MA'. In fact, he is even more internally divided by what seems to be a resurgence of his original autonomous versus meta-reflexive tendencies:

If I had a passion to do anything it would be to work for myself – ultimately I think that's where it lies. But I'm taking the sensible option [the MA] plus the fact that I've got a vested interest so I need to do that. But, given half a chance, that's what I'm going to be taking . . . I'll kick myself if I never give trading at least a try. It will be a bit of an experiment, it will be great, that's where my heart lies at the moment.

Ryan lights up as he talks about his art deco finds and sales, whereas he is explicit that the two-year MA 'would be a pain in the backside. I know what I want to do – follow the artistic side, the Bohemian side, of my character.'

Ryan acknowledges that he is spoilt for opportunities, 'I'm probably overwhelmed with choices to be honest and it's knowing which one to take for the best'. Of course, he has considered combining the two, but the MA may involve him five days a week, meaning the two projects are not complementary. So why does he incline towards the MA? His reasons are a fascinating insight into the dilemmas that the situational logic of opportunity can present: 'I'm going more towards the MA because I don't know if I'll ever get a second opportunity of that again . . . whereas with this selling malarkey, it's always going to be there for me.' In fact he does take up his place on the MA and that may appear to be the official outcome – one more mature working-class student whose talents have been refitted and harnessed to a professional career.

However, this is not where the relational story of this couple ends. At the start, just prior to university, the pair had just been through a trial separation. When both are on the point of graduating, Ryan says of his marriage: 'now that's a partnership and I enjoy it'. The two are not only talking they are engaged in planning together. Vickie had always supported the antique 'malarkey', even as the house became increasingly crammed and her own passion became defined as opening a care home. It seems to be she who first ventured their plan because, in Ryan's words, 'the accumulative side of things [the antiques], that's well reached into Vickie anyway. I mean she even talks about setting up a nursing home in years to come. I think I will be better concentrating on the selling side and earning the money to make that possible as a joint venture.' This is neither pie in the sky, for they have cost out how their house could help capitalize the plan, nor is it a pragmatic compromise. What the couple envisage is creating further relational goods for their son: 'we've got a vested interest in it because of our son. We want to make sure that when he's a teenager he's got his own independence', meaning within a home of individual families with children who have special needs and will always require a special environment: 'I'd love to aim for something like that, that's just perfection, that is. I would love my son to be involved in something like that, it puts your own mind at rest.'

Let Ryan have the last word for the sub-group of meta-reflexives on the theme of their relationship to the situational logic of opportunity: 'If there's one thing I can say about me doing this degree over the past three years it's that now I'm in a situation where I've never been and that is that I can pretty much choose what I want to do. So if there's one thing that I can say this degree has given me, qualifications aside, it would be the choices.'

Conclusion

The aim of this chapter was to identify the distinctive natal relationships that constitute the generative mechanism of meta-reflexivity. Only then would it be possible to account for the linkage between this mode of reflexive practice and the situational logic of opportunity and how meta-reflexives serve to undermine modernity through their antipathy towards both of its Leviathans – the market and the state. Otherwise, the analysis of young, highly educated subjects provides an association between meta-reflexivity and type of career chosen, but not an explanation.

The in-depth interviewing of four subjects alone permits nothing more than tentative hypotheses to be ventured. Nevertheless, their formal similarities at the micro-level were striking. All were the beneficiaries of *certain* relational goods, most importantly of a durable relationship between their parents giving familial stability for which these young subjects expressed their appreciation.[8] In addition, all parents (except the adoptive

---

[8] The lastingness of these marriages endured until the eldest child (as it happened) graduated from university. This means that many of the parents would still be in their forties and could thus contribute to the rise in the national divorce trend after this study is

couple) actively promoted university entry, gave some financial support and offered more, even though the subjects refused to avail themselves of it.

In explaining the disengagement, difference and distancing of the interviewees most importance was attributed to the manner in which persistent parental dissent had problematized key parts of the social order for their children, especially politics and religion in the cases examined. In these and other respects documented above such families were not consensual 'norm circles' fostering normative reproduction in the next generation. On the contrary, they had alerted their children to both the *importance but also the problematic nature* of a central feature of modernity. Although any two parents could manifestly live with their differences, overt disagreements and tensions (presumably because of other but unknown compensations within their relationship), this type of dyad created the greatest obstacle to accommodating a third person (the child) and transforming itself into a working triad. How was the child to fit in? As third parties, the children could not syncretize the mixed messages received because any syncretic formula would be unacceptable to both parents. Nor could they side with one parent against the other, that is, without exacerbating domestic tensions.

It is this that led our subjects to become 'loners' within their domestic settings, young people who confronted micro-level contextual incongruity *within* its confines. They were thus impelled to work out their own orientations towards at least one important part of the social order, as was the explicit intent of some parents, and hence were propelled towards individuation.[9] In other words, they were pressed to make some of their own necessary selections and to do so whilst still growing up.

However, the more extreme the parental dissent the less well equipped were these young people to form their own relationships within the social order and thus to move on to shaping a life that could be found satisfying and sustainable. Hence, Halina and Neville had solved one part of their future *modus vivendi* – their employment after graduation – but had problems rounding this out with friendship and partnership. Conversely, Kate and Ryan compromised or agonized over the former

completed. Whether or not this is the case remains unknown and is merely signalled as a possibility that cannot be ruled out. In Halina's words: 'I think I'm really lucky actually to have had two parents who stayed together'.

[9] Thus Kate reported that she could 'remember from when I was younger that my parents were always very much like "you make your own decisions and you form your own beliefs and we're not going to force you or encourage you into a particular religion or a particular political view or anything".' This appears an increasingly popular strategy for attempting to defuse parental differences.

because they had both established and developed lasting relationships that did not immediately and smoothly dovetail with their occupational concerns.

To different degrees, they all struggled to work out their own attitudes and actions towards that part of the social order that their parents had rendered problematic yet whose *importance* they had succeeded in conveying. This is the main effect of the relational goods they have received. Hence, the use made by all of these subjects, unlike practitioners of other reflexive modes, of their university courses to clarify and articulate their own views. Hence, too, the especial seriousness with which the meta-reflexives took their degrees, not in an instrument rational fashion but because the academic issues, arguments and material to which they were exposed were their raw materials for articulating precisely where they stood in relation to what they cared about most. This also accounts for the meta-reflexives being the one sub-group whose members continuously entertained taking a higher degree or even undertaking a university career. To them academic debates were not a sterile rehearsal and regurgitation of pros and cons to obtain certification but the resources for attaining some (fallible) certitude about the issues their parental dissention had prioritized. In other words, they provide the best exemplification that self-socialization in trans-modernity is a life-long undertaking. Only in this way can they achieve the clarification and discursive substantiation of their own values and inclinations towards courses of action that underlie their practical reasoning in the social order.[10] Both are acquired through a long and active learning process which is the obverse of 'internalization' as an easy and permanent 'fix'.

Of course, it may be objected that family dissention and argument are commonplace, without resulting in the positive responses to the situational logic of opportunity displayed by our subjects through their openness to *inquiry* outside family bounds. This is true, many young subjects may simply 'cut and run', getting away from home by immersing themselves in their peer groups, in cyber social interaction or media induced preoccupations. In fact, it will be ventured that these are the young people who get by domestically on the basis of their 'gut reactions' and their expressive action as will be examined in the next chapter.

What this objection leaves out of account is that the meta-reflexive subjects are recipients of familial relational goods. They distance themselves

---

[10] Here is Kate again on developing one's own values: 'It's very much a personal code of ethics. It's all too easy for you to be told how to live and what to do and what's right and what's wrong. It's a lot more difficult for you to decide for yourself. You feel you've gained a lot more by making those decisions yourself – you feel the decision's been a lot more worthwhile.'

as individuated persons but they have not been subjected to a careless or uncaring domestic fracas provoking unconcern and indifference. On the contrary, they are concerned about sources of difference and their own difference; their parents matter, in particular because they have set the agenda. They are neither to be dismissed as people nor are their differences to be trivialized as purely interpersonal matters of 'getting at one another' or 'not getting on'. What these parental relationships have induced are young people who have to disengage from them in order to re-engage with the social order in terms of their own concerns. Hence, they show openness not only to *inquiry*, in order to define where they stand, but also to the situational logic of opportunity because *novel* openings effectively challenge neither parent yet are expressive of the young subjects' individuation.

7 Fractured reflexives: casualties of the reflexive imperative

The rapid replacement of modernity's 'situational logic of competition' by the 'situational logic of opportunity' undoubtedly places more of a burden on subjects themselves, their familial relationships, natal relational contexts and their chosen social networks. This is because routinely competitive responses by groups, classes and associations are decreasingly appropriate for confronting novelty, as was maintained in Chapter 2. At the same time, 'opportunity' itself is met by a variety of responses. For some (the communicatives), it can be partly but not entirely evaded, for others (the autonomous), it can be seized upon and fallibly exploited, and for yet others (the meta-reflexives), it presents a new horizon of novel possibilities. However, not everyone can practise one of these three reflexive responses towards the 'logic of opportunity', all of which seek to match life outcomes to subjects' life concerns. These are the fractured reflexives.[1]

Whilst 'opportunity' represents the possibility of life being different for the 'rejecters', who have turned their backs on their natal backgrounds and the relational evils they represent, these subjects are regularly so preoccupied by the traumatic events in question that they focus on the immediate needs of survival.[2] This precludes reflexive deliberation about more extended forms of purposeful action. Equally regularly, they admit to huge difficulties in making decisions, in defining courses of action to be consistently pursued and, above all, in engaging in anything more than the survivalist's day-to-day planning.

---

[1] Technically, fractured reflexives were defined as those who scored an average of 4.00 or over on the relevant 'F' questions on ICONI. The distinctions between the sub-categories discussed in this chapter are all derived from the in-depth interview data. Among the entry population, 7.9 per cent (10 students) scored as fractured reflexives, with this rising to 16.9 per cent in the final year. The initial percentage rises to 17.4 per cent (22 students) if the expressive reflexives are added into this sub-group.

[2] See Chapter 3 for the initial discussion of 'rejecters' and other types consequent upon family relations.

Quite different are those who do not number amongst the 'rejecters', yet who encounter some extreme negative contingency with adverse effects for the mode of reflexivity they had previously practised.[3] They find themselves paralysed in conducting internal conversations capable of extricating them from these situations and enabling them to resume purposeful reflexive responses to opportunities. These subjects suffer intensely but, being fixated on their sufferings, they are too disoriented to deliberate about a way out, thus being rendered passive.

Different again are those with 'under-developed reflexivity', i.e. without any fully developed mode of internal conversation enabling them to diagnose (fallibly, of course) the relationship between their personal concerns and their social circumstances, as is necessary for designing constructive courses of action. It is debatable whether or not they should be grouped with the fractured reflexives or be considered as a previously unrecognized mode, one possibly associated with trans-modernity itself. There are two considerations favouring their treatment as a discrete group of practitioners: quantitatively, they do not register 'F' scores and qualitatively their mental processes are peculiarly *expressive* in kind.[4]

Their *expressive* rather than dialogical responses mean they exercise their agency solely in relation to the present moment and current circumstances, rather than assuming any reflexive governance over the shape of their lives. In other words, they respond to the necessity of selection by a series of expressive actions that cannot cumulate into a *modus vivendi* because they lack the coordinated self-monitoring that is essential to the shaping process.[5] It follows that they are not immune to 'opportunity', but that they impulsively seize (instead of intentionally pursuing) a series of appealing opportunities *seriatim*. Since there is nothing to guarantee any coherence between these sequential outcomes and yet the subject has to live with or deal with their consequences, they may well be turning the cutting edge of novel opportunities against themselves in unintended acts of under-reflexive self-harming. The 'situational logic of opportunity' cannot be approached purely situationally as discrete and disconnected episodes, to which expressive responses are random in terms of their

---

[3] Obviously, ICONI is incapable of making such distinctions, which come from the in-depth interview material, since the indicator simply measures scores to questions at the date of its administration.

[4] Instead, expressives are those whose final scores on ICONI were below the mean of 4.00 for *all modes* of reflexivity. The ten recorded as expressive reflexives at point of entry had diminished to five practitioners by the time of graduation. Interestingly, all of the expressives were female, whilst fractured reflexives mirrored the 1:4 ratio of males to females amongst this cohort of undergraduates.

[5] That is coordinated by their hierarchy of concerns and the dovetailing of them.

mutual compatibility. Instead, coherence between these responses over time requires choreography – what Taylor terms having a sense of the 'unity of a life' – which is provided by using our concerns as the compass in order to keep our bearings in the diverse contexts we confront.

On the other hand, expressive reflexives often display an equivalent but consequential distress and regret at the 'mess they have made of things', at how badly they have served those concerns that matter to them and, above all, they share the same uncertainty about how to go forward and what to do next. They accept that their past doings have left a trail of debris, of unfinished business and unresolved issues that still have to be coped with in everyday life as the effect of their past decisions, which were not deliberatively chosen at the time. Because of that, the expressive reflexives will be treated as a form of fractured reflexivity in this chapter, specifically as 'under-developed' reflexives.[6] The main argument for continuing to regard this as a form of 'fracturing' is that *all fractured subjects are primarily expressive*, wounded and regretful, without being able to design a course of action to ameliorate their situation.

The common denominator of all fractured subjects is, as first characterized in *Structure, Agency and the Internal Conversation*, an absence or a lack in the reflexive internal conversation such that 'it supplies the subject with no orientation towards the question "what is to be done". Instead of leading to purposeful courses of action, *the self-talk of the "fractured reflexive" is primarily expressive. Its effect is to intensify affect*.'[7] These are not pathological people or even people with pathologies. In fact, they are courageous subjects and, as the walking wounded, nearly all had concealed their misery from the university authorities, managed to go about their daily student affairs, and to graduate with nothing less than an upper second-class degree.

From the start, fractured reflexivity was not regarded as a homogeneous category. My earliest study differentiated between three sub-categories, which will be retained and refined rather than being replaced here. First, some of the subjects encountered had previously exercised a dominant mode of reflexivity until adverse circumstances had led to the suspension of this personal power. Those were termed '*displaced reflexives*'. What remained unanswerable in that study, because confined to one point in time, was whether or not they could recover their previous reflexive powers and, if so, would they simply resume practising their

---

[6] Further research on a broader population could well succeed in demonstrating that they constitute a distinct sub-group, a conclusion that I neither would nor could resist.

[7] Margaret S. Archer, *Structure, Agency and the Internal Conversation*, Cambridge University Press, 2003, p. 303 (emphasis added here).

earlier dominant mode? The process of recovery and some of the relational conditions for it will be qualitatively examined in this chapter.

Second, there are those who at the initial interview had not developed a mode of reflexivity to the point where it could be exercised to converse internally about relations between self and society. Nonetheless, they showed some bent towards the practice of a particular mode and also shared a similar relational background to its proficient practitioners. These are termed '*impeded reflexives*'.[8] The advantage of this longitudinal study is that the second and third interviews could ascertain if these subjects were able to overcome the problems stemming from their natal backgrounds and begin to practise the reflexive bent to which they appeared inclined.

Third, there is the category about who least is known, namely those who practised very little internal conversation as assessed both quantitively and qualitatively through interview. In the 2003 study only one such subject was encountered, whose extraordinarily limited self-talk led him to be termed a 'near non-reflexive'. In his case this was attributed to the appalling life he had led on the streets since the age of thirteen, more rejected by his family background than a rejecter of it.[9] However, the present findings prompt a refinement of this sub-category.

A cluster of ten '*expressive reflexives*' was detected at point of entry and, although numbers reduced over the three years, half graduated without changing. Clearly they had got by, but how had they got through in seeming defiance of the reflexive imperative? Fortunately, two of those who volunteered for interview are able to tell us. What they reveal is placing great reliance upon their 'gut feelings' as a guide to action, which is not a means of assuming governance over their lives through coherent selection and shaping. In short, the persistence of fractured reflexivity of any form is not only painful in itself but extorts the accumulated penalties of passivity. These subjects themselves would rather that their life courses had been otherwise and could be otherwise. Giving due respect to these differences within the sub-group means dealing with three variants of 'fracturedness': the displaced, the impeded and the expressive.

Of the seven subjects who volunteered for interview, all were female.[10] The six interviewed over the three years divided equally between those of working-class and of middle-class origins. Not one had taken a gap year,

---

[8] This and other sub-categories of Ffractured reflexivity were first discussed in Archer, *Structure, Agency and the Internal Conversation*, pp. 298–341.

[9] See Archer, *Structure, Agency and the Internal Conversation*, pp. 333–341.

[10] Christina, whom we met in Chapter 2, was to drop out after year one and will not be discussed further here.

so the full brunt of their natal relations can be assumed to have impacted directly upon their reactions to entering university.

There is a further finding that sheds light on the fractured group as a whole and to movements into and out of it. This entailed calculating measures of association to discover the relationships between the 'F' scores of practitioners of the other modes of reflexivity upon entering university.[11] The autonomous reflexives have been conceptualized as very different from the fractured in both relations to their natal backgrounds and their 'strategic' rather than passive approach to opportunity. The r value (-0.728 and its p-value $= 0.000$) represents a strong, negative and statistically significant correlation. In other words, autonomous subjects repudiate 'fracturedness' most ruggedly and, it can be hypothesized, are least likely to gravitate into the fractured reflexive group over their three years of study.

Conversely, there was a slight, positive, but not statistically significant relationship between their 'F' scores and the scores of communicative reflexives.[12] This tendency may imply a greater susceptibility to 'fracturing' amongst the communicatives than other types of reflexives and certainly fits the case of Julie to be discussed shortly. A weak, negative, but again not significant correlation was found between 'F' scores and those of meta-reflexives.[13] These two findings may still be of theoretical interest, despite their lack of statistical significance, simply by indicating opposite tendencies: one in the positive direction towards fracturing for the communicatives, whilst the meta-reflexives are (weakly) resilient to it. In the light of the decision to consider the 'expressives' as a variant upon fractured reflexivity, it was also interesting to find a moderate, positive, though not statistically significant association between the 'F' scores and the scores of expressive reflexives.[14] Again, this could be theoretically important in having detected at least a tendency justifying the amalgamation of these two sub-categories in the analysis that follows.

This chapter will work through the three sub-categories of fractured reflexives presenting the same relational analysis of natal backgrounds, friendship groups and career choices as employed in the previous three chapters. Once again, the generic question to answer is: what needed to be the case for young subjects to enter university as fractured reflexives or what happened during their undergraduate careers that led them to enter

---

[11] The measures of association are Pearson's r, ANOVA, and the Bonferroni test procedure. It is important to remember that no one scores zero on any of the other modes of reflexivity, whatever their dominant mode may be and however numerically distanced they may be from a score indicating fractured reflexivity.

[12] Here $r = 0.32$, p-value $= 0.286$.   [13] With $r = 0.163$, p-value $= 0.416$.

[14] $r = 0.304$, p-value $= 0.140$.

this group? The first case to be examined is the sole subject amongst the interviewees who fractured in the course of her studies. It is important to recall that the circumstances involved are expected to be matters of contingency and that she is not anticipated to have natal relations that bear any resemblance to those of the largest group of fractured reflexives, the 'rejecters'.

A displaced communicative reflexive or what led to Julie's fracturing?

When she came to university, Julie was a typical communicative reflexive and a clear 'identifier' (her father is an accountant and her mother a nurse). In listing her three main concerns in life, she places 'my mum' in first place, as distinct from 'my family' which is also listed: 'my mum is very special – so a separate category'. By her final year, her mother remains at the top of the list: 'I mean she's still my best friend and a massive part of my life and she's very, very into family and close to all her side of the family, like my nan and my nan's sister even, and I'm my auntie's child's godmother – and I mean we're very, very close . . . I think I'm just following through with it.'

Julie assumed she would go to university like her two sisters. Nevertheless, she found the decision-making agonizing: 'I was trying to decide whether to come to Warwick or go to university with my boyfriend and it was really tearing me in two directions – and I was asking everyone'. The deciding factor 'was trying to please my dad. He's never really had very high hopes for me . . . So when I got the opportunity to come to Warwick it felt like the first time he's really been proud of me. And hearing him being proud of me, I didn't want to disappoint him.' Not only did Julie propitiate her father rather than her boyfriend, but she compromised with dad over her course and applied for law and sociology, which he considered a better career prospect. However, his view that the aim of his daughters should be the pursuit of lucrative jobs is one that Julie rejects. Mother and father have divergent values with Dad's materialism being at variance with Mum's commitment to caring and continuing to work as a nurse.

Julie describes herself as 'not very confident' and worried about others' opinions of her: 'I like to please people and it does upset me if I think I've upset someone'. Her next comment that 'I like to know what people expect of me and I don't like to get it wrong' shows the normative conventionalism typical of communicative reflexives. In her mother and from outsiders' responses to her, Julie recognizes someone who has solved this in an exemplary manner. During her long vacation, Julie took temporary work in the same hospital: 'I can see the way she affects the patients and they don't know I'm her daughter, but I get a lot of peo-ple coming to me saying "Oh that lovely nurse, I hope she's in again". And it really makes me think wow, she's really doing something here.' However, Julie has already burnt her boats – as far as strict replication is concerned – by propitiating her father and now has to find a different solution for shaping her life, which she resolves by aspiring to work in 'a small local law firm'. As an 'identifier', when asked how she envisages her own future family she clearly wants to replicate those practices she diagnoses as contributing to her closest relationship: 'I would give up my job to look after my children and then maybe go back to work afterwards. That's what my mum did with me and I think that's why we've got such a good relationship.'

Although she and her boyfriend attend different universities, he had already become part of her friendship network ('we're accepted as a couple') and her family before they left home: 'My boyfriend and my mum get on really well. He doesn't have a mum and he's starting to treat my mum like his mum.' This is important for both relationships, given the intensity of Julie's attachment to her mother and the fact that her mother and boyfriend constitute her two home interlocutors, who are never displaced, who survive the course, and help her to survive it. In her first year, Julie tells that 'my mum's learned to email now, so we have day-to-day conversations and I speak to my boyfriend a lot on the phone. In an email I can pop in anything, even like "Do you think this is the right price for a can of beans, Mum?" It's often very trivial. So they're still around quite a lot for me.'

What went wrong in her second year when this pattern communicative unexpectedly returned the score of a fractured reflexive? It is university policy that students live out of halls in year two and common student practice to find accommodation with a small group from the same res-idence. Although Julie had plenty of 'course friends' and some inkling that her housemates were not ideal, she talks of lacking the confidence to seek alternatives and of dreading giving offence. What ensued was the worst of small-group dynamics exacerbated by the worst of geographical contingency. The house they rented was as far from the university as was feasible without a car, off the bus route, and involving a long, dark walk across playing fields, meaning virtual house arrest in winter after 4 pm.

As an ill-assorted group, bickering began between the housemates but Julie became the target of serious bullying after she let slip that she would be moving in with a 'course friend' the following year. The persecution escalated: her belongings were searched, her photos defaced and shopping trolleys parked in her room. She could not use her phone because of eavesdropping and raucous comments, the house had no internet connection, and she would not use the kitchen for fear of abuse, thus fasting between lunch on campus until breakfast there the next morning. 'I couldn't write anything down, I couldn't talk to anyone, it all just built up inside, which I think is why I was just sort of on the brink all the time – I was very emotional'.

In these troubles Julie tried to exercise self-restraint and not over-burden her mother, which almost felt like having lost her, and attempted to do the same with her boyfriend when spending every weekend with him. However, she encountered the same problem with both, for how does anyone censor the rehearsal of her problems when she is a com-municative? Under the combined stress of bullying and of assuming an unwonted self-control in her 'thought and talk' pattern, Julie was being forced into an alien autonomous mode and began to crack.

Why did she not simply pack and leave, as an autonomous reflexive would probably have done? This is because, firstly, she is intrapunitive in believing she has done something to upset her housemates (if only by telling them she will live with other people the following year); secondly, because she feels the expectations of others should be met (she will houseshare with them until the end of the academic year); thirdly, but most importantly, she is deprived of the free-flow of communicativity with her two interlocutors upon which her decision-making depends (going home is a long and complicated journey). Consequently, she tries evasion: staying inside her room, spending a night a week with a 'course friend', and going to her boyfriend as her weekend bolthole. Finally, evasion segues into endurance, counting off the days until her boyfriend's study week, when he will come and stay with her, then her revision period, to be spent at home, only returning to her course friends' accommodation to take her exams (where she receives nightly hate messages from her ex-housemates). Endurance can be another name for the passivity of the fractured reflexive.

Simultaneously, her friendships transmute into relationships of depen-dency. Julie clings to her 'course friends' and the prospect of living with them next year prevents her from dropping out. She becomes yet more attached when late one night they drive out to 'rescue' her in her pyjamas after a whispered phone call. Julie depends on her boyfriend (being the only communicative to have sustained a pre-university relationship) and the weekends with him, when 'I'd spend the first hour crying and the last hour crying'. In this respect, his two weeks spent with her house-mates helped to dilute his perception of her unwarranted dependence and intrapunitiveness:

He got a bit of a shock when he came because they started rifling through his things as well and he was really cross. I mean I had to calm him down because he said 'I just can't believe they've done that. That was outrageous'. It was really strange to me because I thought 'Oh, so it's all right if I get a bit cross when they do this or that to me' because in the past I thought 'Oh, it's probably just me'.

Fracturing strains all relationships and Julie only realized how passively dependent she had become when her mother asked her to order and collect a takeaway meal after her exams: 'Before, I'd been so weak that she'd say "Don't worry, I'll do it" and now she's actually getting me to do things again for myself.'

Whilst Julie's second-year verdict was 'I'm not sure if I'm going to finish university, let alone have a career', by the end of her third year of living with her 'course friends', this has changed to 'it's brilliant, it's like a whole different university'. And she would like to volunteer for 'Nightline', simply to convey the message 'you can come out at the other end'.[15] In that case, why didn't she use it herself and how did she 'come out'? To communicative reflexives, trust is (rightly) regarded as a property emerging between intimates as a relational good that cannot be predicated of an anonymous voice on a helpline. This makes them hard to help, charily reticent about counselling and generically reliant upon their interlocutors. Julie's recovery as a restored practitioner of communicative reflexivity in her third year, one who re-endorses her original replicatory project of returning to live close to home, to marry her boyfriend and to join a high-street law firm, can be attributed to two factors.

On the one hand, without minimizing the pain she went through, her problem was extraneous, of fixed and limited duration, and situational in nature. Indeed, she herself had diagnosed the need to change that situation, except that announcing it was precisely what triggered its deterioration. On the other hand, the strength of her relationships and their positive relationality supported her through this trauma. One final lesson that Julie underscores is that a communicative reflexive will be 'displaced' into the fractured group rather than being able to adopt autonomous reflexivity and practise it in order to save herself alone and unaided.

The 'rejecters': how relational evils result in fractured reflexivity

Relational evils are more than interpersonal cruelty. Although the former certainly do not exclude the latter, it would be a mistake to reduce the nature, receipt and effects of negative relations to individual acts and

---

[15] Nightline is a student helpline, staffed by volunteers, for those in difficulties between 9 pm and 9 am.

their personal consequences for the subject involved. Despite the fact that cruelty can take varied forms, in only one of the three cases to be examined was it unambiguously present, in another it was a contributory factor, and in the third it was absent except as an unintended psychological consequence. Therefore, attention will focus upon the emergent relational effects of natal backgrounds that resulted in their rejection by the subjects reared in them. This is not a necessary outcome because in the same circumstances some succumb to or even collude in their victimization. In other words, two sets of properties and powers are involved, the second being those of the particular person involved.

Even though these personal powers will not have been immune to the relations in question, nevertheless, they remain sufficient to promote 'rejection' itself. In other words, these subjects are resilient enough to retain their fundamental reflexivity, namely 'to consider themselves in relation to their (social) contexts and vice versa'.[16] They are 'normal' rather than 'pathological' because this ability is quintessential to the subjective act of rejection and the volitional but objective act of getting away. Both actions entail 'normal' intentionality, quite apart from the fact that these fractured reflexives participated unremarkably in everyday life including obtaining university degrees. If and when they 'recover', they do not uniformly come to practise the same dominant mode of reflexivity. Again, this is explicable only in terms of the interplay between their personal properties and powers, and the subsequent relational matrix they develop at university.

At point of entry, all three subjects were recorded as fractured reflexives. Since the inability to engage in purposeful courses of action is held to be the defining feature of 'fracturedness', one major paradox to resolve is how their very entry came about. Whilst 'rejection' and getting out of the natal environment might be thought of as spontaneous negative actions, fuelled by emotions such as fear, fury or disgust, getting into university is anything but automatic since it involves selection, decision-making and the subject persisting through the application process.

Relations to their natal contexts

The cases of Shirin, British-born from a broken Asian family, and of Paula, British and with lower middle-class parents, are vastly more dramatic in their courses and consequences than that of Carris, coming from a progressive middle-class background and growing up in a traditional

---

[16] Margaret S. Archer, *Making our Way through the World: Human Reflexivity and Social Mobility*, Cambridge University Press, 2007, p. 4.

university city. All three subjects spent the whole or the majority of their undergraduate careers as 'fractured reflexives'. The concern in this section is to explain how and why their responses to 'contextual incongruity' propelled these young girls to pursue the situational logic of opportunity by the often drastic and costly step of rejecting their natal backgrounds and entering university.

Shirin has the kind of subterranean biography that could have remained unknown throughout her time at university: 'I've had no one to talk to about all this so I'm just kind of blurting it all out to you'. She had spent most of her life trying to have one. Brought up in a strict Pakistani family in the Black Country, as a child Shirin already had problems with her step-mother. When she was ten her step-mother left, taking Shirin's three step-brothers with her and leaving her with all the domestic responsibilities. Her father treated her as the scapegoat for his wife's departure and the loss of his sons, scarcely speaking to her: 'So, I kind of stayed in my room all the time. Even when my step-mother was there I stayed in my room most of the time because she was really horrible to me. I kind of just grew up with TV and books, so that's where I learned my English.' Apparently, this enforced isolation threw her back on her own meagre resources and encouraged her to use whatever opportunities were available.

Soon afterwards, Shirin was stigmatized by much of her extended family, who thus ceased to be a relational resource, because her older cousin had confided to the eleven-year-old that she herself was getting out. As Shirin comments:

There're loads of girls that have run away from home because they just couldn't take the oppressive environment any more . . . She'd run away before as well and they'd got this gangster guy to go and get her back. They took her to Pakistan for a bit and tried to get her married off but she refused so they brought her back and then she ran off again with this other guy, who was a different religion to us. Then, in the end, he left her . . . She had two kids the last time I heard about her, and she didn't finish her A-levels so she just had her GCSEs . . . That's why I've always believed that education is so important so you can provide for yourself, you can be self-sufficient and self-reliant.

Here is the key to why Shirin links 'getting out' with 'getting into' a good education, but how could she obtain it, given little encouragement from her predominantly Asian secondary school?

In her own words, cyberspace supplied the opportunities otherwise closed to her:

I was thirteen and the Internet came about and I was like 'I can learn things' . . . Someone online, in a chat room, told me that Google existed, and

I was like 'Google, what's Google?' and then I found out what Google was and I still use it every day now . . . When I was growing up I didn't have anyone to ask about anything – I was like 'Dad, what does this mean' and he was 'Shut up, I don't know', so I didn't have anyone, like teachers didn't turn up at lessons and kids were busy throwing things at teachers, so I had no one to learn anything from.

She was depressed and wanting to get out but where was the door? Shirin had found it already. By sixteen, and despite strenuous paternal opposition, she was preparing to gain her European Computer Driving Licence, thanks to a few evening classes, usually curtailed by the need to take an early bus home or face her father's anger and possible embargo. Through the Internet, Shirin discovered Warwick bursaries.

Upon entering university, she ceased visiting home. I asked her if she had cut off all relations and she replied that despite the plethora of aunts, uncles and cousins: 'I wasn't close to anyone, so it wasn't like, "Yeah, I'm close to that person but I'm going to cut off all relations". It's just like they were there as a huge restrictive barrier that you want to get rid of – it's a matter of I just want to get away from them.' Not only had Shirin finished with her family, she had also rejected her Muslim background and begun participating in a Buddhist sect during her first year, attracted by its leitmotif that everyone 'has a mission in life and you should all work towards realizing what your mission is and achieving it', which she contrasted with the Islamic list of 'dos and 'don'ts'.

As a 'rejecter', Shirin's critique extends to the Pakistani community in the Midlands, its arranged marriages and its young women with up to fourteen kids who take over the street without recognizing that it is a cul-de-sac:

It's like they don't know anything, and they want you to be the same. They don't want you to be, I don't know whether it's a feeling of being threatened or whatever, they just don't want you to learn, they don't want you to have a good job. It's seen as immoral and Westernized and un-Islamic and they say, you know, you should just get married and stay at home and be a housewife and then pop out the kids and you're just not meant to achieve anything in your life . . . And their lives are so narrow, they don't get out of the area and me, I was like I want out of this area please.

Shirin's rejection of her community and culture comes full circle to the point where she saw her only option as getting out, getting into university and getting the most out of it. Shirin had confronted 'contextual incongruity' as the clash between life in a traditionalist ethnic ghetto and the opportunities proliferating in modern Britain, knowledge of which even infiltrated her bedroom through the Internet. Having rejected the former, Shinin is subjectively willing to grasp the latter but is objectively ill-prepared for this enterprise.

To move from the Black Country to the ancient university city where Carris grew up is also to shift the narrative from brutality and neglect to peer bullying and (perceived) parental over-control. She comes from a highly educated family (her father is a graphic designer and her mother – Oxon and Cantab – is Manager of one of the government's initiatives for early learning). They are progressives: anti-marriage, vegetarians, condemnatory of Tory policies and mix sociably with the like-minded. Although these parents will take on one another, bickering over progressive niceties, they present a formidable united front to their two daughters.

Carris appears to have been acquiescent, until negative relationality engaged between school and home in her mid-teens. Like many all-girls schools, hers was rife with cliques, using derogatory names for one another and expert at the game of inclusion and exclusion, meaning that smooth passage was best assured by adhering to one of them. Carris did not: 'I don't like group behaviour. I just couldn't and didn't fit any of the groups really'. Nor could she weld various individuals into her own friendship group, given that each had more to lose than to gain. Consequently, Carris first became isolated, was then picked-upon and finally suffered full-blown bullying.

The experience was severe but her response was intrapunitive:

At school I did sometimes feel like hurting myself in some way... sometimes I'd be like 'What have I done to deserve this?' and I'd just want to kind of grab hold of my hair or something, so I think a lot of people don't understand where self-harm comes from, but I think I, I can see why or how you would get to that stage.

Intrapunitiveness opened the door to the insecurity, hyper-sensitivity and self-criticism that dogged her at university along with relentlessly high standards and being extremely self-demanding: 'As I was going through school and being bullied, I made a real effort to be a really good person... like be nice to the people who were nasty to me so that I could kind of, I thought that was the way of getting over it. I still try and do that, I still try to see it as my fault if something's wrong, and I need to make the effort.'

Understandably, her mother also made efforts to counteract this negativity by a regime of enforced compensatory achievements. Carris played the piano for eight years, swam for the city, learned Latin:

She really encouraged me to start swimming and then she was very strict that I had to go six times a week... she likes to be in control my mum, and so if I was saying 'I'm not going swimming tonight because I'm going to a friend's house', she'd be like 'well, you haven't discussed it with me, I wouldn't be very happy if you did that'. And then I'd feel like I really should go to please my mum.

Underneath this 'support' Carris believed she could never match her mother's expectations: 'I kind of feel she expects more than I get'. Mother herself had achieved too much: at the same school she had 'definitely been part of the "cool", popular group', she had gained a first-class degree from the best university, had worked her own way through it and was now professionally successful – 'Mum was so amazing'.

Perhaps relationally Mother could impose her strict regime because in Carris' view it was her father who was the dominating or domineering parent, although he comes across as mainly being opinionated. Perhaps, too, Mother was trying her best whilst feeling her way with her first and less independent child, because she later apologized for her over-strictness. Nonetheless, she had effectively set up another competition at home, in parallel to the popularity contest at school, and Carris felt a loser in both settings – 'I just felt like I had to compete with her'. The contrasting but mutually reinforcing negativity of home and school only served to intensify Carris' low self-esteem. Dwelling on these experiences, where neither of her own courses of action – the deliberate exercise of goodwill at school or loyal compliance at home – had produced the desired results, her reflexivity fractured as she confronted a new 'competition', which is how she viewed university.

Being intensely loyal (insisting that she and her mother get on 'amazingly well'), still expecting rejection and failure, and continuing to blame herself in advance for anything that went wrong, she slowly realized that university was not a competition in which she was the foregone loser, but a source of opportunities to become herself and realize her own personal identity. This was contextual incongruity for Carris. Significantly her family slipped from its first place on her list of concerns and daylight started to dawn as she acquired the confidence to become a mild rejecter:

a lot of my ideas about life came from my parents, but more and more now I can look at my parents and be really critical of what they think and I think that's probably a good thing . . . every day now I kind of think more and more how some things my parents do are absolutely absurd. I just can't understand it, whereas before I'd just kind of take it as the norm . . . after a few weeks of being at home over the Christmas holidays, I kind of felt like I really didn't want to be so claustrophobic and crowded by my family anymore, and I don't feel that's a bad thing.

Turning to Paula, it was evident from the first interview that her parents – though especially her mother – functioned as her negative reference group:

I think I've learned from observing my parents what I do and don't want eventually... My mum is pretty much a housewife; she works but then comes in and spends all evening tidying and cooking. She doesn't have many friends or hobbies and I don't think I'd like that at all... My mum's got terribly low self-esteem and always aims low and has thought the same thing about me, but I've realized actually I'm not like that at all and I'm going to aim high... I want a lot more from my life than my parents did.

There is no mention over the three interviews of any relatives, family friends, neighbours or local involvement, giving the impression of a completely isolated nuclear family where everything will turn on its internal relations. The reason for this isolation turns out to be the fact that her mother:

went deaf when she was twenty-one and that caused her to become depressed, she lost all her friends, she lost her job and everything was pinned on me and my sister. So everything I did really affected my mum a lot... once I can remember she ended up crying for about a week because I spilt some paint on my carpet... Even from the age of about three I've had to really think about how everything's going to affect my mum and it seems to have carried over into adulthood.

Paula admits that she was initially sucked into this 'united and very stable family', especially her father's attempts to support and sympathize with his wife, and she considered training to work with the deaf, which would have strengthened the bond between them. However, Paula came to see her mother's depression and her own efforts to please her as a vicious circle in which she was trapped. Its negativity provoked eating disorders which gradually crystallized into the bulimia that still affects her.

Her rejection of confining family values was exacerbated by Paula's attraction to celebrity culture. From the lonely designing of her own clothes, Paula, who avows that she had no friends because of moving school three times from town to town, began to make a few contacts in fashion design when she was sixteen. A year later she had moved into 'glamour' modelling, dazzled by 'the people I was mixing with and the lifestyle I hoped to get, the celebrity lifestyle'. This is contextual incongruity for Paula.

Paula repeatedly insists upon her parents' working-class origin, behaviour patterns and values (although her father is a printing press engineer and her mother a medical microbiologist) to heighten the contrast with her own. Unlike most undergraduates, she does not attribute any of her values to her parents: 'I'm completely different from them... it could come down to the fact that I'm weak in terms of society's pressures, I do feel pressure to be successful and to look a certain way.' That probably lay behind her false start on a university course in Art and Design with a view to entering the fashion business and making high earnings, but one of its effects was to distance her still further from home:

I changed a lot when I first went off to university. I think as you grow up you kind of fit into the family and you go off to university and find out who you are – so when I came home I did feel quite alienated. My parents buy the Sun and the Mail and they've no kind of politics . . . and I found I was quite interested in that kind of thing and realized I'm quite left-wing. And when I tried to talk to them about it they really didn't understand at all.

However, Paula is honest enough to admit that there was another side to her growing mental distancing, which came down to money: 'for some reason all my friends are quite wealthy and they can do things that I can't do, that I can't be part of, and I get really bitter and resentful sometimes and take it out on my family which is really unfair . . . I feel like I've really been limited in my opportunities because I don't have the money to back me up.' Paula instances 'the chance to travel' as symbolic of the whole situational logic of opportunity to which she is straining to respond, including getting back to university.

Desperate to seize opportunity and to negate the three years that her 'false start' had cost her, Paula accepts that 'slowly distancing' herself is the only way to cut the umbilical cord, even if it precipitates another maternal breakdown: 'I feel bad about it because it must have been really hard for her to hear some of the things I said, because I basically have told her that I think she's contributed to some of the problems I've got, which is a horrible thing for a mother to hear, and I really regret having told her that.' Paula now talks seriously about emigrating: 'which is quite horrible and I know that would have a big effect on my mum, but I just think it would be really good for me to have complete independence because even now, every time I go back home I revert back to how I used to be – walking on eggshells'.

This is undoubtedly rejection of her family but Paula also seems to have contributed to her own fracturing and its dilemmas through funding her second chance at Warwick by continuing with 'glamour' modelling. She has paid the price many times over: in disorientation and in persistent bulimia. In addition, she now fears that what is paying her way through university will rebound upon her serious career hopes and prospects. Her website is up, under her own name, and in its dozens of photographs she is easily recognizable, despite the rather austere persona she adopts on campus. The only certainty is that the ongoing modelling, which her parents oppose, has sealed the break from her family and its mindset. As she puts it, 'I've started going home less and less and working more'.

Dependent development: the friendships of fractured reflexives

The nature of the relational evils just examined represent quite different home experiences undergone by these three young subjects. Correspondingly, there is no reason to suppose their negative impacts on their reflexivity will be identical, beyond their common effect of inducing passivity through preventing purposeful action. Thus, what precisely was damaged in each case has to be examined before it is possible to discover the exact consequences of new friendships on these subjects and if they had any healing results for those revealing a bent towards a mode of reflexivity that had been impeded.

As rejecters, all three had either severed contact with their familial backgrounds or distanced themselves from them. In the process, it also transpired that they shed their home friends (if any) in a comprehensive rejection of the natal background. Therefore, the salience of the new university friends they made is expected to be especially influential because they had a clear field, neither competing with nor modified by home influences. Simultaneously, because the 'fracturing' of the three is relational in origin, their ability to form new relationships may be as impaired as their reflexivity is impeded.

At point of entry, Shirin admits to having considerable difficulties with 'decision-making', 'planning' and, especially 'reliving' the painful past – an upsetting mental activity that began when her step-mother left home. She tries to avoid this through blotting out her internal conversation by daydreaming, which she knows is a displacement activity that does nothing to resolve her difficulties – pennilessness, homelessness and friendlessness:

> I tend to avoid thinking about things, I just don't want to think about problems, don't want to deal with them, so I just kind of avoid thinking about it which is really bad because you're not coming to any decision or conclusion either . . . and when I was thinking about I want this to happen, I want that to happen, you have to think about it and then it can cause you to get upset, which is why I kind of avoid it, I blank it out in my head and don't think about it . . . which isn't resolving it but I can't think of a better solution . . . as a little kid, I don't remember avoiding thinking about things, it would just be like ten, eleven onwards.

If she tries to alleviate this by mentioning fragments of her past to people on campus, 'they start giving you funny looks, so you're like okay, I'd better shut up now'. But Shirin realizes that shutting up is also bottling things up and, despite her attempted avoidance of the past in her internal conversations, she becomes paralysed and swamped: 'it just takes over your life and you become really obsessive and I'm trying really hard not to do that about my problems, like I have been doing in the past couple of years'. She knows that greater sociability would at least distract her from this tendency, but she later reflects that 'I was petrified of people when I came to university, I just couldn't come out of my room' and was involved in no campus activities during her first year. Shirin reverted to her reclusive bedroom again, diagnosing whilst deploring her lack of social skills: 'I'm so anti-social, that's not good . . . I have problems with confidence and talking to people because you haven't done it for so long you don't know how to interact with people . . . it's too daunting, too intimidating and I want to run away, especially when they are middle class and self-assured.'

In these quotations it is significant that Shirin frequently substitutes the second-person singular for the first-person, entailing a depersonalization, a shunning of responsibility for self and a shift from active subject to passive object status that has been encountered before among fractured reflexives.[17] What transformed matters was her growing friendship in the hall of residence with a very extrovert and ambitious Bengali student who took Shirin under her wing. In the second year they became housemates and this 'best friend' became a role model, a social coach, the source of a friendship network, an encouragement to take on university offices or employment opportunities, and an introduction to the Buddhist community. Shirin admits that 'she's really helped me. Like I know a lot of people through her, she knows everyone on campus, she's very comfortable around people, so that's made me better at dealing with people . . . I have to say she's been a godsend.' During that year, Shirin left her bedroom retreat behind, becoming a union officer herself and the only female to pioneer a new post in a computer learning facility on campus. Reflecting back the following year, Shirin recognizes that her friend 'helped me be ambitious as well. I [was] like "I shouldn't apply here, I'm aiming too high" and she [was] like "don't be stupid, apply, of course you can do it" . . . so it's [been] really, really helpful to have a friend like that because then you actually do it if you have someone to tell you that you can.' Just as importantly her friend introduced her to a Buddhist group in London, which meant that Shirin 'got to meet a lot more people, really, really nice people and sort of like to have a community and a network of friends'.

Together they went on a short study course with this group where Shirin had to confront her reflexive blocking tactics and mental displacement activities:

[17] See note 8.

If you're chanting about something and you're like, I want to do this, I want to improve that . . . you'll have to think about actually doing something yourself to change it rather than just like 'I hope this will change, God I hope this problem gets fixed', which is not going to happen . . . so it actually encourages you to do more stuff for yourself.

Probably more was involved than this one experience, but it serves to mark Shirin's break with passivity and assumption of active agency. It signified the beginning of the end of her 'impeded' status and released the instrumental rationality that had always been latent in her sheer ability to survive against the odds.

Given Shirin had no further contact with her natal background, there was also no clashing relationality to hold her back from spreading her wings as an autonomous reflexive and one who was to become a very effective practitioner of it. Certainly, she continued to rate her social skills as deficient and to be embarrassed when prominent in social settings, but popularity and ease do not head the agenda of an autonomous reflexive. Her increasing proficiency undoubtedly enabled her to confront the necessity of selection with determination and a sense of purpose in relation to her future career.

Turning to Carris, she is 'impeded' in two quite different respects. On the one hand, so many of her mental activities are pre-occupied with taking the pulse of her interpersonal relationships and hyper-critical analysis of her own performance that she is distracted from deliberating about purposeful action: 'I like everyone to be okay with me, like all the time, and obviously that can't happen. If somebody's fed up with me for any reason, I find it very difficult to move on from that and I have to sort that out.' On the other hand, she has not made the same radical break with her natal background as Shirin and much of this remains to be negotiated before she can define who she is – the person with this particular constellation of concerns – and where she is going. Almost immediately, two relational factors that helped with both of the above came into play. Firstly, she found it 'absolutely amazing', given her history of exclusion, to make instant friends in the student residence and to know by Christmas that she would be living with them next year. Secondly, she met her boyfriend – two years older than her – who steadily helped to dislodge the remnants of well-meaning parental domination. Because her new friends and new boyfriend gelled amicably, their influence was doubled.

At the start of year one, she typically worries 'because I've got to make sure I stay in touch with friends from home, but make sure that I'm not losing out on the friendships I've got here'. Her attempt to amalgamate the two groups by holding a party at home was a disaster: 'they were very, very split, I think they are quite different people. It actually caused an argument – two people didn't get along at all.' Confronted with this need to choose, Carris unambiguously opted for her 'university friends' because they 'know the real me now', rather than clinging on to those 'home friends' who had known her in her bullied and battered state. Thus, she selected 'Option 3', the one that none of the communicatives took, and deliberatively projected herself forward into university life with them, taking up new activities together, such as Ju-jitsu and joining Warwick volunteers to work with young offenders.[18] Significantly, the maternal remedy of competitive swimming receded into a keep-fit activity. Carris' summary is that 'the best thing [about Warwick] is finding the friends I have because that's just made me a happier person'.

From the beginning, her boyfriend systematically challenged Carris every time she repeated familial wisdom: 'haven't you got a mind of your own, do you always think what your family thinks?' He and her parents clashed one evening over politics, with her boyfriend supporting the Tories against what he saw as the progressive 'chattering classes'. This was clearly more problematic for Carris to negotiate: 'I still feel kind of in the middle . . . I think I do tend to take sides with my parents a bit more, but I've been suggesting arguments that my boyfriend's handed me, because my parents are quite extreme.' Symbolically, again, she gave up their vegetarianism. Yet, this was not a selective resolution, with her new relations displacing the old. When her boyfriend graduated and moved to Birmingham, she held back from moving in with him, 'terrified at having someone in the same room all the time' and because she was unsure that this relationship would last.

In her final year she compromised, refusing to become co-owner of the house he was about to buy, but willing to move into one of its rooms alongside other tenants. The problem seems to be that Carris is aware of her past dependency upon and domination by her parents, is attempting to resist transference to her boyfriend and therefore cannot make a commitment to him. Carris is still not fully happy with herself and continues to register as fractured but, in analysing her reluctance to commit to her boyfriend, she reveals a distinct bent towards meta-reflexivity: 'sometimes I worry about if we broke up, because ever since I've been at uni I've known him and the group of friends I'm with. I'm not sure if my happiness is about that package.' She has scruples because unsure whether she is wholehearted and even speculates about a few months apart in

---

[18] Option 3 is to prefer university friends at the expense of home friends. See Chapter 5.

order to discover whether or not she has recovered sufficiently to be comfortable with herself. One sign of both recovery and of meta-reflexivity is the repugnance with which she now looks at dependency: 'I don't like the thought of being kind of reliant on someone to be happy . . . even if we did break up, I can still look back on this and feel I've managed to have a great relationship and some great friends, so I must be quite a decent person that people like.'

Conversely, having largely severed relations with her natal background, Paula's problem is that she seems unable to put any stable relationships in their place. Part of her false start at another university left her with 'horrible memories of really hating the sort of house there that was party life . . . So I think when I came here I wanted a bit of seclusion, a bit of privacy, but it came at a price which was that I didn't make many friends, didn't have much fun, didn't have many experiences.' That was her verdict on year one, but in year two she shared a house with a group of five that produced no friendships and found her not even being offered a lift into campus by the others with cars: 'I don't trust myself to make decisions – it's either what most people say I should do, or the person I care about most . . . but now it's boyfriends.'

It is exceptional that not a single girlfriend features in her three inter-views. The reason seems to lie in the double life that she is leading throughout university. How, as a somewhat older 'glamour model', can she have an ordinary friendship with young women who are still exper-imenting with their hair and clothes, even when this is not their main priority? Either Paula would have to tell all if she revealed her expertise or she would have to maintain the deception that she fosters with her studiedly severe dressing. Given that she has no special interest – or per-haps too many – and joins no society, she cannot gravitate towards other enthusiasts and use this as the springboard to friendship.

At each interview she becomes more open and in her last year admits that 'I don't have the sort of system that most people have in place to work out what they want'. This meant she had propitiated previous boyfriends but now she says 'it's perfect, so I think this is probably going to be the one who goes the distance because I don't need to be anything I'm not, he seems to like me for who I am'. Despite what she has just said, her new boyfriend, a law student who is three and a half years younger, clearly understands her incapacity to make decisions and has taken her in hand: 'I think he knows what's best for me, which is for him not to help, so I always turn to him to try to get him to make decisions for me and he refuses to . . . he's trying to get me to learn to do it for myself. So even little things like where we go for dinner, he'll make me choose everything, if we go to see a film he'll make me choose because he's trying to get me used to doing that.' This is inverted dependency.

He is her sounding board and she tries out innumerable career possibilities on him, journalism being Paula's aim at that point. However, when she rehearses its uncertainties to him he sticks to his policy and tells her to go for what she wants and to forget about the money. Hushing the inner voice that is whispering 'but what if we split up', Paula starts to think of living with him and writing as a freelancer. She goes further, admitting that she would marry him now, move wherever he was located and have children immediately. In other words, she reaches for the easy fix to her career quandaries by endorsing the traditional female role. But 'he doesn't like me saying that because he's twenty-one, so when I start going on about marriage and babies, I think he'd prefer to wait a few years.'

The extent of her dependency is illustrated when Paula talks about her ongoing bulimia: 'he knows about it and he monitors me quite a lot', though she still does it, 'but next year when I'm living with him that's going to be impossible, he won't let it carry on, which is what I really need'. What she is rather careful not to reveal is how much he knows about her continuing modelling activities. These now involve her being 'the face of a porn channel', about which she manifests ambivalence and receives ambivalent responses. On the one hand, to Paula, exposing her face is not displaying her body but, it also seems to her that 'all my morals have a price'. On the other hand, she is further confused because 'people' are often quite impressed to learn she features in Playboy. To this mélange of mixed internal and external messages, she responds with passivity: 'I'd like to live in a world where we don't need to do that kind of thing, but I just accept that's the way it is and I might as well exploit it.'

Nevertheless, her passive acquiescence is not her boyfriend's and, as an aspirant barrister, he may feel threatened by its disclosure. In short, Paula is sustaining negative relationality between her network of contacts in this seedy underworld and the boyfriend who seems concerned to counteract the very passivity that leaves her in it. Is Paula really asking this second year student to offer her marriage and a new life as the means of shedding the contradictions between the double life she currently leads? If so, he has said 'not yet' and thus – knowingly or unknowingly – has left an explosion waiting to happen. Paula herself is not lacking in insight but remains trapped in passivity: 'its worrying me because I rely on him so much, emotionally and in other ways as well, so I think if we split up I'd be a bit of a wreck. I feel everything would fall apart again if we split up, which isn't how things should be but I can't help it.'

Career choice: the dilemma of selecting from variety

As has already been suggested (in Chapter 3), one of the main engines of the reflexive imperative is the necessity of selection itself. Given the proliferating number and range of career opportunities available (to graduates), some process is required for the reduction of variety to a scope with which subjects can cope. This is unavoidable because choice of employment – even if later revised – is the coping stone that completes personal identity and binds it to the social identity of each and every subject.[19] It entails the use of practical reason to answer the questions 'who am I?' and 'how do I wish to live?' by selecting a role from the array on offer. Effectively, though fallibly, the role that is chosen states 'this is the "you" I seek to become' (social identity) by 'personifying it in my own way' (personal identity). Of course, this does not complete the shaping of a life because all subjects still have to design a *modus vivendi* expressive of their main concerns, in which each is accorded its place in due order and where their careers are not necessarily their ultimate concerns. Therefore, successfully meeting the necessity of selection is a predicate of shaping a life.

The last three chapters have shown how the different dominant modes of reflexivity constituted distinctive processes through which the reduction of variety was achieved: replication for the communicative reflexives, instrumental rationality for the autonomous reflexives and value commitment for meta-reflexives. In turn, the development and maintenance of these modes was seen to be underpinned by equally distinctive patterns of relations to the natal backgrounds of 'identifiers', 'independents' and the 'disengaged'. Such relational differences provided a preliminary orientation to the world of work, highlighting some sectors and eliminating others. The subsequent pattern of relations that developed in the course of their undergraduate years then operated as a finer filter guiding reflexive deliberations and fine tuning their selection of future employment within each of the sectors already pre-selected.

Although the working of these relational processes was neither automatic nor hydraulic in kind, which is precisely why each subject had to assume the burden of responding to the reflexive imperative, they are all in a radically different situation from the fractured reflexives. In a nutshell, this is because 'rejecters' have jettisoned the preliminary process for the reduction of variety because to repudiate *any form of directional guidance* from the natal background is to leave the field of careers wide

---

[19] Margaret S. Archer, *Being Human: The Problem of Agency*, Cambridge University Press, 2000, pp. 222–249 and 283–305.

open with nothing to reduce variety to 'bounded variety'. Almost everything then hangs on the relations formed at university, which furnish the sole filter for coping with the situational logic of opportunity. Yet, as has just been examined, the relational networks established by the three fractured subjects were extremely different in kind and in quality. Thus, the last leg of investigating the 'rejecters' is to ask how they coped with the reduction of variety and whether or not this enabled them to deal with the necessity of selection. The expectation is that those who appeared to be 'on the mend', as evidenced by signs of some proclivity towards practising a mode of reflexivity, would fare more constructively than anyone who did not.

Perhaps lone survival encourages autonomous reflexivity by definition, for those who do succeed. Conversely, the absence of backup and recurrent setbacks could send some spiralling down into a pit of purposelessness. Shirin has exactly £2,000 a year (fees paid) from her bursary and thus the dual task of working to maintain herself for twelve months (no home base during vacations) and of planning her career (which must start to pay fast after graduation). As a 'rejecter', she not only wants out of her natal background but also up the social scale, being overt about her quest for social mobility. Her first two years could have been extremely discouraging, given the rebuffs she received. Instead, she honed the instrumental rationality, necessary for paying her way, into a highly strategic course of action that melded her temporary jobs with the career she sought.

In year one she became a student caller for the university, as a living advert to raise further bursaries, where she felt a complete failure because of her lack of 'people skills'. Simultaneously, having learned about the fast track into the civil service from the Internet when she was sixteen – and also about its Oxbridge bias – she applied for a summer placement and failed to gain an interview because of her performance on the psychometric tests. The following year was the fulcrum and also coincided with her dependent friendship and mentoring by her Bengali friend.

In the September before year two began, she recalls, 'I just applied for lots and lots of jobs because I cannot be a student caller again, I don't raise any money for them, so it's really horrible that they give me more money than I raise'. Shirin not only seeks money but believes in giving value for money and extending her own skills. Thus she was delighted to gain the job of Student Computing Advisor, which maintained her until graduation. At the same time and unashamedly attracted by the pay, she was sufficiently intrigued by investment banking to attend a Goldman Sachs symposium on campus. She was interviewed there and then, got through to the final round in London, but failed to gain the internship. The nature of her disappointment is revealing: 'They push you to learn so many skills – that would have been the whole point of doing it. There are still a few places looking for interns so, amongst doing essays and work and going to lectures, I'm applying to do internships as well. I mean you have to keep trying because if you don't try, you won't get anywhere.' One problem is that Shirin is getting no feedback, another is that she is using a spray shot approach and simply applying for everything advertised.

We have already seen how her friend encouraged her to become an officer in the students' union, to expand her interests and to develop her social skills. Whether this was intended or not, Shirin begins to think strategically: 'I'm trying to use the Warwick name to push myself forward for the best jobs possible and trying to get involved in really good things with the students' union and, you know, make the most of the advantages you have.' She recognized her lack of 'outside interests' and turned to her friend: 'I was like please help me find hobbies and things to do . . . I don't know what I'm interested in, I don't know what I like doing – help.' Help she did and Shirin thoroughly grasped the knack of strategic self-presentation: 'Yeah, I'll get involved in that, Oh okay, I'll do a bit of voluntary work, it's meant to look good on your CV. I'll just do stuff actually to have stuff, it's not really because "Oh yes I love chairing the committee", so I'll chair the committee.' There are so many resonances here with the autonomous subjects in Chapter 5 that Shirin's time as an impeded reflexive is nearly up.

In her final year, her instrumental rational approach is marked and she has moved from strategy to tactics. Whereas

last year I applied for research in lots of different investment banks, I had no idea, because I don't hang around with merchant bankers . . . but this year I was like I'll just apply to Goldman Sachs and I applied for the graduate scheme and got rejected. So then I found a very roundabout way of applying for the internship because they're not really for finalists, so I applied for operations, which is a support desk, so this time I changed tactics.

She discovered this from the internet, temporarily lowered her sights to operations, and she got it, together with a 60–70 per cent chance of being offered a full-time post afterwards. 'So that's how I got it by being really strategic, very cunning' or, another way of putting it, is by having graduated as an unimpeded autonomous reflexive.

If necessity and availability had to some extent 'bounded variety' for her, Shirin is fully aware of the need to shape a life. She does not want a career in an investment bank, just five years to train and to save, after which she believes interviewers will simply be impressed by seeing 'Goldman Sachs' as she slips into forensic accountancy or the like to investigate corporate corruption. This new capacity for long-term planning is another sign of recovery. As her good friend had told her 'you can make money and you can create value in your life, it's not one or the other' and Shirin freely admits 'basically I caught this from her, this bug'.

In comparison, we have seen that Carris did not make the same radical and decisive break with her family but stepped back and gradually distanced herself by evaluating their progressive views and forming her own social conspectus. Although much of this inspection and selection was prompted by her relationship with her boyfriend, she did not simply exchange their outlook for his. For all her lack of confidence in social interaction, Carris appears morally unimpeded. In her first and most tentative year, she had already joined a giving scheme to Oxfam. In the following two years she experienced little difficulty in career planning and selecting what she found worthwhile in her family's practices, yet synthesizing these with her own attitudes and, above all, experiences. In exercising this ability to turn back upon her own relational evils and then to deliberate about turning these to good social effect, she showed all the signs of meta-reflexivity. Such syncretism is how she achieved the 'reduction of variety' and thus accomplished the necessity of selection.

Carris steadily refined her vocation in a manner that indicated she was shedding much of her impeded status. She still had difficulties in shaping a life – in common with many non-fractured subjects – but even in that, her vocational assurance and her listing her career as her main concern showed that she was well advanced in developing a personal and social identity, which are the obverse of fractured reflexivity.

During her first year, her mother's impact remained strong in both evaluative and practical terms. Carris reviewed her mother's work approvingly: in 'my mum's job you're making a difference every day because she's working with troubled kids – giving people a better start. She's only helping on a small scale but it's going to make a difference to certain people's lives. I think that would be quite important to me.' Practically, her mother also acted as the gatekeeper and when Carris developed an interest in homeless youth for one of her course projects, she took vacation work in a residential hostel: 'I could easily gain access to this place because my mum has a friend who's a manager there'. However, as a relief worker she spent most of her time with the young people but concluded that a permanent post would not be for her because too much time was diverted to managerial tasks that, sub-textually, were more suited to her mother.

During her second year, Carris was drawn towards work with young offenders and used her vacation jobs to investigate the field and to narrow down her options. 'That kind of experience made me realize I wouldn't like to go into social work as such because I think . . . Social workers are so interfering in your lives, whereas if I'm working in a kind of residential home, people are coming to me to get help.' In moving towards this decision, it is significant that Carris pursued this quite independently of her mother: 'I haven't discussed it at all . . . me and my mum used to be so close and discuss everything, but I don't think she knows about all these things that are going on at the moment . . . it's been my idea anyway what I want to do.' Equally, she does not allow her future vocation to hang upon her boyfriend, the fact that he is now in Birmingham and is wanting her to join him. 'When I'm making this decision I don't know if I'll consider my boyfriend as a priority. I think I'll just apply to particular jobs in areas that I'm interested in, no matter where they are based . . . I'd put it that if we want to be together then we'll make it work wherever we are.' However, Carris does recognize that this constitutes a problem of reciprocity in their relationship because his basing himself in Birmingham 'has shown that I'm a priority in where he wants to be'.

With her university friends, she had already joined Warwick Volunteers but, in her third year, directed this expressly to working with young offenders. She undertook the training and made the commitment to mentoring an offender for a year, despite her lack of confidence that the young subjects would respect her or value what she had to offer. Since this went well, Carris is currently applying to work in a youth offending scheme, where she believes that, particularly with the girls, her own negative experiences can be turned to good use, for example, her ability to understand the impulse behind self-harming.

As she sums it up, since

I'm not money-driven at all, I just think supporting other people in any way I can will make me really happy. It sounds silly but I feel I'm quite good at listening to other people. I don't know what I'd have to offer, but I feel quite strongly that it's a problem and I really would like to try to address this. And I'd feel better as a person doing that than working in finance or something for example, which doesn't appeal to me at all.

Carris has made her selection for meta-reflexive reasons and shows further signs of her 'recovery' by her new found ability for mid-term planning and the dovetailing of her concerns. After two years in this post she intends to obtain an MA in Social Work, because the qualification will improve her employability, and to register at Birmingham University, thus acknowledging her commitment to her boyfriend. In many ways, Carris has not only succeeded in making her necessary selection, but is also more advanced in shaping her life than many of those who did not have to overcome fractured reflexivity.

Unfortunately, Paula's case is the exact opposite. She is literally thrown by the necessity of selection from start to finish ('there are just so many options') and never learns how to produce 'bounded variety' and then to narrow it down to a specific career choice as Carris did. She can be considered a victim of the situational logic of opportunity, with which she never learns to cope. As nascent morphogenesis engages there are likely to be an increasing number of such casualties because the task can only be accomplished by the subject (in relation with others), but not by family socialization – especially for a 'rejecter'.

The crux of her problem, as Paula herself knows, is determining what she wants from her career. The desire for success, money and helping others are at war with one another because no *desideratum* dwarfs the others into subordination and yet she cannot (if it can be done) define a post that makes the three commensurable and compatible. As she rightly says at the end of her first year,

If I don't really know who I am then I don't really know what I want and it's hard to make a career decision based on that. I just feel I'm massively behind most people. Most people have dealt with their identity . . . but I really need to find myself, find out who I am and what's important to me and I think career is just going to be put on pause, probably just over the summer.

She laughs at herself for sounding 'very Oprah Winfrey', but her analysis is impeccable for the root of fractured reflexivity does stem from an absence of personal identity, from not knowing what matters to the subject and in what order of priority.

In her second year, Paula frequently reverts to the opportunities she has missed but opportunity is precisely what she cannot deal with. She has not begun the reduction of variety but is attracted in a multiplicity of directions without one predominating or any being excluded. Thus we discuss the range of careers that she is seriously considering: journalist, solicitor, teacher, counsellor, charity worker or entering the civil service or arts administration. How does someone narrow these down if their fear of the risk involved is reinforced by their fear of commitment? In a demonstration of self-knowledge, Paula reflects upon the three years' cost by her false start: 'I really don't want to make another mistake. But I also don't want to be so tentative that I don't end up doing what I want to do through fear. There're quite a few things I'd love to do but they've all got some element of risk so I'm shying away from them,' including journalism to which she seems most drawn. Her conclusion is starkly honest: 'The chances are I probably will end up just taking a job for money because I'm too worried about taking the step that's got a bit of risk'.

By year three, Paula comments, 'I'm still in the same position as in the first year' and sadly that is the case for she again rehearses a comprehensive list of possible careers, now augmented by having enrolled for two MA courses. She is trying to change and avoid the passivity of letting others decide but 'it's really hard, I hate making decisions, it's agonizing for me, just the thought of it going wrong again . . . but by being so indecisive nothing gets done, I've gone in so many different directions but nothing's been done. My CV doesn't look very good . . . I'm still flailing.' More positively, Paula has got everything lined up for journalism: work experience, course enrolment and a placement with a local paper. The hope is that if comparative risk assessment didn't work for reducing variety the previous year, then her enhanced commitment will override fear of failure in the coming year.

She knows starting is the hardest thing and has been advised to write something every day, but she cannot because 'people keep asking to see my work and I'm really scared of showing them because I'm worried that they'll think it's crap, especially my boyfriend.' For all his care and concern, she cannot reciprocate with confidence. Thus, Paula's internal conversation goes round in circles: she cannot start through fear of criticism; journalists get so many rejections and have to be thick-skinned; even then not everyone gets a 'big break'. Paula concludes, 'I'm really not sure if it's the right thing to do and I think I'll probably chicken out at some point as well, which is a shame . . . I'm not sure whether I'd just prefer money, just try to earn as much as possible, because I do like money.'

Regretfully, she ends where she started, possibly yet more fractured by her defeats in the face of the logic of opportunity, which simply presents too many options: 'It's not that there's nothing I want to do, it's just that there's so much' and she cannot cope with the necessity of selection. As I write, four years on, her modelling website has expanded into one of many.

Expressive fracturing or Carole and contingency

The reflexive ability to choose and to shape becomes increasingly pressing as opportunities proliferate. Absence of any purposeful response to the situational logic of opportunity is most marked among certain members of this sub-group, two of whom initially stated that they did not engage in internal conversation at all.[20] While some who

---

[20] On ICONI, these are subjects – ten in number at point of entry – who scored less than the mean of 4.00 on all modes of reflexivity *including* fractured reflexivity.

entered university as expressives soon adopted other modes of reflexivity, two did go through their undergraduate careers and exited with their 'underdeveloped' reflexivity unchanged. Fortunately, both had volunteered for interview.[21] The question is simply how was this possible for them?

Of the remaining eight, we have already met two in Chapter 4 – Ruth and Kirsty – who by the second year had become assimilated into the communicative group from which they were indistinguishable in terms of relations to their natal backgrounds and also in being strong 'identifiers'. I would hypothesize that until separated from their families, the distinctive communicative pattern of 'thought and talk' was much stronger on the latter element. In other words, because co-habiting with and being very close to all their family members, most of the business of the internal conversation was conducted through ordinary external conversation.

The only other subject already encountered is Emily, a communicative until her final year, who was found (Chapter 4) trapped in negative relationality between her home and university networks from which she could not extricate herself because of her attachment to both. This raises the intriguing but wholly tentative hypothesis that when overwhelmed by their difficulties, certain subjects may blot out their problems by refraining from reflexive activities that defeat them, thus quasi-volitionally opting for a passive agential status in which circumstances are allowed to determine outcomes. However, the data collected are insufficient to substantiate this hypothesis.[22]

The remaining five cases oscillated during the undergraduate period between fractured scores and expressive ones, but none of these volunteered for interview. In brief, far too little is known about this sub-group, but such oscillation reinforces the appropriateness of dealing with expressive reflexivity as part of the fractured category. Since it is impossible to provide any meaningful relational account on the basis of one subject, what follows is a speculative exploration which seems worthwhile because the expressive group was as large as the fractured category amongst these undergraduate entrants.

The flavour of 'expressive reflexivity' is immediately conveyed by the two first-year interviews with Sally and Carole, which showed remarkable similarities. Sally is from a middle-class background and Carole has working-class origins. Since we will have less chance to listen to Sally, let us picture the minimal use of internal conversation by

---

[21] Unfortunately, the material collected is partial for one subject because of failure of the audio recorder in her second-year interview.

[22] The one other subject recording the same pattern did not volunteer for interview.

expressives through simply listing her responses to the ten mental activities into which reflexivity is initially broken down in the first interview (Figure 7.1).[23] Her telegrammatic responses are a condensed characterization of how the expressive subject operates in the social order.

Événementalisme *or 'stuff happens'*

If subjects remark no pattern in their social circumstances, no repetitions representing regularities and no changes whose trajectories signal in which direction, what do they make of such an unpatterned social order? If no previous event is seen to stand in any determinate relationship with what follows, the sequence of events is kaleidoscopic and its indeterminacy defies predictability. Such subjects would view their social environments as matters of contingency – or, as the young put it, 'stuff happens'. What occurs would be perceived as shapeless happenstance because congruence (or incongruence) entails a pattern whilst complete contingency is the absence of one. In a closed system, this would be the randomness of Brownian movement; in an open one it is perceived as novel contingent permutations which, as it were, defeat complexity theory in advance. 'Stuff' does, indeed, just 'happen'.

Given that action is inescapable in everyday life, what enables the expressives to act at all, since intentional action is not a set of random responses? It seems that they do so by responding to the discrete and proximate events that they confront *seriatim*. They produce 'bounded variety' simply by limiting selection to dealing with situational 'chunks'. They live by 'presentism' because to them there is no 'big picture' but simply a succession of events that command their attention from day to day.

It follows that a 'presentist' selection is at odds with shaping a life and that their life histories will be the shapeless accumulation of these relatively discrete responses, produced without any agential eye to their overall complementarity. As *événementalistes* they do not attempt to achieve governance over their lives as a whole because the conviction that contingency rules precludes the whole process of <Discernment → Deliberation → Dedication>, whose completion yields personal identity as the person-with-this-constellation-of-concerns. Carole, who undoubtedly cares about her four grown-up children, does her caring on an

---

[23] Questions were not put to subjects in the bald one-word way used in Figure 7.1. These ten mental activities have been used throughout the trilogy and a fuller formulation is found in Archer, *Structure, Agency and the Internal Conversation*, p. 161. Sally's responses were sometimes longer than presented here, but without modifying the tenor of what has been reproduced.

Planning: 'I don't really tend to plan anything, it's more of a get up and do if the time arises and the opportunity's there.'

Rehearsing: 'No, you can't predict what's going to happen and anything could just come up. So, hold yourself open and take anything that's thrown at you.'

Reliving: 'Things that are personal and close to me I look back on and try to learn what I've done wrong or right at the time, but I wouldn't say I ponder on a lot really. I think it's more what went wrong than what I did wrong, because I think that you don't do anything wrong – you don't because you feel it's right. So I think it's more what went wrong.'

Mulling over: 'I think it's more on the smaller scale with me, to do with me and the close people around me, my family and friends.'

Imagining: 'Occasionally, not too often really.'

Deciding: 'The majority of the time I'd make a snap decision rather than sit there and debate.'

Prioritising: 'It comes more readily to me than having to think about it. I wouldn't say I have to think about prioritising things, I just go with the flow. I prefer to go with the flow than against it.'

Clarifying: 'If it's something that doesn't really interest me or I don't have a huge opinion on or I'm just not bothered about, then I'm not the sort of person who would sit down and try to figure out what it was.'

Holding imaginary conversations: (Laughs) 'No!'

Budgeting: 'Not particularly, no. I'm kind of bad at budgeting.'

Figure 7.1 Expressive responses to the mental activities constituting reflexivity

episodic basis, attending to emergencies and thus treating parenting as day-to-day crisis management. It also follows that if the DDD sequence is not tackled, and thus cannot be completed, then neither can such subjects complete the sequence of <Concerns → Projects → *Modus vivendi*>, which secures social identity. In other words, their method of 'reducing variety' by attending to the pressing and the proximate is a response to the necessity of selection, governed by situational immediacy and intensity alone. The implication is that these subjects accept 'shape-less lives' because, in effect, they have rescinded the agential power to become (something of) their own 'sovereign artificers'.[24] Another way of putting this is that rather than making their way through the world, they accept that they *ad hoc* their way through it.

Although this may resonate with Luhmann's anxious, non-purposive and self-referential conception of the (non) 'subject', there are four major differences that excuse a long detour through his thought.[25] Firstly, expressive subjects, as a sub-group of fractured reflexives with under-developed reflexivity, are the exact obverse of Luhmann's characterization of human beings in general, ones who struggle self-despairingly to give meaning to their lives.[26] Here, instead, they are seen as people who lack the architectonic principle supplied by personal identity but ones who do not recognize this absence as a lack. Secondly, I am dealing with epistemic subjects (their perceptions) instead of advancing a general ontology of the (non-)'subject'. Thirdly, despite the absence of deliberative selection and shaping among expressive subjects, this does not deprive their unit acts of intentionality or meaningfulness in their episodic contexts. Finally, they are engaged in the world through their human concerns, despite the absence of prioritization or dovetailing, and hence, are not exemplars of Luhmannian 'futility'.

Let us return to the skein of unanswered questions: how do these subjects get by as more than lottery players? How do they act in a meaningful, if not very consistent, way? Ultimately, on what basis do they act at all? The answer they give is their 'gut feelings'. Sally, who disavows having any specific moral code, responds to unavoidable choices by 'an instant yes, I think I'll get on okay with this or not with that'. She agrees she works by gut feelings: 'I try to trust them – gut instincts – I haven't had a huge setback... your emotions guide you a lot, so I think you usually

---

[24] See Martin Hollis, *The Cunning of Reason*, Cambridge University Press, 1987, pp. 1–14.
[25] For a comparison that economically singles out similarities and differences, see Andrea M. Maccarini and Riccardo Prandini, 'Human Reflexivity in Social Realism: beyond the Modern Debate', in Margaret S. Archer (ed.), *Conversations about Reflexivity*, London, Routledge, 2010, pp. 79–91.
[26] See Niklas Luhmann, *Social Systems*, Stanford University Press, 1995, p. 426f.

trust them'. Carole speaks in the same vein, using the same semantics: 'I'm quite confident about how I feel, it's not very often that I think I was wrong, I mean in my gut reaction. I feel quite confident in that if something feels right you'll go along with it, it's only when things probably aren't going – your hackles are raised and you think there's something not right here.'

Although emotive action is indisputably self-referential, since it is obviously the subjects' own feelings that are consulted, I again part company with Luhmann in maintaining that emotions always have intentionality, they are about something in the world rather than being a threat to it.[27] Elsewhere, I have developed the argument that because of our human constitution, the way the world is made and the necessity of interaction between the two, everyone unavoidably has concerns in their physical well-being (natural order), performative competence (practical order) and self-worth (social order).[28] Each cluster promotes first-order emotions as 'commentaries upon their concerns', for example, fear promotes flight; boredom prompts a cessation of work; shaming leads to social withdrawal. All of these are spontaneous responses resulting in impulsive actions. However, most of us recognize the dilemma that since we receive three sets of commentaries, we cannot respond impulsively to our 'gut feelings' (except in exceptional circumstances such as a fire in a building) because each commentary may damage our other concerns vested in different orders – for example, the soldier under fire feels fear but knows that if he flees, he will face a court-martial. It is from this necessary engagement with the world and the conflicting commentaries received from it that most subjects derive the impetus to prioritize their first-order concerns and to resist impulsiveness. In so doing, they begin to define their personal identities.

This is precisely what the expressives do not do and cannot do because of their *événementalisme*. To consider what combination of concerns matters most to a subject, in what order, and with what degrees of accommodation, subordination and exclusion entails a comparative consideration of situations and potential events – imaginative, fallible and corrigible – but a comparison nonetheless. However, this comparative exercise will only be conducted by those who *know that to heed every 'gut reaction' will result in their downfall* sooner rather than later. It is why most of us, for example, refrain from the expression of the 'road rage' that we temporarily feel with intensity.

---

27 *Ibid.*, p. 430.
28 Archer, *Being Human*, pp. 193–221. For an abbreviated version, see 'Emotions as Commentaries on Human Concerns', in Jonathan H. Turner, *Theory and Research on Human Emotions*, Amsterdam, Elsevier, 2004, pp. 327–356.

As prioritization, accommodation and so forth are achieved, emotions are transvalued into second-order feelings and commentaries.[29] The resulting emotional commentaries then prompt purposeful actions such that those promoting or defending one concern do not endanger others. They enable us to serve multiple commitments through 'joined-up caring' across the wide variety of events encountered, allowing us to be engaged with a plethora of situations rather than dealing with each sequentially.

The 'under-developed' reflexives with whom we are dealing remain at the mercy of their first-order emotional commentaries, resulting in impulsive, spontaneous actions that are *expressive* in kind. Terming them expressive signals two things: firstly, they do indeed express the subject's self-referential feelings in a given situational context but, secondly, they may be *merely* expressive because once a particular event is over, nothing ensures that the next 'gut reaction' will be consonant with the previous one.

Finally, there is a last question to pose of our expressive subjects. Since emotions have both an affective and a cognitive component, how do these intelligent university students consistently downplay the cognitive element, as is necessarily the case if they continue to abide by their 'gut feelings'? They do so by regularly subordinating the cognitive to the 'gut reaction' through a selective perception that picks out only those parts of information that confirm the inerrant nature of their emotive responses. Let us briefly illustrate how these points – reliance on emotivism, *événementalisme*, dependence on strong first-order feelings and use of the verification principle in practical reasoning – operate to oppose the shaping of a life.

Metaphors help to enter into Carole's world. Her landscape of contingency conforms to the image of her environment as one of 'blooming, buzzing, confusion'. Alternatively, picture a blizzard that confines perception to what is close at hand, blanketing out not only possible pathways forward but also faraway peaks. Then, imagine the sense of powerlessness this would instil in a hiker who knows she has to keep moving or succumb to hypothermia – a trope for complete social passivity – yet lacks a compass or map because contingency precludes such orientation devices. Into this landscape, insert a warm-hearted human being, pulsing with inchoate concerns, and ask how she takes any step forward rather than becoming an exemplar of Luhmannian 'despair'.

---

[29] That there is some second-order processing within our emotional sets commands broad agreement. Jon Elster refers to it as 'transmutation' (*Alchemies of the Mind*, Cambridge University Press, 1999), John D. Greenwood as 'transformation' (*Realism, Identity and the Emotions*, London, Sage, 1994), and Charles Taylor as 'transvaluation' (*Human Agency and Language*, Cambridge University Press, 1985).

The most Carole can do to explicate the origins of her epistemology of contingency is the contrast she provides between her warm familial relations when growing up and her encounters with wider tracts of social reality: 'I can remember feeling angry when I was learning about the world and I sort of blamed my mum because my mum was so nice I thought everyone was so nice, so I was quite shocked at how horrible the world was and how horrible people could be.' This seems to have sparked her strong feelings of social justice, but these are tempered in action by her equally firm conviction that little can be done beyond proximate acts of personal kindness. Although she is sometimes tempted to attribute this feeling of powerlessness to her subordinate working-class status or to sexual politics, she frequently proffers these discourses only to withdraw them as inadequate to the complexities involved. In other words, she eagerly stretches out a hand to these promised orientation devices but cannot clasp them because she recognizes their unfitness for purpose. Perhaps Carole senses that these conceptual handles are as unequal as she is herself to dealing with perceived contingency. Perhaps both are recent victims of the variety already generated in the transition towards morphogenetic society, which has gathered speed throughout her lifetime.

Instead, Carole resorts to her situational 'gut feelings' as guidelines to action, battling against complete agential passivity and refusing to be reduced to the status of an object determined by shifting external causal powers. She recognizes that in following her inner promptings – 'I'm not sure where it comes from, it's like a sweeping feeling' – her successive and expressive actions add up to what she brands as failure: 'there's such a lot in life that makes you think you're a failure' – especially with regard to her four children.

Her expressive mode of action seems to have begun early, but each episodic and emotive response has prompted a selection which has not led anywhere apart from the accumulation of their unintended consequences. For example, at school she rejected the engendered options and selected 'gardening' because 'I was off the female role model'. However, she understood little about the nutritional values of vegetables until she had been a vegetarian for years and currently has a 'messy garden' that she knows her father would censure.

Carole married at eighteen, welcomed the arrival of her children but, needing to supplement the family income, she had the impulse to drive a truck and actually became a bus driver. This way of life was shattered eighteen years later when her husband became bankrupt, the house was repossessed and divorce ensued. Her elder daughter, who had been through drugs and become a single mother, was their refuge until the family obtained social housing by Carole pretending her daughter had evicted them. Subjectively, Carole presents this as her nadir, frequently reverting to 'having lost the house' as representing her 'failing her children', although she does not appear to have been in any way responsible.

Conversely, when matters are awry with the children (her elder daughter was on hard drugs, as was her second son, which precipitated schizophrenia, and most are dyslexic), these are occurrences that Carole regards in the light of misfortunes. She copes with their outcomes but feels no responsibility for their onset. With little money and numerous grandchildren between them, much time is spent in one another's houses: 'we're all close and we laugh too, we all cope – any sort of problems and we all laugh . . . So we're going through quite a nice phase until we'll all be going off later in life, but it's nice at the moment.' The pleasures are in the present tense but recognized to be transient. Yet Carole cannot see any further ahead to some way of coping with this overload of difficulties: 'how can I sort this out? I'm not coming up with any solution – other than winning the lottery or meeting some rich bloke!' Thus, the only antidote to negative contingency is conceived of as positive contingency.

However, Carole has been through an access course and gained entry to university. Why does she not see this as the gateway to social mobility, against the odds, and the opening up of new opportunities for herself and her family? Basically, because she is convinced that contingent social reality precludes planning and her 'gut reactions' are proving stubbornly silent. Thus, 'I'm hoping, sort of on the way, I'll start finding a bit of direction and a focus. It's all a bit new and I'm a bit overwhelmed at the moment.' This is a fair comment in year one, but the next year she voices the same passive sentiment of waiting upon circumstances to decide: 'I think something's going to say . . . if nothing does after Christmas or Easter, then I'll just have to force myself to pick something and that's it'. In her final year she has not brought herself to do so and, very like Paula, says 'I've got a few [careers] in my mind but I haven't sort of decided, I would find it hard, but that's I think because I would like to do them all'. She mentions 'something to do with the community' or work with children or young offenders, but the only form of inner selective guidance she detects is a strong affective repugnance towards business and consumerism: 'my gut feelings would still be in this [above] group rather than, say, go into business. I wouldn't have any interest in advertising, trying to get people to buy meaninglessness. You know, my gut feeling just wouldn't be there . . . and I couldn't go in, I couldn't.' However, neither the necessity of selection nor the shaping of a life can be tackled by elimination, expressive or otherwise.

Let us try to go further in understanding why Carole's reliance on her emotive lodestar actually prevents her from planning, decision-making and, most importantly, from any serious and lasting form of active social engagement. Clearly, occurent emotions surface at a given point in time, even if they are recurrent in kind. For those whose actions are governed by them, the very occurrence (and fading) of these affective states serves to punctuate any course of action, both by initiating it and by inserting a full stop. This is *événementalisme*, meaning that each tract of the life course is chopped into episodic segments where action is restricted to being expressive in form. It is not that the first-order emotions vary inconsistently with similar circumstances over time, but rather that the perception of successive episodes as being discrete confines each action to the bounds of that given episode. The effects are that, on the one hand, what do turn out to be lasting concerns (by the repeated attention given to them) are fragmented into separate events precluding any overall engagement. On the other hand, a single, intense, but negative experience can kill an inchoate but potential course of action that could otherwise have resulted in a serious commitment if sustained. Carole provides many examples of how her 'presentism' militates against continuous, concerted and concerned action.[30]

For example, each year Carole lists 'my children's well-being' amongst her main concerns in life. There is no reason to doubt her, yet there is every reason to question whether her *événementaliste* approach – tantamount to crisis management – is the way to promote their longer term well-being. As she reflects: 'I've always enjoyed the children very much. Obviously, when they were teenagers and had all these different problems it was awful but I've always got over it, sort one out and then sort something else out with another one.' Working as a single mother of four, it would be hard not to sympathize with her phenomenal feel. However, she continues: 'As they get older I just leave them to get on with it. It would have to be a bit of a crisis [for me to act] but then I think it just sort of comes naturally, it's spontaneous.' Without denying that Carole likely evidences many signs of caring for each child between crises, the issue remains whether her 'presentism' is not, in fact, the enemy of her genuine concern. With her second son, variously diagnosed as schizophrenic or obsessive, it is understandable that she acts and successfully appeals when he is sectioned under the Mental Health Act. Nevertheless, when she risks controlling his medication on the basis of her spontaneous feelings about his condition at the time, without seeking a second opinion or making some attempt to resolve the conflicting medical diagnoses,

---

[30] Obviously, this interpretation will not be welcomed by supporters of 'emotional intelligence'.

such *événementalisme* provokes some discomfort even though she might, indeed, know what is best for him.

One very bad experience can deter most of us from continuing with a certain activity, but for Carole this seems a regular pattern. In her mid-forties, after a varied employment history, she became a support worker in a centre for people with severe learning difficulties and challenging behaviour where she 'got on better with the clients than with the group of so-called normal staff.' Conflicts ensued over the petty inflexibility of the latter (such as manhandling a client out of the car after a trip) and culminated in an official confrontation ending with Carole saying 'I think it's best if I just go, I don't want to be in this situation'. Her reflection, several years later, is pertinent because she admits that leaving prevented her from 'doing anything else' – a withdrawal from commitment into passivity that only ended when she enrolled on the access course: 'I've moved on though, I'm not going to think about it anymore . . . I did try and understand it for quite a while, but then I thought no more, it's not something I'm going to understand. So I put it behind me, but it did stop me doing anything for quite a while, it did.'

Doubtless, most of us can resonate with that experience, but from her being a bus driver to taking most of the gender modules available on her degree, Carole displayed a quarter of a century's affinity with feminism. Yet one early experience of joining a women's group deterred her from further feminist involvement: 'I was just a normal working-class girl and they were all university-educated and were coming out with what they'd researched and I didn't have a clue what they were on about, so I didn't stay there very long . . . when they asked I just didn't know what to say and I'd just say "oh I don't know nothing", so that didn't work out.' As isolated episodes these are unremarkable, but cumulatively their frequency spells an *événementalisme* in which her life course is fragmented and defeats any follow through.

If we take Carole's following statement that 'you don't think logically, you just go, if something feels right you'll go along with it', this raises the traditional problem about the role of the cognitive in human emotions.[31] It is particularly relevant to her progress through university since she has been acquiring a wider knowledge base which might contradict or at least qualify some of her spontaneous emotive reactions. Her following response, made just before graduation, shows how she articulates the relationship between the cognitive and the affective:

---

[31] Jon Elster, *Strong Feelings*, Cambridge, Mass., MIT Press, 1999, p. 108f. Also see Andrew Ortony, Gerald L. Gore and Andrew Collins, *The Cognitive Structure of Emotions*, Cambridge University Press, 1988.

You have a conversation with your sort of logical side. If your gut feelings don't marry up, yes they would take precedence I'd say. Obviously, if it was ridiculous, your logical side would kick in, but no, I think our gut feelings tell us a lot. I suppose if you don't go by them, then it's a bit like a kind of gnawing feeling. You know they are going to be there and you're not going to be truly happy with what you're doing because you hadn't listened to them.

Thus, the affective prompt takes precedence but, in fact, the cognitive plays a bigger role than simply booting out ludicrous inclinations.[32] Although subordinate, cognitive reasoning plays a crucial role *in rationalizing affect by working on the verification principle*.[33] It provides *articulation* for the sensed feeling, *confirmation* for the rightness of that feeling and *justification* for expressive action based upon that feeling: 'things in the past that you'd felt and didn't know very well how to express and then you read and say "yes that's right". I like that feeling . . . because sometimes you get emotions and then you think "why did I?", but then you think "Well, yes, you were right to".'

To make the final link with expressive action, we can take Carole's account of her vegetarianism. This she traces to a childhood aversion towards eating chocolate animals, which she later followed up by visits to the public library: 'I just wasn't happy with that and I did some reading about the battery hens and the factory [farming], and I thought "well, that's not right and that's something you can do straight away".' Thus, at nineteen and married, she became a life-long vegetarian and brought her children up likewise. To begin with she felt tired and unwell, admitting that she knew little about nutrition and rectifying this by reading. However, when the role of the cognitive is confined to the verification principle, it clearly cannot gainsay 'gut feelings' but it can amplify them. Carole has read on and now thinks of turning vegan. In brief, university education has served to make her a more sophisticated expressive reflexive, thus accounting for why it is possible for such 'expressive reflexives' to graduate unchanged.

In sum, the overall consequence of *événementalisme* is for the subject to rely exclusively upon first-order emotions. In turn, a stable prioritization of their concerns is impossible and Carole agrees that these vary according to age and stage. It is significant that when listing her three main concerns in life during each year of her undergraduate career she (and Sally) always include 'health and happiness'. Instead of this

---

[32] In the second interview, Carole questioned if one's feelings on the day would not affect how ICONI was completed. Although I suspected this was to confuse 'feelings' with 'moods', such a question was inserted at the end of ICONI when it was administered in the third year. There were no significant findings or even tendencies.

[33] Karl Popper, *The Logic of Scientific Discovery*, London, Hutchinson, 1962.

being a generic phrase doing duty for the good life, it is a pointer to the deep self-referentiality of the expressive subject, whose only compass for making their way through the world is the consultation of their occurent emotions in each episodic situation. The paradox is that this extreme form of self-reference co-exists with the absence of a clear personal (and social) identity, thus precluding the development of a satisfying *modus vivendi* and effective forms of engagement with the social world.

Obviously, this section lacks the empirical basis for even starting to specify the conditions making for the expressive reflexives. Nevertheless, some entirely speculative pointers are advanced for exploration. Given the general relational approach adopted, what is most striking is Carole's poverty of enduring or extensive social relations. In short, Carole is isolated: her parents have moved far away and rarely visit, no mention is made of long-term or local friends, as a mature student she makes none at university, and her lack of engagement denies her the networks of those promoting particular concerns. She endorses this by talking about the 'little world' she and her gown-up children inhabit. Marrying young, having four children in quick succession and taking whatever jobs would ease the family finances, also contributes to the overburdening effects of material poverty: its stop-gap shifts, relentless fixation on today's needs and constant settling for the sub-optimal. Add to this the loss of community, the unknown neighbours, the retreat from street brutality and this means the 'network society' confronts single mothers like Carole with nothing but its holes.[34]

It is not that the reflexive imperative is any less exigent in cases like hers but that she has no resources with which to meet it constructively because what has been termed her 'presentism' is structurally induced. Her enormous respect for contingency is precisely because her life course has been directed by real and apparent contingencies, making the future seem entirely contingent. From the cultural system the message of messianic contingency – the lottery win, achievement-less celebrity, the X Factor – is entirely reinforcing. Given these micro- and macro-contexts, it is less than surprising that Carole resorted to her 'gut feelings' as her sole guide, and her lonely struggle for personal integrity deserves respect in the absence of sociality that seemingly necessitated it. If there is anything in these speculations, they open up the prospect of an increase in expressive reflexivity during the transition to morphogenetic society,

---

[34] However, this should not be taken as an exclusively working-class phenomenon, although it is in these particular manifestations. We must remember that Sally is middle class.

especially amongst the victims of modernity who are worst placed to avail themselves reflexively of the situational logic of opportunity.

Conclusion

In developing this relational analysis of the breaking of human reflexivity, subjects' natal and chosen relationships have been presented as helping to produce 'bounded variety', in very different ways, but providing directional guidance when confronting the necessity of selection. Thus, subjects 'displaced' by contingent occurrences could return to their earlier mode of reflexivity if circumstances became more favourable and provided that their relations supported their return (as in Julie's case). 'Impeded' subjects had a negative point of reference in the rejection of their natal backgrounds but could only begin to practise the mode of reflexivity to which they were inclined given effective support from their chosen network of friends (as in the cases of Shirin and Carris). 'Expressive' subjects like Carole could not overcome their reflexive 'under-development' in the absence of such a network. Instead, she developed a more sophisticated mode of verifying her emotive inclinations that seemed to promote 'drift' rather than supplying guidance that facilitated selection and enabled her to begin the task of shaping a life. In sum, fractured reflexivity can be overcome given the appropriate relational conditions and, with it, passive agency can be left behind. In the absence of such relationships, the subject continues drifting without aspiring to an active agency that seemingly evades them (as for Paula and Carole).

Returning to the macroscopic level, what is it about nascent morphogenetic society that generates these tendencies themselves, specifically a high level of fractured reflexivity?[35] Whilst modernity's situational logic of competition undoubtedly gave rise to a large quotient of objective losers, the advent of morphogenetic society's quite different logic of opportunity makes for a larger proportion of casualties among those whose subjectivity precludes their engagement with purposeful action. Subjects who cannot work as effective practitioners of any dominant mode of reflexivity accrue objective penalties as the dark side of their inability to comply with the reflexive imperative. Subjectively, they undergo profound mental distress and experience a disorientation that is qualitatively distinct from the anger and unfairness experienced by many in

---

[35] It should be recalled that whilst the percentages of fractured subjects more than doubled in the course of the study whilst those of expressive subjects halved, this leaves the combined proportions at entry and exit in net increase.

modernity.[36] The picture is darker still in that many struggle with their 'fracturing' in the absence of the collective support forthcoming within modernity: those similarly placed, geo-locally rooted and frequently collectively organized, who could at least understand modernity's 'victims'.

Although a morphogenetic social order promotes new and different modalities of relational association, it will be maintained in the conclusion that the increasing incidence of fractured reflexivity will not be a transitional phenomenon unless the proliferation of 'variety', right down to the level of the singular subject, is distributed and integrated as 'diversity' at the level of civil society.

---

[36] The latter have been dwelt upon by Helena Flam, 'Emotion, and the Silenced and Short-circuited Self', in Archer (ed.), *Conversations About Reflexivity*, pp. 187–205, but without making the distinction that is held to be crucial here.

8   Conclusion

As is often the case, to come to the end of a book is to start the next one. This is so here because a small qualitative study, which cannot pretend to be representative even of university students within one institution, furnishes no basis for inferential statistics and no justification for extrapolation to the increasingly varied groups constituting the population of Britain. However, as a theoretico-empirical study, what it does provide is food for further theoretical consideration; for something between unregulated speculation and theoretical propositions warranted by empirical substantiation. In short, the findings presented have implications worth entertaining in theorizing about future transformations of the social order. Their examination is itself a response to the 'situational logic of opportunity', since it too involves an exploration of 'contingent compatibilities' that are the ultimate constituents of the increase in 'variety' today.[1]

The patterns and processes involved in the making and breaking of reflexivity – the dominant mode developed, practised and sometimes fractured – amongst this small cohort of sociology students is summarized in Figure 8.1 below. These are largely qualitative findings about educated young people in late modernity. Tempting as these findings are for hypothesis formation, various forms of inference or extrapolation simply cannot be supported from the empirical work undertaken and presented in chapters 4, 5, 6 and 7: (i) from the interviewed group to the rest of the entrance cohort, because interviewees were volunteers, self-selected rather than being matched with the larger group in their composition; (ii) from the interviewees to students entering the same university at the same time to study other disciplines or courses, partly again because of self-selection but also partly because of different entry requirements and a penumbra of factors which influenced their possession; (iii) from the

---

[1]   Much of this argument is based upon Margaret S. Archer, *Culture and Agency*, Cambridge University Press, 1988, for this work is also a theory about the growth of knowledge, despite that not being appreciated by certain reviewers. See pp. 219–226 and 235–270.

	% in entry group	Relations with natal background	Relations with home friends	Relations with new friends based on	Career sought for	Career sought in	Response to situational logic of opportunity
Communicative reflexives	13.5	Identifiers	Retention	Commonalities	Replication	Family example	Rejection
Autonomous reflexives	19.0	Independents	Selection	Interests	Material benefits	Financial and public services	Competetive adaptation
Meta-reflexives	38.6	Disengaged	Rejection	Values	Promoting change	Third sector	Embrace
Fractured reflexives	17.4	Rejecters	Absence	Dependency	Ephermeral appeal	Uncertain	Passivity

Figure 8.1 Summary of findings

Warwick interviewees to those at other British universities, where the definition of sociology, *desiderata* for entrants, and the repute of different institutions contributed to defining different populations at point of entry; (iv) from those interviewed to the same age cohort in the British population and so forth. These are very real limitations but they do not necessarily entail the banal conclusion that 'there is need for much further research' and no more can be said. Undoubtedly there is such a need but simply to rectify the methodological limitations itemized would be interesting, but extremely expensive and would not in itself contribute to more than descriptive accuracy on a representative basis. Its implications for the social order would require the same theoretical exploration as is now the case.

Moreover, this trilogy on reflexivity has not been undertaken out of an intrinsic interest in one aspect of human subjectivity per se. It began from seeking to answer the theoretical question about how structure and culture got in on our personal acts for those of us who were dissatisfied with both positivistic 'social hydraulics' and Parsonian 'internalization'. In their place, 'reflexivity' was advanced in *Structure, Agency and the Internal Conversation* as the process responsible for mediating between structural and cultural 'conditioning' and human agents, without entailing the obliteration or suspension of the agential properties and powers of persons.[2]

In the second volume, *Making our Way through the World: Human Reflexivity and Social Mobility*, which did use a sample of the local population of Coventry, stratified by age, gender and socio-economic position, the aim was to ascertain whether or not a personal emergent property (in this case dominant mode of reflexivity practised) governed the type of social mobility desired and achieved under people's own descriptions. These patterns of mobility (i.e., social stability, upward mobility or lateral volatility) were held to result from actions arrived at through the reflexive deliberations of singular subjects in social contexts not of their own making. Reflexivity thus acquired a stronger claim for mediating between one macroscopic aspect of the social order – the patterning of social mobility – and the personal 'projects' pursued by subjects through their reflexive internal conversations, which defined the precise courses of action taken by them.

It will be evident to those who have read the present volume from beginning to end that a similar kind of theoretical preoccupation prompted this study. The huge question here is 'will nascent morphogenesis turn into

---

[2] SEPs (structural emergent properties) and CEPs (cultural emergent properties) influence PEPs (personal emergent properties) but never completely override them.

morphogenesis unbound and supersede modernity?' The second and equally big question is 'what kind of morphogenetic society would this tend to be?' Satisfactory answers would require examining a range of considerations that have not even been raised in this small study of the making and breaking of reflexive practices amongst a non-representative group of students. Thus, what follows is no more than a sketch of preliminary thoughts whose refinement must await the next book.

Since the present volume has been overtly based upon 'relational realism', so too will be my approach in responding to the above questions.[3] However, it will begin from the contributions of systems theory to sociology even though it will end with their critique. Of course, that invokes the old joke about someone asking for directions and the riposte, 'well, if I wanted to get to x I wouldn't start from here'. Why do I, since I have always seen myself as a critic of 'complex adaptive systems theory?[4] The reason is that lay-thinking would almost certainly agree with statements about the increasing pace of social change, the novelties people have already encountered in their lifetimes, and their expectations for new variety to continue to grow during those of their children. Nevertheless 'change', 'novelty' and 'variety' remain imprecise terms and are usually addressed anecdotally by references to the new ubiquity of mobile phones, to holidaying in previously inaccessible places, eating foreign food and so forth. The reverse face of this within social theorizing is the exorbitation of new 'risks', which is rarely counter-balanced by a parallel accentuation of new 'opportunities'. In fact, it is only the protagonists and heirs of cybernetics who have sought to give any *precision* to the notion of 'variety', an absence also lacking in Luhmann and his followers. Nevertheless, this 'precision' is limited because cybernetics continues to bear the marks of its origins in information theory. However, the reservations that follow are not restricted to consequences of this pedigree. They are, rather, signposts to where reconceptualization is needed.

Generically, the difficulties are rooted in the fact that most of the influential pioneers concerned themselves with 'variety' alone without giving significant attention to sociological questions about its distribution and diffusion. As always, I return to David Lockwood's crucial distinction between 'systems integration' and 'social integration', to endorsement

---

[3] The two independently developed forms of realism are fully compatible. See Pierpaolo Donati, 'Critical Realism as Viewed by Relational Sociology' in his *Relational Sociology: A New Paradigm for the Social Sciences*, London, Routledge, 2011, pp. 97–119. See also Margaret S. Archer, 'Critical Realism and Relational Sociology: Complementarity and Synergy', *Journal of Critical Realism*, 9:2, 2010, 199–207.

[4] Even though my friend William Outhwaite begs to differ, *The Future of Society*, Oxford, Blackwell, 2006, pp. 88–90.

of his argument that the two can vary independently, and to my own conviction that unless the two co-exist there is no chance for the development of a robust civil society and economy.[5] On the contrary, systems theory in general has shown a marked tendency to neglect the conditions necessary for new forms of 'social integration' and given almost exclusive attention to 'variety' as the main or sole driver of social transformation. Necessarily, this preoccupation with endlessly increasing differentiation between people arrives at the terminus of what I will call 'transactional individualism'. Not only does this represent an extrusion of modernity but it also constitutes a denial of both the human need for social relations and the emergent relational goods that these generate for society. Social integration is integral to a civil society and economy, which both promote it and under which it prospers. Fundamentally, this omission is because the key concepts used to capture morphogenesis continue to be used in ways that are incongruous with the conceptualization of a morphogenetic society that does not derogate social integration in order to privilege social innovation.[6] Highlighting this one-sidedness, however briefly, gives a job specification to be completed before it can properly be said that there is a social theory of morphogenetic society.

The key to developing such a theory lies in acknowledging that *there is no such social formation as 'the' morphogenetic society*. Like markets based on the exchange of equivalents that are central to modernity, differences in the mode of production compared with the mode of distribution are essential *inter alia* for capturing the multiple forms of modernity – to recognizing how different Sweden and Switzerland are from China and Chile and the latter pair from one another. The same needs to be the case for discussion of 'morphogenetic societies'. Why this was not and still is not the case is because when morphogenesis first began to be discussed within cybernetics in the 1950s, attention became riveted upon the effects of the 'variety' *produced* to the detriment of the simultaneous consequences of its *distribution*.[7]

[5] David Lockwood, 'Social Integration and System Integration', in G.K. Zollschan and W. Hirsch, *Explorations in Social Change*, London, Routledge and Kegan Paul, 1964. Stefano Zamagni, 'Reciprocity, Civil Economy, Common Good', in Margaret S. Archer and Pierpaolo Donati (eds.), *Pursuing the Common Good: How Solidarity and Subsidiarity Can Work Together*, Proceedings of the 14th Plenary Session of the Pontifical Academy of Social Sciences, Vatican City Press, 2008, pp. 467–502.

[6] To characterize the social order, as opposed to the analytical 'morphogenetic approach' that provides an explanatory framework for examining when, whether and why structural, cultural and agential elaboration versus replication will result from a given period of social interaction.

[7] Ross Ashby held that 'the concept of "variety"' was 'a concept inseparable from that of "information"', p. 140. W. Ross Ashby, *An Introduction to Cybernetics*, London, Chapman and Hall, 1957.

Thus, it seems useful to pinpoint why some of the key terms frequently employed in this study (particularly 'variety') have entirely different connotations and denotations in cybernetics – whether the first, second or third cybernetics. The implication is that the social sciences cannot simply borrow concepts, propositions and theories to produce an instant 'social cybernetics'. Interdisciplinarity can, at best, stimulate ideas. What it cannot and should not result in is a shuffling and shuttling of concepts between them that is damaging for both.

'Variety' for social science

In this work, the constitution of 'variety' has been held to derive from 'contingent compatibilities' between elements lodged in the cultural system. This means elements that are objectively complementary and *may* be brought together in productive juxtaposition and sometimes synergy by those who spot them. In this way they come to constitute a novel addition to what is known and may be used. Such new items can remain confined to a small research group, may 'pass the test' of technological applicability or the quite different one of attracting public attention.[8] These are matters for the sociology of science to address, but ones already indicating that questions of distribution arise immediately after any given 'novelty' has been detected, articulated and published.

However, an important feature of 'contingent complementarities' is that because 'complementarity' between any two items in the cultural system is real (ontologically a 'complementarity' exists as an emergent property independently of its epistemological detection), the number of these potential items of 'variety' is incalculable. As Popper once noted, we are incapable of knowing all the implications of a single proposition or finding. It follows that we humans would require omniscience to be capable of numbering the potential compatibilities existing at any given time (and if we could number them, they would already have been discovered).

It also follows that in sociology and allied trades the meaning of 'variety' has to be confined to 'known variety'. We can theorize about the social conditions propitious to making the necessary connections and we can theorize about their consequences for the social order. But we are always theorizing about a finite domain of 'known variety', at any given time and place, whose real totality remains unknown – defying enumeration. What this means is that social theorists cannot employ

---

[8] See Margaret S. Archer, *Being Human: The Problem of* Agency, Cambridge University Press, 2000, pp. 177–188.

the same definition of 'variety' as used in early cybernetics where the *quantity of variety* was always measurable. Thus, to Ashby, working in terms of information theory, the 'word "variety"', in relation to a set of distinguishable items, will be used to mean either (i) the number of distinct elements, or (ii) the logarithm to the base 2 of the number'.[9] Hence, the preoccupation of early cybernetics with 'codes', very varied in kind but always with a *finite number* of possibilities necessarily capable of enumeration (such as the information given by traffic lights). Hence, too, the operationalization of 'variety', such that in a 'given set' this is a question 'of how many distinguishable elements it contains. Thus, if the order of occurrence is ignored, the set *c, b, c, a, c, c, a, b, c, b, b, a* which contains twelve elements, contains only three *distinct* elements – a, b and c. Such a set will be said to have a *variety* of three elements.'[10] In other words, 'variety' in the 'first' cybernetics is an objective, aggregate concept, best suited to coded information where effort has been given to making distinctions sufficiently clear to exclude subjective interpretation and to reduce any that may nonetheless intrude to the status of human error.[11]

Without going further, least of all entering into the mathematical intricacies and superstructure that cyberneticians have erected, let us simply note three basic differences between how the term 'variety' is used by Ashby and the ways in which it is not helpful to incorporate this concept into conceptualizing morphogenetic society.

Firstly, as defined above, such that it can be said that a set 'has a variety of X elements', the concept is that of an objective aggregate. What is included as 'an element' is not problematic within information theory because the purpose of clearly communicating something delineates it in advance. However, if the set comprises two cities that are being compared for their 'variety', different criteria will be needed depending on the purpose of the comparison (the health of their citizens or the efficiency of their transport systems). Equally, if maintaining that nascent morphogenesis is more advanced in one set than another (for example, in Britain today compared with fifty years ago), a crucial distinction has to be made between 'variety per se' and 'novelty' or 'new variety'. This is because the effect of novelty is often the displacement of old 'properties' (for example, radio sales dropped as those of television rose). Thus, in the social order, aggregate variety frequently diminishes with certain

[9] Ashby, *An Introduction to Cybernetics*, p. 126.   [10] *Ibid.*, pp. 124–125.

[11] Ashby does admit that 'a set's variety is not an intrinsic property of the set: the observer and his powers of discrimination may have to be specified if the variety is to be well defined.' *Ibid.*, p. 125. However, the insight is not followed up.

innovations,[12] meaning that aggregates of distinguishable elements are not merely unhelpful but can be completely deceptive about the extent of change.[13]

Secondly, the aggregate approach is atomistic. It is capable of recording only those 'elements' that can be counted in units or on a *per capita* basis. This means that 'variety' necessarily excludes 'relational goods' unless these are reduced to individual terms, yet reducibility is precisely what the concept denies. This is because disaggregation would entail the erroneous premise that 'common goods' are divisible, that people's 'share' of a marriage, a football team or an orchestra can be portioned out, which is a contradiction in terms because the 'elements' making for a 'great team' are not aggregates as in an addition sum. Attempts to incorporate relational goods by disaggregation would also imply a fallacious notion of individual substitutability (for example, that a national orchestra simply needs any trained cellist). The aggregative approach basically deals with individuals and quantifiable things. It thus cannot include those forms of variety or novelty that are collective, qualitative and above all relational properties.

Thirdly, the computational approach to defining 'variety' is confined to the incidence of 'elements' but mute about their distribution. Thus, the same numerical count representing 'a variety of three elements' is compatible with the three being distributed amongst different tracts of the population or all being concentrated in the same hands. Certainly, it is usually the case that if incidence has been counted then the distribution can also be calculated. But, that will only happen if distributions are considered to be as important as aggregates. As far as our question about what kind of morphogenetic social order is the referent, distributional issues are as important as matters of aggregate variety.

Indeed, this whole study about how young people responded to 'opportunity' was an attempt not merely to show that 'new varieties' of employment had increased for the cohort of undergraduates studied but also that what was decisive for their take-up were subjective differences in subjects' dominant modes of reflexivity. These affected both the distribution of *new variety* and the amplification of nascent morphogenesis. In other words, the different modes of reflexivity and both their differential and selective take-up of new opportunities served to explain the distribution of this *new variety*. What this study itself could not even begin to address were the effects of the distribution of this variety within the

[12] Although this is also the case in industrial technology, displacements are less susceptible to changes in fashion or manipulated consumption.
[13] This is without entering the methodological and evaluative issues surrounding the designation of 'an element' itself, let alone when it acquires the above adjectival prefixes, all of which are challenges to or for the supposed 'objectivity'.

population as a whole (even within one country) and its consequences in that particular area. Yet it is the *integration* of this growing variety (or its absence) that holds the key to the kind of morphogenetic social order capable of developing.

In the 'second cybernetics', as Maruyama termed his approach, his examination of positive, deviation-amplifying feedback was allied to some discussion of the *distribution of variety*. The issue at stake is whether his huge corpus of work brings us any closer to being able to differentiate between different types of morphogenetic societies and, within them, to begin to discern those features making for a strong civil society and economy.[14]

From the start, Maruyama dealt exclusively with 'deviation–amplifying mutual causal processes' i.e. 'processes that are loosely termed as "vicious circles" and "compound interests"; in short, all processes of mutual causal relationships that amplify an insignificant or accidental initial kick, build up deviation and diverge from the initial condition.'[15] The illustrations given are the enlargement of a crack in a rock by water collecting, freezing and widening the fissure and the 'kick start' of a town from the accidental death of a horse or loss of a wheel leading someone to settle in that spot, rather than elsewhere on an otherwise homogeneous plain. From then on, homogeneity gives way to heterogeneity as the first homestead gradually attracted other residents and later prompted the opening of shops, facilities and transport, as the generative mechanism for variety to stimulate more variety engaged.

Forty years later, Maruyama was to complain that although his emphasis on the quantitative side of change-amplifying causal loops had been well received, most 'readers did not even notice the more important qualitative side: *the necessity, desirability and increase in interactive heterogeneity.*'[16] The latter is the point that he continuously stressed over the next four decades, namely that 'interaction among heterogeneous elements can genuinely create new information, not just a new combination of old information, and the way the amount of information can increase.'[17]

Here *variety* embraces *new variety* or *novelty*, as the product of *heterogeneity*, entering into 'symbiosis' with other heterogeneous elements.

[14] See Per Nyfelt, *Professor Maruyama's writings*, http://heterogenistics.org/maruyama/bibliography/bibliography.html.
[15] Magoroh Maruyama, 'The Second Cybernetics: Deviation–Amplifying Causal Processes', *American Scientist*, 5:2, 1963, 164–179.
[16] Margoroh Maruyama, 'Causal Loops, Interaction, and Creativity', *International Review of Sociology*, 13:3, 2003, 607–628 (italics added).
[17] *Ibid.*, p. 618.

'Symbiosis' is not synonymous with the concept of 'contingent compatibilities' that I have used to theorize how *new variety* originates ideationally. This is because symbiosis entails mutual benefits for both parties, meaning by definition that every symbiotic development is positive-sum for those involved. What, however, about those (in any given population) who are not involved? Does a gap widen between a new elite, adept at initiating symbiosis and benefitting from it and a new mass of 'others'? In that case, it is impossible to ignore the plummeting of social integration that would ensue from such a *divided* morphogenetic society.

What is of concern is Maruyama's growing preoccupation with *heterogeneity* (differences) alone and his disregard of *homogeneity* (similarities) in a population. The latter is relegated to the bad old days when theories of 'socio-cultural adaptation implied the desirability of sociocultural homogeneity.'[18] Of course 'one knows what he means' and I have consistently railed in unison with him against the common equation of 'culture' with 'shared meanings'.[19] Nevertheless, an integrated society cannot be based upon *heterogeneity alone.*

Differences are necessary amongst members (as valid expressions of their differing capacities) but so are similarities and both should be valued: the former create the *novelty* resulting in new opportunities, the latter continue to supply a bonding that links together members of a group (community, team or enterprise) that accentuates their human commonalities and makes their belongingness something more than rational instrumental opportunism. If similarities are progressively eroded whilst differences increase (through variety generating more variety amongst those most responsive to the situational logic of opportunity) this is a formula for a serious decline in social integration that should be regretted by all. Such a progressive fall in social integration is not a loss that can be offset by *Heterogenistics* or the socially engineered symbiosis-for-all that Maruyama advances as the solution.[20] It is only by the manipulated involvement of nearly everyone (via social policy interventions) in the process of generating *new variety* that Maruyama thinks is capable of intensifying morphogenesis whilst avoiding the divided morphogenetic society.[21]

---

[18] *Ibid.*, p. 624.

[19] Margaret S. Archer, 'The Myth of Cultural Integration', *British Journal of Sociology*, 36:3, 1985, 333–353. The debate continues, see Margaret S. Archer and Dave Elder-Vass, 'Cultural System or Norm Circles? An Exchange', *European Journal of Social Theory*, 2011, 1–23.

[20] Magoroh Maruyama, 'Heterogenistics and Morphogenetics: Toward a New Concept of the Scientific', *Theory and Society*, 5:1, 1978, 75–96.

[21] 'Individuals in a culture, or cultures of the world, among which symbiotic combinations can be found, can be hooked up in a network. For example, old people who like to be

Thus, paradoxically in his paper on 'Interwoven and Interactive Heterogeneity in the 21st Century', instead of dwelling upon the extension of symbiotic interaction – whether voluntary or engineered – as promoting *heterogeneity*, he immediately returns to his earlier work in which subjects of different 'epistemological types' are held responsible for the promotion of morphostasis or morphogenesis.[22] These different 'mindscapes', as he terms them, are partly innate and partly learned, but in either case are psychological and mean the whole approach to who works in terms of negative feedback loops versus positive ones (thus, promoting social stability or change), becomes a matter of psychological reductionism. Yet, if that is the case, then it contradicts the social policy of 'heterogenistics'. Moreover, it begs the whole question about the generation of *new variety*, its distribution and the *integration of variety as diversity* for the nature of a morphogenetic social order. Although these 'mindsets' are neither exclusive nor set in concrete, their modification is seen as an individualistic process of 'self-heterogenization', sometimes accompanied by actual migration, and 'comes from increased accessibility to different cultures, life styles, entertainments, foods, and languages'.[23] Hence, the part played by social relations and relationality in shaping the new social order – into something other than the *divided* morphogenetic society – largely make their exit.

Thus, it is precisely when attention is focussed exclusively upon *heterogeneity*, because its intensification fosters more and more morphogenesis, that any concern for social integration disappears. If, in consequence, the distribution of variety is confined to a minority of any given population (those with the appropriate 'mindscape'), their unrestrained pursuit of the situational logic of opportunity would result in finer and finer forms of differentiation between them. They could not even be deemed an elite because, by definition, every elite is held to have binding interests in common – however much these are at variance with other sections, or the entire remainder, of the population. This is why the accentuation of *heterogeneity* alone is always a formula for 'individualism'. It is so because the differences characterizing each agent so overwhelm any

with children can be housed near families who need babysitters. On the other hand, those among whom no symbiotic combinations can be found need to try different networks.' *Ibid.*, p. 94.

22 Magorah Maruyama, 'Interwoven and Interactive Heterogeneity in the 21st Century', *Technological Forecasting and Social Change*, 45, 1994, 93–102. Regarding his earlier work on subjects of different 'epistemological types', this is spelt out in most detail in Magorah Maruyama, 'Interrelations among Science, Politics, Aesthetics, Business Management, and Economics' in Maruyama (ed.) *Context and Complexity: Cultivating Contextual Understanding*, New York, Springer-Verlag, 1992.

23 Maruyama, 'Interrelations among Science', p. 96.

communalities with others that they increasingly engage in transactions with the system 'as a whole' (meaning raiding it for the detection of 'contingent complementarities' and exploiting these novelties). In this process, subjects who can accumulate this new variety are differentiated still further from their peers, prompting a sedulous reduction in what remained of social integration based upon similarities. As these subjects acquire more new variety, their association with other social units becomes less and less rewarding and prompts a multiplication of the number of smaller and smaller social units that follows. For example, the existing number of political parties can no longer represent the extent of their differentiation.

This is why 'symbiosis' seems to be an inappropriate concept for capturing the dynamics of morphogenetic intensification, because not everyone can be a beneficiary and 'those among whom no symbiotic combinations can be found need to try different networks.'[24] In other words, let them migrate elsewhere. The 'third generation' have revised their terminology and increasingly use the notion of 'transactions' and 'transacting' between heterogeneous individuals and the system. This meaning of 'transaction' does not entail reciprocal exchange or the exchange of equivalents. It is qualitatively different from even the wealthy art collector, who acquires canvases for his private delectation, because he has to engage in market exchange with his art dealers. Of course, in neoliberal economics, market exchanges somehow generate the hidden hand producing social cohesion as the rabbit out of the hat of self-interest. Now, even that magical consequence is dispensed with. A 'transaction' on the part of the super-differentiated subject may involve no one else and entails no human relationship. Already this can be seen in the development of investment supermarkets where individuals no longer follow their hunches about the likely success of specific products, or in the erection of apartment buildings with no particular inhabitants in mind and no consultation of their particularistic preferences. In such cases, the investor already transacts with systemic 'market trends' rather than with a market made up of human buyers.

What is increasingly lost as growing *heterogeneity* deprives the ultra-differentiated of some person or group with sufficient similarities to constitute a trading partner is the potential for such human relations to be 'positive sum', which itself has an integrative valence. The suggestion of using 'heterogenistics' as the basis of a social policy to bring about marriages of symbiotic convenience (such as the lone old ladies as babysitters) is to take a systemic view of human relations and to neglect the

---

[24] See note 22.

human characteristics precluding or potentially stymying such relationships; some old ladies may wish to retire early, may detest the children's music and may feel threatened by groups of teenagers hanging out on the streets. Such manipulated fixes are themselves dehumanizing and constitute no solution to the deficit in social integration.

Recognizing this problem, 'third generation' cybernetics pays considerably more attention to the distribution of variety throughout a population, whose diversity increases until the newly distributed item reaches 50 per cent and then represents a shift towards integrative similarity.[25] Typical examples would be the spread of radio and television, the latter now accessed by 97 per cent of the British population. Yet, here, the ghost of Ashby's 'objective', 'measurable' and 'aggregate' definition of 'properties' returns to vitiate the argument. The above figure means that the Queen and the homeless person sleeping in a refuge both watch television, but does this constitute a similarity or contribute to social integration? Qualitatively programmes are designed for different viewers, qualitatively people's differences filter their viewing and qualitatively their re-differentiation has led growing numbers to supplement and then supplant the role of passive spectator by interaction on the Internet. In short, the problem of diminishing social integration resurfaces, precisely because it cannot be tackled in the restricted terms and definitions of cybernetics where a morphogenetic society always ends up at variance with a dynamic civil society.

A conclusion is not the place in which to engage in a detailed overview of interdisciplinary contributions to thinking about morphogenetic society. I have only used examples from cybernetics to introduce a problem that has not been given the attention that it warrants, namely the 'sociological deficit' in the thinking of those who have given most attention to the *process* of morphogenesis in the social domain. This deficit consists in focussing almost exclusively on the *generation of new variety* that in one sense carries society (now one and global) forward and a corresponding neglect of what holds it together or pulls it apart. In other words, to examine morphogenetic society in such terms is like discussing feudalism without reference to fealty or protection or capitalism without mentioning class divisions or class conflict. Conversely, to ponder upon *the integration of variety as non-divisive diversity* is an attempt to reduce the 'sociological deficit' by attending to the conditions necessary for the elaboration of an *integrated morphogenetic society*. This represents a new

---

[25] See Henry Teune and Zdravko Mlinar, *The Developmental Logic of Social Systems*, Beverly Hills and London, Sage, 1978, who devote a chapter to precisely this issue, pp. 127–146.

agenda for social theory that has only been cursorily introduced here, but is vital to develop it if we are to be able to envisage superseding modernity by an integrated rather than a divided morphogenetic society.

Giving their due to social relations

Finally, returning to the start of the chapter, what contributions to this issue are made by the findings presented about the making and breaking of different modes of reflexivity in late modernity? Speculative as these must be, they deal in entirely different terms with nascent morphogenetic society – that is, in terms of personal concerns and human relations rather than the aggregation and distribution of properties. At the end of each substantive chapter a brief assessment was provided about the likely future trajectory of each of the four dominant modes of reflexivity: communicative reflexivity was deemed to be in decline; autonomous reflexivity to be stable, whilst both meta-reflexivity and the various kinds of fractured reflexivity were anticipated to be on the increase. Were these expectations found to be broadly correct, the final question I want to raise is whether or not this points towards a different kind of morphogenetic social order from that presented by cyberneticians and systems theorists in general. In particular, does it hold out any greater hopes for an integrated civil society and economy than is the case for the anti-social 'transactional individualism' just examined?

As far as the communicative reflexives are concerned, their demise seems to me irreversible. The speed and penetration of change in the advanced parts of the world is fundamentally destructive of the 'contextual continuity' upon which communicative reflexivity depends. Morphogenetic change destroys the *modi vivendi* continuous from the past but also defies the re-establishment of new continuities on the basis of residence, community, occupation, religion, ethnicity and kinship. What is unprecedented, in so far as some do struggle to maintain a small shelter of 'contextual continuity' for themselves and a few significant others, is that this is also a matter of reflexive deliberation and it now comes at a price. The costs are in terms of refusing geographical mobility and of rejecting the full extent of occupational advancement offered by higher education. This is a choice, not a default option or fall-back position. It has to be made, it carries a price tag, it is based upon personal commitment and is hostage to it. In turn, the main consequence of this decline in communicative reflexivity is to precipitate the reduction in social solidarity that was seen to have been treated with little concern, at least in the 'first' and 'second' cybernetics. However, recalling that throughout this trilogy communicative reflexivity was not found to be associated with socio-economic position, it follows that the shrinkage of this group will have repercussions throughout the social order – ones that are both cultural and structural in kind.

On the one hand, the normative conventionalism of the communicatives has been mentioned frequently in the course of this book. If their progressive demise is indeed the case, then normativity is fast losing its social anchorage in a group whose clarity about rectitude once stood as a firm reminder to others. When conventions decline there is nothing – despite their being arbitrary in nature – that ensures another set will replace them. On the contrary, when premiums become attached to innovatory actions, to seizing novel opportunities and to exploring and exploiting new connections, there is a severely reduced sense in which actions of this type can be norm-governed. Action needs to be at least recurrent in kind in order for norms to develop to cover it. When successive and successful creative acts become increasingly rewarded, this defies stable expectations coalescing into normativity. The 'decencies' for which the communicative collectivity used to provide aggregate support – loyalty, appreciation, gratitude, consideration – are losing their strongest protagonists and exemplars.

Correspondingly, and especially in those areas where innovation is morphing most rapidly, even legal regulation is left limping behind: as in biotechnology, the protection of intellectual and artistic property rights, or the privacy of communication in daily life. Instead, innovation outruns codification and trying to catch up with it is like trying to open the fridge door fast enough to see the light come on. Bureaucratic regulation is no substitute, because getting things done fast and flexibly is impeded by fixed protocols. Consequently, more and more specialist groups are becoming normatively self-regulating, according to their own shifting definitions (as within the IT community, its users and abusers). If normativity declines, as a generalized medium of social life, an inversion that appears to be occurring will intensify. Namely, it will become subjects' own involvements that determine under what tract of regulation they place themselves, until this is renegotiated.[26] Yet negotiated norms lack the binding power of the generalized normativity that communicative reflexivity used to promote and becomes more akin to temporary wage settlements.

On the other hand, the structural bastion of the communicative reflexives was the traditional family but it has been see how as 'identifiers',

---

[26] To some extent this has always been the case; those who do not drive are only subject to the rules of the road as pedestrians, cyclists, etc. but not as motorists.

who seek to replicate their natal backgrounds, this sub-group is already in a small minority compared with the 'independents', 'disengaged' and 'rejecters'. Moreover, they find replication difficult, in large part because their partners do not share the same background but also because job location draws them away from it. The evidence on marital breakdown, 'amalgamated', 'patchwork' and 'rainbow' families is well-known and such variants are likely be augmented as the ranks of the communicative reflexives decrease. One implication that has been traced is the seemingly enhanced importance of friendship networks for young people. Yet friendship was often perceived as fragile and ephemeral, demanding effort and concessions to maintain it because it is simply not 'there' in the way that the family once was. The resort to mobile phones, socially interactive websites and those sad Facebook entries addressed to 'my one thousand friends' but, in fact, to no one particular other, are symptomatic of the loss in social integration spelt by the diminution in the conditions necessary for the production and reproduction of communicative reflexives.

I trust that no one who has accompanied me through more than 300 pages is going to ask the question that might come from some of those who have started at the end, namely 'what then happens to the communicative reflexives?' Clearly, the answer is 'nothing' because without the social conditions (of 'contextual continuity') for their production, there are none. This form of social subjectivity – like all others – is relational through and through. Dominant modes of reflexivity do not mean their practitioners share a personality type that will somehow surface regardless of social conditions. The fact that social integration seems likely to plummet as a consequence of the diminution of communicative reflexivity should concern us all but, in terms of theorizing, will only be disturbing to any who still hold complex social systems to be adaptive.

Thus, although there is no basis whatsoever for thinking that because there seems to be a negative correlation between the decrease in communicative reflexivity and an increase in fractured reflexivity, that this means the former sub-group has moved into the latter *en bloc*. Certainly, individuals may change their dominant mode of reflexivity, but there is no sense in which the fall in social solidarity can be regarded as a problem confined to (or attributable to) a particular sector of the population (i.e. the fractured) either sociologically or psychologically.

On the one hand, this is because every social formation is expected to harbour some (unfixed) quotient of fractured subjects who have encountered the contingent adversities of life in an open system. Where formations differ most is probably less in the incidence of fracturing of this kind than in their relational capacities to provide support rather than neglect for these subjects. On the other hand, and potentially of greater concern for sharpening the downward reduction in social solidarity, is the (tentative) discovery that 'under-developed' reflexivity, in the form of expressive reflexive subjects, accounted for the highest proportion of 'fracturedness' amongst the cohort at time of entry. At first, because not knowingly having encountered such subjects before, they were semi-jokingly classified as 'refuseniks', by virtue of their low ICONI scores on all modalities. But, despite this label turning out to be quite apposite, it is no joke for these subjects who turn their backs on the reflexive imperative and pay for it in phenomenological terms by bearing the brunt of low social integration, seen as both the cause and effect of expressive reflexivity – as is perfectly possible with deviation–amplifying processes.

These subjects are hypothesized to be products of a lifelong 'relational deficit', becoming isolates whose inclinations towards particular 'concerns' may never connect up with a network capable of nurturing them into commitments, by presenting a bigger picture that enabled them to discount passing snubs and discouragements. Another way of putting this is that they never become fully fledged members of any 'norm circle', because even if they are on the periphery of several, they never form sufficiently close relational bonds to experience the relational goods deriving from engagement that encourage resilient dedication to a group or 'cause'. Their retreat into *événementalisme*, where responses to (what are perceived of as) discrete situations are guided by 'gut feelings' and justified by selective perception guided by verificationism. This condemns them to the agential passivity of 'presentism'. Their resulting 'shapeless' lives of regrets and feelings of failure stand as a human reproach to those sociological theorists who vaunt 'situationalism' and defend the formation of courses of action within action itself, unrelated to any durable social engagement anchoring lasting actions tendencies.

The expressive subject can neither wholeheartedly respond to any social source of normativity nor seriously contribute towards one since 'gut feelings' cannot even be the source of a consistent emotivism. Nor are they responsive to the opportunities that they have helped to make available for themselves, since even these are regarded as contingencies rather than possible trajectories. If there is anything in my conjecture that a persisting 'relational deficit' is the root of persistent expressive under-developed reflexivity, there are two additional factors that exacerbate the already low state of social integration. Firstly, objective indicators of social isolation are on the increase (the predominant type of household in Britain is now constituted by the lone occupant; most people do not know the names of their neighbours and so forth). Thus, for the young who start down this track and do not form a lasting partnership there are diminishing integrative resources at their disposal, which is one way in which the deviation–amplifying process works.

Secondly, the increasing use that the under-thirties make of their ear-phones to listen to music in public places (when walking and travelling) means that the practice of reflexivity is being blocked out during the most available interludes. If Elster is correct that music affects mood rather than emotion (the former lacking the intentionality and commentary on our concerns supplied by the latter), it is plausible the mood shifts produced act more powerfully on 'gut feelings' to which expressive subjects would be most susceptible.[27] In any case, this evasion of occasions for internal conversation will reinforce reflexive under-development amongst this sub-group yet be all the more attractive to them because it blankets out their own feeling of isolation and conceals it from others. Possibly, this may be doubly counter-productive in depriving expressive subjects, in particular, of spaces in which self-talk could develop or where social contact might be initiated.[28] If so, it will confirm both their undeveloped reflexive mode and its grounding in relational poverty, serving to intensify their already low level of social integration and their poignant feelings about being 'confirmed isolates'.[29]

Is the competitive buoyancy of the autonomous reflexives and the anticipation that this sub-group will remain (proportionately) stabile in the immediate future a finding that runs counter to any expectation about the transformation of modernity? These successful 'independents' confidently compete for positions in finance capitalism, in the multi-nationals, corporate life in general, and now have expanded outlets in the public services, since these became run on lines of managerial performance. Why, then, is there any question mark hanging over their future role in perpetuating the 'situational logic of competition', fundamental to modernity's institutions with their winners and losers? Since this logic is fundamentally socially divisive, why are these subjects not automatically seen as the prime agents who will foster future social division and determine that nascent morphogenesis will necessarily assume the divided form? This question arises from another that was not answered when these subjects were characterized as upholding a new 'spirit of social enterprise', namely where does it come from if it is not merely dismissed ideologically as 'bad faith'? If it is allowed to be authentic, as least amongst these young subjects, then we should not slip into a facile nominalism that assumes them to be the same group as their employers and predecessors simply because they occupy many of the same posts, reap many similar advantages and appear to be seeking much the same objective material rewards.

---

[27] Jon Elster, *Strong Feelings*, Cambridge, Mass., MIT Press, 1999.

[28] It may be pertinent that Carole met her current ('sort of') boyfriend in the street.

[29] Recall how Carole evaluated her time surrounded by her problematic children and their grandchildren as 'quite good' because of its social intensity, whilst being fully aware that this was a phase in her life cycle that would pass.

This would be to disregard the social, cultural and structural crises that confront modernity's main enterprise and that cannot be understood at the aggregate level of individuals' attitudes and behaviour. Instead, it is necessary to introduce the counter-movements and collective critiques that have bombarded 'capitalism' in the last two decades and its responses to them.[30] Until the 1990s the main ideological challenge to liberal economics came from different parts of the socialist spectrum confronting it with a 'constraining contradiction'.[31] It was constraining because profit depended upon labour however much unionist organization was forcefully resisted. From its inception the full brunt of 'eliminative' action could not be turned against organized labour and ended in the political incorporation of unionism.

The varied oppositional groupings developing from the late 1980s onwards also constituted 'constraining contradictions': feminism could initially be treated to 'tokenism', but not to eliminative exclusion with more than half of women now working; likewise the 'greens' as ongoing consumers spelt minor concessions such as restrictions on the use of plastic bags; similarly the advocacy of more family-friendly policies had to be met at least gesturally since all workers had families. This is not the place to attempt even a broad sketch of these intricate forms of protest and ideological critique. The only point I want to make here is that the full range of capitalist enterprise was caught in the toils of the 'constraining contradiction'. Its socio-cultural logic meant that whilst liberal interests would initially make the most minimalist concessions to their critics and opponents, their survival compelled them towards more 'generous' forms of syncretism.

The advent of New Labour highlighted how far syncretism had gone and how much further the Party wished to go. The point is not about 'good faith' or 'bad' but concerns corporate practice and its practitioners.[32] Very quickly personnel departments turned into human resources, taking 'human bonding' exercises into schools and melding them with heroic-sounding survivalist weekends in the Highlands,

---

[30] A valid point made by Frédéric Vandenberghe, 'The Archers – Final Episode?', *European Journal of Social Theory*, 8:2, 2005, 227–237.

[31] See Archer, *Culture and Agency*, pp. 148–171.

[32] Christine Hemingway shows how variable this was amongst corporate executives, although only a tiny minority overtly challenged it, 'The Conditions and Character Traits of Corporate Social Entrepreneurship: Insights From a UK-based Multi-national Corporation', presented at the 23rd European Business Ethics Network (EBEN) Annual Conference, University of Trento, Italy, 2010. See also, Christine A. Hemingway, Corporate Social Entrepreneurship: Integrity within the Socially Responsible Organisation, in the series *Business, Value Creation, and Society* (eds. R. Edward Freeman, Stuart L. Hart and David Wheeler), Cambridge University Press, forthcoming.

living on lichen and camaraderie; business schools spawned 'business ethics' curricula; multi-national accountants adopted schools for the under-privileged; global corporations paid for street access to computers for street-kids and corporate charitable initiatives mushroomed.[33] In short, corporate social responsibility took its place on capitalism's agenda.

What was the source of our autonomous reflexives' new 'spirit of social enterprise'? In part, the very corporate enterprises they were inclined to join and the assimilation of their rhetoric, taken in 'good faith' by some of the interviewees. In equal part, from the arguments of the social movements that had increased in social salience throughout their school-days, not by making converts from amongst these unlikely candidates but by normalizing the lowest common denominator of their charters. In other words, a positive feedback loop had engaged here too with its consequence of deviation–amplification. The legitimate expression of autonomous reflexivity was now significantly different from its post-war versions. Yet, does it make a real difference to social integration, sufficient to reduce the chances of a divided morphogenetic social order emerging in Europe?

Structurally, the recent economic crisis laid bare the vacuity of talk about 'liquid society' made up of shapeless, evanescent and, above all, unstructured flows. It should have been a painful lesson about the inter-locking financial structures of late modernity had it not been deflected through personalization into the relative trivialities of bankers' bonuses. Now that Europe is scrambling to return to 'business as usual', evidence points to the poorer sectors bearing the brunt of politico-economic retrenchment. In brief, today's young autonomous reflexives talk the new talk whilst their bosses walk the old walk. Nevertheless, time passes, our interviewees will gain promotion and the firm itself will become an increasingly interesting place of division itself over the divisive and unbridled 'logic of competition'. The anticipated stability of the sub-group of autonomous reflexives in the immediate future will serve to insert their 'spirit of social enterprise', sandpapering away the rougher edges of the profit motive and bringing corporate social responsibility into the company rather than, as now, looking benignly on the voluntary extra-mural activities of their employees. If so, the newly recruited autonomous subjects will be pre-disposed to make some incremental

---

[33] See Balihar Sanghera, 'Charitable Giving, Everyday Morality and a Critique of Bour-dieusian Theory: An Investigation into Disinterested Judgements, Moral Concerns and Reflexivity in the UK', forthcoming. The different forms of charitable giving described coincide exactly with the four modes of reflexivity discussed here.

contribution offsetting the prospects of a divided morphogenetic social order.

More important, however, than civilized corporatism is the effect that increasingly rapid morphogenesis will have upon already outdated notions of vested material interests. These have such a weight and length of history as hierarchical, functional and stratified 'givens' that it takes a reflexive mental shake – even from academics – to recognize that we ourselves no longer have them. Certainly, we care about reputational goods but these are conferred by a diffuse, global constituency in ways that largely defeat instrumental rational strategies. They are not enhanced by receipt of an extra pay increment at one's local university. Ironically, this local institution is of diminishing importance except in one respect – it is where we engage in free-giving to our students in defiance of performance indicators! In fact, most of us have no vested material interests in our local universities because what keeps us going is neither materially nor institutionally based. Instead, it is the quite small group of geographically dispersed friends (and a vastly larger one of friendly acquaintances) who furnish relational goods defying commodification: stimulus above all but also constructive criticism, a readiness to read and improve first drafts, a sharing of their reactions to new material and a reference if you can't locate it. This is not a diversion but is intended to illustrate that what meta-reflexives seek is not utopian. We live it, even if we are not fully self-conscious that *homo academicus* is dead and that what should appear on his death certificate is 'morphogenesis'.

He died from the speed of change that precludes hierarchical sclerosis, a demise that we recognize elsewhere (in geeky thirty-something Heads of IT). In short, we now live by relational and not positional, let alone material goods; we have an intellectual position to defend, not a cabbage patch; and we are moved by what we care about, which is ideational, not material. In other words, we have a 'cause', like the meta-reflexives or, as Weber rightly called it, a 'vocation'. Yet, most of us are not utopians.

What is encouraging is that the young meta-reflexives understand that this kind of life is possible and preferable to modernity's zero-sum game plan. They are personally unmoved by class, status and power because their aim is 'to make a difference' and morphogenesis makes this realistic. But to making what kind of morphogenetic society do they contribute? As critics of market and state they are protagonists of civil society who manifest a distinct predilection for work in the third sector, regardless of its rewards or lack of them. Thus, practitioners of meta-reflexivity showed a greater willingness to consider if not to conclude for employment in the voluntary sector. It would have been feasible to concentrate upon this in the present work and would not have been irrelevant to the future of the historic bond between modernity and capitalism.

However, to have focussed on exploring a (hypothesized) shift towards the third sector would also have been to endorse its centrality in the transition from modernity by moving it to centre stage.[34] However, the institutionalized third, voluntary, social–private or not-for-profit sector is more contentious, even or especially for those who cherish hopes for the emergence of a genuine civil society and economy.

An intrinsic part of political centrism is an increased reliance upon the 'voluntary sector' to reinforce both of the old and ailing Leviathans of modernity. This has become increasingly clear in Britain with the attempt to put the crisis of finance capitalism in the past tense. It becomes more glaring with the advent of the new Coalition government and the ideological role assigned to voluntary work in its advocacy of the 'Big Society', but this is not novel.[35] Regardless of party, centrist government has regularly passed part of the bill for 'public services' to voluntary agencies – in education, health and care of the aged and so forth – and ideologically appropriated the ethos of 'free giving'. Yet, giving does not remain 'free' once subject to governmental controls and expectations; moreover the recognition of voluntary provisions becomes increasingly blurred with and indistinguishable from outsourcing to for-profit enterprises.

What young meta-reflexives seek is considerably more important to the kind of morphogenetic society they will help to shape and structure than their support for the third sector as we know it in Britain and in its much more developed and variegated forms in other parts of Europe.[36] Indeed, in Italy with her much richer spectrum of voluntary organizations, the motivational patterns of three 'generations' of supporters and workers has been shown to change quite considerably over time.[37] Generically, what meta-reflexives want for themselves and for all is something that many of us privileged academics already have, which is why we were introduced above.

---

[34] Such an endorsement is problematic and quite unlike the procedure that could be adopted by Luc Boltanski and Eve Ciapello, *The New Spirit of Capitalism*, London, Verso, 2005, who could focus upon the capitalist enterprise and the significance of its changing spirit precisely because they could rightly presume its enduring importance in late modernity (and its indubitable centrality in the previous two centuries).

[35] New Labour had already instituted ministerial control over the 'third sector' and provoked predictable conflict over 'faith schools' and certain adoption agencies.

[36] Pierpaolo Donati, *Sociologia del Terzo settore*, Rome, NIS, 1996.

[37] Matteo Orlandini, 'Third Sector Cultures and Engagement with the World', paper presented at the Annual Conference of the International Association of Critical Realism, Padua, Italy, 2010. See also, Riccardo Prandini, 'La morfogenesi culturale del Terzo settore' in Ivo Colozzi and Andrea Bassi (eds.), *Cultura, organizzazione e terzo settore*, Impresa Sociale, 2010. Both are based on life history research

Having already turned their backs on modernity's Leviathans and rejecting the confines of 'friends and family' – even though they want both – the meta-reflexives recognize that it is only in between the macro and the micro, that within like-minded association and associations they can be both generators and beneficiaries of the relational goods they hold worthwhile: solidarity in pursuit of a common cause, multi-faceted friendship, meaning and purpose in daily life and making a communal contribution that exceeds their aggregate exertions. Another way of putting this is that they use the situational logic of opportunity to discover congenial 'corporate agents' with whom they can live and work.

Just as importantly, the young meta-reflexives are explicitly inclusive. Their signature tune, the 'desire to make a difference' is often followed up by them adding, 'if only to one person'. In other words, they are seeking the 'common good' rather than the 'total good', an addition sum whose result is higher if those doing less well on whatever criterion are discounted.[38] The meta-reflexives are unwilling to discount the well-being of anyone. Socially, their mission is fully inclusive; individually they will go after the lost sheep. What they seek to do is to *integrate* the less fortunate by extending the availability of opportunities to these groups, ones they consider themselves to have enjoyed as an unmerited privilege. From the start of their university careers they were free-givers who contracted into to making regular donations to charities, as undergraduates they intensified their efforts for causes and for individuals in difficulties, and at the point of graduation they are prepared to dedicate themselves to this in their careers. Another way of putting this is that they are bent upon the extension of variety and its integration as diversity. Yet another is that to them a good society cannot be a divided morphogenetic society.

And the outcome?

To maintain that the process of morphogenesis will continue and gather speed through its generative mechanism for variety to produce more variety, is only a social theorist's way of putting what a survey of ordinary people would almost certainly endorse. To venture what kind of morphogenetic society will ensue is quite another matter and to do so would be to fly in the face of realism's well-grounded refusal to make predictions because of the complexity of intertwining generative processes and

---

[38] A point first made by Stefano Zamagni, who goes on to say that the 'common good' is more akin to a multiplication sum. If one entry is zero, so is the total. Margaret S. Archer and Pierpaolo Donati (eds.), *Pursuing the Common Good: How Solidarity and Subsidiarity Can Work Together*, Vatican City Press, 2008.

the openness of every social system to contingency. More specifically, it would constitute a performative contradiction for the 'morphogenetic approach'. I have always maintained that it is what happens between different sets of individuals and groups in their socio-cultural interaction between T2 and T3 that alone determines the outcome at T4. In other words, whether structural elaboration (or morphostasis) ensues is entirely activity-dependent upon interaction. There is no finalism whatsoever. Nothing but agential doings, agential engagement with other groups and agential commitment (individual and collective) shapes and reshapes the social order.

The absence of finalism is true in two ways. To begin with, we can have no idea how the shifting patterns of reflexivity will pan out: in Britain, in Europe or in the one world. In any case, aggregate patterns are nothing without real relations animating them. Even at this level, it has to remain opaque what autonomous reflexives imbued with a genuinely new 'spirit of social enterprise' will actually do and whether there is scope for combined action with the commitments of meta-reflexives, which is only to focus on the two collectivities overtly seeking to reshape the social order. It should not be taken to mean that practitioners of other modes will exert no influence. Moreover, sociologically we cannot remain at this level, neglecting action networks, social movements, institutional structures and power, including the power of ideas, in the elaboration of the social order.

To end with, we literally don't know what we are talking about. This conclusion has been cast in simple terms by making a distinction between a divided and an integrated morphogenetic society and asking what current aggregate changes in modes of reflexivity contribute to the one or the other. Conceptually, almost none of the work has been done to prepare the ground for posing the key question about the future configurations possible for morphogenetic society: how do we define variety and its distribution; what turns variety into concrete if quintessentially changing opportunities; can all forms of variety be diffused as diversity and with what effects if some cannot; is every patterning of diversity amenable to integration or do some tend in the opposite direction? For the time being, I am much richer in question marks than in the necessary clarifications, which is why this is, indeed, the start of another book.

Methodological appendix

This study is based upon all entrants to the undergraduate degrees in sociology (including joint honours with other social sciences, law and French) in 2003/2004 when I was giving the lectures on the obligatory foundation course. Students were administered ICONI (Internal Conversation Indicator) but told they were free not to participate. Details for the construction of this indicator can be found in the Methodological appendix to *Making our Way through the World*.[1] ICONI was administered in the auditorium, before the start of that week's lecture, in order to maximize returns and to ensure that through supervised administration it was completed by individual students without collaborating with their neighbours or friends. This would have been the drawback to the alternative, namely emailing the form to students and requesting its return.

One of the negative trade-offs involved was that the usual quota of absentees from the lecture did not participate. No attempt was made to follow up those absent because they may have been influenced by conversation with those who had been present. This was their first experience of participating in university research and a brief explanation was given about the project's aims, the ideas behind it and its relation to the ongoing Coventry study (a stratified sample of the general population). In addition, quite a large group of students remained behind at the end for further discussion. Therefore, although tracking down absentees was possible, there was no guarantee that they would still have remained 'naïve subjects', given the frequency of exchanges amongst students since all were housed in campus residences in their first year.

After administering ICONI, each student was asked to complete a background demographic data sheet, covering parental socio-economic status (current or last post held by father and mother), educational history, geographical mobility and whether or not they had previously studied sociology. They were also asked to list the 'three most important

[1] Margaret S. Archer, *Making our Way through the World: Human Reflexivity and Social Mobility*, Cambridge University Press, 2007, pp. 329–334.

areas of your life now'. Finally, volunteers were requested, who would be willing to be interviewed in-depth about the kind of topics included on the indicator and their decision-making process about choice of future career. They were told that this would involve the same type of interview in each of their three years as undergraduates.

This group of thirty-six volunteers constitute the students interviewed in-depth and upon whose accounts and responses the empirical part of this book is based. The reason for using volunteers was that I had no right to abuse the power relationship involved by any suggestion that participation was an expectation on the part of the department or university. Also, no financial compensation was being offered for their gift of time. This means of selection entailed two limitations. Firstly, there was no way of guaranteeing that these thirty-six were representative of the 126 students who made valid returns on ICONI (i.e. gave a response to every question). Indeed, from names, appearances and also coming to know approximately fifty of them from teaching seminar groups, it is fairly certain that undergraduates from overseas and those who were second-generation migrants to Britain were more reticent about volunteering. The seemingly disproportionate number of females among the thirty-six is not, in fact, out of line since they constituted 80.2 per cent of those present at that particular lecture and reflected the percentages of males and females registered on the foundation course.

Secondly, since the volunteers came forward during the same session in which they had completed ICONI, they were not in any way selected *for* their dominant mode of reflexivity at that time because their responses had obviously not yet been coded. When we come to the analysis of the 126 respondents, it will be possible to determine how closely their composition reflected that of the group as a whole *in this respect*. Beyond that, there is no way of establishing their typicality but, in such a new area of research it is impossible to specify what factors would qualify as typical. Thus, it is advisable to regard the volunteers as nothing more than an exploratory group whose responses form the basis for advancing tentative hypotheses inviting further investigation.

This is reinforced by the fact that although all thirty-six generously collaborated during their first year, some were lost in subsequent years for various reasons: several turned out to be taking the course as an 'outside' option from other departments, one withdrew from the university, two changed their registration to degrees not involving sociology, another suffered illness in her second year and was away from campus for several months, and a further participant had to fly home for family reasons before the date scheduled for her final third-year interview. Only one

Communicative reflexives: Those whose internal conversations require completion and confirmation by others before resulting in courses of action.

Autonomous reflexives: Those who sustain self-contained internal conversations, leading directly to action.

Meta-reflexives: Those who are critically reflexive about their own internal conversations and critical about effective action in society.

Fractured reflexives: Those whose internal conversations intensify their distress and disorientation rather than leading to purposeful courses of action.

Figure A.1 Dominant modes of reflexivity

volunteer declined a further interview, an option that was offered to all in years two and three.

In analysing the ICONI responses of the foundation course group, it is necessary to provide a brief summary of the different modes of reflexivity that were being measured in the light of *Structure, Agency and the Internal Conversation* (Cambridge University Press, 2003), where these modalities were first ventured, and of *Making our Way through the World*, where ICONI was developed and first used (Figure A.1).

To contextualize the results gained from the first-year sociologists, they can be compared with those gained from the Coventry population, which was of a similar size, but consisted of a sample stratified by gender, age and socio-economic status.

A cognate PhD thesis by Mark Carrigan is well underway and he is using much the same method (administration of ICONI plus asking for volunteers for interview). Figure A.4 shows his distribution of dominant modes of reflexivity for first-year sociologists following the same foundation course in 2010.

We lack the necessary information to explain differences in the two distributions. Relevant factors may include the fact that the 2010 percentages are recorded more than five years later than those in Figure A.3 and, meanwhile the world had experienced two years of economic recession. It is possible that this is reflected in the much reduced proportion of 'meta-reflexives', if young people are now more pessimistic about 'making a difference', and in the increased proportion of those entering as 'fractured reflexives', if family relations have suffered through circumstances such as involuntary redundancy and mortgage difficulties. However, it would need to be established if these students were also family 'rejecters' – the relational factor held in this study to be closely associated with 'fracturing'. On the other hand, although we know that entry years vary in some respects (academics have always talked about

Mode of reflexivity	Frequency	Percentage	Cumulative percentage
Communicative	27	21.1	21.1
Autonomous	35	27.3	48.4
Meta-	29	22.7	71.1
Fractured	28	21.9	93.0
Expressives*	3	2.3	95.3
Unclassified	6	4.7	100.0
TOTAL	128	100.0	100.0

* The term refers to subjects who scored less than 4 on C, A, M or F. The reasons for deeming

Figure A.2 Modes of reflexivity endorsed in the Coventry sample

Mode of reflexivity	Frequency	Valid percentage	Cumulative percentage
Communicative	17	13.5	13.5
Autonomous	24	19.0	32.5
Meta-	49	38.6	71.4
Fractured	10	7.9	79.4
Expressives*	12	9.5	88.9
Unclassified	14	11.1	100.0
TOTAL	127	100.0	100.0

* The term refers to subjects who scored less than 4 on C, A, M or F.

Figure A.3 Modes of reflexivity endorsed by first-year university sociology students

Mode of reflexivity	Frequency	Valid percentage	Cumulative percentage
Communicative	17	16.67	16.67
Autonomous	29	28.43	45.1
Meta-	22	21.57	66.67
Fractured	21	20.59	87.26
Expressives	0	0	87.26
Unclassified	13	12.75	100.01
TOTAL	102	100.0	100.0

Figure A.4 Modes of reflexivity endorsed by first-year sociologists five years on. Reproduced by courtesy of Mark Carrigan

Percentages	Sociology	WBS*	English Lit.	Physics
C	16.67	14.52	15.79	13.04
A:	28.43	37.1	21.05	40.58
M/R:	21.57	25.81	39.48	21.74
F:	20.59	14.52	15.79	10.14
Other:	12.75	8.06	7.89	14.49

* Warwick Business School

Figure A.5 Modes of reflexivity of entrants to different departments, 2010. Reproduced by courtesy of Mark Carrigan

particularly 'good years' and their opposite), we necessarily remain ignorant about the range of variation from year to year and whether or not there has been any particular trajectory in recent years.

Neither of the factors cited above as potentially being relevant to these variations seems plausible if the 2010 sociologists are compared with Carrigan's findings across faculties, since there are no grounds for arguing that sociologists-to-be had been disproportionately influenced by them.

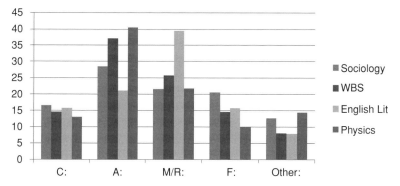

Figure A.6 Assigned scores as percentage of total populations. Reproduced by courtesy of Mark Carrigan

Mode of reflexivity	Frequency	Percentage	Cumulative percentage
Communicative	5	18.5	18.5
Autonomous	4	14.8	33.3
Meta-	8	29.6	62.9
Fractured	4	14.8	77.7
Expressives	4	14.8	92.5
Unclassified	2	7.4	99.9
TOTAL	27	99.9	99.9

Figure A.7 Modes of reflexivity at point of entry among those interviewed over their undergraduate course

However, the further relevance of Carrigan's data is that it does confirm a
hypothesis we both entertained, namely that students entering university
to study different disciplines would be self-selected and at least partly in
terms of their mode of reflexivity.

The original volunteers who were interviewed in each of their three
undergraduate years recorded dominant modes of reflexivity upon entry
in the frequencies and proportions shown in Figure A.7. These neither
constitute a perfect fit with the proportions listed in Figure A.3, nor are
they grossly out of line with the distribution of all 'sociologists' entering

	Fathers Valid* N = 108	Mothers Valid = 112
Managerial and professional occupations	70.4% (N = 76)	51.8% (N = 58)
Intermediate occupations	18.5% (N = 20)	19.6% (N = 22)
Routine and manual occupations	10.2% (N = 11)	10.0% (N = 19)
Never worked and long-term unemployed	0.9% (N = 1)	11.6% (N = 13)

* Invalid ' and excluded responses are those that could not be classified on NS-SEC. For example, because recorded as 'hospital employee' or 'works for Marks and Spencer'.

Figure A.8 The socio-economic background of first-year respondents' parents

that year. Nevertheless, it is reassuring to note that 'willingness to volunteer' did not come disproportionately from practitioners of any particular mode of reflexivity. (It must not be assumed that all continue to practise the same mode with which they entered and the reasons for some of their changes are tracked in the text.)

Relationship between mode of reflexivity on entry and demographic characteristics

As was known in advance from statistics on Warwick University's student recruitment, the undergraduate population is highly skewed towards offspring of middle-class parents and even more so towards those with fathers in 'managerial and professional occupations'. On the simplified three-class version of the *National Statistics Socio-Economic Classification* (NS-SEC)[2] entrants to sociology mirrored this marked bias. Therefore, there is no question of extrapolating from these students to the rest of their age cohort. In addition, given the very small absolute numbers of those with fathers and/or mothers in 'routine and manual occupations', even though these were (fortuitously) captured as interviewees in relation to their proportion among the 'volunteers', the small numbers coming from working-class backgrounds may be qualitatively swamped (see Figure A.8). This is quite a serious difficulty. Any future attempt to

[2] See *National Statistics Socio-economic Classification User Manual*, Basingstoke, Palgrave Macmillan, 2006, p. 10f.

correct this deficiency by conducting a similar investigation at a different university with a more socially representative intake would simultaneously introduce concomitant variations in other student characteristics: especially student grades at A-level and the proportion schooled in the private sector. These two features are associated with the rank order of universities on a variety of official league tables.

Cross-tabulating the socio-occupational status of respondents' fathers with modes of reflexivity that students endorsed at point of entry showed no statistically significant relationship between the two variables at the conventional 0.05 level (chi-squared score $= 19.685$ and p-value $= 0.073$). Performing the same operation for mothers' occupation also yielded no significant relationship (chi-squared $= 6.345$ and p-value $= 0.898$).

The frequency distribution of respondents' gender was as follows:

Male	Female
(Valid N $= 126$) 19.8% (N $= 25$)	80.2% (N $= 101$)

Again, no statistically significant relationship was found between gender and mode of reflexivity during year one at university (p-value $= 0.348$). A similar lack of relationship was the case for two other variables.

The first of these concerned students' previous study of sociology and their (presumed) interest in it, given the degree course on which they had enrolled. Since it was seen above that there is self-selection amongst students enrolling in different disciplines and faculties, the specific question here was whether or not prior familiarity with sociology was responsible for the 'meta-reflexives' forming the numerically largest group of entrants (in 2003 although not five years later). Just over a quarter (27.8 per cent) of those entering in 2003, had not previously studied sociology, whilst 69.1 per cent had taken it successfully at A-level and a further 3.1 per cent had other qualifications in it (usually by having attended access courses). Since no statistically significant relationship was identified, prior study does not seem to account for the large proportion of meta-reflexives found.

The second factor explored, if only to eliminate its potential interference with modes of reflexivity as registered on ICONI, was the mood of the subjects at the time of its administration. Subjects were asked to consider their mood on the day they completed ICONI and to record if they were feeling 'better than usual', 'about average' or 'feeling rather down'. One specific possibility in mind was that 'feeling down' might inflate the proportions of those being classified as 'fractured reflexives'. However, once again, no statistically significant findings resulted.

Relationships between different modes of reflexivity in the first year

With a handful of exceptions, everyone had a score for each mode of reflexivity and, under particular circumstances we all make use of every kind. At least that theoretical assumption was empirically warranted in *Making our Way through the World*. The same was found in this investigation when the composite scores on ICONI were inspected for individual subjects. Indeed, the category of 'unclassifiables' was made up of those with tied scores for two different modes. One of the most interesting of the volunteers was a young man who gained the top score of 7 for both autonomous and meta-reflexivity!

However, the different modes are meant to discriminate between distinct types of practitioners. On ICONI, this should mean that those scoring 'high' on a given cluster of questions should also register 'low' or 'lower' scores on the other three clusters. Nevertheless, some modes are more antithetic to one another than others. This was the finding in the Coventry survey but, since undergraduates are a very different population, it was necessary to re-check this finding.

As far as scores for 'fractured reflexivity' (FR) were concerned, the expectation was that the weaker the FR score (indicating little proclivity towards 'fracturing'), then the stronger would be the endorsement of 'autonomous reflexivity' (AR), 'communicative reflexivity' (CR), and 'meta-reflexibity' (M-R) (expressive reflexivity, as an unknown in such numbers was also included). In total four bivariate correlations were calculated with Pearson's r for each pair of variables always including FR.

The ARs are the extreme opposites of the FRs in almost every respect (especially in decisiveness and the ability to conclude their deliberations alone). Thus, in terms of the theoretical framework, the more extreme are the subjects' AR scores, the more they are expected to respond negatively to those items indicative of 'fracturedness'. Pearson's r was calculated twice. The first r is -0.332 and its p-value is 0,098, obtained from the full sample ($N = 126$). The second r is -0.728 and its p-value is 0.000, obtained from the same sample with two outliers being excluded, which is statistically significant. However, since this is not an independent random sample (because it over-represents the age group 18–21, those of middle-class backgrounds and the more highly educated) no inferences can be made from this finding to the population at large. All other results were in the expected direction but did not attain statistical significance (i.e. M-R and FR showed a weak negative correlation ($r = -0.160$, p-value = 0.300), perhaps because the two do have 'self-questioning' in common; CR and FR showed a slight positive correlation ($r = 0.232$, p-value = 0.286) perhaps because, despite their differences, blurring may occur as both share the quality of self-mistrust; and a moderate positive relation was found between ER and FR scores for those subjects who endorsed E ($r = 0.304$, p-value = 0.140) which merits further qualitative clarification (provided in Chapter 7).

ANOVA was then used to explore the relationship between FR scores and the various modes of reflexivity to test the null hypothesis that average FR scores do not differ among CR, AR, M-R and E. The lowest average F score was recorded by the AR sub-group, followed by the M-Rs and then the CRs (the Es were excluded here because their smaller numbers would have violated the assumptions of ANOVA). The F-ratio is 8.457 and the p-value is statistically significant at 0.000 (N = 93), meaning that the null hypothesis can be rejected outright. The pairwise comparisons of the average F scores for CR, AR and M-R highlight two statistically significant differences. Firstly, the difference between the average F scores between CR and AR (the mean difference is 2.943, p-value = 0.001) confirms the hypothesis. Secondly, so does the difference between M-R and AR (with a mean difference of 2.5192, p-value = 0.002). Using the Bonferroni test procedure, both differences are statistically significant. In turn, if indirectly, this also reinforces the distinctiveness of each of the four different modes of reflexivity.

Changes over time

Without doubt, attempts to chart changes over the three years using the 'background population' (the 126 starting sociology at the same time) as a check upon whether or not the findings from the 'volunteer population' were in line with them, is the least satisfactory part of the research design. This was largely a function of student accessibility. In the first year, all entrants were together on the foundation course, but at the time this research was being conducted, that was the only compulsory course taken during their undergraduate degree(s) (single and joint-honours). My particular interest was in a broad comparison of the whole group at point of entry and close to graduation. However, the third-year curriculum was a free choice of three options plus an (individually supervised) dissertation. Since the menu of options was broad, including the choice of taking modules outside the department, there was no teaching situation where they were all gathered together.

Even if the concern about collusion had been pocketed, administration in the third year would have meant that some were being asked to complete ICONI two or three times over, depending upon their option choices, whilst a significant number following a given module would not have been part of the original foundation group because they were taking it as an 'outside option', as Erasmus students or as those on Junior Year Abroad programs. Consequently, the decision was taken to make use of a third-year meeting at which all students were addressed by the head of department. Because attending the meeting was not obligatory, only fifty-nine of the original 126 respondents on entry (just under half) were administered the indicator on this occasion. This was manifestly unsatisfactory. Conversely, it seems unlikely that more than half would have attended a specially designated meeting for the purposes of this research project. Given timetabling constraints, this could only have been convened in an evening and would have entailed students coming in specially (in their third year, the majority are living off-campus).

Therefore, because there is no way of ascertaining that this 'half' of the original population did not deviate from the rest in important ways, the two findings reported below for those in their final year must be treated cautiously. At most, they *may be* indicative, but there is no way of cross-checking this.

Stability and change in mode of reflexivity

Among those repeating ICONI in their final year, 49 per cent registered a dominant mode of reflexivity *unchanged* from that with which they entered university. If that finding can be reconfirmed, it would mean that half of those (mainly middle-class) students leaving school/college at eighteen have already developed the dominant reflexive modality that will see them through school leaving, through their undergraduate degrees, and into employment. If that were generally the case, one implication would be that the 'making of reflexivity', in the sense of the stable practice of a dominant mode, occurs before subjects legally come of age. Again, this would reinforce paying more detailed attention to the quality of family relations and those at school and college.

Of the equal number whose dominant mode changed during the course of their first degree the two most common trajectories were constituted by:–
(i) Those who registered as communicative, autonomous or meta-reflexives or 'E' on entry being recorded as 'fractured reflexives' when close to graduation. The FR sub-group had more than doubled (which, were one to assume comparability, would represent

an increase in the proportion of 'fractureds' from 7.9 per cent to 16.9 per cent). It seems prudent merely to be alert to some growth in fractured reflexivity in the undergraduate careers of the cohort as a whole. Fortunately, one such case was found among the 'volunteers' and is examined in Chapter 7.

(ii) Those whose first recorded scores were 'E', meaning that they did not clear the threshold (a mid-way score of 4) for any of the other modes, halved in number because of some shifting to one of the other four modes (a third of them becoming fractured). Bearing in mind that we are dealing with single-digit numbers, the most that might possibly be entertained is that the 'expressives' enter university as 'under-developed reflexives', which in *Structure, Agency and the Internal Conversation* was regarded as a variant upon fractured reflexivity. The pros and cons of this interpretation are examined in Chapter 7.

The importance of what they care about

When ascertaining students' main concerns ('the three most important areas of your life now – those that you care about deeply?') respondents were given three spaces at the end of ICONI and asked to list what mattered to them in order of preference. They were invited to record their concerns in their own words because I had no conviction about knowing sufficiently well what mattered to eighteen-year-olds to present them with pre-coded categories. However, this made for two kinds of difficulties. Firstly, some amalgamated 'friends and family' whilst others separated them; secondly, it was hard to know to what, for instance, a generic concern for 'happiness' or 'university' referred.

On the basis of the Coventry study, the concerns listed by respondents were originally coded into fourteen categories but this yielded some cells with a single respondent. Following the practice employed in the Coventry investigation, these fourteen were coded as concerns typical of CR (interpersonal relations), AR (careers/performative skills), and M-R (moral causes and issues) as follows:

> Communicative concerns = 'family and friends'; 'family'; 'friends; 'relationship' (singular); 'university social life'.
>
> Autonomous concerns = 'university work'; 'money'; 'performative interests' (mainly sport, music, and drama).
>
> Meta-reflexive concerns = 'socio-political causes' (including social movements); 'faith'

This left 'university in general', 'health', 'happiness' and a few single entries, such as 'doing my best' or 'fulfilling my potential' as 'unclassified'.

Because most of the variables involved are nominal in nature, these were then cross-tabulated with mode of reflexivity using Fisher's exact test. The statistically significant results for autonomous and meta-reflexives all concentrated within their 'exit' year, thus giving some reinforcement to the argument that the processes of *discernment* and *deliberation* are actively ongoing during the three undergraduate years. However, the small numbers involved make such conclusions tentative at best. That an A concern was the prime concern of the autonomous reflexives (with unclassified subjects excluded from analysis) and was significant at the 5 per cent level [p = 0.031: N = 55]. The same cross-tabulation for the meta-reflexives, with unclassified subjects also excluded, was also statistically significant at the 5 per cent level [p = 0.001: N = 56]. This served to reinforce the notion that it was worthwhile tracking the undergraduates year by year to discover in the first person how their ultimate concerns crystallized and their rank ordering of what mattered to them was indeed being clarified and consolidated during the period of their first degree.

Results were not statistically significant for those scoring as communicative reflexives and mentioning a C concern as their most important in life or listing at least one C concern amongst their three most important concerns. This absence of significant result is plausibly explained by the popularity of C concerns among the respondents, regardless of their dominant mode of reflexivity. In the data sets for the university 'entrants' and for those at the point of 'graduation', over 75 per cent listed a C concern as their most important concern in life (although not necessarily the same one), whilst less than 5 per cent of the students did not mention any C concern amongst their three. If a comparison is made with the Coventry population (N = 128) used in *Making our Way through the World* the importance attached to the family as a prime concern was the case for 78 per cent, with only ten respondents failing to list it among their three and with C concerns, as defined here, totalling 92.2 per cent of all those listed.

Since the Coventry population was made up of those aged from 16 to 80 plus, it is more realistic, if not strictly comparable, to focus upon the responses of the youngest age group (16–24 year olds) in relation to those of the undergraduates at their point of entry. Large differences immediately surface for their first concerns. Whilst 53 per cent of the Coventry youth listed 'family' first, only 30 per cent of the students did so. If we now add in listing a partner as the first concern, then the student total rises to 43 per cent compared with 69 per cent for Coventry youth.

(This latter result is probably because 44 per cent of the Coventry young stated that they were in a relationship of at least two years' duration, which vastly outnumbered students in the same position.)

What if we take all of their three listed concerns together for the two different populations? For the Coventry youth, the 'family' retains its pride of place, accounting for 30 per cent of their total listed concerns, which is only slightly lower than the 33 per cent accorded to it by the total sample of the Coventry population. Those in the Coventry 16–24 age cohort are much more similar to the older residents of the city than they are to the students, whose top overall concern was for 'university work' (23 per cent), rising to 28 per cent if 'university social life' was added in and to 34 per cent if 'university in general' was included.

Despite drawbacks in the comparability of the data, it is hard to resist the conclusion that the family, under their own descriptions, matters more to young people in the general population (some of whom are also graduates) than it does to the university entrants investigated. This is in line with the overall hypothesis that the *contextual discontinuity* represented by the great break that going away to university involves for the majority of students (who now represent nearly 40 per cent of the age cohort), also entails a major and often irreparable caesura with the 'solidary', geo-local family. Necessarily, such data can tell nothing about the qualitative break entailed by *contextual incongruity*, which is the point where the in-depth interviewing has to take over.

Index